CONNECTIONIST MODELS OF DEVELOPMENT

Studies in Developmental Psychology
Published Titles

Series Editor
Charles Hulme, University of York, UK

The Development of Intelligence
Mike Anderson (Ed.)

The Development of Language
Martyn Barrett (Ed.)

The Social Child
Anne Campbell and Steven Muncer (Ed.)

The Development of Memory in Childhood
Nelson Cowan (Ed.)

The Development of Mathematical Skills
Chris Donlan (Ed.)

The Development of Social Cognition
Suzanne Hala (Ed.)

Perceptual Development: Visual, Auditory, and Speech Perception in Infancy
Alan Slater (Ed.)

The Cognitive Neuroscience of Development
Michelle DeHaan and Mark H. Johnson (Eds.)

Connectionist Models of Development

Developmental Processes in Real and Artificial Neural Networks

Edited by

Philip T. Quinlan
Department of Psychology, University of York, UK

Ψ Psychology Press
Taylor & Francis Group

HOVE AND NEW YORK

First published 2003
by Psychology Press
27 Church Road, Hove, East Sussex, BN3 2FA

Simultaneously published in the USA and Canada
by Psychology Press
29 West 35th Street, New York, NY 10001

Psychology Press is a part of the Taylor & Francis Group

Copyright © 2003 Psychology Press

Typeset in Times by RefineCatch Limited, Bungay, Suffolk
Printed and bound in Great Britain by
Biddles Ltd, Guildford and King's Lynn
Cover design by Bob Rowinski at Code 5 Design

British Library Cataloguing in Publication Data
A catalogue record for this book is available from the British Library

Library of Congress Cataloging-in-Publication Data
Connectionist models of development / edited by Philip T. Quinlan.
     p. cm. – (Studies in developmental psychology)
Includes bibliographical references and index.
     ISBN 1-84169-268-9 (alk. paper)
     1. Developmental psychology. 2. Connectionism. I. Quinlan, Philip T.
II. Series
     BF713.5 .C67 2003
     155–dc21   2002010901

ISBN 1-84169-268-9 (hbk)

Contents

List of contributors

Eliana Colunga, Department of Psychology, Psychology A128, Indiana University, Bloomington, IN 47405, USA

Matt H. Davis, MRC Cognition and Brain Sciences Unit, 15 Chaucer Road, Cambridge, CB2 2EF, UK

Melissa Dominguez, Department of Computer Science, University of Rochester, Rochester, NY 14627, USA

Michael Gasser, Department of Computer Science, Lindley Hall 215, Indiana University, Bloomington, IN 47405, USA

Robert A. Jacobs, Department of Brain and Cognitive Sciences, University of Rochester, Rochester, NY 14627, USA

Ping Li, Department of Psychology, 28 Westhampton Way, University of Richmond, Richmond, VA 23173, USA

Bodo Maass, Department of Experimental Psychology, South Parks Road, Oxford, OX1 3UD, UK

Peter McLeod, Department of Experimental Psychology, South Parks Road, Oxford, OX1 3UD, UK

Denis Mareschal, Centre for Brain and Cognitive Development, School of Psychology, Birkbeck College, University of London, Malet Street, Bloomsbury, London, WC1E 7HX, UK

J. Bruce Morton, Department of Psychology, University of Western Ontario, London, Ontario, N6A 5C2, Canada

Yuko Munakata, Department of Psychology, 345 UCB, University of Colorado at Boulder, Boulder, CO 8309-0345, USA

David C. Plaut, Carnegie Mellon Institute 115-CNBC, 4400 Fifth Avenue, Pittsburgh, PA 15213-2683, USA

Steven R. Quartz, Division of Humanities and Social Sciences, and Computation and

Neural Systems Program, H&SS, 228-77, California Institute of Technology, Pasadena, CA 91125, USA

Philip T. Quinlan, Department of Psychology, The University of York, Heslington, York, YO10 5DD, UK

Douglas L. T. Rohde, Massachusetts Institute of Technology, NE20 437E, 3 Cambridge Center, Cambridge, MA 02139, USA

Thomas R. Shultz, Department of Psychology, McGill University, 1205 Penfield Ave, Montreal, Quebec, H3A 1B1, Canada

Sylvain Sirois, Department of Psychology, The University of Manchester, Manchester, M13 9PL, UK

Jennifer Merva Stedron, Department of Psychology, University of Denver, 2155 South Race Street, Denver, CO 80208, USA

Mark T. Wallace, Department of Neurobiology and Anatomy, Wake Forest University School of Medicine, Winston-Salem, NC 27157, USA

Modelling human development: In brief

Philip T. Quinlan
Department of Psychology, The University of York, UK

This book has grown out of a longstanding interest in the potential for uniting studies of brain development with studies of artificial neural networks—uniting the study of "model" brains with the study of "real" brains (Quinlan, 1991, 1998). Although the book is intended for those who have a general interest in the psychological underpinnings of development and those whose primary interests are in attempting to model human development with connectionist networks, some of the chapters contain details of neurobiological aspects of development. In this way, research on real and artificial brains has been brought together in one book. All of the chapters deal with developmental processes but no attempt has been made to impose a uniform approach or theoretical framework. I placed no constraints on what topics the authors chose to write about and therefore the current volume reflects both the depth and breadth of what it is that these contributors feel is currently most important. The variety of methods and approaches described reflects the diversity and liveliness of the field.

The book assumes some basic knowledge of the basic connectionist concepts and some familiarity with what a fully connected (multilayered) back-propagation network is. This is the most popular kind of neural network that has featured in the psychological literature and there are now many step-by-step accounts of the operation of these networks (Marcus, 2001; McLeod, Plunkett, & Rolls, 1998; Plunkett & Elman, 1997; Quinlan, 1991). It is also the case that the individual authors have taken great care to explain novel techniques or architectures in some detail. So although there is some

1

technical material included, I feel that the content is generally understandable given a basic familiarity with the more central concepts.

A PERSONAL PERSPECTIVE

In a review that I wrote some time ago (Quinlan, 1998) I started by taking a hard look at what was then known about brain development. At that time, a dominant view was that the neurons that were present at birth were not likely to increase in number. In this respect, the term "brain development" was something of a misnomer because neurons died and were not replaced, so that essentially development could be characterised as a process of sculpting a neural network from a fixed number of units and their random interconnections. More particularly, brain development was seen as Darwinism operating at the neural level (Edelman, 1987). By this account, weak, redundant or just plain irrelevant neurons and their interconnections are simply weeded out by a process of natural selection. I am sure that there are still serious proponents of such a view, but on a much more careful reading of the literature other accounts appeared to be far more plausible: Brain development is characterised by both regressive and progressive changes. Regressive changes such as neural cell death are well documented (Ellis, Yuan, & Horvitz, 1991) but it is also clear that many other forms of progressive structural changes take place (Purves, 1994) and because of these, simple neural Darwinism accounts appeared to be inadequate.

Moreover, there was some consensus that during early brain development the making and maintaining of connections between neurons may be due to both activity-dependent and activity-independent processes (Shatz, 1996). At the neural level these aspects seemed to reflect, in part, environmental and genetic factors, respectively. Issues concerning nature versus nurture clearly permeate thinking about human development down to the cellular level. The fact that connectionist models typically deal only with activity-dependent processes came across as being something of a shortcoming. Weight changes are seen to be the products of a given learning regimen and because of this they provide almost no insights into activity-independent processes. Moreover, although many grandiose claims have been made about the biological plausibility of connectionist nets (see Page, 2000, for a discussion) at a very basic level the models failed to simulate neural development. For instance, in real brains the notion that the pattern of interconnectivity is random is simply wrong. Neurons can be extremely selective in choosing the right sorts of other neurons to synapse with. So even before beginning an in-depth look at the then current modelling literature some interesting limitations of fixed-architecture neural networks—as a biologically plausible account of human brain development—were apparent. Now, of course, it is possible to argue that these models were never intended to be taken as literal accounts of brain development but it nevertheless seemed timely to try to explore how models of real neural development might inform models of human development.

Having summarised the basic facts about neurological development, a second aim was to review the relevant connectionist literature on models that at least on the surface appeared to be more brain-like in their methods than simple fixed architectures. Again there was a reasonably large literature to cover and in attempting to bring this literature together I coined the term "dynamic neural network" (or, more simply, "dynamic networks"). A dynamic network is defined as any artificial neural network that automatically changes its structure through exposure to input stimuli. As might be imagined, there turned out to be numerous types of models that could be defined as dynamic networks. There were various accounts of regressive changes. For instance, there were models of neural cell death—models that removed both units and connections—and models that just removed connections but left units intact. In addition, there were generative models that added units and connections. Perhaps the most elaborate (and perhaps most unwieldy) models were those marrying regressive and progressive changes. Development in this account consists of cycles of growth and then shrinkage of structures.

So, overall, many aspects of brain development had been incorporated into various connectionist models of development either by design or incidentally. Nonetheless, two serious problems remained. First, it seemed important to be able to tie together the psychological with the physical because the central assumption in reviewing the work was that some changes at the physical level have observable effects at the psychological level.

One provocative example relates to studies involving brain development in the rhesus monkey (Goldman-Rakic, 1987). It had been discovered that the density of synapses in the brain of the developing monkey increases dramatically over the last third of gestation and that this increase continues up until about 4 months postnatally (Rakic et al., 1986). It had also been noted that there is a marked overproduction of synapses between 2 and 4 months and that the incidence of synapses is actually greater than that observed in the adult brain. The complete developmental progression revealed that after 4 months there is a significant decrease in synapses over the next year and then a more gradual decline in numbers over the remaining life-span. Also, from the available data, it seemed that this developmental pattern held for all areas of the brain studied.[1]

---

[1] The notion that the same developmental trend holds for all brain regions has been questioned with respect to human development. Something of an issue now exists over the degree to which brain development, and in particular the growth and recruitment of synapses, follows the same developmental trend across the human brain. For a dissenting view see Huttenlocher and Dabholkar (1997).

The marked overproduction of synapses between the second and fourth month seemed to be intimately related to changes taking place at the cognitive level. To examine this possibility, Goldman-Rakic (1987) studied how the infant monkeys performed on a version of a standard Piagetian task of human infant object permanence—the A-not-B task (a detailed account of this task is given in Chapter 3 by Munakata, Morton, & Stedron). In the standard task the child is presented with two containers (e.g. an A cup and a B cup). The experimenter shows the child a small object and hides it under the A cup. The child may then retrieve the object from under the A cup. After doing this several times, the experimenter hides the object under cup B. In committing the A-not-B error the child will then try to retrieve the object from under cup A. This is despite the fact that both cups are in view, are within easy reach, and the child has actually seen the object being placed under cup B. For a brief period, children of around 7 months of age will commit the A-not-B error. Prior to 7 months they will fail to search for hidden objects and after about 12 months of age children successfully retrieve hidden objects.

The basic findings of the studies with monkeys revealed that the developmental progression shown by human infants did occur in the developing monkeys. Critically, although humans make the A-not-B error at around the seventh month, monkeys were found to make the error between approximately 2 and 4 months of age. The central point was that the occurrence of the error in monkeys accompanied the overproduction in synapses. As a consequence it was argued that the ability to carry out these tasks was contingent upon the growth of a critical mass of cortical synapses and that competent performance was eventually predicated upon "the elimination of excess synapses that occurs during adolescence and young adulthood." (Goldman-Rakic, 1987, p. 601).

Clearly this is quite a strong claim given the data, and indeed alternative accounts of performance are provided in Chapter 3, but at the time, this was quite a striking example of research that took seriously the possibility that cognitive development reflects underlying structural changes at the neural level. Other data can also be used to support the idea of close links between physical and psychological changes but in many cases important neurological changes occur during gestation and, because of this, their psychological correlates remain a mystery. Nevertheless, the fact that there is significant brain development during the early years of life (see Johnson, 1997, pp. 32–39; Quartz, 1999, p. 53) suggests fruitful work that attempts to link physical with psychological changes should be possible. At the very least it would be surprising if brain development during these early years has no consequences for psychological development.

Having considered possible links between brain development and psychological development, it was then pertinent to ask what psychological insights had been gained from the connectionist work on dynamic networks. Progress here had been very limited indeed and there was only one example that provided tantalising suggestions as to a causal link between a structural change and a corresponding functional transition. This example was provided by the work of Shultz, Mareschal, and Schmidt (1994) in relation to learning about the properties of a simple balance-beam, as originally described by Piaget. Again, for those unacquainted with the task, children are presented with a balance-beam that is configured with various weights. Different configurations of weights are used and the distances of the weights from the fulcrum vary. The beam is stabilised and the child has to say whether the configuration would balance, or, if not, which side would drop when no longer supported. As with the object-searching (A-not-B) task discussed before, performance on this task follows a distinct behavioural progression through a series of conceptual stages. The account is best conveyed in the manner set out by Raijmakers, van Koten, and Molenaar (1996) and in this formalism two dimensions—weight and distance from the pivot—are defined and one of the dimensions is classified as *dominant* and the other as *subordinate*. Four general rules describe the developmental trend:

Rule 1: consider only the dominant dimension.
Rule 2: consider the subordinate dimension if, and only if, the values on the dominant dimension are equal.
Rule 3: consider both dimensions and in case of conflict guess.
Rule 4: consider both dimensions in a proper way.

The work reported by Shultz et al. (1994) in modelling this developmental progression followed on from McClelland's earlier account. McClelland (1989) configured a fully connected back-propagation network to do the task. In a given simulation, the net was trained with input stimuli, each of which represented a balance-beam configuration. Similar novel stimuli were then used to assess the model's acquired knowledge about the problem. The results showed that the net progressed through—essentially—a series of discrete stages, at each of which the outputs were predominantly in line with one of the four rules stated above. There then appeared to be an abrupt change to behaviour more in keeping with the next rule in the sequence. Although McClelland (1989) noted that these abrupt changes came about through a genuinely continuous learning process, on a more careful analysis Raijmakers et al. (1996) showed that the network actually exhibits only continuous and not discrete transitions between periods of particular rule-like behaviour.

Perhaps the major shortcoming of this work was that the net was unable to achieve behaviour commensurate with Rule 4 without also regressing to Rule 3 behaviour. This particular shortcoming was addressed by Shultz et al. (1994) in their simulations with a dynamic network known as the cascade-correlation algorithm. A comprehensive account of the cascade-correlation algorithm is provided by Sirois and Shultz in Chapter 1: Suffice it here to note that the algorithm is a constructivist method whereby new units are generated and recruited as learning proceeds. So, from a minimal architecture comprising a layer of input units each connected to a single output unit, the network is capable of growing new intermediate (hidden) units and connections as learning proceeds. Summarising the results greatly, Shultz et al. (1994) replicated McClelland's findings in all major respects, except that their nets were able to successfully produce Rule 4 responses in the absence of regressing and producing Rule 3 responses.

From the analyses undertaken by Shultz et al. (1994), it became evident that the addition of hidden units throughout the course of learning enabled the nets to capture fine-grained distinctions between differences on the weight and distance dimensions. Such distinctions appeared to underlie the network's ability to respond more appropriately as the training regime proceeded. Of particular interest, though, is the finding that the recruitment of a new hidden unit tended to accompany the quick progression from one stage of development to the next. Simply put, this finding seemed to show that growth in neural structures may underpin stage transitions at the psychological level. By this view there appears to be a pleasing rapprochement between evidence from neurobiology, psychology, and finally, modelling. Moreover, statements about the neural implausibility of dynamic networks that generate new units over time are themselves thrown into doubt given the recent discovery of neurogenesis taking place in adult brains (see Scharff, 2000, for a review). It really does appear that the generation, recruitment and survival of new neurons in adult brains takes place.[2]

In many respects, the foregoing merely sets out my interest in dynamic networks and is intended to convey my own personal view of what I take to be important developmental issues. What I also have tried to do is provide a justification for considering models of psychological development alongside discussion of brain development. The past 20 years of connectionist research is a testament to the fact that a great deal has been learnt from studying these kinds of models. Moreover, as many of the ensuing chapters reveal, many nonintuitive results are still being produced by studying such architectures.

THE STRUCTURE OF THE BOOK

I conclude my contribution with a very brief synopsis of the different chapters. I have intentionally glossed over the details, and also over some of the contradictions that become evident as you read through the chapters. There are opposing views expressed in the book, particularly with respect to

---

[2] The paper by Schultz et al. was eventually published in 1998 (Quinlan, 1998).

constraints on development, but it is not for me to pre-empt the debates nor to attempt to settle them. Although some may find the disagreements unsettling, I take this to be a sign of the liveliness and intellectual interest that exist in the field.

Although there are no explicit structural markers included in the book I have divided the material into roughly three sections. The first section primarily contains material about general conceptual development and comprises the chapters by Sirois and Shultz (Chapter 1), Mareschal (Chapter 2), and finally Munakata et al. (Chapter 3). All of the chapters in this section deal directly with basic issues in developmental psychology and all explore, to differing degrees, how best to model performance in standard Piagetian tasks.

Chapter 1 provides a detailed exposition of the cascade-correlation algorithm and Sirois and Shultz show how certain key Piagetian concepts can be explained by analogy to the operation of this kind of generative connectionist architecture. Not only does this chapter provide a good grounding in describing the operation of a particular dynamic architecture, but it also provides an example of how certain, difficult to define, concepts may be operationalised. Indeed, Sirois and Shultz provide several examples of how this algorithm can be used to model performance in certain classic Piagetian (e.g. conservation/seriation) tasks.

In Chapter 2, Mareschal provides an integrative review of some of his own work on modelling cognitive development. He covers a range of abilities (infant categorisation, word learning and phoneme discrimination, and again, object permanence). A variety of different architectures are described in order to model these different abilities. As Mareschal states, though, this allows him to explain a range of different domains in terms of a common set of (connectionist) mechanisms. Interestingly, he concludes with a brief digression on a possible framework for thinking about static and dynamic architectures. He claims that whereas "networks with fixed connectivity are good models of learning in infancy, . . . networks that developed their own connectivity are better models of later learning and development" (p. 78). This is an interesting possibility and he admits that it raises the issue of how the static connectivity system develops into the dynamic connectivity system.

In Chapter 3, Munakata et al. provide a useful example of how thinking about the brain can inform modelling. More particularly, they are keen to link the functioning of prefrontal cortex with perseveration and describe variants on the same sort of fixed architecture as providing some instructive insights into this possibility. Again, much of this work concerns Piagetian tasks and Piagetian concepts and, again, there are in existence proofs that connectionist architectures can simulate detailed characteristics of the development of human behaviour.

The second section of the book focuses on linguistic development and comprises chapters by Li (Chapter 4), Davis (Chapter 5), Rohde and Plaut

(Chapter 6), and, finally, Gasser and Colunga (Chapter 7). Li examines the phenomena in first language acquisition of over- and undergeneralisation of different inflected forms. This is quite a striking contribution in that he describes the operation of models of self-organisation. Here, unlike the standard back-propagation networks, no teaching signal is provided for a given input stimulus: The models evolve via processes that are sensitive to the internal structure of the input stimuli themselves and their statistical characteristics. Central to the back-propagation algorithm is the idea of an error signal that is computed for each input pattern. The error signal is defined as some measure of the discrepancy between the actual output the net produces for a given input and the desired output provided as a teaching signal. This error signal is then used in adjusting the weights on the connections throughout the net (for a much more exact account see Hinton, 1999). Given the importance of the teaching signal in back-propagation it is referred to as a *supervised* method of learning. Li, however, concentrates on *unsupervised* methods in which no explicit instruction is given and shows how these methods can be used to model structural development within and between different linguistic stores (i.e. within and between a phonological lexicon and a semantic store).

As Li suggests, one literal reading of the back-propagation algorithm— that for every input stimulus there is an external teacher supplying the exact desired output—is simply a hopeless construal of how first language acquisition takes place. By this view, back-propagation is clearly an implausible characterisation of language acquisition processes. Li then uses the limitations of back-propagation to, in part, motivate his choice of unsupervised methods. Although these particular points are well taken, the strict dichotomy between supervised and unsupervised learning algorithms is perhaps not so clear as it may appear, particularly in cases where an internally generated teaching signal is used to adjust connection weights in the absence of any externally supplied information. Although such examples are rare, they do exist (see Becker & Hinton, 1995, and for further discussion of these issues see also O'Reilly, 1998).

In Chapter 5, Davis explores issues concerning vocabulary acquisition with various recurrent architectures made famous by Elman (1990). Such nets as these incorporate additional hardware (i.e. units and connections) that operate as a kind of additional memory buffer in which the immediately preceding hidden unit representation is incorporated into the current training case. As Chater (1990, p. 8) states in this respect "activation from past inputs recirculates around the network thus enabling it to have a continuing influence on the outputs at future time-steps". Such nets have typically been used to simulate sequence/grammar learning. However, in a novel application Davis uses a recurrent architecture to simulate the ability to segment a continuous stream of characters (i.e. phonemes) into lexical units. Of additional interest, though, are the human-like developmental trends that the extended model exhibits.

In Chapter 6, Rohde and Plaut concentrate on a more traditional application of recurrent networks: the learning of grammatical sequences. There is no doubting the fact that this chapter is provocative because it stands in direct opposition to the "less-is-more" hypothesis previously advanced by Elman (1993). In its original form, this hypothesis appeared to have computational support from the demonstrations that simple recurrent networks could learn the structure of an artificial (English-like) grammar, but only when memory resources were increased over training or when the input started simple and increased in complexity over time. Simply put, Rohde and Plaut have been unable to replicate these findings and, as well reporting a systematic series of simulations, they present a critical and thought-provoking discussion of similar claims that have been advanced in the literature. Their chapter extends their previous research on the topic (Rohde & Plaut, 1999) and until a robust defence of the less-is-more hypothesis is published it is difficult to see what the response could be.

The final chapter in the "linguistic section" is Chapter 7, by Gasser and Colunga. Something that became apparent during the course of editing the book was the incredible impact that the work of Saffran and colleagues has had (Saffran, Aslin, & Newport, 1996) on the field. Such work is repeatedly referenced throughout this book and it has clearly spawned both further work (Marcus, Vijayan, Bandi Rao, & Vishton, 1999) and controversy (see Marcus, 2001, Chapter 3). In this regard, the chapter by Gasser and Colunga is a welcome contribution because they summarise the basic findings succinctly and also provide thought-provoking simulations. A central issue here is with the degree to which concepts such as *identity* can be incorporated into a connectionist model, although the work also speaks to more general issues concerning the nature of learning in infancy. Gasser and Colunga might feel that I have done them something of a disservice in having included their chapter in a section on language development because they couch their work in terms of pattern learning. Although they do discuss work in relation to language learning, the implication is that the mechanisms that they describe have a general applicability outside the problems posed by grammar learning. In this regard the work is clearly in keeping with the idea that, at some fundamental level, both linguistic and nonlinguistic domains may be dealt with by similar learning mechanisms (see Saffran, Johnson, Aslin, & Newport, 1999, for discussion of the same point).

The third and final section deals, essentially, with biological processes or, at the very least, biologically inspired processes. It starts with Chapter 8 by Dominguez and Jacobs, who are concerned with the development of visual abilities and pick up on some of the themes about developmental constraints discussed in Chapter 6 by Rohde and Plaut. The primary concern in

Chapter 8 is with an aspect of stereo vision, namely the development of binocular disparity sensitivities, and the details of the simulations they describe are closely tied to known properties of the human visual system. In addressing this issue, Dominguez and Jacobs examine how the mature performance of a multilayered network is affected by the type of input that it is exposed to during the course of learning, specifically, how altering the type of input affects the eventual mature state of the network. They compare three different learning regimens: (1) in which the quality of the input remained unchanged throughout learning; (2) a coarse-scale-to-fine scale learning regimen; and (3) a fine-scale-to-multiscale regimen. In the second case, the network was initially provided with inputs that carried only gross visual information about the content of the input, and it was only over the course of training that the inputs were changed such that the fine detail became exposed; this patterning of the input was reversed for the final case, in which fine details were provided from the start and only later did the inputs carry the gross characteristics. Compared with the no-change control case, both of the models that had ordered inputs showed better levels of eventual improvements in performance.

The next two chapters, by Quartz (Chapter 9) and Wallace (Chapter 10), deal with aspects of real brain development and it is these chapters that provide the reader with the opportunity to judge the degree to which research on real and artificial neural networks converge. Quartz takes the opportunity to extend his constructivist manifesto (Quartz & Sejnowski, 1997) and discusses a conceptualisation of development in which both learning as statistical inference and learning as the construction of efficient representations are considered. Central to the discussion is the notion of development constraints that are rooted in dynamic brain development. Clearly, the personal perspective outlined above is very much in keeping with this particular account.

Chapter 10 provides a fascinating account of cross-modal neural integration in which Wallace traces the development of multisensory neurons in the superior colliculus. One reason I feel that this work is of such importance is that it speaks directly to an old issue in developmental psychology—namely whether (essentially) perceptual development should be construed primarily as a process of sensory integration or as sensory differentiation. Bower (1974) was clear that development should be construed according to a differentiation hypothesis, claiming that "It is apparently easier for an organism to grow with undifferentiated perceptual system than with differentiated sensory modalities." (p. 120). A more measured conclusion, however, is provided by Wallace in Chapter 10, and it is clearly the case that no such simple hypothesis can explain the wealth of data that supports a much more subtle account of neuropsychological development.

The book closes with Chapter 11, by McLeod and Maass, which returns to the consideration of characteristics of artificial rather than real neural networks. The authors review some previous work on "so-called" evolutionary connectionism and then go on to report new simulations of a child learning to catch a ball. Obviously this particular example is very different from the more cognitive abilities discussed elsewhere in the book, yet the content of the chapter provokes thought about fundamental issues concerning human development. It is tempting to argue that the work also provides something of a common framework for thinking about more general issues in debates about nature versus nurture.

In closing, I take this opportunity to thank several people who have provided help during the production of the book. Both Julian Pine of the Department of Psychology, Nottingham University, and Tim Rogers of the MRC Cognition and Brain Sciences Unit, Cambridge, provided in-depth comments on all of the chapters. Their contributions helped me greatly during the editorial process and their insightful comments considerably influenced my own thinking about the content of the book. I would also thank Gareth Gaskell, who perhaps unwittingly helped in engaging with me in discussion. His enduring optimism about connectionist modelling is a constant source of encouragement. Finally, I thank Charles Hulme for his invitation to edit this book and for his comments on this opening chapter.

REFERENCES

Becker, S., & Hinton, G. E. (1995). Spatial coherence as an internal teacher for a neural network. In Y. Chauvin & D. E. Rumelhart (Eds.), *Backpropagation: Theory, architectures, and applications* (pp. 313–349). Hillsdale, NJ: Lawrence Erlbaum Associates, Inc.

Bower, T. G. R. (1974). *Development in infancy*. San Francisco: W.H. Freeman and Co.

Chater, N. (1990). *Learning to respond to structure in time*. Unpublished manuscript. Department of Psychology, University College London.

Edelman, G. (1987). *Neural Darwinism: The theory of neuronal group selection*. New York: Basic Books.

Ellis, R. E., Yuan, J., & Horvitz, H. R. (1991). Mechanisms and functions of cell death. *Annual Review of Cell Biology, 7*, 663–698.

Elman, J. L. (1990). Finding structure in time. *Cognitive Science, 14*, 179–211.

Elman, J. L. (1993). Learning and development in neural networks: The importance of starting small. *Cognition, 48*, 71–99.

Goldman-Rakic, P. S. (1987). Development of cortical circuitry and cognitive functions. *Child Development, 58*, 601–622.

Hinton, G. E. (1999). Supervised learning in multilayer neural networks. In R. A. Wilson & F. C. Keil (Eds.), *The MIT encyclopaedia of the cognitive sciences* (pp. 814–816). Cambridge, MA: The MIT Press.

Huttenlocher, P. R., & Dabholkar, A. S. (1997). Regional differences in synaptogenesis in human cerebral cortex. *Journal of Comparative Neurology, 387*, 167–278.

Johnson, M. H. (1997). *Developmental cognitive neuroscience*. Oxford: Blackwell.

Marcus, G. F. (2001). *The algebraic mind*. Cambridge, MA: The MIT Press.

Marcus, G. F., Vijayan, S., Bandi Rao, S., & Vishton, P. M. (1999). Rule learning by seven-month-old infants. *Science, 283*, 77–80.

McClelland, J. L. (1989). Parallel distributed processing: Implications for cognition and development. In R. G. M. Morris (Ed.), *Parallel distributed processing: Implications for psychology and neurobiology* (pp. 8–45). Oxford: Clarendon Press.

McLeod, P., Plunkett, K., & Rolls, E. T. (1998). *Introduction to connectionist modelling of cognitive processes*. Oxford: Oxford University Press.

O'Reilly, R. C. (1998). Six principles for biologically based computational models of cortical cognition. *Trends in Cognitive Science, 2,* 455–462.

Page, M. (2000). Connectionist modelling in psychology: A localist manifesto. *Behavioral and Brain Sciences, 23,* 443–512.

Plunkett, K., & Elman, J. L. (1997). *Exercises in rethinking innateness: A handbook for connectionist simulations*. Cambridge, MA: The MIT Press.

Purves, D. (1994). *Neural activity and the growth of the brain*. Cambridge: Cambridge University Press.

Quartz, S. R. (1999). The constructivist brain. *Trends in Cognitive Science, 3,* 48–57.

Quartz, S. R., & Sejnowski, T. J. (1997). The neural basis of cognitive development: A constructivist manifesto. *Behavioral and Brain Sciences, 20,* 537–596.

Quinlan, P. T. (1991). *Connectionism and psychology: A psychological perspective on new connectionist research*. Hemel Hempstead, UK: Harvester Wheatsheaf.

Quinlan, P. T. (1998). Structural change and development in real and artificial neural networks. *Neural Networks, 11,* 577–599.

Raijmakers, M. E. J., van Koten, S., & Molenaar, P. C. M. (1996). On the validity of simulating stagewise development by means of PDP networks: Application of catastrophe analysis and an experimental test of rule-like network performance. *Cognitive Science, 20,* 101–136.

Rakic, P., Bourgeois, J.-P., Eckenhoff, M. E., Zecevic, N., & Goldman-Rakic, P. S. (1986). Concurrent overproduction of synapses in diverse regions of the primate cerebral cortex. *Science, 232,* 232–235.

Rohde, D. L. T., & Plaut, D. C. (1999). Language acquisition in the absence of explicit negative evidence: How important is starting small? *Cognition, 72,* 67–109.

Saffran, J. R., Aslin, R. N., & Newport, E. L. (1996). Statistical learning by eight-month-old infants. *Science, 274,* 1926–1928.

Saffran, J. R., Johnson, E. K., Aslin, R. N., & Newport, E. L. (1999). Statistical learning of tone sequences by human infants and adults. *Cognition, 70,* 27–52.

Scharff, C. (2000). Chasing fate and function of new neurons in adult brains. *Current Opinion in Neurobiology, 10,* 774–783.

Shatz, C. J. (1996). Emergence of order in visual system development. *Proceedings of the National Academy of Science USA, 93,* 603–608.

Shultz, T. R., Mareschal, D., & Schmidt, W. C. (1994). Modeling cognitive development on balance scale phenomena. *Machine Learning, 16,* 57–86.

CHAPTER ONE

A connectionist perspective on Piagetian development

Sylvain Sirois
Department of Psychology, University of Manchester, UK

Thomas R. Shultz
Department of Psychology and School of Computer Science, McGill University, Montreal, Canada

The significance of Jean Piaget's contribution to the study of cognitive development has gained the status of a truism. Even today, some of his original ideas such as object permanence spawn significant theoretical debates (e.g. Baillargeon, 2000; Bogartz et al., 2000), generating contributions from connectionist and other computational approaches as well (see Mareschal, 2000, for a review). However, Piaget's heuristic value is not limited to the identification of several robust empirical regularities, however useful these may be to benchmark developmental theories.

Piaget's contribution to the study of cognitive change can be divided, for convenience, into four distinct areas. First, as alluded to in the previous paragraph, his work led to the identification of several robust findings about infants' and children's cognitive abilities. Notions such as object permanence, conservation, and seriation, for example, spawned hundreds of studies that replicated, extended, or refined Piaget's earlier work.

Second, his many original findings stemmed from a novel methodological approach that stressed underlying cognitive operations rather than the usual success or failure assessment of performance. In the clinical interview, for instance, a child's errors prompt researchers to inquire about the justifications for the child's behaviour. These justifications provide insights into the underlying conceptual system of the child that elude traditional, quantitative assessment approaches.

Third, Piaget proposed a unifying framework to discuss cognitive competence. His structural theory argued that any level of cognitive functioning from infancy into adulthood, was a function of a general information-processing structure, the nature of which changed over the course of a person's interaction with the environment.

Finally, Piaget proposed mechanisms of cognitive change. Notions such as assimilation, accommodation, equilibration, and abstraction refer to the processes involved in the various changes observed over infancy, childhood, and adolescence. It may prove useful to bear these four aspects of Piaget's legacy in mind when assessing his contribution to developmental psychology.

Piaget's theory as a whole is no longer tenable nowadays, which is the second truism of this introduction. However, rejecting the whole of Piaget's contribution on the basis of criticisms of specific aspects of his work could prove detrimental for current research. Piaget has been proved wrong in many respects, but quite right in others, and sometimes just too vague for proper assessment (Boden, 1994). For instance, some of his empirical findings rely heavily on the specific methodology he used. Diamond (1985) showed how performance on object permanence tasks can be altered by modifying the delay between disappearance and search, for example. Furthermore, Piaget's suggestion that a general structure, or *structure d'ensemble*, sustains all of cognition proves untenable (Karmiloff-Smith, 1992). That is, progress in different domains can follow different trajectories and, at times, suggest different levels of competence. However, despite these and other criticisms, current connectionist research independently supports one of Piaget's central claims: that cognitive change is a function of self-organisation and adaptation.

This chapter examines how neural network research might help to clarify the crucial yet vaguely specified mechanisms of cognitive change in Piaget's theory. It has been argued that notions such as assimilation and accommodation were too vague to be useful (Klahr, 1982). Neural networks escape such criticism because they are fully specified, and it may prove fruitful to assess whether Piaget's vague intuitions have correlates in these dynamical mechanisms. We focus on a particular algorithm—cascade correlation (henceforth the CC algorithm), which has been used successfully to model a host of developmental phenomena, including Piagetian tasks. It must be stressed that the purpose of the chapter is to draw analogies between aspects of Piaget's theory and aspects of connectionist models. We are not attempting to express one theory in terms of the other. Rather, Piagetian research can benefit from the specification and computational power inherent to neural network research, and connectionist work can benefit from the broad theoretical framework laid down by Piaget.

The first section of the chapter outlines the mechanisms of cognitive change discussed by Piaget, and stresses how these mechanisms relate to learning and development. The second section presents the CC algorithm (Fahlman & Lebiere, 1990) and suggests how aspects of the model are analogous to Piagetian mechanisms. The third section discusses the success of the CC algorithm at modelling number conservation, a landmark Piagetian task. The fourth section, to highlight the broad applicability of the model, discusses the application of the algorithm to a typical empiricist problem: discrimination shift learning. Finally, the discussion argues that generative neural networks such as the CC algorithm can provide the building blocks of a general framework for cognitive development and, in the process, provide a novel level of specification to some of Piaget's important but ill-specified ideas.

PIAGET'S MECHANISMS OF CHANGE

Piaget's developmental theory is articulated around the notion that cognition is a function of a general knowledge structure. Within a given structure (i.e. a level of development), three processes strive to optimise representations: assimilation, accommodation, and equilibration. When an optimised structure nevertheless fails to adequately represent information from the environment, the process of reflective abstraction generates a higher-level structure aimed at improving the child's understanding of the world.

Assimilation is the process through which information from the environment is distorted to fit the current cognitive structure of the organism, and accommodation is the adaptation of the structure to environmental input. Assimilation prompts accommodation, and accommodation improves further assimilation (Piaget, 1980). Equilibration is the process that maintains a balance between assimilation and accommodation, ensuring that (only) enough accommodation takes place to promote satisfying assimilation. Piaget called these three processes (assimilation, accommodation, and equilibration) *functional invariants*. He assumed that they were part of the infant's innate endowment (along with a few motor reflexes), and that the processes never changed over the course of life. That is, he considered the functional invariants to be impervious to experience. These invariant functions built the mind, using experience and the current state of the mind as materials.

The process of equilibration, with respect to assimilation and accommodation, produces a state of equilibrium. For Piaget, equilibrium was the goal of a self-organising, adaptive mind (Boden, 1994). But this equilibrium is only temporary if it is the current best solution from an inadequate structure. That is, a child can be satisfied with his or her solution to a problem only as long as it is his or her best comprehension of the problem, even in the face of failure. But the repeated conflict between the child's assimilation–accommodation achievement and disconfirming environmental feedback will eventually prompt a structural reorganisation.

Structural changes are possible through the process of abstraction, of which Piaget (1980) distinguishes two forms[1] whose functioning is also regulated by a process of equilibration. Reflective abstraction involves a functional reorganisation of a cognitive structure in order to promote higher-level assimilation–accommodation. Reflective abstraction itself consists of two distinct processes: (1) reflecting, which is a projection to a higher level of what is at a lower level; and (2) reflexion, which is reorganisation at a higher level. The other form of abstraction is reflected abstraction (or reflected thought), which concerns making explicit and integrating functional structures generated through reflective abstraction. For Piaget (1972, 1980), the semiotic function (i.e. the capacity to represent objects through symbols) is essential for abstraction, and language is especially important in reflected abstraction.[2]

Recent attempts to discuss Piaget in neural network terms (McClelland, 1995; Shultz, Schmidt, Buckingham, & Mareschal, 1995) did not quite succeed at this endeavour, mainly because they focused on assimilation and accommodation, ignoring the notion of abstraction. This focus on the twin processes of assimilation and accommodation may reflect a common belief; namely, that these are the fundamental developmental mechanisms in Piaget's theory. In his critique of Piaget, for example, Klahr (1982) described assimilation and accommodation as the "Batman and Robin" of cognitive development. With this analogy, Klahr stressed the mysterious nature of the processes, and thus the need to go beyond vague statements with respect to the mechanisms underlying cognitive change.

Although legitimate, Klahr's severe evaluation of Piaget is surprising for two reasons. First, for many Piagetians, equilibration—the "Superman" of development—is far more mysterious than assimilation and accommodation (Furth, 1972; Gallagher & Reid, 1981). Second, the process of abstraction is probably the most important developmental aspect of Piaget's structural theory (Case, 1999), and not assimilation and accommodation as many believe (Nersessian, 1998; Siegler, 1998). An outstanding question, not addressed by the Batman and Robin analogy, concerns the nature of learning. Piaget acknowledged that there was learning and not just development, but never clearly outlined how learning was achieved or how it interacted with development (Gallagher & Reid, 1981).

To discuss Piaget's mechanisms of change with respect to learning and development, we first need to introduce definitions we have outlined

---

[1] Actually, there is a third form of abstraction called empirical abstraction (Piaget, 1980), which concerns the acquisition of object properties (i.e. content rather than competence acquisition). Empirical abstraction allows the storage of factual information from the environment.

[2] This section presents a significantly simplified account of Piaget's theory, on which he worked for over 50 years. Conservative estimates suggest that on cognitive development alone, Piaget published over 40 books and 100 articles (Miller, 1989). This section presents a summary of key elements in Piaget's theory based mostly on one of his later papers (Piaget, 1980), where his work-in-progress was possibly most explicit.

elsewhere (Sirois & Shultz, 1999). We defined learning as parametric change *within* a processing structure in order to adapt to the environment. This broad description was meant to be compatible with general statements about learning, such as found in nativistic (Fodor, 1980) and developmental (Carey 1985; Piaget, 1980) accounts. A key element in this definition of learning is the quantitative nature of the process. In contrast, development was defined as change *of* an existing structure to enable more complex parametric adaptations. This definition highlights a key idea for most developmental theories: a qualitative change in the structure supporting cognitive activity. For instance, our definition of development is compatible with Carey's (1985) conceptual change, and Karmiloff-Smith's (1992) representational redescription. We argued that such functional definitions of learning and development allow for useful distinctions between the two processes. There is no overlap between the processes, which constrains their unique contribution to cognitive change: learning as parameter adjustment within a given structure, and development as structural change that enables further learning.

Discussing the mechanisms of change in Piaget's theory within this formal distinction between learning and development, a specific interpretation emerges. Assimilation and accommodation can be construed as the learning component in Piaget's work, a different interpretation than typical Piagetian accounts that view accommodation as a developmental mechanism (Gallagher & Reid, 1981; Siegler, 1998). We suggest that accommodation only results in quantitative changes within the existing cognitive architecture. Essentially, information is assimilated in the system and, if the discrepancy between the internal representation and the external information is important, the system accommodates (i.e. adjusts its parameter values). The process of equilibration, which strives to move the system towards a state of equilibrium, ensures that enough accommodation takes place given the current level of assimilation. Learning is thus the quantitative process that adapts the current representational structure to the input it receives. A system in equilibrium is one where further accommodation would not improve assimilation.

Development is the more radical process by which an inadequate architecture is qualitatively transformed in order to promote further learning. Reflective abstraction describes this developmental process. The current representational structure is reformulated at a more adaptive level (reflecting), whereby the new structure can be used for further parametric adaptations (reflexion). Furthermore, the construction of the new structure makes use of the same mechanisms involved in learning. The new structure assimilates the previous representations and accommodates towards a new level of equilibrium. Whereas learning consists of adapting the current structure, development involves learning new structures. This suggests a rather compact model with few primitives (the three functional invariants) implementing two functionally different processes (external adaptation versus internal restructuring).

This interpretation of mechanisms of change in Piaget's theory marks a departure from recent attempts (McClelland, 1995; Shultz et al., 1995). These approaches focused on assimilation and accommodation as developmental mechanisms, which misrepresents Piagetian development. Assimilation and accommodation do not produce higher-level representational structures; rather, these mechanisms work within the confines of the current structure. The key developmental process in Piagetian theory is reflective abstraction (Case, 1999). What we propose in this chapter, then, is a framework that explores the full range of functional change mechanisms in Piaget's work.

We will discuss the usefulness of this interpretation in a later section. For now, we should acknowledge that our description of Piagetian learning and development remains rather abstract. Piaget was vague about how his theory could be implemented and his lack of mechanical specification is reflected in our review. However, it is useful to turn to neural network models for the level of specification we ultimately strive for and which renders the theory operational and testable. The next section presents a neural network algorithm that exhibits some unique properties to aid in this enterprise.

THE CC GENERATIVE ALGORITHM

The cascade correlation (CC) algorithm is a feedforward neural network algorithm. Such networks are trained to acquire the functional dependency that exists in pairs of input and output patterns (i.e. that a set of target output activations Y is some function of a set of inputs X). At any time in training, network error is defined by the discrepancy between the target output activations and the network's current output. The structure of the network (the number of modifiable weights, the activation functions of the units, and how units are connected to one another) defines a multidimensional error surface. Training involves navigating on this error surface towards (ideally) its global minimum.

The learning rule in CC is called quickprop and, as the name implies, it is both similar to and quicker than back-propagation. Connection weights are changed as a function of the discrepancy between actual and desired output, as in back-propagation, but it uses the second-order derivative of the unit activation (the curvature of the error surface) as well as the first-order derivative (the slope of the error surface). That is, the learning rule uses the change in slope over time, as well as the slope at a given time. This results in comparatively faster leaning.

Another important feature of CC is its ability to build a network topology as it learns. At the onset of training, CC networks consist only of an input layer, a bias unit,[3] and an output layer, as well as initially random weights from input and bias units to the output layer. Such two-layer networks are able to learn linear functions. In case of more complex (i.e. nonlinear) functions, the networks alter their topologies over the course of training in order to increase their computational power.

There are two training phases in CC, input and output training, and networks switch between these phases as a function of their performance (see Fahlman & Lebiere, 1990, for a full description). Training in a new network begins with output training. This training phase is so named because only the weights coming into the output units are adjusted in order to reduce network error. Training goes on until the error reaches a satisfactory low level, in which case training ends, or until error reduction stagnates above the tolerable error level. When error is still high and can no longer be reduced, the network switches to input training.

During input training, weights to the output units are temporarily frozen. A pool of candidate hidden units (typically, eight) is constructed, and random weights are generated between the input and bias units and each candidate. Using the quickprop algorithm, these weights are modified in order to increase the absolute correlations of the candidate units' activations with residual error measured at the output units. For each candidate, the correlation between its activation and output error is computed, which is an index of the unit's ability to represent the main source of error for the network's current structure. The procedure entails that candidates are trained to capture the largest source of residual error. When correlation increments stagnate, the candidate unit with the largest absolute correlation with the network's residual error is added to the network. Weights coming into the new hidden unit are permanently frozen (see Johnson, 1997, for neurophysiological support), and random connections are generated between the new unit and each output unit. Other candidate units are discarded.

The network then resumes output training. Weights from input and bias units are unfrozen and can be further modified. The weights from the new hidden unit to output units are also trained. The computational power of the network has thus been increased. Stagnation of the learning process motivated the alteration of the network's structure. Each new hidden unit is trained to capture residual error with respect to the task the network is trying to acquire. The permanently frozen weights coming into a hidden unit, after it could no longer improve its correlation with error, ensure that the hidden unit will remain a specialised error detector, dedicated to some specific aspect of the problem.

---

[3] The bias unit is a convenient way to implement modifiable thresholds in neural networks. It acts as an input unit but its activation value is a constant. Units downstream from the input bank can modify their activation threshold through a learnable connection from the bias unit.

Many problems require more than a single hidden unit before network error is reduced to a satisfactory level. Training in CC involves an alternation of output and input training phases. Each input phase begins when error reduction stagnates. Furthermore, candidate units receive input activations not only from input and bias units, but also from all previously recruited hidden units. This cascaded addition of units allows the network to acquire progressively abstract representations of the environmental input, with new units able to integrate previous processing. Figure 1.1 shows different learning phases in a CC network.

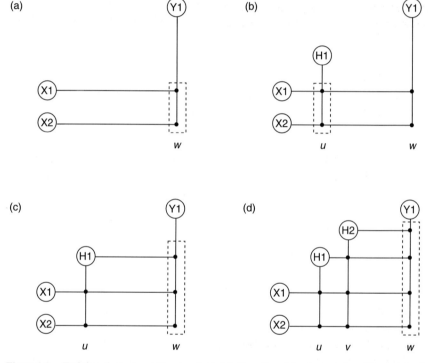

Figure 1.1.   Training phases in a CC network. In (a), the network begins training with a minimal architecture connecting both input units X1 and X2 to the output unit Y1. During the initial output training phase, connection weights w (identified by the dotted rectangle) are modified to reduce network error. When learning stagnates and fails to reduce error to a satisfactory low level, the network switches to input training. In (b), a candidate-hidden unit H1 is trained (only one candidate is shown, for clarity). Input training involves modifying the connection weights u to maximise H1's absolute correlation with network error. When correlation maximisation stagnates, the candidate unit with the largest correlation is incorporated in the network and output training resumes, as shown in (c). Connection weights w are trained to further reduce network error. Finally, in (d), a network with two hidden units is shown. As can be seen, hidden unit H2 receives signals from the input units and from the previous hidden unit through connection weights. Output training with such a network involves, as before, modifying only weights w.

At the onset of training, CC networks consist only of a set of input units and a bias unit (not shown) connected to a set of output units, such as depicted in Figure 1.1(a). The initial representational power of this network can be expressed as:

$$Y = f(wX) \tag{1.1}$$

where Y is the output vector of the network, f is the activation function of the output unit (typically, the S-shaped sigmoid function), w the weights between X and Y, and X the input vector. This network can initially represent output functions that are a linear combination of input. When this fails to solve the problem at hand, the network alters its topology. The first hidden unit recruited is trained to correlate with the network's residual error. Its representational power is expressed as:

$$H_1 = f(uX) \tag{1.2}$$

where H_1 is the hidden unit's activation, f is the activation function of the hidden unit (typically, the sigmoid function), u the weights between X and H_1, and X the input vector. The values of weights u are learned in Figure 1.1(b).

When the new hidden unit is incorporated in the network, however, the representational power of the network changes substantially, as shown in Figure 1.1(c). From Equation 1.1, where the network could represent linear functions, the representational power has grown into:

$$Y = f(w(X \mid f(uX))) \tag{1.3}$$

where Y is the output vector, f the sigmoid function, w the weights feeding into output units, X the input vector, and u the weights feeding into the first hidden unit. Similarly, the representational power of the network, after a second hidden unit is recruited, can be expressed as:

$$Y = f(w(X \mid f(uX) \mid f(v(X \mid f(uX)))))) \tag{1.4}$$

where Y is the output vector, f the sigmoid function, w the weights feeding into output units, X the input vector, u the weights feeding into the first hidden unit, and v the weights feeding into the second hidden unit.

The topology-modifying properties of the CC algorithm have many implications compared to static architecture networks. First, there is no need to figure out beforehand what is an appropriate topology for a given problem, because the network grows the necessary computational power as it learns. General-purpose mechanisms build the necessary representational space for a given problem. Moreover, a network only grows a sufficient topology; the network will not grow too powerful and merely memorise the input–output training pairs.[4] Finally, the network is also less likely to get stuck in a local

---

[4] A network with too many hidden units might memorise the training pairs because it is not pressured to abstract an underlying function relating inputs to outputs.

minimum, because the number of units and modifiable weights contribute to define the error surface. Trapped locally, a CC network would recruit a new hidden unit, which would increase the dimensionality of the error space and consequently redefine the error surface.

With this introduction to CC, it is now possible to draw analogies with Piagetian mechanisms of change. Output training, where the structure is maintained and only quantitative changes are made, is analogous to assimilation–accommodation processing. The network computes an output based on the input it receives (assimilation), and adapts its weights based on environmental feedback (accommodation). The process of equilibration is implemented by the learning rule, which computes change (accommodation) as a function of current output (assimilation). When assimilation–accommodation equilibrium is reached, either the network has learned the problem (error is within a tolerable low level), or structural changes are required (error can no longer be reduced significantly and performance is still conflicting with environmental feedback).

Hidden unit recruitment in CC is akin to reflective abstraction. Candidate hidden units receive input from all lower-level units and are trained to capture residual error of the network's performance (reflecting). The candidate with the best correlation with network error is incorporated in the network, which allows the network to integrate the new representation into its solution (reflexion). The cascaded architecture that is developed allows for higher-order abstractions in the most recent units, permitting developmental stages (e.g. Piaget's "spiral of knowing"; Gallagher & Reid, 1981). Again, the learning rule provides equilibration in this reflective abstraction phase. In essence, candidate hidden units assimilate input when their activations are computed, and units accommodate to the network's residual error by weight adjustment.

The "functional invariants" that permit overt learning are also involved in the construction of new representations. New units redescribe the network's current knowledge through a process of equilibration. What is different, however, is the learning target. During output training, the target is the desired output. During input training, the learning target is error, the inability of the current structure to capture the desired output. In this framework, target behaviours and new internal representations are learned, as these involve only parametric changes (i.e. weight adjustment). The developmental mechanism is the one that assesses learning failure, prompts learning that redescribes current representations, and incorporates the new representation into the network. These aspects of the CC algorithm result in a qualitative change in network architecture (and, thus, increased representational power), and are analogous to Piaget's notion of reflective abstraction.

CC networks can thus illustrate an implementation, in computational terms, of the vague mechanisms at the core of Piaget's theory. Not surprisingly then, such networks have been successful at modelling a variety of developmental phenomena, including seriation (Mareschal & Shultz, 1993, 1999), the acquisition of velocity, time and distance concepts (Buckingham & Shultz, 2000), conservation (Shultz, 1998), the acquisition of personal pronouns (Oshima-Takane, Takane, & Shultz, 1999; Shultz, Buckingham, & Oshima-Takane, 1994), and the balance-scale (Shultz et al., 1995). Moreover, using the same principled framework, such networks were also able to capture age-related change in a variety of discriminative learning tasks (Sirois & Shultz, 1998a, 1998b).

The next two sections review two of these simulations to assess the usefulness of a constructivist framework such as CC. First, a model of conservation (Shultz, 1998) is reviewed; this is a classical Piagetian task and is associated with robust empirical regularities. Whereas object permanence was the quintessential achievement of infancy, conservation was Piaget's comparably crucial test of developmental change during childhood, and the ability of CC to successfully model these tasks would provide useful information as to how Piaget's vague ideas may or may not explain such changes. Next, a model of discrimination shift learning (Sirois & Shultz, 1998a, 1998b) is reviewed. These tasks are also associated with a robust literature and involve some age-related phenomena. In recent years, so-called neo-Piagetian theorists have argued that developmental approaches should try to explain such data stemming from the empiricist tradition (Case, 1999). In the context of this chapter, which argues that learning is a crucial component of Piaget's developmental theory, it is important to examine this research.

A MODEL OF CONSERVATION

Conservation is the belief in the continued equivalence of physical quantities despite perceptual transformations that alter only the appearance of one of the initially equal quantities. Figure 1.2 shows various transformations used in number conservation tasks. The child is initially required to agree that both rows of objects, prior to a transformation, have an equal number of objects. The experimenter then transforms one of the two rows. For example, objects in one row may be moved closer to one another, thus compressing the row (as shown at the bottom of Figure 1.2). The experimenter then asks the child whether both rows still have the same number of objects, or whether one has more. Such tasks require that the child distinguish transformations that alter quantities from those that preserve quantities (Siegler, 1981). Piaget (1965), and many others who followed, observed that children below the ages of 6 or 7 performed differently than older children. On conservation problems that preserve number, such as compression or elongation, the younger children tend to respond that one row (usually the longer one) has more items. By contrast, older children answer correctly on transformations that maintain number.

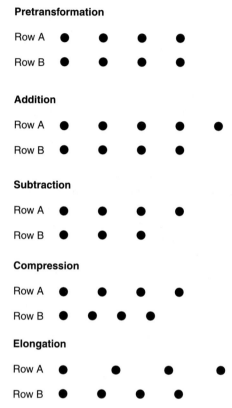

Figure 1.2. Various transformations in a number conservation task. The child must first agree that both pretransformation rows are equal. The experimenter then modifies one of the rows by adding or subtracting an element, or by changing the density of one row, thereby compressing or elongating it. After the transformation, the child is asked again about the equality of the two rows.

For Piaget, the shift from nonconservation to conservation reflected a major and central shift in underlying conceptual structure, whereby children come to understand the invariance of certain properties such as number despite the transformation of other features such as length (Flavell, Beach, & Chinsky, 1966). Although current theorising (Karmiloff-Smith, 1992) would question whether conservation acquisition reflects a general developmental shift such as acquiring concrete operational thought, it remains that conservation is one of the most studied phenomena in psychology (Shultz, 1998). Moreover, varied and robust findings make conservation an ideal target to assess models of cognitive development.

Shultz (1998) proposed a CC model of number conservation. The main aim of this research was to capture four main regularities found in the conservation literature. First, there is a shift from nonconservation to

conservation around the ages of 6 or 7 for large quantities. This is the acquisition effect, and it can be abrupt. Second, correct conservation judgements
initially emerge for small quantities. This is referred to as the problem size
effect. Third, children who do not conserve tend to choose the longer row
as holding more objects, which is known as the length bias effect. Finally,
nonconservers continue to conserve until they actually see the results of a
transformation. When a transformation is screened, young children can
make correct conservation judgements, although they revert to incorrect
judgements when they see the transformation. This is the screening effect.

What constitutes naturally occurring, relevant experience for the acquisition of conservation is unclear and, as such, Shultz (1998) aimed to model
conservation in an environment with few built-in assumptions. Rows were
described in terms of perceptual characteristics, their length and density.
Providing networks with the number of items in each row would make the
problem trivial, and would also thwart Piaget's (1965) efforts to prevent or
limit the child's use of number estimation (which would, similarly, defeat the
purpose of the task, which aims to study the understanding of conservation
rather than fluency in numerical comparisons). Shultz (1998) used the
common transformations depicted in Figure 1.2: addition, subtraction,
compression, and elongation.

Networks in these simulations had thirteen input units and two output
units: two inputs for the perceptual features of each of the two rows before
and after the transformation (for a total of eight), one input for the identity
of the transformed row, and four inputs for the nature of the transformation.
Perceptual features of rows (length and density) ranged in value from 2 to 6.
The identity of the transformed row was coded as −1 for the first row, 1 for
the second row. Addition was coded as 1 −1 −1 −1, subtraction as −1 1 −1 −1,
elongation as −1 −1 1 −1, and compression as −1 −1 −1 1, such that transformation information was presented arbitrarily (i.e. the networks had to
learn how these binary inputs relate to specific numerical comparisons).
These thirteen input units were connected to two output units. The output
units used the sigmoid activation function, with an output range between
−0.5 and 0.5. The task that networks were required to learn consisted of
turning only the first output on if the first row had more items, turning only
the second output on if the second row had more items, and leaving both
outputs off if both rows had an equal number of items. Figure 1.3 depicts
how a particular conservation problem is presented to a network.

Shultz (1998) used 5 levels of length and 5 levels of density, for a total of
25 possible rows. Initial rows could have an equal number of elements, or one
row could have an additional element.[5] These three combinations (A = B,

---

[5] Although rare in the literature, initial inequality of the two rows should not pose a problem
for competent conservers (Shultz, 1998).

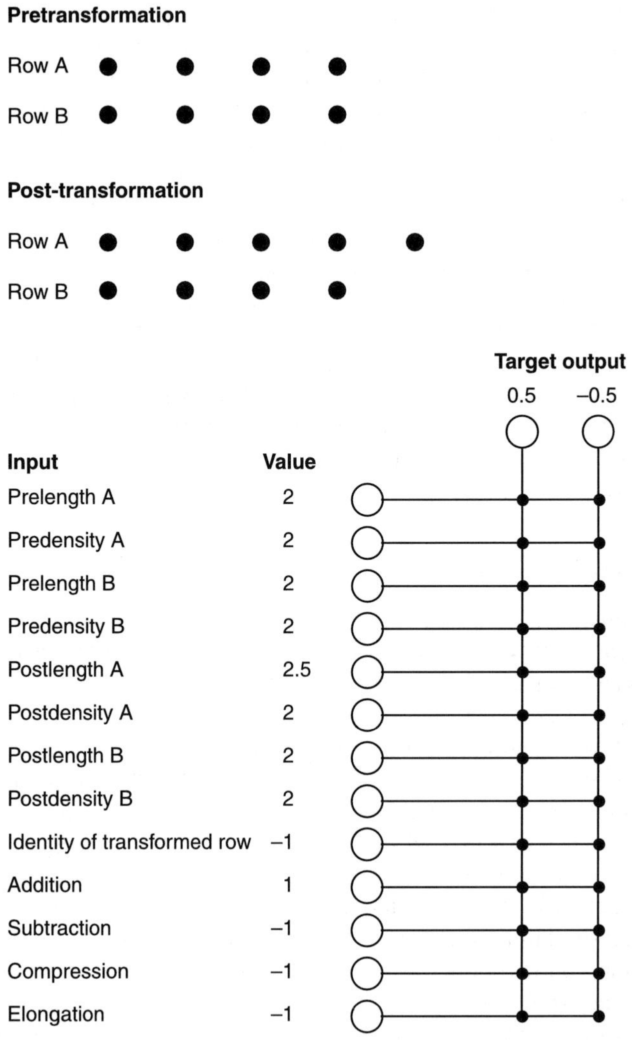

Pretransformation

Row A   ●   ●   ●   ●

Row B   ●   ●   ●   ●

Post-transformation

Row A   ●   ●   ●   ●   ●

Row B   ●   ●   ●   ●

Target output

0.5   −0.5

Input	Value
Prelength A	2
Predensity A	2
Prelength B	2
Predensity B	2
Postlength A	2.5
Postdensity A	2
Postlength B	2
Postdensity B	2
Identity of transformed row	−1
Addition	1
Subtraction	−1
Compression	−1
Elongation	−1

Figure 1.3. Example of a conservation problem and its implementation for the simulations. The top portion of the figure shows the rows before the transformation, with each holding four elements, and both rows after the transformation, where row A has an additional element. The bottom portion of the figure shows how this particular problem is presented to a network. The network shown has yet to recruit hidden units. The first eight units (from the top) encode perceptual features as real valued numbers. The identity of the transformed row, A or B, is coded as −1 or 1, respectively. Each transformation type (addition, subtraction, compression, and elongation) has one input unit. For a given transformation, the appropriate unit is given a value of 1, and the other three units receive −1.

A > B, B > A) multiplied by the number of rows yields 75 initial pairs of rows. Either row could be transformed in any of the four ways we have identified (addition, subtraction, compression, or elongation), resulting in $2 \times 4 = 8$ possible transformations. The number of initial pairs of rows, 75, times the number of possible transformations, 8, allows for a bank of $75 \times 8 = 600$ number conservation problems. For each network in these simulations, 420 training problems and 100 test problems were selected randomly from the bank. Test problems allow researchers to evaluate the ability of a network to generalise outside of the training space. When the effects of interest can be assessed on test problems (i.e. those problems the network was never trained on), one can safely assume that network performance is not merely bounded to the specific training set used. Networks in these simulations used the default parameter values specified by Fahlman (1991), with the exception of input-epsilon and output-epsilon, which were set at 0.01 (compared to 1.0 and 0.35, respectively).[6] These were lowered to prevent error fluctuations during learning.

Conservation acquisition

In a first simulation, 20 networks were trained on conservation problems as described in the previous section. Each network is unique in terms of initial random weight values (its "heredity") and the order in which it encounters problems (its "environment"). As such, the 20 networks used are analogous to sampled participants in empirical studies. The networks required an average of 1305 epochs[7] to solve the problem, and recruited an average of 8.3 hidden units. Network performance on test problems closely matched performance on training problems and, at the end of training, the average proportion correct on test problems was .95.

All 20 networks showed sudden increases in performance. For 12 networks, the largest jump followed the recruitment of a second hidden unit. The largest jump followed the third unit in 6 networks, the fourth unit for 1 network, and the eighth unit for the last network.

Overall, the performance of CC networks shows that the networks can acquire correct conservation judgements and that these generalise to novel instances of conservation problems. Networks do not merely memorise input–output pairs; rather, they abstract the underlying function in this conservation task.

---

[6] Epsilon values control the amount of linear gradient descent to use in updating weights. Input-epsilon does this for input weights (i.e. weights entering hidden units) and output-epsilon takes care of output weights (i.e. weights entering output units).

[7] An epoch is defined as the presentation of all training problems (in this case, 420), akin to a block of trials in human experiments.

The problem size effect

In this simulation, test patterns were defined as small if the numerosity of the smaller row was less than 12, and large if it exceeded 24. The proportion correct for each type of pattern was recorded over the course of training. Networks made significantly more errors on larger problems than on smaller problems. The effect was not observed in the first few epochs, however, as networks have yet to learn enough to show the effect. Moreover, the effect disappeared by the last stages of training, where networks essentially master conservation and performance is nearing ceiling.

As observed with children, networks proved sensitive to problem size. This effect is not limited to conservation tasks, however. Similar effects can be observed in number comparison tasks, for instance (Sekuler & Mierkiewicz, 1977). Shultz (1998) argued that the problem size effect can be simulated in connectionist networks through analogue encoding of magnitude.

The length bias effect

Nonconserving children typically make erroneous conservation judgements based on one salient dimension (Piaget, 1965). Children may judge the longer of two numerically equal rows as having more items, ignoring the larger density of objects in the shorter row. Similarly, they may consider that a taller beaker contains more liquid than a shorter one, failing to compensate for the larger width of the shorter beaker.

Whether CC networks would show the length bias effect was examined in two simulations (Shultz, 1998). Analysing the results of a first simulation, it was found that length bias accounted for roughly 80 per cent of network errors, a figure comparable to empirical data obtained with children (Siegler, 1995). To explain the origins of this bias, it is useful to note that number-altering transformations (i.e. addition and subtraction) typically involve a change in length for one row, which becomes longer or shorter while density remains constant. Therefore, length bias may be learned rather than reflecting the intrinsic salience of length over density. It follows that a density bias could be induced by uncorrelating length and numerosity on number-altering transformations, and thus varying density.

In a second simulation, Shultz (1998) trained 20 networks in an environment where length remained constant on addition and subtraction problems. That is, adding an item to a row made it denser, and subtracting an item made it sparser. The results showed that, when length is constant on number-altering transformations and thus density becomes the better predictor of number, a density bias similar to the usual length bias emerges. Networks, as children, appear sensitive to perceptual dimensions that best correlate with the results of transformations.

The screening effect

Nonconserving children can provide correct conservation judgements when the transformation is screened (Bruner, Olver, & Greenfield, 1966). For example, the child is told that one of the initially equal rows is stretched (behind a screen) so as to make it longer. The child responds that the two rows still have an equal number of items. When shown the result of the transformation as the screen is removed, however, younger children revert to nonconservation.

Screened problems can be easily simulated by not providing input values for the length and density of the transformed row after the transformation. Like the children in screened tests, networks can receive input only about the initial rows, the identity of the transformed row, the nature of the transformation, and the unchanged row after transformation. Networks in this simulation were tested on both screened and unscreened problems.

Results from this simulation showed that performance of networks was better on screened problems than on standard problems for the first few hundred epochs of training. As with children, then, removing misleading perceptual information improves a network's performance. When networks have developed a more abstract representation of the problem, however, reliance on perceptual information drops (such as shown with the length bias) and screened problems are no longer easier than standard problems.

Discussion

CC successfully captures a variety of robust effects associated with number conservation. Not only can networks successfully acquire conservation, but also all networks exhibited a large sudden jump in performance over the course of training, the sort of discontinuity considered the hallmark of developmental change (van der Maas & Molenaar, 1992). For most networks, this occurred soon after the recruitment of the second or third hidden unit. Beyond mere acquisition, networks exhibited various perceptual effects identified in the literature, namely problem size, length bias, and screening.

These successes stem from a neural network algorithm that alters its topology as a function of experience. We have argued that the mechanisms in CC implement the vague notions used by Piaget to discuss such developmental changes. A further advantage of this mechanically precise framework is that the underlying representations in networks can be scrutinised to a finer level than is possible with children. Shultz (1998) further analysed conservation networks using a technique called contribution analysis. Contributions are the products of sending activations and weights feeding into output units. A pattern by contribution matrix is created and is submitted to a principal components analysis (PCA), which is used to evaluate the most important dimensions of variation in a network's activity. This technique is useful to characterise how networks represent information from the input units and, if applicable, from hidden units. The technique can be applied at any stage of training but is most informative when conducted at the end of output training phases, a point when the current structure has reached equilibrium (which may be temporary if the solution is beyond the current representational power of the network).

Results from these analyses suggest that the time course of a network's acquisition of conservation involves a shift from how the rows look, in terms of their length and density, to a concern with the nature of the transformation and the identity of the transformed row. Therefore, networks do not merely fit data but also conform to psychological evidence that understanding transformations is crucial for acquiring conservation (Siegler, 1981).

In Piagetian terms, we could say that output training on conservation problems corresponds to assimilation–accommodation learning. Initially, and after every new hidden unit is installed, a network adjusts the weights entering its output units in order to gradually reduce error, using a learning rule that implements equilibration. In this process, weight changes (accommodation) are a function of the discrepancy between actual outputs (assimilation) and target outputs (contributed by environmental feedback about whether or not the rows are numerically equal). Periods of temporary equilibrium (a balance of assimilation and accommodation) are reached as error reduction stagnates, creating a relative plateau in conservation performance as measured by some continuous variable such as proportion correct. At this point, a network recruits a new hidden unit, during input training, a phase analogous to Piaget's reflective abstraction. Here, weights entering candidate hidden units are adjusted (accommodation) so as to better track the network's current error. This corresponds to the aspect of reflective abstraction known as reflecting, as conservation problems get reformulated at a higher level of abstraction. In this reformulation, the network uses everything it knew about conservation before recruitment to re-represent particular conservation problems in terms of the amount of judgemental error that they still produce. These input-side weight adjustments are made with the same equilibration learning rule involving accommodation of weights to track network error at the outputs, using assimilation of problem inputs to produce the outputs. Once the correlations between hidden unit activations and network error stagnate, the best correlating hidden unit is installed into the network, and then integrated into a solution, a process corresponding to Piaget's other aspect of reflective abstraction, reflexion. Here again, the equilibration learning rule tries to achieve a balance between assimilation (actual outputs) and accommodation (change in output weights to reduce error). Spurts in the proportion of correct responses to conservation problems typically followed shortly on the heels of these hidden unit recruitments.

The knowledge representations achieved by the increasingly more powerful network revealed a decrease in attention to inputs of length and density of the rows and an increase in attention to transformation inputs. Relative plateaux in the proportion of correct responses to conservation problems typically marked the gradual stagnation of error reduction as the network finished integrating its new computational power through continued output weight adjustment (reflexion).

The simulations reported by Shultz (1998) provide a clear illustration of how competence such as conservation may be acquired and represented. But the learning ideas behind neural network models such as CC, despite similarities with Piaget's structuralist approach, owe more to the empiricist tradition than to any mentalist approach. It should prove interesting, therefore, to examine how the framework embodied in CC can be applied to a representative empiricist problem. Combining the empiricist tradition with Piagetian ideas into a single, coherent framework is at the core of neo-Piagetian approaches (Case, 1985, 1999; Pascual-Leone, 1970). The next section reviews a CC model of discrimination shift tasks.

A MODEL OF DISCRIMINATION SHIFTS

Discrimination shift tasks represent a basic form of concept learning tasks and are associated with a vast literature in which robust findings have been observed (Esposito, 1975; Wolff, 1967). Although the tasks originate in the animal conditioning literature and are linked to researchers such as Karl Lashley (1929) and Kenneth Spence (1956), later research with humans suggested to some researchers that discriminative learning taps basic cognitive development, and that the representations held by young children are radically different to those held by older children and adults (Kendler & Kendler, 1962, 1975). Therefore, a developmental framework with a formal learning component such as we are proposing might offer unique insights into these tasks.

Basic shift learning tasks are shown in Figure 1.4. In such experiments, pairs of stimuli with mutually exclusive attributes on three binary dimensions (e.g. shape, colour, and position) are shown repeatedly and participants must learn to pick the stimulus in a given pair exhibiting a target attribute (e.g. *circle*). Learning is feedback-driven (i.e. participants are told whether their choice on a given trial is correct or wrong) and lasts until a success criterion is reached (typically, eight correct responses in ten consecutive trials). When initial learning is successful, a shift in reward contingencies is introduced (usually without explicitly telling the participant). Shift learning phases can be distinguished based on the new target's dimension and on the stimuli used. Shifts within the initially relevant dimension imply that the new learning target is the other attribute of the previously relevant dimension (e.g. from *circle* to *square*). Conversely, shifts between dimensions imply that the new

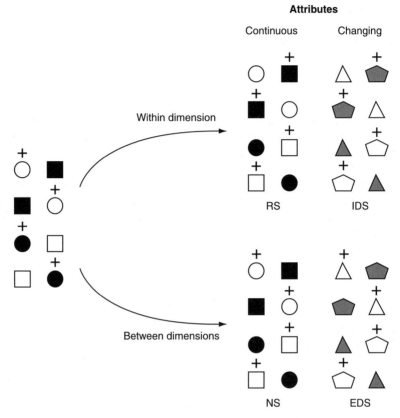

Figure 1.4.   Basic shift learning tasks. To the left are four stimulus pairs used in initial training, with *circle* as the target attribute; plus signs identify which stimulus in a pair is rewarded. The right-hand side of the figure shows reward contingencies for four types of shift, depending whether the shift is within or between dimensions, and whether attributes from the initial learning phase are used continuously or are changed at shift onset. For RS (within, continuous), the shift is from *circle* to *square*. For NS (between, continuous), the shift is from *circle* to *white*. For IDS (within, changing), the shift is from *circle* to *pentagon*, whereas for EDS (between, changing), the shift is from *circle* to *light grey*. EDS, extra-dimensional shift; IDS intra-dimensional shift; NS, nonreversal shift; RS, reversal shift.

target is from one of the initially irrelevant dimensions (e.g. from *circle* to *black*). Continuous shift learning tasks imply that the same attributes (e.g. *circle* and *square*) are used for both initial and shift learning, whereas total change tasks involve the use of new attributes (e.g. *triangle* and *pentagon*) at the onset of shift learning.

Despite over 40 years of research, no general and inclusive theoretical account of data obtained with various discrimination shift tasks had been formulated, partly because of methodological variations between subsets of tasks within which theories were articulated. Before presenting our CC model of these tasks (Sirois & Shultz, 1998a, 1998b), we review the relevant phenomena that successful accounts must capture.

Empirical regularities

In continuous shift learning tasks, shifts within the initially relevant dimension are called reversal shifts (RS). In an RS, all previous responses must be changed. A shift to a previously irrelevant dimension is called a nonreversal shift (NS), and requires that only half of responses be changed. Adults and children above the age of 10 typically require fewer trials to learn an RS than to learn an NS (Wolff, 1967), which is contrasted with the performance of preschool-aged children, for which both shifts are equally difficult, despite an incorrect assumption in some of the literature that preschoolers solve an NS more quickly than an RS (Sirois & Shultz, 1998a).

During an NS, responses to half of the stimulus pairs remain unchanged (e.g. half of the circles are white). Performance on these unchanged pairs remains high throughout the shift learning phase for preschool-aged children. In adults, the initially correct performance on unchanged pairs typically drops during the first few trials of the shift learning phase. It increases again as participants solve the new learning contingency.

Optional shift tasks (OS), however, have three phases (Figure 1.5). After an

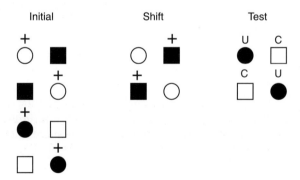

Figure 1.5. Depiction of the optional shift task. On the left, the four stimulus pairs used for initial training are used, with plus signs identifying reward. In this example, the initial target is *circle*. After initial training is successful, reward contingencies are changed for half the pairs, and only these are used for shift learning, shown in the middle. At this point, the nature of the shift is equivocal: the new target could be either *square* or *black*, in the example. When shift training is complete, testing takes place with the remaining pairs (i.e. those that were not used in the shift phase). As each pair is presented, participants merely pick the stimulus that should provide reward, as before. The question of interest is whether the shift has generalised to these pairs. Behaviour can be changed (identified by C) or unchanged (identified by U) with respect to initial training.

initial learning phase using all four stimulus pairs and one target attribute (e.g. *circle*), a shift learning phase is introduced. During this second phase, only half of the stimulus pairs are used for shift learning. These pairs are chosen so as to make the shift equivocal. That is, the new target attribute cannot be identified from this subset of stimulus pairs. In a third phase, participants are tested on the remaining stimulus pairs (i.e. those not used in the shift learning phase). The purpose of this test phase is to assess whether partial shift learning in the second phase generalises to the remaining pairs. Preschool-aged children do not typically generalise a partial shift to the remaining stimuli, whereas older children and adults do. It is as if preschool-aged children respond to individual stimuli, whereas older people respond to stimulus dimensions (and thus generalise to all instances along the same dimensions).

In total change tasks, shifts within the initially relevant dimension are called intra-dimensional shifts (IDS). Participants must learn to select a new attribute from the previously relevant dimension (e.g. from *circle* to *pentagon*). Although the previous dimension is relevant, previous responses are not because new attributes are used. The procedure makes the onset of the shift obvious, however. Shifts to a previously irrelevant dimension in total change tasks are called extra-dimensional shifts (EDS). As with the NS, the new target is an attribute from a previously irrelevant dimension (e.g. from *circle* to *light grey*). Preschool-aged children, older children, and adults typically execute an IDS more quickly than an EDS.

A model of discrimination shifts

Modelling age-related phenomena from discrimination shift tasks posed unique problems compared to previous developmental work with CC. First, as the conservation simulations exemplified, models of development examine the changes in performance and representations over the time course of the acquisition of successful performance on a task. In discrimination shifts, however, both the younger children and adults can successfully learn the tasks. They merely differ in their ease of learning the various shifts and on generalising partial learning to unchanged (EDS) or untrained (OS) stimuli. Moreover, there is nothing inherently better in the pattern of adult performance (save for average acquisition speed). Second, the tasks are simple from a computational perspective. Discrimination shift tasks are linear problems, and networks do not recruit hidden units to solve them. These two problems are related, however, as we found a single solution for both of them.

There exists in the shift learning literature an interesting phenomenon called the overtraining effect. By providing a few training trials beyond the usual success criterion (between 10 and 30 extra trials usually works), preschool-aged children can be made to perform in similar ways to adults:

they execute an RS more quickly than an NS, show the temporary decrease in performance on unchanged pairs of the NS, and generalise partial shift learning to test pairs in OS tasks. We thus proposed that the pattern of performance of older children and adults stemmed from extensive, iterative processing of stimuli, which would result in spontaneous overtraining (Sirois & Shultz, 1998a). Levine (1966) had observed that adults in concept learning tasks rehearsed their current hypothesis about the target during learning. Moreover, the memory literature suggests that the development of spontaneous rehearsal in children occurs over the same age period as changes in discrimination shift patterns are observed (e.g. Flavell, 1963). Spontaneous overtraining was thus our working hypothesis for these simulations.

We trained CC networks on the various shift learning tasks discussed in the previous section. To model adult performance, we reduced the default value for the allowable discrepancy between current and target output values. This would, all other things being equal, result in additional training trials for adult networks. Inputs to the networks were binary representations of two dimensions for two stimuli, each at a unique position (left or right). These input units were connected to two output units. The learning tasks involved turning on the appropriate output unit, depending on whether the target attribute was at the left or right position.

Networks successfully captured all phenomena under investigation (Sirois & Shultz, 1998a, 1998b). Adult networks learned an RS more quickly than an NS, an IDS more quickly than an EDS, showed impaired performance on unchanged pairs of an NS, and generalised partial shift learning to test pairs of an OS. Preschool networks, on the other hand, learned RS and NS equally fast, learned an IDS more quickly than an EDS, maintained high performance on unchanged pairs of the NS, and showed no generalisation in OS tasks. A series of network analyses showed that the deeper learning of adult networks, compared with preschool-aged networks, resulted in significantly more emphasis on relevant inputs, and that adult networks better ignored irrelevant information (Sirois & Shultz, 1998a). That is, weights grew large for relevant dimensions while they neared zero for the irrelevant dimension. As such, a network trained on *circle* behaved as a function of *shape*. This substantial reliance on relevant information, coupled with little consideration for irrelevant inputs, made shifts within the initial dimension easier and resulted in the generalisation of partial shifts to test items.

Preschool-aged networks did not segregate relevant and irrelevant information very much. Their responses to individual stimulus pairs were instead a function of the specific combination of both types of information, akin to rote learning. That is, preschool-aged networks behaved as a function of the compound properties of stimulus pairs. They thus failed to benefit from shifts within the initially relevant dimension and did not show generalisation. These networks did learn something about the relevant dimension, however, as their performance on total change tasks shows. Introducing new attributes removes the effects of rote learning and allows the networks to exhibit some dimensional learning.

Discussion

CC successfully modelled basic shift learning tasks, providing the best coverage of this literature to date (Sirois & Shultz, 1998b). In contrast to conservation acquisition, these shift learning tasks are linear problems that do not require the recruitment of any hidden units. Consequently, in Piagetian terms, there is no need for reflective abstraction; the entire performance can be characterised as assimilation–accommodation learning. The accommodation that occurred during this learning was deeper for adult networks than it was for child networks, due to a parameter setting that tolerated less network error for adults than for children. This deeper accommodation in the adult networks was reflected in crisper knowledge representations, focusing more clearly on the relevant stimulus dimensions, and in adult-style shift performance.

Moreover, novel predictions were derived from this work. For instance, the spontaneous overtraining hypothesis suggests that adults would perform as preschoolers if extensive, iterative processing were prevented. Our preliminary results from shift learning tasks performed with a cognitive load support this prediction. Adults still execute an IDS more quickly than an EDS, but fail to execute an RS faster than an NS. Another prediction is that preschool-aged children would perform at chance on a classification task following pairwise training. This prediction is derived from network analysis suggesting that behaviour in preschool-aged networks is a compound function of attributes of both stimuli. Again, preliminary results from an experiment offer some support for this prediction, as preschool-aged children trained to the usual criterion on pair-wise discrimination show a classification performance only slightly above chance, and significantly lower than the performance of overtrained preschool-aged children.

The theoretical framework for learning and development embodied in CC networks thus applies to age differences in learning. In the case of discrimination shift tasks, a small change in depth of learning is sufficient to explain age-related changes in performance. As such, the model questions the suggestion that preschool-aged children and adults represent discriminations in qualitatively different ways. The nature of spontaneous overtraining remains to be determined, however. We have argued that it likely reflects a general-purpose mechanism, similar to suggestions found in Case (1985). But whether it is learned, developed, or is simply a function of maturation is an open question. This observation highlights an important limit of the current framework (and of all currently viable theories of cognitive development as well): Models are limited to simple tasks and must make use of assumptions with respect to crucial mechanisms that are beyond the scope of their purpose. We return to this point later.

This review of our shift learning work illustrates the broad applicability of the proposed framework for cognitive change. Here we have a demonstration of a model that captures domain-specific changes within the constraints of postulated domain-general changes. More importantly, the framework instantiates the crucial mechanisms of a formal developmental theory yet is readily applicable to phenomena originating from a learning, empiricist tradition. Ever since Pascual-Leone's (1970) attempt to discuss Piaget's schemata (i.e. the simplest unit of representation) in terms of classical conditioning, an important goal for many developmental psychologists has been to bridge learning and developmental traditions (Case, 1999). Our proposed framework achieves that.

GENERAL DISCUSSION

We raised two complementary questions in the introduction of this chapter. Can Piagetian theory gain from connectionist research? Alternatively, can connectionist research on development benefit from Piaget's work? To evaluate these questions, we should briefly review the four distinct contributions of Piaget to developmental psychology: unique empirical findings, novel methods, a broad theoretical framework, and developmental mechanisms. The first two of these contributions need not be questioned here. Piaget's original findings are still influential in contemporary theorising (Mareschal, 2000), and the methods he devised have helped to shed unique light on the process of developmental change. The latter two types of contributions are worthy of further discussion.

Although Piaget was severely criticised for the vagueness of the mechanisms he proposed to account for cognitive change (Klahr, 1982), it doesn't follow that he was wrong. Piaget argued that small, continuous changes were instantiated by assimilation and accommodation, the companion processes at the core of equilibration. These can be construed as the learning component in Piaget's theory. He further argued that the states of equilibrium thus reached may be suboptimal, and that a process of abstraction was necessary to generate a new level of representation that would allow for better equilibrium. He suggested that the same process of equilibration (i.e. a mixture of assimilation and accommodation) was involved in the construction of new representations. We have proposed that key features of CC correspond to these mechanisms. Equilibration is made possible by the learning rule, in which input is passed through the current structure (assimilation) and where the resulting error is used to adjust connection weights (accommodation). These correspond to the output-phase learning component of CC. When learning fails, a new hidden unit is trained to represent the network's current failure, allowing for a new level of representation, akin to abstraction in Piaget. Moreover, the same learning rule is used to train this new representation. Although Klahr's (1982) critique was legitimate, a neural network algorithm such as CC certainly meets the current standards of specification for cognitive theories with respect to how knowledge is represented and processed (Thagard, 1996). Piagetian theory thus has much to gain from the connectionist perspective.

How can connectionist approaches to development gain from Piagetian theory? At the end of the previous section, we alluded to an important limitation in most neural network models of development: the fact that they are typically limited to a very narrow subset of cognitive competence, thus lacking a broader perspective on cognitive change. The simulations reported in this chapter are no exception. A crucial assumption in our shift learning model is that adults iteratively process information, but there is no such processor in our model. Although the model enables us to evaluate a novel, promising perspective with respect to the shift learning literature, we have yet to implement this core assumption, let alone how such processing might change over time. A similar problem exists for the conservation model reviewed here. Number conservation is but a subset of conservation tasks. Although various types of conservation (e.g. number, liquids, mass) are acquired at different times over development, it may ultimately prove inaccurate to discuss the acquisition of a single type of conservation independently of progress on other forms of conservation. More generally, an important limitation of common neural network models is that they do not tell their story as dynamical elements of a broader system.

Piaget suggested that the mechanisms of development, striving for equilibrium, served the more general task of building the *structure d'ensemble* that underlies general cognitive competence (Boden, 1982, 1994). Recent empirical and theoretical work has suggested that a general cognitive structure is not a tenable construct as there is substantial domain-specific cognitive activity (Carey, 1985; Karmiloff-Smith, 1992). Although Piaget's theory is not compatible with a multiplicity of competencies, his crucial suggestion was that the functional invariants (assimilation, accommodation, and equilibration) build the cognitive architecture from domain-specific experiences. We can reject the suggestion of a domain-general design, but we might still wish to consider the elegance of a limited set of primitives underlying the construction of higher-order, integrative abilities. To the question of how to integrate the currently isolated models of highly specific competence, Piaget's suggestion would be to apply the same mechanisms used to construct the individual model in order to incorporate them into a progressively general structure.

The notion of the brain as a network of networks gains substantial appeal, in our view, when it can be argued that a limited, pervasive set of processes could build the individual parts as well as the progressively general modules. It has been argued that modularity is an emergent property of neural networks (Elman et al., 1996). Building networks of networks may implement this property, providing a well-specified alternative to Piaget's notion of *structure d'ensemble*. Evidence from the neurosciences suggests that the human brain is highly plastic (Quartz & Sejnowski, 1997), which further underscores the need to develop mechanisms that explain how networks of networks might emerge. Piaget's idea that a few simple processes might sustain this sort of construction may prove useful for the next generation of connectionist models of development.

In related work, a new algorithm called knowledge-based cascade correlation (KBCC) was found to speed learning by recruiting relevant, previously learned networks as well as single hidden units (Shultz & Rivest, 2000a, 2000b, 2001). This allows existing knowledge to influence new learning through automatic integration of network-based modules. Basically, networks already in the system compete with each other and with single hidden units for recruitment into a network learning a new problem. As we begin to apply KBCC to psychological tasks, perhaps the promise of a computational specification of knowledge integration across cognitive developmental tasks will be realised.

ACKNOWLEDGEMENTS

Preparation of this chapter was supported by a postdoctoral fellowship from the Natural Sciences and Engineering Research Council of Canada (NSERC) awarded to S.S. and an NSERC grant to T.R.S.

REFERENCES

Baillargeon, R. (2000). Reply to Bogartz, Shinskey, and Schilling; Schilling; and Cashon and Cohen. *Infancy, 1*, 447–462.

Boden, M. A. (1982). Is equilibration important? A view from artificial intelligence. *British Journal of Psychology, 73*, 165–173.

Boden, M. A. (1994). *Piaget*. London: Fontana Press.

Bogartz, R. S., Cashon, C. H., Cohen, L. B., Schilling, T. H., & Shinskey, J. L. (2000). Reply to Baillargeon, Aslin, and Munakata. *Infancy, 1*, 479–490.

Bruner, J. S., Olver, R. R., & Greenfield, P. M. (1966). *Studies in cognitive growth*. New York: Wiley.

Buckingham, D., & Shultz, T. R. (2000). The developmental course of distance, time, and velocity concepts: A generative connectionist model. *Journal of Cognition and Development, 1*, 305–345.

Carey, S. (1985). *Conceptual change in childhood*. Cambridge, MA: MIT Press.

Case, R. (1985). *Intellectual development*. New York: Academic Press.

Case, R. (1999). Conceptual development in the child and in the field: A personal view of the

Piagetian legacy. In E. Scholnick & S. Gelman (Eds.), *Conceptual representation: The Piagetian legacy* (pp. 23–52). Mahwah, NJ: Lawrence Erlbaum Associates, Inc.

Diamond, A. (1985). Development of the ability to use recall to guide action as indicated by infant's performance on AB. *Child Development, 56*, 868–883.

Elman, J. L., Bates, E. A., Johnson, M. H., Karmiloff-Smith, A., Parisi, D., & Plunkett, K. (1996). *Rethinking innateness: A connectionist perspective on development*. Cambridge, MA: MIT Press.

Esposito, N. J. (1975). Review of discrimination shift learning in young children. *Psychological Bulletin, 82*, 432–455.

Fahlman, S. E. (1991). *Common Lisp implementation of cascade-correlation learning algorithm* [computer program]. Pittsburg, PA: Carnegie Mellon University, School of Computer Science.

Fahlman, S. E., & Lebiere, C. (1990). *The cascade-correlation learning architecture* (Technical Report CMU-CS-90-100). Pittsburgh, PA: Carnegie Mellon University, School of Computer Science.

Flavell, J. H. (1963). *The developmental psychology of Jean Piaget*. New York: van Nostrand.

Flavell, J. H., Beach, D. R., & Chinsky, J. M. (1966). Spontaneous verbal rehearsal in a memory task as a function of age. *Child Development, 37*, 283–299.

Fodor, J. (1980). Fixation of belief and concept acquisition. In M. Piattelli-Palmarini (Ed.), *Language and learning. The debate between Jean Piaget and Noam Chomsky* (pp. 143–149). Cambridge, MA: Harvard University Press.

Furth, H. (1972). Furth's reply to Piaget's paper on the problems of equilibration. In C. F. Nodine, J. M. Gallagher, & R. H. Humphreys (Eds.), *Piaget and Inhelder on Equilibration* (pp. 21–29). Philadelphia, PA: The Jean Piaget Society.

Gallagher, J. M., & Reid, D. K. (1981). *The learning theory of Piaget & Inhelder*. Monterey, CA: Brooks/Cole Publishing Company.

Johnson, M. H. (1997). *Developmental cognitive neuroscience*. Cambridge, MA: Blackwell Publishers.

Karmiloff-Smith, A. (1992). *Beyond modularity: A developmental perspective on cognitive science*. Cambridge, MA: MIT Press/Bradford Books.

Kendler, H. H., & Kendler, T. S. (1962). Vertical and horizontal processes in problem solving. *Psychological Review, 69*, 1–16.

Kendler, H. H., & Kendler, T. S. (1975). From discrimination learning to cognitive development: A neobehavioristic odyssey. In W. K. Estes (Ed.), *Handbook of learning and cognitive processes* (Vol. 1, pp. 191–247). Hillsdale, NJ: Lawrence Erlbaum Associates, Inc.

Klahr, D. (1982). Nonmonotone assessment of monotone development: An information processing analysis. In S. Strauss (Ed.), *U-shaped behavioral growth* (pp. 63–86). New York: Academic Press.

Lashley, K. S. (1929). *Brain mechanisms and intelligence*. Chicago: University of Chicago Press.

Levine, M. (1966). Hypothesis behavior in humans during discrimination learning. *Journal of Experimental Psychology, 71*, 331–338.

Mareschal, D. (2000). Object knowledge in infancy: Current controversies and approaches. *Trends in Cognitive Science, 4*, 408–416.

Mareschal, D., & Shultz, T. R. (1993). A connectionist model of the development of seriation. *Proceedings of the Fifteenth Annual Conference of the Cognitive Science Society* (pp. 676–681). Hillsdale, NJ: Lawrence Erlbaum Associates, Inc.

Mareschal, D., & Shultz, T. R. (1999). Development of children's seriation: A connectionist approach. *Connection Science, 11*, 149–186.

McClelland, J. L. (1995). A connectionist perspective on knowledge and development. In T. J. Simon & G. S. Halford (Eds.), *Developing cognitive competence: New approaches to process modeling* (pp. 157–204). Hillsdale, NJ: Lawrence Erlbaum Associates, Inc.

Miller, P. H. (1989). *Theories of developmental psychology*. New York: Freeman.

Nersessian, N. J. (1998). Conceptual change. In W. Bechtel, & G. Graham (Eds.), *A companion to cognitive science* (pp. 157–166). London: Blackwell.

Oshima-Takane, Y., Takane, Y., & Shultz, T. R. (1999). The learning of first and second pronouns in English: Network models and analysis. *Journal of Child Language, 26*, 545–575.

Pascual-Leone, J. (1970). A mathematical model for the transition rule in Piaget's developmental states. *Acta Psychologica, 32*, 301–345.

Piaget, J. (1965). *The child's conception of number.* New York: Norton.

Piaget, J. (1972). *Problèmes de psychologie génétique.* Paris: Denoël/Gonthier.

Piaget, J. (1980). The psychogenesis of knowledge and its epistemological significance. In M. Piattelli-Palmarini (Ed.), *Language and learning. The debate between Jean Piaget and Noam Chomsky* (pp. 23–34). Cambridge, MA: Harvard University Press.

Quartz, S. R., & Sejnowski, T. (1997). The neural basis of cognitive development: A constructivist manifesto. *Behavioral and Brain Sciences, 20*, 537–596.

Sekuler, R., & Mierkiewicz, D. (1977). Children's judgment of numerical inequality. *Child Development, 48*, 630–633.

Shultz, T. R. (1998). A computational analysis of conservation. *Developmental Science, 1*, 103–126.

Shultz, T. R., Buckingham, D., & Oshima-Takane, Y. (1994). A connectionist model of the learning of personal pronouns in English. In S. J. Hanson, T. Petsche, M. Kearns, & R. L. Rivest (Eds.), *Computational learning theory and natural learning systems: Vol. 2. Intersection Between Theory and Experiment* (pp. 347–362). Cambridge, MA: MIT Press.

Shultz, T. R., & Rivest, F. (2000a). Using knowledge to speed learning: A comparison of knowledge-based cascade-correlation and multi-task learning. *Proceedings of the Seventeenth International Conference on Machine Learning* (pp. 871–878). San Francisco: Morgan Kaufmann.

Shultz, T. R., & Rivest, F. (2000b). Knowledge-based cascade-correlation. *Proceedings of the International Joint Conference on Neural Networks, Vol. V* (pp. 641–646). Los Alamitos, CA: IEEE Computer Society Press.

Shultz, T. R., & Rivest, F. (2001). Knowledge-based cascade-correlation: Using knowledge to speed learning. *Connection Science, 13*, 1–30.

Shultz, T. R., Schmidt, W. C., Buckingham, D., & Mareschal, D. (1995). Modeling cognitive development with a generative connectionist algorithm. In T. J. Simon & G. S. Halford (Eds.), *Developing cognitive competence: New approaches to process modeling* (pp. 205–261). Hillsdale, NJ: Lawrence Erlbaum Associates, Inc.

Siegler, R. S. (1981). Developmental sequences between and within concepts. *Monographs of the Society for Research in Child Development, 46* (Whole No. 189).

Siegler, R. S. (1995). How does change occur: A microgenetic study of number conservation. *Cognitive Psychology, 28*, 225–273.

Siegler, R. S. (1998). *Children's thinking* (3rd ed.). Upper Saddle River, NJ: Prentice Hall.

Sirois, S., & Shultz, T. R. (1998a). Neural network modeling of developmental effects in discrimination shifts. *Journal of Experimental Child Psychology, 71*, 235–274.

Sirois, S., & Shultz, T. R. (1998b). Neural network models of discrimination shifts. *Proceedings of the Twentieth Annual Conference of the Cognitive Science Society* (pp. 980–985). Mahwah, NJ: Lawrence Erlbaum Associates, Inc.

Sirois, S., & Shultz, T. R. (1999). Learning, development, and nativism: Connectionist implications. *Proceedings of the Twenty-First Annual Conference of the Cognitive Science Society* (pp. 689–694). Hillsdale, NJ: Lawrence Erlbaum Associates, Inc.

Spence, K. W. (1956). *Behavior theory and conditioning.* New Haven, CT: Yale University Press.

Thagard, P. (1996). *Mind: Introduction to cognitive science.* Cambridge, MA: MIT Press.

van der Maas, H., & Molenaar, P. (1992). Stagewise cognitive development: An application of catastrophe theory. *Psychological Review, 99*, 395–417.

Wolff, J. G. (1967). Concept-shift and discrimination-reversal learning in humans. *Psychological Bulletin, 68*(6), 369–408.

CHAPTER TWO

Connectionist models of learning and development in infancy

Denis Mareschal
Centre for Brain and Cognitive Development, School of Psychology, Birkbeck College, University of London

The real challenge for developmental psychology is to explain *how* and *why* behaviours emerge. One way to address this challenge is to posit a set of mechanisms for learning, and to implement these mechanisms as a working computer model (a computer program). The model then provides a tangible tool for exploring whether behaviours can emerge or be caused by the interaction of this set of well-defined mechanisms with some equally well-defined learning environment.

The use of computer modelling in developmental psychology is not new (Boden, 1980; Klahr & Wallace, 1976; Mareschal & Shultz, 1996; McClelland, 1989; Papert, 1963; Shultz, Schmidt, Buckingham, & Mareschal, 1995; Simon, 1962; Young, 1976). However, until relatively recently there have been few attempts to model infant development. This is somewhat surprising because infancy is such a rich period of development in which many behaviours are closely tied to the development of perceptual and motor systems, and there is a long history of providing computational models of perceptual and motor learning in adults (Posner, 1989).

In this chapter, I will describe four connectionist computational models of infant learning and development that I have worked on. Connectionist models are loosely based on neural information processing. However, they are not meant as neural models, but rather as neurally plausible information processing models. The four models target behaviours across a range of different domains. The topics covered are infant categorisation, word learning and phoneme discrimination, object-directed behaviours, and the perception of object unity. The models are presented in order of complexity, from the simplest to the most complex. That is, each successive model embodies a greater number of constraints on the information processing.

The model of perceptual categorisation involves processing information from one source only (vision). The model of word learning and phoneme discrimination involves processing information from two separate sources (vision and audition). These two models have minimally prestructured architectures. The two other models illustrate how progressively greater information processing constraints (that help determine what representations are developed by a network) can be embodied in the form of initial architectural structuring. The model of object-directed behaviours has two prestructured processing pathways and biases in the associative mechanisms operating in each of these pathways. Finally, the model of the perception of object unity makes use of a large number of prewired and computationally encapsulated modules. When considered together, these models illustrate how the debate between empiricism and nativism can be better reformulated in terms of the degree to which information processing constraints are in place from the onset of adaptation (Elman, Bates, Johnson, Karmiloff-Smith, Parisi, & Plunkett, 1996).

PROCESSING A SINGLE SOURCE OF INFORMATION: THE CASE OF PERCEPTUAL CATEGORISATION

This section presents a simple connectionist model of perceptual categorisation in early infancy. This is the most basic connectionist model presented in this chapter. It illustrates how information is processed in feedforward networks.

Perceptual category learning in infants

Categories and concepts facilitate learning and reasoning by partitioning the world into manageable units. Even 3- to 4-month-olds have been shown to categorise a range of real world images. Research by Quinn and Eimas demonstrates that such infants can categorise photographs of cats, dogs, horses, birds, tables, and chairs (see Mareschal & Quinn, 2001, or Quinn & Eimas, 1996, for detailed reviews). However, the perceptual categories do not always have the same characteristics as might be expected from the adult concepts. In particular, the extension and exclusivity of infant categories (i.e. the range of exemplars accepted or rejected as members of the category) may differ from that of adult categories.

Quinn, Eimas, and Rosenkrantz (1993) used a familiarisation/novelty-preference technique to determine if the perceptual categories of familiar animals (e.g. cats and dogs) acquired by young infants would exclude perceptually similar exemplars from contrasting basic-level categories. This is the level of categorisation for which the ratio of between-category variance to within-category variance is the highest (Rosch, Mervis, Gray, Johnson & Boyes-Braem 1976). Quinn et al. found that when 3- to 4-month-olds are familiarised with six pairs of cat photographs presented sequentially (12 photographs), the infants will subsequently prefer to look at a novel dog photograph rather than a novel cat photograph. Because infants prefer to look at unfamiliar stimuli (Fantz, 1964), this was interpreted as showing that the infants had developed a category of cat that included novel cats (hence less looking at the cat photograph) but excluded novel dogs (hence more looking at the dog photograph). However, if the infants were initially famil-iarised with six pairs of dog photographs sequentially (12 photographs), they then showed no subsequent preference for looking at either a novel dog or a novel cat. Furthermore, control conditions revealed that: (1) the infants would prefer to look at a novel test bird after initial familiarisation with either dogs or cats; (2) there is no *a priori* preference for dogs over cats; and (3) the infants are able to discriminate within the cat and dog categories. Taken together, these findings led Quinn et al. to suggest that the 3- to 4-month-olds had formed a perceptual category of dog that included novel dogs but *also* included novel cats. Mareschal, French, and Quinn (2000) suggest that per-formance on these categorisation tasks reflects the way in which information is stored in an associative system with distributed representations. The model below was built to test this hypothesis.

Building the model

Infant perceptual categorisation tasks rely on preferential looking or habitu-ation techniques based on the finding that infants direct more attention to unfamiliar or unexpected stimuli. The standard interpretation of this behaviour is that infants are comparing an input stimulus to an internal repre-sentation of the same stimulus (Charlesworth, 1969; Cohen, 1973; Sokolov, 1963). As long as there is a discrepancy between the information stored in the internal representation and the visual input, the infant continues to attend to the stimulus. While attending to the stimulus, the infant updates its internal representation. When the information in the internal representation is no longer discrepant with the visual input, attention is directed elsewhere. This process is illustrated in Figure 2.1. When a familiar object is presented there is little or no attending because the infant already has a reliable internal repre-sentation of that object. In contrast, when an unfamiliar or unexpected object is presented, there is more attending because an internal representation has to be constructed or adjusted. The degree to which a novel object differs from existing internal representations determines the amount of adjusting that has to be done, and hence the duration of attention.

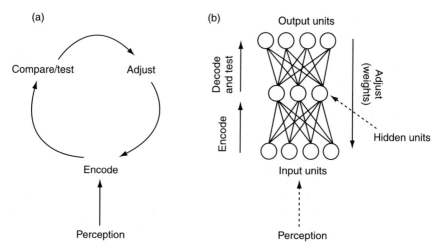

Figure 2.1. The process of representation construction in (a) infants and (b) autoencoder networks (after Mareschal & French, 2000). Copyright © 2000 Lawrence Erlbaum Associates Inc. Reprinted with permission.

We (Mareschal & French, 2000; Mareschal et al., 2000; Schafer & Mareschal, 2001) have used a connectionist autoencoder to model the relation between attention and representation construction. An autoencoder is a feedforward connectionist network with a single layer of hidden units (Figure 2.1(b)). It is called an autoencoder because it associates an input with itself. The network learns to reproduce on the output units the pattern of activation across the input units. It relies on a supervised learning algorithm but, because the input signal serves as the training signal for the output units, no teacher other than the environment is hypothesised. In an autoencoder, the number of hidden units is smaller than the number of input or output units. This produces a bottleneck in the flow of information through the network forcing the network to develop a more compact internal representation of the input (at the hidden unit level) that is sufficiently rich to reproduce all the information in the original input. Information is first compressed into an internal representation and then expanded to reproduce the original input. The successive cycles of training in the autoencoder constitute an iterative process by which a reliable internal representation of the input is developed. The reliability of the representation is tested by expanding the representation and comparing the resulting predictions to the actual stimulus being encoded. Similar networks have been used to produce compressed representations of video images (Cottrell, Munro, & Zipser, 1988). Note, however, that in its current form, this model says nothing about how an infant's looks are shared between the multiple competing stimuli.

We suggest that during the period of captured attention infants are actively involved in an iterative process of encoding the visual input into an internal representation, and then assessing that representation against the continuing perceptual input. This is accomplished by using the internal representation to predict what the properties of the stimulus are. As long as the representation fails to predict the stimulus properties, the infant continues to fixate the stimulus and to update the internal representations (see also Di Lollo, Enns, & Rensik, 2000, for a similar recurrent, re-entrant processing account of adult object recognition).

This approach to modelling novelty preference has several implications. It suggests that infant looking times are positively correlated with the network error (where error is the sum-squared difference between the network's output and its target value—namely, the corresponding inputs). The greater the error, the longer the looking time. Stimuli presented for a very short time will be encoded less well than those presented for a longer period. However, prolonged exposure after error (attention) has fallen off will not improve memory of the stimulus. The degree to which error (looking time) increases on presentation of a novel object depends on the similarity between the novel object and the familiar object. Presenting a series of similar objects leads to a progressive error drop on future similar objects. All of this is true of both autoencoders (where output error is the measurable quantity) and infants (where looking time is the measurable quantity).

The modelling results reported below are based on the performance of a standard 10-8-10 feedforward back-propagation network and are reported in more detail elsewhere (Mareschal et al., 2000; Mareschal, Quinn, & French, 2002). The data for training the networks were obtained from measurements of the original Cat and Dog pictures used by Quinn et al. (1993). There were 18 dogs and 18 cats classified according to the following ten traits: head length, head width, eye separation, ear separation, ear length, nose length, nose width, leg length, vertical extent, and horizontal extent.

Networks were trained for a fixed 250 epochs per pair of stimuli. This was done to reflect the fact that in the Quinn and Eimas studies infants were shown pictures for a fixed duration of time. The results are averaged over 50 network replications, each with random initial weights.

Twelve items from one category were presented sequentially to the network in groups of two (i.e. weights were updated in batches of two) to capture the fact that pairs of pictures were presented to the infants during the familiarisation trials. The remaining six items from each category were used to test whether the networks had formed categorical representations.

The development of cat and dog categories

Like infants, these networks form both Cat and Dog categories. Figure 2.2 shows the initial error score (the sum-squared error across output units), the error score after 12 presentations of either cats or dogs, and the average error score (after training) for the 6 remaining exemplars in either the Cat or Dog category. After learning, error is lower, suggesting that the network has developed a reliable internal representation of cats or dogs. The generalisation error rises slightly, showing that the networks recognise these exemplars as novel. Infants are also able to distinguish individual exemplars within the category (Quinn et al., 1993). However, the generalisation error remains well below the initial error suggesting that the new exemplars are assimilated within the category representation formed by the networks across the hidden units.

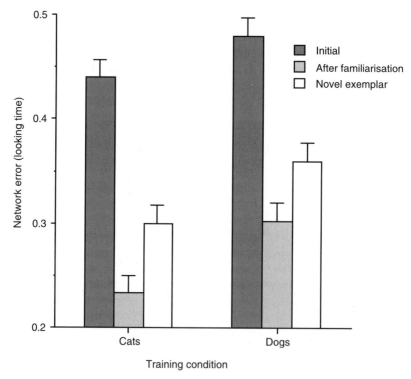

Figure 2.2. Network responses to Cat and Dog exemplars before and after category learning (after Mareschal et al., 2000). Copyright © 2000 by the American Psychological Association. Reprinted with permission.

The asymmetric exclusivity of the Cat and Dog categories

Eimas and Quinn found that there was an asymmetry in the exclusivity of the Cat and Dog categories developed by infants. Figure 2.3 shows what happens when networks trained on cats are presented with a novel cat and a dog, and when networks trained on dogs are tested with a novel dog and a cat. When the networks are initially trained on cats, the presentation of a dog results in a large error score, corresponding to the results observed with infants in terms of a longer looking time. Dogs are not included within the category representation of cats. In contrast, when the networks are initially trained on dogs, the presentation of a cat results in only a small increase in error suggesting that the cats have been included in the dog category.

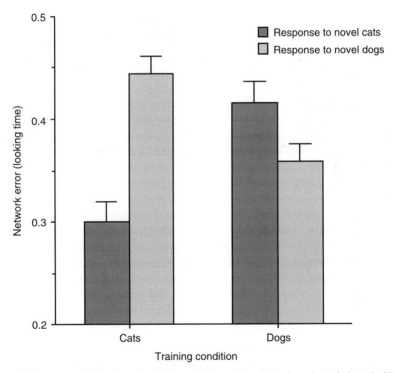

Figure 2.3. Asymmetric exclusivity of Cat and Dog categories (after Mareschal et al., 2000). Copyright © 2000 by the American Psychological Association. Reprinted with permission.

The source of the asymmetry

One advantage of building a model is that it can be taken apart to explore what causes the observed behaviours. Connectionist networks extract the correlations between features present in their learning environment. The variation of the internal representations (developed across the hidden units) reflects the variation of the corresponding categories in the environment. Figure 2.4 shows the frequency distributions of the 10 input features for both cats and dogs. Each feature has been fit to a normal distribution. In almost all cases the distribution for each Dog trait (represented by the dark line) subsumes the distribution for the corresponding trait for cats. The narrower distributions for most Cat traits, on the other hand, do not subsume the range of values for the corresponding Dog traits. In other words, cats are possible dogs but the reverse is not the case: most dogs are not possible cats.

The key distribution feature of the data is that Cat features are (in general) subsumed within the distribution of Dog features. It is not just the added variability of dogs along certain features, but the subset relationship that is crucial for explaining the asymmetry. Connectionist networks develop internal representations that reflect the distributions of the input features. Thus, the internal representation for Cat will be subsumed within the internal representation for Dog. It is because the internal representations share this inclusion relationship that an asymmetry in error (looking time) is observed. The behaviour arises because of an interaction between the statistics of the environment and the computational properties of the learning algorithm.

Mareschal et al. (2000) then used the model to explore what the effects of learning with a mixed set of exemplars would be. They presented the networks with training sets of either eight cats and four dogs (the Mostly-cats group), or eight dogs and four cats (the Mostly-dogs group). Under these conditions, the networks in the Mostly-cats group developed a category that included novel cats but excluded novel dogs. In contrast, the networks in the Mostly-dog group developed a category that included novel dogs but also included novel cats. Thus, the category asymmetry was predicted to persist even when both kinds of exemplars were presented during familiarisation. A further study with 48 3- to 4-month-olds revealed that this was also the case with infants, thereby confirming the model's prediction and corroborating the model as a valid mechanistic account of early infant perceptual categorisations. Additional predictions of asymmetric interference in the sequential category learning of Cat and Dog perceptual categories by 3- to 4-month-olds have also been confirmed (Mareschal et al., 2002).

If the infant looking behaviours reflect bottom-up processing rather than the top-down application of Cat and Dog category schemas, then we should be able to subtly alter the cat and dog images such that the inclusion relation in the feature distributions is reversed, but that the images still appear to be

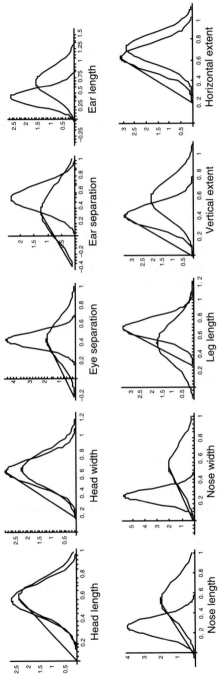

Figure 2.4. Normalised frequency distributions of feature values in Cat (thin line) and Dog (thick line) exemplars (after Mareschal et al., 2000). Copyright © 2000 by the American Psychological Association. Reprinted with permission.

cats and dogs to adults. This is indeed what French, Mermillod, Quinn, and Mareschal (2001) found. By selectively morphing a few cat and dog images, they produced a set of images with an inverted inclusion relation (i.e. the cat feature distributions tended to include the dog values). This led to a reversal of the looking time patterns in 3- to 4-month-olds but had no change in adult classification performance. Hence, infant behaviours really do appear to be bottom-up driven.

In summary, this model illustrates how categorical representations of visually presented stimuli can be acquired within a single testing session. An associative system that parses stimuli into distinct features and develops distributed representations will also develop categories with the same exclusivity asymmetries as 3- to 4-month-olds when presented with the same stimuli as these infants. This analysis constitutes a novel explanation of the infant data that emerge from the construction of a computational model.

PROCESSING MULTIPLE SOURCES OF INFORMATION: THE CASE OF PHONEME DISCRIMINATION

The model described above demonstrates how a connectionist autoencoder extracts information from a single source and develops an internal representation that captures the essence of that information. The same mechanism can be used when information arrives from different modalities or sources. For example, at some basic level, word learning consists of matching auditory input (the label) to a visual stimulus (the object). The model in this section (described in more detail in Schafer & Mareschal, 2001) explores how the integration of information from two sources impacts on the network's internal representations. The representations acquired within the context of word learning constrain the type of auditory discriminations that can subsequently be made.

Word learning and speech sound discrimination in young infants

Occasionally, development is accompanied by a reduction in a given ability rather than an improvement in that ability. This is the case with phoneme discrimination. Until the age of about 8 months, infants respond in a categorical fashion to phonemic contrasts that do not appear in their native language. However, older infants and adults find these contrasts difficult to detect (Trehub, 1976; Werker & Lalonde, 1988; Werker & Tees, 1983, 1984a; but see Best, McRoberts, & Sithole, 1988 for a case of detection of non-native contrasts by older infants). Werker and Pegg (1992) have argued that the changes in infants' performance in such speech sound discrimination tasks are diagnostic of distinct stages in infants' speech processing.

Stager and Werker (1997) investigated the possible relationship between word learning and speech sound discrimination, using a bimodal habituation task. Infants were habituated to stimuli presented in both auditory and visual modalities, for example, a stimulus comprising a sound and an image. The authors suggested that such a task invoked the mechanisms subserving the learning of words, that is, learning that a given label (sound) goes with a given object (image). During subsequent testing, a change was made in the sound, but not the image. The extent to which infants dishabituated to this new sound–image combination was interpreted as an index of the specificity of the binding between the habituated sound and the (unchanged) image. Infants who have habituated to a given sound–image combination will dishabituate only if they perceive the difference between the sound heard during prior habituation phase and the sound heard during subsequent testing phase.

Stager and Werker found that within the label–object associative learning paradigm described above, 8-month-olds in an English language environment could discriminate the label [*bih*] from the label [*dih*] whereas 14-month-olds appeared unable to do so. However, the older infants *could* discriminate a more distinct pair of labels such as [*lif*] and [*neem*]. The 14-month-old infants could also discriminate [*bih*] from [*dih*] in a simple auditory discrimination task. Furthermore, the 14-month-olds were not capable of discriminating [*bih*] from [*dih*] when the task involved learning about *two* label–object tokens (i.e. [*bih*] + object 1 and [*dih*] + object 2). Stager and Werker argued that, taken together, these data suggest a functional reorganisation of the language system occurring between the ages of 8 and 14 months. As a consequence of this reorganisation, infants of different ages react differently to identical stimuli. Schafer and Mareschal (2001) constructed a connectionist model to explore whether simple associative systems, whose adaptive properties do not change over time, could also account for the apparent discontinuity in processing.

Building the model

To model infant performance, connectionist networks were taught to autoencode labels and objects, in a homologue of looking and listening by the infant. Three-layer autoencoder networks were trained to reproduce, on their output units, the label–object pairs that had been presented at the input (Figure 2.5). This task requires the networks to develop an internal representation across the hidden unit layer, merging the information from these two sources of information (Chauvin, 1989; Plunkett, Sinha, Møller, & Strandsby, 1992). As in the previous section, the networks were trained using

Outputs

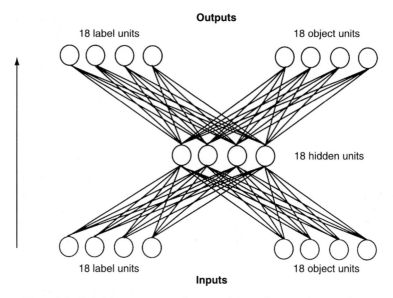

Figure 2.5.   Label–image autoencoder network. Not all connections are shown.

the back-propagation learning algorithm. Labels were represented as consonant-vowel-consonant (CVC) strings, with each phoneme represented by six binary bits (cf. Plunkett & Marchman, 1991). The six bits represented the following features of each phoneme: consonantal (one bit), voiced (one bit), manner (two bits), place (two bits). It should be stressed that although this coding scheme is based on phonemes, it can be thought of as representing any nonarbitrary feature of words, for example, phones.

The "language" that networks were exposed to was created in the following manner. Labels were generated by randomly selecting a consonant, and then a vowel, and then a consonant, from the list of phonemes. Our artificial language comprised 240 label–object pairs. This is 5 per cent of the $20 \times 12 \times 20 = 4800$ possible CV combinations. Object input vectors were then generated by duplicating the list of 240 18-bit label vectors, shuffling this list and assigning each of the resultant randomly ordered object vectors to a label vector.

The networks were trained according to a two-stage procedure: (1) a language exposure phase; and (2) an experimental phase. Networks were initially exposed to a linguistic "environment", in which label–object pairs were successively presented to the network for a predetermined fixed period, reflecting the "age" of the network at testing. To reflect the differential language exposure of the 8- and 14-month-old infants, "older" networks received more language exposure trials before testing than did "younger" networks. Following this "language exposure" process, the experimental phase *per se* began.

First, networks were habituated to a label–object pair. The same interpretation of habituation was used as in the previous section. Finally, after habituation, a dishabituation stimulus was presented and the error (looking time) was calculated.

"Language exposure" was modelled as follows. All the networks were trained to autoencode the same randomly generated bank of 240 label–object pairs. Following each language exposure trial, the label–object pair was returned to the bank and another pair selected at random. "Younger" networks received 1000 such trials; "older" networks received 10,000 trials.

Networks were tested on a homologue of Stager and Werker's (1997) four experiments, against a background of this language exposure. The procedure for modelling Stager and Werker's Experiments 2 and 3 was as follows. During the habituation phase, a network experienced 100 habituation trials. Each habituation trial used the same label–object pair (e.g. "bih", plus a corresponding object). During the dishabituation phase, the label segment of the input vector was replaced by the to-be-tested label (e.g. "dih"). Thus, in the dishabituation phase, the network was presented with a familiar object but a novel label, as had been the case with the infants. Following Stager and Werker, we refer to this as a "switch" trial. In contrast, during a "same" trial, the label–object pair presented was the same as had been used during habituation. As described above, the response to the novel pairing is an index of the amount of stimulus processing that has occurred during habituation, and the specificity of the binding achieved, during habituation, between label and object.

Minor modifications allowed this procedure to be used for modelling Experiments 1 and 4. In the case of Experiment 1, two label–object pairs were used in the habituation phase. In each trial, one pair was selected at random to be presented to the network. In the case of Experiment 4, all input bits coding image information were set to 0.5 (midway between the 0 and 1 binary values used to encode object information) thereby conveying no object information. These modifications correspond to analogous modifications in the procedure used by Stager and Werker for testing infants in Experiments 1 and 4.

There were 20 networks in each experimental group, all with different initial connection weights. These were randomly set at the outset to values between −1.0 and 1.0.

Model results

Figure 2.6 illustrates the performance of the networks. The model results are remarkably similar to those obtained with infants (see Stager & Werker, 1997, Figure 1). In particular, consider the data of Experiments 2 and 3: "Older" networks showed poorer discrimination of the similar pair ("bih" and "dih")

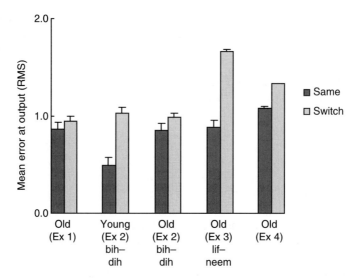

Figure 2.6. "Young" and "old" network performance on phoneme discrimination tasks (after Schafer & Mareschal, 2001). Copyright © 2001 Lawrence Erlbaum Associates Inc. Reprinted with permission.

than the "younger" networks; the "older" networks were nevertheless able to discriminate the more distinct pair ("lif" and "neem").

To investigate the effect of language experience on the responses of the networks, we compared the relative novelty preference of networks at different ages (i.e. differing degrees of language exposure) in the bih/dih and lif/neem discrimination trials. First, novelty preference was nonmonotonic with age. For both similar (bih–dih) and dissimilar (lif–neem) pairs, novelty preference exhibits two minima in the range of language exposure evaluated. Overall, novelty preference (in the networks) reaches a minimum at around 10,000 language exposure trials, then increases again with further language exposure. This sort of nonmonotonicity is reminiscent of human behaviour in the detection of non-native speech contrasts. Young infants are initially able to make these distinctions, but lose this ability at some point before their first birthday (Werker & Tees, 1983, 1984a); nonetheless, adults are, in certain circumstances, able to make these distinctions (Werker & Tees, 1984b).

Second, the extent of a release from habituation in the networks follows a different time course for the two types of stimulus pairs. Assuming that release from habituation is observed when novelty preference exceeds some arbitrary but constant threshold, then there is a period during which a release from habituation will occur for dissimilar pairs but not similar pairs.

Further analyses suggest that the developmental profiles arise as an interaction between the computational requirements of the different test conditions (i.e. the bih–dih or lif–neem habituation tasks) and the differential language experience of the "young" and "old" networks. The representations of linguistic knowledge in the networks (in the form of connection weights) are continuously evolving in response to increasing linguistic exposure. The way in which those representations evolve is independent of the fact that the networks will subsequently be tested on bih–dih or lif–neem discriminations (as these syllables are not in the training set). The behaviour on these tests will be determined by some interaction between the ability of the networks to perform the task *per se*, and their current level of linguistic representation. Because connectionist networks extract the statistical regularities of their environments, that interaction is determined by the relationship between the test syllables (bih–dih and lif–neem) and the distribution of similar syllables in the background linguistic environment.

In summary, this model has shown how the representations developed by an autoencoder can integrate information from different sources or modalities. Behaviour on any given task occurs within the context of prior learning. Representations developed in one learning context may determine the feasibility of subsequent learning in a different context, or even on a different (but related) task.

THE IMPACT OF ARCHITECTURAL CONSTRAINTS: THE CASE OF INFANTS AND OBJECTS

This section describes a model that incorporates more neurophysiological constraints than the models in the two previous sections. The models discussed in the previous sections had minimal initial architectural constraints. The model in this section provides a mechanistic account of the infant's developing abilities to interact with objects that move in and out of sight, and is reported in more detail in Mareschal, Plunkett, and Harris (1999).

The two models above show how associative learning mechanisms can interact with the statistics of the environment to produce task appropriate internal representations. In the sections below we show how architectural constraints gleaned from neuropsychology and neurophysiology can help shape the network architecture. The initial architecture provides added constraints on the flow of information, and on the developmental profile of behaviours that emerges from the network. These constraints are one way in which innate knowledge can be built into a connectionist network. The model is made up of a number of modules, each of which uses a different neural network technique (e.g. supervised versus unsupervised learning). It illustrates how complex systems can be built up from relatively simple components.

Infant object-directed behaviours

Newborn infants possess sophisticated object-oriented perceptual skills (Slater, 1995) but the age at which they are able to reason about hidden objects remains unclear. Using manual search to test infants' understanding of hidden objects, Piaget concluded it was not until 7.5 to 9 months that infants understand that hidden objects continue to exist because younger infants do not successfully reach for an object hidden behind an occluding screen (Piaget, 1952, 1954). More recent studies using a violation of expectancy paradigm have suggested that infants as young as 3.5 months do have some understanding of hidden objects. These studies rely on nonsearch indices such as surprise instead of manual retrieval to assess infant knowledge (Baillargeon, 1993; Baillargeon, Spelke, & Wasserman, 1985). Infants watch an event in which some physical property of a hidden object is violated (solidity). Surprise at this violation (as measured by increased visual inspection of the event) is interpreted as showing that the infants know: (1) that the hidden object still exists; and (2) that the hidden object maintains the physical property that was violated (Baillargeon, 1993). The nature and origins of this developmental lag between understanding the continued existence of a hidden object and searching for it remain a central question of infant cognitive development.

The lag cannot be attributed to a delay in manual control because infants as young as 4.5 months reach for a moving visible object and, by 6 months, can reach around or remove an occluding obstacle (Von Hofsten, 1989). Nor can it be attributed to immature planning or problem-solving abilities because infants have been shown to solve problems involving identical or more complex planning procedures (Baillargeon, 1993; Munakata, McClelland, Johnson, & Siegler, 1997).

Clues may be found in recent work on cortical representation of visual object information. Anatomical, neurophysiological, and psychophysical evidence points to the existence of two processing routes for visual object information in the cortex (Goodale, 1993; Milner & Goodale, 1995; Ungerleider & Mishkin, 1982; Van Essen, Anderson, & Felleman, 1992). Although the exact functionality of the two routes remains a hotly debated question, it is generally accepted that they contain radically different kinds of representations (Johnson, Mareschal, & Csibra, 2001). The dorsal (or parietal) route processes spatial–temporal object information, whereas the ventral (or temporal) route processes object feature information.

The dorsal and ventral routes both project into the frontal lobes (Goodale, 1993). As a whole, the frontal lobes play a crucial role in learning what responses are appropriate given an environmental context (Passingham, 1993). They have been closely tied to the development of planning and underlie the execution of voluntary actions, particularly in the context of manual search by human infants (Diamond, 1991).

Voluntary retrieval such as manual search for an occluded object must involve the integration of spatial–temporal information concerning the location of the occluded object with surface feature information concerning its identity. The surface feature information is required to decide whether an object is desired or not, and spatial–temporal information is required to direct the response. Furthermore, the cortical representation of these two types of information must be sufficiently well developed for accurate integration to occur. We suggest that early in development only visible objects offer the degree of representational precision needed to support an accurate integrated response because cell activations diminish when a target is no longer visible.

One possible explanation is that the lag occurs whenever it is necessary to integrate two potentially imprecise sources of information: (1) spatial–temporal information about the location of the occluded object; and (2) featural information about the identity of the occluded object. This explanation predicts that tasks requiring access to only one imprecise source of information or tasks that are performed with a visible object will not result in a developmental lag. In contrast, any task that calls for the integration of cortically separable representations will fail unless performed with a visible object or with precise cortical representations. This account does not attribute the lag to any difficulties the infant might encounter in attempting to remove or circumvent the occluder in manual retrieval tasks. In addition, the lag does not depend on the response modality. Instead, it arises from information processing considerations associated with voluntary, object-directed behaviours. Surprise reflex responses, which may subsequently be manifested by an increased inspection time or spontaneous visual search behaviours, can be elicited by access to only one of the object representations.

Building the model

Figure 2.7 shows the model in schematic outline. It consists of a modular architecture. Each functional module is enclosed by a dashed line. Some units are shared by two modules (e.g. the 75 hidden units are shared by the response integration and trajectory prediction networks) and serve as a gateway for information between the modules. In accordance with the neurological evidence reviewed above, spatial–temporal information about objects in the world is processed independently of feature information. Information enters the network through a two-dimensional retina homogeneously covered by feature detectors. It is then funnelled concurrently into one pathway that processes the spatial–temporal history of the object and another pathway that develops a spatially invariant feature representation of the object.

The retina consists of a 4×25 cell grid. Each cell contains four feature detectors responding to different properties (e.g. light/dark, high/low contrast, red/green, soft/hard). If a projected image overlaps with a grid cell, the

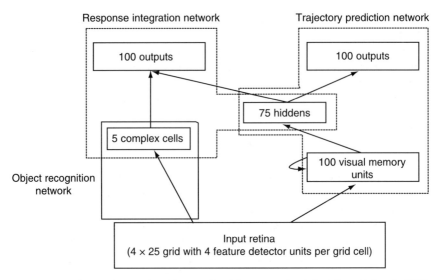

Figure 2.7.   Schema of network architecture for object processing (after Mareschal et al., 1999). Copyright © 1999 Blackwell Publishing, Oxford. Reprinted with permission.

cell's feature detectors take on the value +1.0 if the feature is present and −1.0 if the feature is absent. Cells on which the object image is not projected are quiescent and take on the value 0.0. An occluding screen is also projected onto the retina. The retinal cells corresponding to the screen's image have a constant activation of 1.0.

The network experiences four different objects with correlated features: (−1 1 −1 1), (−1 1 1 −1), (1 −1 1 −1), (1 −1 −1 1). All object images are 2 × 2 grid cells large. For each object presentation, an object moves once back and forth across the retina, either horizontally or vertically. All horizontal movements across the retina involve an interim occluding event whereas vertical movements across the retina can result in either nonoccluding or partially occluding events. Completely occluded vertical movements are never observed because the occluder height is identical to height of the retina. At any specific time step there are four possible next positions for the object: up, down, left, or right. Predicting the next object position can only be resolved by learning to attend to the trajectory of the object.

The object recognition module generates a spatially invariant representation of the object by using a modified version of the unsupervised learning algorithm developed by Foldiak (1991). Initially, a bank of five complex cells is fully and randomly connected to all feature detectors. The algorithm exploits the fact that an object tends to be contiguous with itself at successive temporal intervals. Thus, two successive images will probably be derived from the same object. At the end of learning each complex cell becomes associated with a particular feature combination wherever it appears on the retina.

The trajectory prediction module uses a partially recurrent, feedforward network trained with the back-propagation learning algorithm. At each time step, information about the position of the object on the retina is extracted from the 100 retinal grid cells and mapped onto the visual memory layer. The retinal grid cells with which the object image overlaps become active (+1.0) whereas the other cells remain inactive (0.0). The network is trained to predict the next instantaneous, retinal position of the object. The prediction is output onto a bank of 100 units coding position in the same way as the inputs into the module. The network has a target of +1.0 for those units corresponding to the next object position and 0.0 for all other units.

All units in the visual memory layer have a self-recurrent connection (fixed at $\mu = 0.3$). The resulting spatial distribution of activation across the visual memory layer takes the form of a comet with a tail that tapers off in the direction from which the object has come. The length and distinctiveness of this tail depend on the velocity of the object. The information in this layer is then forced through a bottleneck of 75 hidden units to generate a more compact, internal re-representation of the object's spatial–temporal history. As there are no direct connections from the input to the output, the ability of the network to predict the next position is a direct measure of the reliability of its internal object representation. We interpret the response of the trajectory prediction network as a measure of its sensitivity to spatial–temporal information about the object.

The output of the response integration network corresponds to the infant's ability to coordinate and use the information it has about object position and object identity. This network integrates the internal representations generated by other modules (i.e. the feature representation at the complex cell level and spatial–temporal representation in the hidden unit layer) as required by a retrieval response task. It consists of a single-layered perceptron whose task is to output the same next position as the prediction network for two of the objects, and to inhibit any response (all units set to 0.0) for the other two objects. This reflects the fact that infants do not retrieve (e.g. reach for) all objects. In general, infants are not asked or rewarded for search. The experimental set-up relies on spontaneous search by the infant. Some objects are desired (e.g. sweet) whereas others are not desired (e.g. sour). Any voluntary retrieval response will necessarily require the processing of feature information (to identify the object as a desired one) as well as trajectory information (to localise the object).

The model embodies the basic architectural constraints on visual cortical pathways revealed by contemporary neuroscience: an object-recognition network that develops spatially invariant feature representations of objects, a trajectory-prediction network that is blind to surface features and computes appropriate spatial–temporal properties even if no actions are undertaken towards the object, and a response module that integrates information from the two latter networks for use in voluntary actions. We suggest that surprise can be modelled by a mismatch between the information stored in an internal representation and the new information arriving from the external world. More specifically, in the trajectory-prediction module, surprise occurs when there is a discrepancy between the predicted reappearance of an object from behind an occluder and its actual reappearance on the retina. In the object-recognition module, surprise occurs when there is a discrepancy between the feature representation stored across the complex units and the new representation produced by the new image.

Model results

The trajectory-prediction network learns very quickly to predict an object's next position when it is visible. However, the hidden unit representations that are developed persist for some time after the object has disappeared and allow the network to keep track of the object even when it is no longer directly perceptible. The object-recognition network also maintains a representation of the features of the object that persists beyond direct perception. When an object is surreptitiously changed while occluded, there is a delayed recovery in reliability. This reflects the fact that the new object features are different from those that are stored in the recognition module's internal representations. The rate of recovery is directly related to the similarity between the new object features and the original object features.

The model was designed to test the hypothesis that the developmental lag between voluntary retrieval and surprise-based indices arises from the difference in the integration demands of the two tasks. Network responses when presented with an unoccluded desired object, an occluded desired object, and an occluded undesired object are depicted in Figure 2.8. The reliability of a module is computed as (1 – sum-of-squares error of outputs) averaged over the output units and patterns involved in the event. Because the networks begin with random weights, the initial (untrained) output activations are also random. The initial network response is to turn off almost all output units. This results in an immediate increase in reliability (decrease in error) but it only reflects a blanket inhibition of output activity (including some cells which should be active). Hence, this stage of learning does not reflect the acquisition of position-specific knowledge. To normalise for this, the plotted reliabilities are linearly scaled to range between 0.0 and 1.0 with the origin of the scale (the baseline) corresponding to the reliability value obtained when all output units are turned off. Any increase in reliability above this origin corresponds to an increase in the ability to predict the object's next position. The baseline reliability

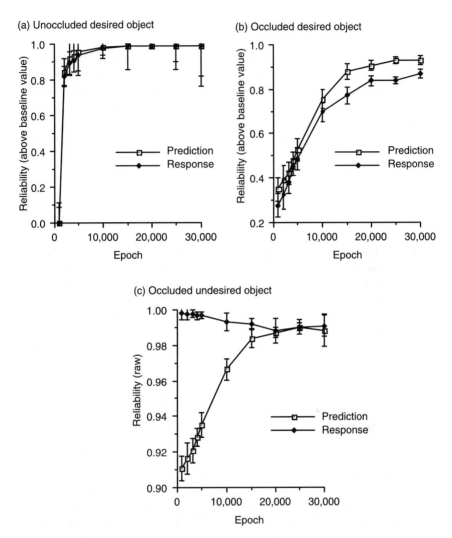

Figure 2.8. Network performance on tracking and responding to (a) a desired unoccluded object, (b) a desired occluded object, and (c) an undesired occluded object.

value was 0.863 since on average about 86 per cent of the units will be silent in producing an accurate response.

Figure 2.8(a) shows the average network performance ($n = 10$) on both the position prediction and retrieval tasks when presented with an unoccluded, desired object. We interpret network behaviour by assuming that a threshold of reliability over and above the previously mentioned baseline level is required to control an accurate prediction/response. Consider the case where this threshold is set to 0.8. At this level, it can be seen from Figure 2.8(a) that the network learns very quickly (within 1000 epochs) not just to predict the position of the desired object but also to produce an appropriate retrieval response.

When the object is occluded the network's behaviour is very different (Figure 2.8(b). Predictive localisation and retrieval responses are initially equally poor. The internal representations are not adequately mature to support any reliable response. However, the reliability of tracking develops faster than that of retrieval. By 10,000 epochs the prediction response has achieved the requisite level of reliability whereas the retrieval response does not achieve this level until approximately 20,000 epochs. In other words, the network replicates the well-established finding that infants exhibit a developmental lag between successful predictive tracking of an occluded object and successful retrieval of an occluded object.

The output required for retrieval of a desired, occluded object is identical to that required for predictive localisation. Moreover, both sets of output units receive exactly the same information from the hidden units about the spatial–temporal history of the object. The two modules differ only in that the retrieval-response module must also integrate information coming from the object-recognition module. Thus, the developmental lag in the network arises from the added task demands of integrating information concerning the location and identity of an occluded object.

An advantage of modeling is that we can test this hypothesis directly using a manipulation that would not be possible with infants. If the lag is due to the need for information integration concerning the location and identity of an occluded object, then it should disappear on a task that does not require such integration. Undesired objects do not require information integration because it suffices to attend only to the identity representation in order to elicit an appropriate response. An inhibitory output can then be emitted, which does not require any spatial–temporal information. Figure 2.8(c) shows the performance of the network when presented with an undesired object. Here, raw reliabilities are plotted because the correct response is to turn all output units off. The network learns to inhibit any attempt at retrieval because it can ignore information from the spatial–temporal channel, even though it is still learning to predict the object's position. In short, inspection of Figure 2.8(c) shows, as predicted, that the developmental lag disappears on tasks not requiring integration of information across modules.

The model is successful in demonstrating how the requirement to integrate information across two object representations in a voluntary retrieval task can lead to a development lag relative to performance on surprise tasks that only require access to either spatial–temporal information concerning an occluded object or surface feature information accessed separately. Early mastery of surprise tasks that claim to show the coordination of position and feature information (Baillargeon, 1993) have—on close scrutiny—provided evidence only for the use of positional information in conjunction with size or volume information. Both size and volume are spatial dimensions that are encoded by the dorsal route. Thus, processing information in these tasks only requires accessing a single cortical route. Note that early surprise responses can arise from feature violations, from spatial temporal violations and even from both types of violation arising concurrently and independently, but not from a violation involving the integration of feature and spatial–temporal information concerning an occluded object. The model predicts that infants will show a developmental lag not just on manual search tasks but also on surprise tasks that involve such integration. Evidence supporting this prediction has now been repeated (Mareschal & Johnson, in press).

In summary, this model shows how specialised modules can emerge through basic constraints in the form of different assumptions about the associative mechanisms that operate in a network and the original architecture of a network. This model also demonstrates that different connectionist modelling techniques can be combined within the same model. Connectionist models are not necessarily synonymous with homogeneous processing systems.

ENCAPSULATED PROCESSING MODULES: THE CASE OF THE PERCEPTION OF OBJECT UNITY

This section provides an example of highly constrained learning. The model in this section differs from previous ones in that there are many built-in constraints that take the form of encapsulated preprocessing modules. This section describes a model of the developing ability to perceive object unity in displays involving partially occluded objects (Mareschal & Johnson, 2002). A network learns to associate the presence of low-level visual cues with the presence of a unified object, and thereby learns to predict when an ambiguous, partially occluded stimulus event arises from one object rather than two distinct partially occluded objects.

The perception of object unity by young infants

Neonates appear to perceive the moving and partly occluded rod in Figure 2.9 as consisting of two disjoint objects (Slater, Morison, Somers, Mattock, Brown, & Taylor, 1990). By contrast, 4-month-olds (and adults) perceive such a partly occluded rod as consisting of a single unified object. Early studies of the cues that support the perception of object unity concluded that common motion of the rod parts was the primary visual cue used by infants in determining that the rod parts belonged to a common object (Kellman & Spelke, 1983; Kellman, Spelke, & Short, 1986).

However, more recent studies have called this finding into question by systematically varying the cues available in a display. Three-dimensional depth cues were not found to be necessary for the perception of unity as 4-month-olds still perceived a two-dimensional (computer generated) rod-and-box display, in which two rod parts moved above and below a stationary box, against a textured background as a single unified rod (Johnson & Nanez, 1995). However, in the absence of a textured background, there was no systematic preference for a unified over two disjoint rods when tested with a two-dimensional display (Johnson & Aslin, 1996). The relatability of the two rod segments (the fact that, if extended, they would meet behind the screen) was also found to be important in determining the infants' perception of unity (Johnson & Aslin, 1996).

Currently, there are few accounts of how the developmental shift could take place. Spelke (1990; Spelke & Van de Walle, 1993) has suggested that young infants' object perception is tantamount to reasoning, in accord with a set of core principles. However, infants' performance on object unity tasks is dependent on the presence or absence of motion, edge alignment, accretion and deletion of background texture, and other cues, implying that low-level perceptual variables strongly influence object perception, rather than reasoning from core principles (Johnson & Aslin, 1996; Kellman & Spelke, 1983). Two-month-olds are found to have an intermediate response between that of neonates and 4-month-olds (Johnson & Nanez, 1995). Whereas neonates perceive the stimulus in Figure 2.9 as arising from two disjoint objects and 4-month-olds perceive it as arising from a single unified object, 2-month-olds do not show a preference and are equally likely to respond as though the stimulus is unified or disjoint. In this section we explore whether the perception of object unity can be learned by experience with objects and events in early infancy.

Building the model

Figure 2.10 illustrates the model architecture. The models received input via a simple "retina". The information presented to the retina represented objects, their orientation and motions, and the background. This information was processed by seven encapsulated perceptual modules, each of which identified the presence of one of the following cues during specific portions of training and test events: (1) motion anywhere on the display; (2) co-motion of objects in the upper and lower halves of the display, whether in-phase or out-of-phase; (3) common motion of objects in the upper and lower halves of the display; (4) parallelism of object edges in the upper and lower halves of the display; (5) relatability of object edges in the upper and lower halves of the display; (6) texture deletion and accretion; and (7) T-junctions. We chose these particular cues because of the importance of motion (i.e. cues 1, 2, and 3), edge orientation (cues 4 and 5), and depth (cues 6 and 7) to young infants'

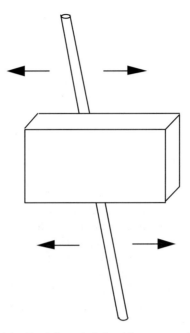

Figure 2.9.   Partially occluded ambiguous test stimulus.

perception of object unity (Johnson & Aslin, 1996; Kellman & Spelke, 1983).

Each perceptual module fed into a layer of hidden units with sigmoid activation functions, which in turn fed into a response (output) layer. The response units determined the model's decision as to whether the ambiguous stimulus (i.e. the partly occluded rod) contained a single object, two disjoint objects, or neither (a response we termed "indeterminate"). Unity was also a "primitive", like the other cues, in that a model could perceive it directly in unambiguous cases (i.e. when the object was visible to one side of the occluder). These types of response to unity are consistent with evidence from human neonates. In the absence of any occlusion, neonates can discriminate between a broken and an unbroken visible rod. Indeed, this is a necessary precondition for interpreting the looking-time behaviours of neonates in experimental studies of the perception of object unity (Slater et al., 1990). In the absence of direct perception (i.e. when the objects were partly occluded) the perception of unity was mediated by its association with other, directly perceivable, cues.

We do not wish to make the claim that a mediated route is unique to the percept of unity. There may well be a highly complex and interactive network of connections in the brain that allow any set of not-directly perceivable cues to be indirectly computed from the activation of other directly perceivable

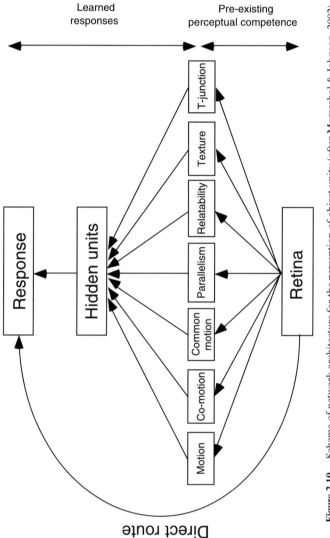

Figure 2.10. Schema of network architecture for the perception of object unity (after Mareschal & Johnson, 2002). Copyright © 2002 Blackwell Publishing, Oxford. Reprinted with permission.

cues. However, in the interest of clarity, we have only considered the one mediated route.

The bottom half of the network embodies pre-existing abilities. We assume that neonates are able to perceive the components of each of these cues. Indirect evidence suggests that this is the case (Slater, 1995). There is no learning in any of these encapsulated modules. The top half of the network embodies the learning that can occur through interactions with the environment.

The network "sees" a series of images from the world and responds with whether a perceived object is unified or not. The response is coded across two output units: (+1, −1) signifies that the object is unified; (−1, +1) signifies that the object is *not* unified. (+1, +1) or (−1, −1) is interpreted as an ambiguous response.

The input retina consists of a 196-bit vector mapping all the cells on a 14×14-unit grid. In the middle of the grid is a 4×4-unit occluder. All units corresponding to the position of the screen are given a value of 1. When background texture is required, all other units on the retina are given a value of 0.0 or 0.2, depending on the texture pattern. Units with values of 0.2 correspond to position on which there is a texture element (e.g. a dot). Units corresponding to the position of an object are given a value of 1.0. Figure 2.11 shows a snapshot taken from the "ambiguous" portion of all 26 events in the environment.

An object event is made up of a series of snapshots like this one, in which the rod moves progressively across the retina. All events begin with the object moving onto the retina from the side. We will call this the unambiguous portion of the event. The object then moves across the retina, passing behind the area occupied by the occluding screen. We will call this the ambiguous portion of the event. Finally, the object reappears on the other side of the screen and continues off the retina.

All events except 5 and 6 involve motion. The presence of texture, T-junctions, relatability and colinearity are varied systematically. All events with motion involve motion in the upper and lower half of the retina (co-motion) but only half of those involve common motion (relatable motion). This leads to a total of 26 possible events. Although alignment has been manipulated as a cue in some infant studies, note that two objects are aligned if, and only if, they are colinear and relatable. Thus, colinearity and relatability are more primitive cues than alignment in the sense that the latter cannot be computed without computing (at least implicitly) the former, whereas the converse is not true (i.e. both colinearity and relatability can be computed independently of alignment).

Learning is driven by direct feedback from the environment. When the object is visible, the environment provides immediate feedback about the unity of the object via the direct perception link. When the object is not

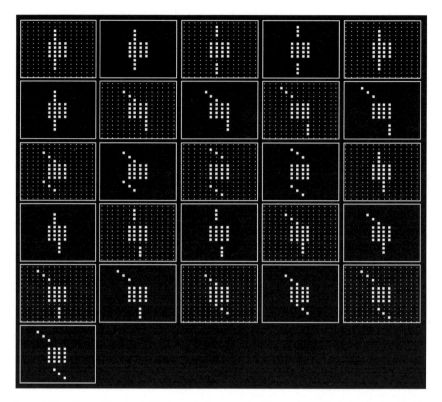

Figure 2.11.   Complete set of object events (top panel) with corresponding visual cues (bottom panel) (after Mareschal & Johnson, 2002). Copyright © 2002 Blackwell Publishing, Oxford. Reprinted with permission.

completely visible, the environment cannot provide feedback about the unity of the object. The model has a short-term, rapidly decaying memory that encodes unity information obtained while the object was entirely visible. Immediately following occlusion there is a clear trace of the state of the rod before occlusion (i.e. a kind of short-lived visual memory). After a short delay, that information has decayed away completely and can no longer be used for learning.

The interaction between memory and direct perception is embodied in the target signal used to train the connection weights between the perceptual cue modules and the unity output. This signal has two components. One component arises from direct perception whereas the other component arises from memory. In the absence of direct perception (i.e. when the object is partly occluded) the perceptual component is zero and the memory component determines the value of the training signal.

When direct perception is possible, the model's prediction of unity (via the

Events	Perceptual cues						
	Motion	Co-motion	Common motion	Parallelism	Relatability	Texture	T-junctions
Event 1	●	●	●	●	●	●	●
Event 2	●	●	●	●	●		●
Event 3	●	●	●	●	●	●	
Event 4	●	●	●	●	●		
Event 5				●	●	●	●
Event 6				●	●		●
Event 7	●	●	●		●	●	●
Event 8	●	●	●		●		●
Event 9	●	●	●		●	●	
Event 10	●	●	●		●		
Event 11	●	●	●	●		●	●
Event 12	●	●	●	●			●
Event 13	●	●	●	●		●	
Event 14	●	●	●	●			
Event 15	●	●		●		●	●
Event 16	●	●		●			●
Event 17	●	●		●		●	
Event 18	●	●		●			
Event 19	●	●				●	●
Event 20	●	●					●
Event 21	●	●				●	
Event 22	●	●					
Event 23	●	●		●		●	●
Event 24	●	●		●			●
Event 25	●	●		●		●	
Event 26	●	●		●			

Figure 2.11. (bottom panel).

mediated route) can be compared to the signal coming from direct perception. The degree to which the prediction is correct when direct perception is not possible reflects how well the model's ability to fill in missing information matches that of infants tested on ambiguous events. The degree to which the prediction is corrected when direct perception is possible reflects how well the network has extracted general object occlusion knowledge that applies across its entire learning environment.

Model results

In Mareschal and Johnson (2002), we discuss in detail how differences in the learning environment effect the bias to perceive an ambiguous event as arising from a single unified object or two disjoint objects. Here, we report only the model's performance in the best condition, which involved training the model with events 1, 2, and 17 to 22. This reflects the assumption that the majority of events that an infant observes arise from unrelated objects moving about. Under such conditions, the mediated route is learned very quickly (by 10 epochs) to detect correctly the presence of one or two objects in the unambiguous portions of all test events.

The key question is how the networks respond when tested with the ambiguous portions only of the events. Figure 2.12 shows the performance of 10 networks tested with the ambiguous portions of all 26 events. Consider first the events on which the model was trained. By the end of training, the networks achieved high levels of performance in seven of the eight familiarisation events (events 1, 2, and 17 to 21), and half the networks responded appropriately in the eighth (event 22). Initially, the networks perceived the single object in event 1 as arising from two disjoint objects, a tendency that was not overcome until after 4000 epochs. There was then a period (from about 5000 to 7000 epochs) in which an increasing proportion of the population of networks perceived this stimulus as arising from a single unbroken object. There was much variation across the networks, therefore, as to how this event was perceived. The variation arose from the sequence of events experienced by the networks during training (i.e. a preponderance of disjoint objects), and the initial random weights prior to training. By 8000 epochs, nine of the ten networks perceived this ambiguous event as arising from a single unbroken object, indicating that they had learned to go beyond a general default response that was consistent with the majority of training events (recall that the majority of training events arise from two distinct objects).

A slightly different pattern emerged when tested for unity perception in event 2. As in event 1, the networks perceived disjoint objects during the initial training period, but were able to overcome this tendency more quickly to respond appropriately to the object's unity. The only difference between events 1 and 2 is the presence of texture in event 1, which seems to have made perception of object unity more difficult, a counterintuitive result that is at odds with human performance (Johnson & Aslin, 1996). This is because the networks are powerful statistical learners that have picked up on a spurious correlation in their simplified environments. Indeed, they experience slightly more texture events associated with disjoint responses, and therefore learn that this is a weak predictor of the presence of two objects (see Mareschal & Johnson, 2002, for a more detailed discussion of this point).

Consider next performance on events to which the networks were not exposed during training. By the end of 8000 epochs, the networks achieved accurate performance on 14 of these 18 events (77.8). In events 5 and 6, in which there is no motion, unity is perceived accurately by 1500 epochs. This percept is achieved more quickly than in comparable displays with motion (events 1 and 2), suggesting that motion is a cue that biases *against* unity perception early in development. As in the case of the texture cue described previously, this counterintuitive result (relative to human performance) can be accounted for by appealing to the nature of the training set. Recall that the majority of training events consisted of disjoint objects, and these all contained co-motion as a cue (but not common motion). Motion, therefore, in the form of co-motion, became associated with disjoint objects; later in training, common motion (available as a cue in events 1 and 2 in the training set) became associated with unity.

If perception of unity in events 1 and 2 was not achieved primarily on the basis of motion, what cue or cues led to accurate performance? Note that alignment (the combination of parallelism and relatability) was present in these two events but none of the other training events, leading the networks to associate alignment to unity, rather than to disjoint objects. In the absence of motion, therefore, the networks more quickly perceived unity when alignment was available (events 5 and 6). The networks also seemed to use parallelism and relatability separately as cues for unity, even though this led to inaccurate performance: Unity was perceived in events 7 and 8, each with relatability but not parallelism, and events 23 and 24, each with parallelism but not relatability. This response pattern was due to the association of each cue to unity in training events 1 and 2. This tendency to perceive unity from parallelism and relatability was overcome, however, with the additional information for disjoint objects provided by the lack of T-junctions in comparable displays (events 9 and 10, and events 25 and 26, respectively). Lack of T-junctions was associated consistently with separate objects during training in events 17, 18, 21, and 22.

In summary, the networks learned to perceive either unified or disjoint objects in a wide range of new events. Performance was superior relative to Model 1, due to the provision of a richer training set. Cases in which the model's performance diverged from that of infants could be explained appealing to the limitations of the training environment and the power of

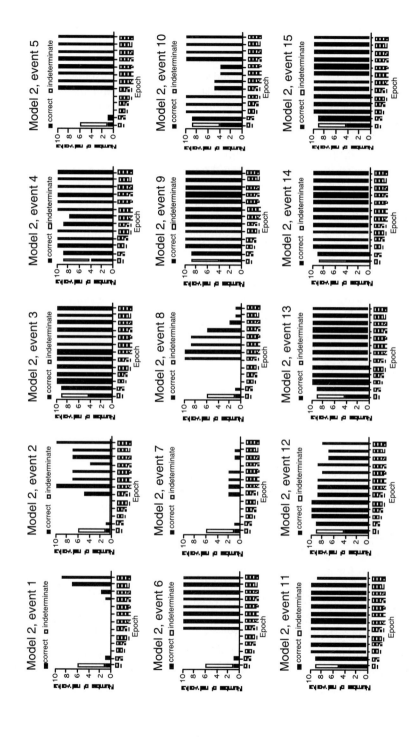

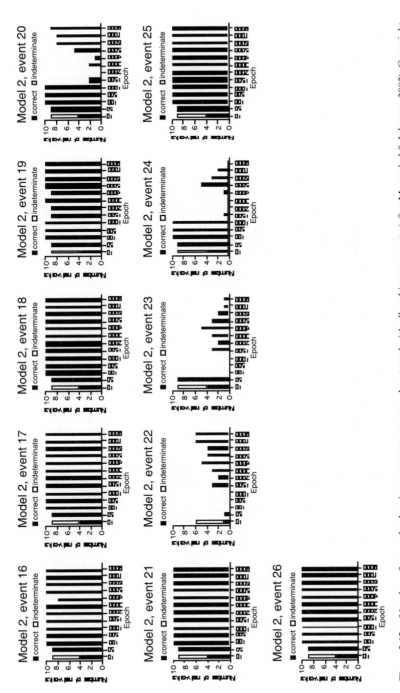

Figure 2.12. Number of networks showing a correct response when tested with all ambiguous events (after Mareschal & Johnson, 2002). Copyright © 2002 Blackwell Publishing, Oxford. Reprinted with permission.

connectionist systems to learn from even very small correlations. These powerful statistical learners extracted regularities that were unique to their training environment and that did not reflect regularities inherent in the human environment. Increasing the richness and complexity of this environment (thereby bringing it more in line with the infant's environment) should eradicate these spurious correlations. For these networks, therefore, their responses were *not* inaccurate (strictly speaking), given the perceptual environment they were provided.

This model has shown how initial architectural constraints coupled with a simple associative learning mechanism result in rapid learning of a complex high-level ability (namely, the apparent perceptual inference of unity). Of course, this remains a preliminary model. For example, the current model does not have access to three-dimensional depth cues, and is therefore not a full model of infant behaviour. Nevertheless, it illustrates how associative mechanisms could drive the developmental profiles observed with infants.

GENERAL DISCUSSION AND FUTURE DIRECTIONS

This chapter reviewed four connectionist models of infant learning and development. Each successive model introduced more and more processing constraints than the previous models. The first was a model of infant categorisation that also illustrated the basic connectionist information processing mechanisms. Autoencoder networks were found to develop the same categories as 3-month-olds when presented with the same stimuli used to test these infants.

The second model demonstrated how information from different sources or modalities could be integrated within a single internal representation. Acquiring representations that enabled the networks to learn one task (word learning) constrained their subsequent ability to perform on another task (phoneme discrimination). This illustrates how differences in levels of general experience can explain age differences in performance on a particular task.

The third model illustrated how functionally distinct modules can emerge from the same environmental experience. Networks with initially different associative mechanisms differed in the type of object information they came to process. The appearance of object-directed behaviours was related to the ability to integrate information across multiple object representations.

Finally, the fourth model showed how complex high-level behaviours could arise from the combination of encapsulated low-level visual processes. Inferring the continuity of a partially occluded object could be achieved by learning the associations between unity and low-level perceptual cues. This model also illustrated how a variety of mechanisms could be hardwired into a connectionist system to embody initial knowledge constraints.

Together, these models illustrate how a range of diverse infant behaviours can be explained in terms of neurally plausible information processing mechanisms. The models provide an *explanation* for these behaviours in terms of the interaction between neural information processing and the characteristics of the infant's environment. Both components are equally important. Because connectionist networks extract statistical regularities, the distribution of features in the environment determines the type of representations developed. Similarly, constraints such as the different initial architectures or different associative learning mechanisms also determine the type of representations developed. Finally, the way these representations interact in a complex multimodule system causes the observed behaviours.

While there are generally no "innate" representations in connectionist networks, innate knowledge can be implemented through different learning mechanisms and architectures that promote the rapid learning of domain-specific information. Thus, what is interpreted as innate knowledge in very young infants may actually reflect the rapid learning of a highly constrained associative system.

These models provided a mechanistic account of infant behaviours. They allow us to explain behaviours across a range of different domains in terms of a common set of mechanisms. In turn, these mechanisms can be speculatively related to the brain (Johnson, 1997). Of course, these models remain very simple. Nevertheless, they allow us to raise causal questions about *how* learning and development occur rather than simply describing the consequences of learning and development. By showing how the same family of mechanisms can explain behaviours from such a diverse set of domains, these and other connectionist models of infant development (Changeux & Dehaene, 1989; Dehaene & Changeux, 1993; Munakata, 1998; Munakata et al., 1997; Quinn & Johnson, 1997; Schlesinger & Parisi, 2001; Sirois, Buckingham, & Shultz, 2000) lay the groundwork for an explanatory synthesis of infant development.

One added advantage of mechanistic accounts of infant development is that they provide a handle with which to start asking how infant competence gets transformed into the abilities of older children and even adults. For example, we have begun to explore how the categorisation abilities of young infants can account for the performance of 3- and 4-year-olds on inductive reasoning tasks that oppose perceptual category information with label category information (Loose & Mareschal, 1997).

Models also allow us to address an issue that is flagged in the title of this chapter; namely: Are there mechanistic differences between learning and development? This is an issue that has hounded developmental psychology since the advent of information processing approaches that attempted to provide mechanistic accounts of development (Collins, 1982; Liben, 1987, see also Chapter 1). The answer, pervasive throughout this chapter is a resounding no. Both learning and development are modelled through the use of identical associative learning mechanisms within connectionist networks that differ only in architecture.

All the models in this chapter describe networks in which the connectivity is fixed from the onset. Although the weights are adjustable, the initial connectivity provides constraints that guide the rapid learning of basic perceptual and cognitive skills. However, there are networks that develop their own connectivity as part of the learning process (Mareschal & Shultz, 1996). We have argued elsewhere (Shultz & Mareschal, 1997) that networks with fixed connectivity are good models of learning in infancy (during which the basic building blocks of cognition are developing), whereas networks that developed their own connectivity are better models of later learning and development (in which there are fewer *a priori* constraints on what will need to be learned, e.g. learning a particular arithmetic system is culturally specific whereas learning about object unity is universal). This raises the question of how one system (the static connectivity system) develops into the other systems (the dynamic connectivity system).

Finally, although connectionist models aspire to provide explanations of behaviour in terms of neurally plausible mechanisms, they are a far cry from the full complexity of the human brain. One direction in which these models need to develop is to incorporate more constraints from the neurosciences. More realistic learning mechanisms need to be considered. However progress in this direction cannot proceed any faster than our knowledge of brain functioning.

ACKNOWLEDGEMENTS

I am very grateful to Robert French, Paul Harris, Scott Johnson, Kim Plunkett and Graham Schafer for their help with the projects described in this chapter. The writing of this chapter was supported by in part by European Commission Grant HPRN-CT-2000-00065 and Economic and Social Research Council UK Grant R000239112.

REFERENCES

Baillargeon, R. (1993). The object concept revisited: New directions in the investigation of infants' physical knowledge. In C. E. Granrud (Ed.), *Visual perception and cognition in infancy* (pp. 265–315). Hove, UK: Lawrence Erlbaum Associates Ltd.

Baillargeon, R., Spelke, E. S., & Wasserman, S. (1985). Object permanence in 5-month-old infants. *Cognition, 20*, 191–208.

Best, C. W., McRoberts, G. W., & Sithole, N. N. (1988). The phonological basis of perceptual loss for non-native contrasts: Maintenance and discrimination among Zulu clicks by English-speaking adults and infants. *Journal of Experimental Psychology: Human Perception and Performance, 14*, 345–360.

Boden, M. A. (1980). Artificial intelligence and Piagetian theory. In M. Boden (Ed.), *Minds and mechanisms: Philosophical psychology and computational models* (pp. 236–261). Ithaca, NY: Cornell University Press.

Changeux, J. P., & Dehaene, S. (1989). Neuronal models of cognitive function. *Cognition, 33*, 63–109.

Charlesworth, W. R. (1969). The role of surprise in cognitive development. In D. Elkind & J. Flavell (Eds.), *Studies in cognitive development. Essays in honor of Jean Piaget* (pp. 257–314). Oxford, UK: Oxford University Press.

Chauvin, Y. (1989). Towards a connectionist model of symbol emergence. In *Proceedings of the 11th annual conference of the Cognitive Science Society* (pp. 580–587). Hillsdale, NJ: Lawrence Erlbaum Associates, Inc.

Cohen, L. B. (1973). A two-process model of infant visual attention. *Merrill-Palmer Quarterly, 19*, 157–180.

Collins, W. A. (1982). *The concept of development*. Hillsdale, NJ: Lawrence Erlbaum Associates, Inc.

Cottrell, G. W., Munro, P., & Zipser, D. (1988). Image compression by backpropagation: An example of extensional programming. In N. E. Sharkey (Ed.), *Advances in cognitive science* (Vol. 3, pp. 208–240). Norwood, NJ: Ablex.

Dehaene S., & Changeux J.P. (1993) Development of elementary numerical abilities—a neuronal model. *Journal of Cognitive Neuroscience, 5*, 390–407.

Di Lollo, V., Enns, J. T., & Rensik, R. A. (2000). Competition for consciousness among visual events: The psychophysics of re-entrant visual pathways. *Journal of Experimental Psychology: General, 129*, 481–507.

Diamond, A. (1991). Neuropsychological insights into the meaning of object concept development. In S. Carey and G. Gelman (Eds.), *The epigenesis of mind: Essays on biology and cognition* (pp. 67–110). Hillsdale, NJ: Lawrence Erlbaum Associates, Inc.

Elman, J. L., Bates, E. A., Johnson, M. H., Karmiloff-Smith, A., Parisi, D., & Plunkett, K. (1996). *Rethinking innateness: A connectionist perspective on development*. Cambridge, MA: MIT Press.

Fantz, R. L. (1964). Visual experience in infants: Decreased attention to familiar patterns relative to novel ones. *Sciences, 164*, 668–670.

Foldiak, P. (1991). Learning invariance from transformation sequences. *Neural Computation, 3*, 194–200.

French, R. M., Mermillod, M., Quinn, P. C., & Mareschal, D. (2001). Reversing category exclusivities in infant perceptual categorisation: Simulation and data. In J. D. Moore & K. Stenning (Eds.), *Proceedings of the twenty-third annual conference of the Cognitive Science Society* (pp. 307–312). Hove, UK: Lawrence Erlbaum Associates Ltd.

Goodale, M. A. (1993). Visual pathways supporting perception and action in the primate cerebral cortex. *Current Opinion in Neurobiology, 3*, 578–585.

Johnson, M. H. (1997). *Developmental cognitive neuroscience*. Oxford: Blackwell.

Johnson, M. H., Mareschal, D., & Csibra, G. (2001). The functional development and integration of the dorsal and ventral visual pathways: A neurocomputational approach. In C. A. Nelson & M. Luciana (Eds.), *The handbook of developmental cognitive neuroscience* (pp. 339–351), Cambridge, MA: MIT Press.

Johnson, S. P., & Aslin, R. N. (1996). Perception of object unity in young infants: The roles of motion, depth, and orientation. *Cognitive Development, 11*, 161–180.

Johnson, S. P., & Nanez, J. E. (1995). Young infants' perception of object unity in two-dimensional displays. *Infant Behaviour and Development, 18*, 133–143.

Kellman, P. J., & Spelke, E. S. (1983). Perception of partly occluded objects in infancy. *Cognitive Psychology, 15*, 483–524.

Kellman, P. J., Spelke, E. S., & Short, K. R. (1986). Infant perception of object unity from translatory motion in depth and vertical translation. *Child Development, 57*, 72–86.

Klahr, D., & Wallace, J. G. (1976). *Cognitive development: An information processing view.* Hillsdale, NJ: Lawrence Erlbaum Associates, Inc.

Liben, L. S. (1987). *Development and learning: Conflict or congruence?* Hillsdale, NJ: Lawrence Erlbaum Associates, Inc.

Loose, J. J., & Mareschal, D. (1997).When a word is worth a thousand pictures: A connectionist account of the percept to label shift in children's inductive reasoning. In G. W. Cottrell (Ed.), *Proceedings of the 19th annual conference of the Cognitive Science Society* (pp. 454–459). Hove, UK: Lawrence Erlbaum Associates Ltd.

Mareschal, D., & French, R. M. (2000). Mechanisms of categorisation in infancy. *Infancy, 1*, 59–76.

Mareschal, D., French, R. M., & Quinn, P. (2000). A connectionist account of asymmetric category learning in infancy. *Developmental Psychology, 36*, 635–645.

Mareschal, D. & Johnson, M. H. (in press). The "What" and "Where" of infant object representations. *Cognition.*

Mareschal, D., & Johnson, S. P. (2002) Learning to perceive object unity: A connectionist account. *Developmental Science, 5*, 151–172.

Mareschal, D., Plunkett, K., & Harris, P. (1999). A computational and neuropsychological account of object-oriented behaviours in infancy. *Developmental Science, 2*, 306–317.

Mareschal, D., & Quinn, P. C. (2001) Categorisation in infancy. *Trends in Cognitive Science, 5*, 443–450.

Mareschal, D., Quinn, P. C., & French, R. M. (2002) Asymmetric interference in 3- to 4-month-olds' sequential category learning. *Cognitive Science, 26*, 377–389.

Mareschal, D., & Shultz, T. R. (1996). Generative connectionist networks and constructivist cognitive development. *Cognitive Development, 11*, 571–603.

McClelland, J. L. (1989). Parallel distributed processing: Implications for cognition and development. In R. G. M. Morris, (Ed.), *Parallel distributed processing: Implications for psychology and neurobiology* (pp. 8–45). Oxford: Oxford University Press.

Milner, A. D., & Goodale, M. A. (1995). *The visual brain in action.* Oxford: Oxford University Press.

Munakata, Y. (1998). Infants perseveration and implication for object permanence theories: A PDP model of the AB task. *Developmental Science, 1*, 161–211.

Munakata, Y., McClelland, J. L., Johnson, M. H., & Siegler, R. S. (1997). Rethinking infant knowledge: Towards an adaptive process account of successes and failures in object permanence tasks. *Psychological Review, 104*, 686–713.

Papert, S. (1963). Intelligence chez l'enfant et chez le robot. In L. Apostel, J. Grize, S. Papert, & J. Piaget (Eds.), La filiation des structures. *Etudes D'Epistemologie Génétiques, 15*, 131–194.

Passingham, R. E. (1993). *The frontal lobes and voluntary action.* Oxford: Oxford University Press.

Piaget, J. (1952). *The origins of intelligence in the child.* New York: International Universities Press.

Piaget, J. (1954). *The construction of reality in the child.* New York: Basic Books.

Plunkett, K., & Marchman, V. (1991). U-shaped learning and ferquency effects in a multilayered perceptron: Implications for child language acquisition. *Cognition, 38*, 43–102.

Plunkett, K., Sinha, C., Møller, M. F., & Strandsby, O. (1992). Symbol grounding or the emergence of symbols? Vocabulary growth in children and a connectionist net. *Connection Science, 4*, 293–312.

Posner, M. I. (1989). *Foundations of cognitive science.* Cambridge, MA: MIT Press.

Quartz, S. R., & Sejnowski, T. J. (1997). The neural basis of cognitive development: A constructivist manifesto. *Behavioural and Brain Sciences, 20*, 537–596.

Quinn, P. C., & Eimas, P. D. (1996). Perceptual organization and categorisation in young infants. *Advances in Infancy Research, 10*, 1–36.

Quinn, P. C., Eimas, P. D., & Rosenkrantz, S. L. (1993). Evidence for representations of perceptually similar natural categories by 3-month-old and 4-month-old infants, *Perception, 22*, 463–475.

Quinn, P. C., & Johnson, M. H. (1997). The emergence of perceptual category representations in young infants. *Journal of Experimental Child Psychology, 66*, 236–263.

Rosch, E., Mervis, C. B., Gray, W. D., Johnson, D. M., & Boyes-Braem, P. (1976). Basic objects in natural categories. *Cognitive Psychology, 8*, 382–439.

Schafer, G., & Mareschal, D. (2001). Modeling infant speech sound discrimination using simple associative networks. *Infancy, 2*, 7–28.

Schlesinger, M., & Parisi, D. (2001). The agent-based approach: A new direction for computational models of development. *Developmental Review, 21*, 121–146.

Shultz, T. R., & Mareschal, D. (1997). Rethinking innateness, learning, and constructivism. *Cognitive Development, 12*, 563–586.

Shultz, T. R., Schmidt, W. C., Buckingham, D., & Mareschal, D. (1995). Modelling cognitive development with a generative connectionist algorithm. In T. Simon & G. Halford (Eds.), *Developing cognitive competence: New approaches to process modelling* (pp. 347–362). Hillsdale, NJ: Lawrence Erlbaum Associates, Inc.

Simon, H. A. (1962). An information processing theory of intellectual development. *Monograph of the Society for Research in Child Development, 27* (2, Serial No. 82).

Sirois, S., Buckingham, D., & Shultz, T. R. (2000) Artificial grammar learning by infants: An autoassociator perspective. *Developmental Science, 3*, 442–456.

Slater, A. M. (1995). Visual perception and memory at birth. *Advances in Infancy Research, 9*, 107–162.

Slater, A. M., Johnson, S. P., Kellman, P. J., & Spelke, E. S. (1994). The role of three-dimensional depth cues in infants' perception of partly occluded objects. *Early Development and Parenting, 3*, 187–191.

Slater, A. M., Morison, V., Somers, M., Mattock, A., Brown, E., & Taylor, D. (1990). Newborn and older infants' perception of partly occluded objects. *Infant Behaviour and Development, 13*, 33–49.

Sokolov, E. N. (1963). *Perception and the conditioned reflex.* Hillsdale, NJ: Lawrence Erlbaum Associates, Inc.

Spelke, E. S. (1990). Principles of object perception. *Cognitive Science, 14*, 29–56.

Spelke, E. S., & Van de Walle, G. (1993). Perceiving and reasoning about objects: Insights from infants. In N. Eilan, R. A. McCarthy, & B. Brewer (Eds.), *Spatial representation: Problems in philosophy and psychology* (pp. 132–161). Oxford: Blackwell.

Stager, S., & Werker, J. F. (1997). Infants listen to more phonetic detail in speech perception tasks than in word-learning tasks. *Nature, 388*, 381–382.

Trehub, S. (1976). The discrimination of foreign speech contrasts by infants and adults. *Child Development, 47*, 466–472.

Ungerleider, L. G., & Mishkin, M. (1982). Two cortical visual systems. In D. J. Ingle, M. A. Goodale, & R. J. W. Mansfield (Eds.), *Analysis of visual behaviour* (pp. 549–586). Cambridge, MA: MIT Press.

Van Essen, D. C., Anderson, C. H., & Felleman, D. J. (1992). Information processing in the primate visual system: An integrated systems perspective. *Science, 255*, 419–423.

Von Hofsten, C. (1989). Transition mechanisms in sensori-motor development. In A. De Ribaupierre (Ed.), *Transition mechanisms in child development: The longitudinal perspective* (pp. 223–259). Cambridge: Cambridge University Press.

Werker, J. F., & Lalonde, C. E. (1988). Cross-language speech perception: Initial capabilities and developmental changes. *Developmental Psychology, 24*, 1–12.

Werker, J. F., & Pegg, J. E. (1992). Infant speech perception and phonological acquisition. In C. A. Ferguson, L. Menn, & C. Stoel-Gammon (Eds.), *Phonological development: Models, research, implications.* Timonium, MD: York Press.

Werker, J. F., & Tees, R. C. (1983). Developmental changes across childhood in the perception of non-native speech sounds. *Canadian Journal of Psychology, 37*, 278–286.

Werker, J. F., & Tees, R. C. (1984a). Cross language speech perception: Evidence for perceptual reorganisation during the first year of life. *Infant Behaviour and Development, 7*, 49–63.

Werker, J. F., & Tees, R. C. (1984b). Phonemic and phonetic factors in adult cross-language speech perception. *Journal of the Acoustical Society of America, 75*, 1866–1878.

Young, R. (1976). *Seriation by children: An artificial intelligence analysis of a Piagetian task.* Basel: Birkhauser.

CHAPTER THREE

The role of prefrontal cortex in perseveration: Developmental and computational explorations

Yuko Munakata
Department of Psychology, University of Colorado at Boulder, USA

J. Bruce Morton
Department of Psychology, University of Western Ontario, Canada

Jennifer Merva Stedron
Department of Psychology, University of Denver, Colorado, USA

INTRODUCTION

One of the hallmarks of "higher" intelligence is the ability to act flexibly and adaptively, rather than being governed by simple habit. For example, we may drive the same route to and from work each day but we can pull ourselves out of this habit when necessary (e.g. to stop to do some shopping on the way home). Many findings point to the critical role of the prefrontal cortex in such flexible behaviour. However, the exact nature of its role is uncertain. In this chapter, we use neural network models to explore the role of the prefrontal cortex in the development of flexible behaviour in the first years of life.

Infants often demonstrate a lack of flexibility by perseverating, repeating prepotent or habitual behaviours when they no longer make sense. For example, as soon as infants will search for a toy that is presented and then hidden, they search perseveratively, continuing to reach back to old hiding locations after watching as the toy is hidden in a new location (Diamond, 1985; Piaget, 1954). Infants will even perseverate when objects are fully visible in front of them. For example, when faced with two towels to pull—one with a distant toy on it and one with a toy behind it—infants will choose the towel with the toy on it. However, if the towels are switched so that the towel that was to the infants' left (e.g. with the toy on it) is now to the infants' right, they perseverate, continuing to pull the towel on the same side as before, although it does not yield the toy (Aguiar & Baillargeon, 2000).

These perseverative behaviours are not limited to infancy; children also demonstrate them quite reliably. For example, most 3-year-olds can correctly sort cards according to experimenter instructions (e.g. with all of the blue cards going into one pile, and all of the red cards going into another pile). However, when instructed to switch to a different sorting rule (e.g. to sort the cards by their shape rather than their colour, with all of the trucks going into one pile, and all of the flowers going into another pile), 3-year-olds persever-ate, continuing to sort by the initial instructions (Zelazo, Frye, & Rapus, 1996). Six-year-olds show the same pattern when asked to judge a speaker's feelings from utterances with conflicting emotional cues (e.g. a sentence with happy content—"I won a prize" spoken in a sad tone of voice; Morton & Trehub, 2001). When instructed to judge the speaker's feelings from the con-tent of her utterances, most 6-year-olds succeed. However, when instructed to switch and judge the speaker's feelings from her tone of voice, many 6-year-olds perseverate, continuing to base their judgements on content (Morton & Munakata, 2002b; Morton, Trehub, & Zelazo, unpublished).

In all of these cases, infants and children appear quite sensible in their initial behaviours—searching in the correct location for the hidden toy, pull-ing the appropriate towel, and sorting cards and judging utterances according to experimenter instructions. However, they appear quite inflexible in their subsequent behaviours, perseverating with their previous responses when they no longer make sense—searching in the incorrect location for the hidden toy (making the "A-not-B" error), pulling the inappropriate towel, and sorting cards and judging utterances without apparent regard for the experimenter's current instructions.

Interestingly, even as infants and children perseverate with their previous responses, they sometimes seem to indicate through other measures that they have some awareness of the correct response. That is, they show dissociations in their behaviour. For example, even as infants reach perseveratively to a previous hiding location for a toy, they occasionally gaze at the correct hiding location (Diamond, 1985; Hofstadter & Reznick, 1996; Piaget, 1954). Fur-ther, in violation-of-expectation variants of the A-not-B task, infants look longer when a toy hidden at B is revealed at A than when it is revealed at B, following delays at which they would nonetheless search perseveratively at A (Ahmed & Ruffman, 1998). Perhaps even more compelling, even as children sort perseveratively according to a previous rule, they can correctly answer questions about the new rule they should be using, such as where trucks should go in the shape game (Zelazo et al., 1996), or what aspect of a speaker's voice they should be listening to (Morton & Munakata, 2002b; Morton et al., unpublished). These dissociations in infants' and children's behaviour provide an important constraint on theories of perseveration.

Further, behavioural dissociations are a salient aspect of development more generally (Berthier, DeBlois, Poirier, Novak, & Clifton, 2000; Hood & Willatts, 1986; Piaget, 1952; Spelke, Breinlinger, Macomber, & Jacobson, 1992). Understanding such dissociations may thus be an important step in understanding the development and organisation of our cognitive systems (Munakata, 2001a; Munakata & Stedron, 2002).

Another important constraint on theories of perseveration is the remarkable decalage (Piaget, 1941, 1967), or temporal uncoupling of similar cognitive developments (Flavell, 1963), observed across various tasks. That is, infants succeed in the A-not-B task years before they succeed in the card-sorting task, and children succeed in the card-sorting task years before they succeed in the speech interpretation task. Children's apparent abilities to overcome perseveration and respond flexibly thus depend heavily on exactly what task they face.

The prefrontal cortex plays a critical role in reducing perseveration and in supporting flexible behaviour more generally (Diamond, 2002; Miller & Cohen, 2001; Miyake & Shah, 1999; O'Reilly, Braver, & Cohen, 1999; Roberts & Pennington, 1996; Stuss & Benson, 1984). For example, impaired prefrontal functioning often leads to perseverative behaviours. Some of the most dramatic examples come from human adults with prefrontal damage, who may exhibit environmental dependency syndrome—inappropriately carrying out habitual responses supported by particular environmental stimuli (Lhermitte, 1986). For example, one such patient, upon entering her physician's home and seeing dirty dishes in the kitchen, began to wash them. Another patient, upon seeing paintings on the floor next to a hammer and nails, began hanging the paintings. Such patients have also put on multiple pairs of glasses when presented with them individually, and even used a makeshift urinal when presented with it (Lhermitte, 1986). In all of these cases, patients simply carried out prepotent responses to particular stimuli, rather than responding flexibly based on the particular context, in which it would have been more appropriate to inhibit those behaviours. The prefrontal cortex has also been implicated in more systematic tasks like those described above. For example, patients with prefrontal damage perseverate in tasks like Zelazo et al.'s (1996) card-sorting task (Milner, 1963). When the sorting rule is changed, patients respond based on habit (the first sorting rule) rather than responding flexibly to feedback indicating that the rule has changed. Similarly, adult monkeys with lesions to the prefrontal cortex perseverate in the A-not-B task (Diamond & Goldman-Rakic, 1986, 1989). And, human infants' eventual success in this task is correlated with event-related potential measures recorded over frontal cortex (Bell & Fox, 1992).

Thus, there is general agreement that the prefrontal cortex plays a role in reducing perseveration, that there is a decalage in when children succeed in overcoming perseveration, and that behavioural dissociations emerge in tasks that require flexibility, with one measure yielding perseveration and another measure suggesting awareness of the correct response. In this chapter, we use neural network models to explore three remaining questions about perseveration in infancy and childhood:

- *How* does prefrontal development reduce perseveration?
- *Why* are dissociations observed in perseveration?
- *Why* do children show the remarkable decalage in their flexibility, overcoming perseveration at such different ages across various tasks?

We consider each of these questions in turn, and close by comparing the answers that emerge from our neural network explorations to other accounts of perseveration.

PREFRONTAL CORTEX AND PERSEVERATION

Neural network models have helped to understand how the development of the prefrontal cortex can reduce perseveration (Dehaene & Changeux, 1989, 1991; Morton & Munakata, 2002a; Munakata, 1998; Stedron, Munakata, & Sahni, 2002). In this chapter, we explore an account based on a distinction between "active" and "latent" memory traces (Munakata, 2001b). In the neural network framework, active traces take the form of sustained activations of network processing units (roughly corresponding to the firing rates of neurons), and latent traces take the form of changes to connection weights between units (roughly corresponding to the efficacy of synapses). According to the active–latent account:

- Perseveration occurs based on a competition between latent memory traces for previously relevant information and active memory traces for current information.
- Latent memory traces, subserved primarily by posterior cortex, result when organisms change their biases toward a stimulus after processing it, so that they may respond differently to the stimulus on subsequent presentations. These latent traces are not accessible to other brain areas, because synaptic changes in one part of the brain cannot be communicated to other areas. Rather, latent traces can only influence processing elsewhere in the system in terms of how they affect the processing of subsequent stimuli, and resulting patterns of activation.
- Active memory traces, subserved primarily by prefrontal cortex, result when organisms actively maintain representations of a stimulus. Unlike latent traces, such active representations may be accessible to other brain areas in the absence of subsequent presentations of the stimulus, because neuronal firing in one region can be communicated to other areas.

- Flexible behaviour can be understood in terms of the relative strengths of latent and active memory traces. The increasing ability to maintain active traces of current information, dependent on developments in prefrontal cortex, leads to improvements in performance on tasks such as A-not-B.

Behavioural and physiological data motivate the active–latent distinction central to the proposed theory of perseveration. For example, neurons can "remember" information in two distinct ways: through sustained firing for a stimulus (active), or through changes in firing thresholds or synapses that affect neurons' subsequent firing to a stimulus (latent). When monkeys performed a task that required memory for a specific stimulus item, neurons in the prefrontal cortex showed sustained firing for the stimulus, across intervening stimuli (Miller, Erickson, & Desimone, 1996). This active memory is consistent with a number of neural recording and imaging experiments in the prefrontal cortex (Cohen et al., 1997; Fuster, 1989; Goldman-Rakic, 1987). In contrast, on an easier task that required memory for any familiar stimulus, monkeys solved the task using some form of latent memory in neurons in the inferotemporal cortex; these neurons showed no maintained firing signal but showed reduced firing when familiar stimuli were presented again (Miller & Desimone, 1994). Monkeys appeared to simply process stimuli and as a result, laid down latent memory traces for them, resulting in facilitated processing (i.e. reduced firing) when they were repeated. Neurons in prefrontal and posterior parietal cortex have shown the same active–latent distinction for memories of spatial locations (Steinmetz, Connor, Constantinidis, & McLaughlin, 1994). Finally, humans with frontal lobe damage show deficits in working memory, but are unimpaired in discriminating novel and familiar stimuli (see Petrides, 1989, for a review). Such recognition memory might depend on latent memory traces that do not require the prefrontal cortex, whereas working memory requires information to be kept active for manipulation.[1]

The active–latent account shares several features with and builds on existing accounts and computational models of perseveration. Many accounts and models similarly posit perseveration to arise based on a competition between two kinds of information, and describe something akin to the latent or active elements of the active–latent account (Butterworth, 1977; Dehaene & Changeux, 1991; Diamond, 1985; Harris, 1986; Thelen, Schoner, Scheier, & Smith, 2001; Wellman, Cross, & Bartsch, 1986). Further, many accounts and models have similarly emphasised working memory as a primary mechanism of prefrontal cortex, with other functions (e.g. inhibition

---

[1] We view active memory as only one component of (rather than equivalent to) working memory.

of prepotent responses) emerging from this more basic mechanism (Cohen & Servan-Schreiber, 1992; Goldman-Rakic, 1987; Kimberg & Farah, 1993; Miller & Cohen, 2001; O'Reilly et al., 1999; Roberts, Hager, & Heron, 1994). In this view, prefrontal cortex subserves the ability to maintain and manipulate information in working memory, in the absence of supporting stimuli (e.g. across delays) or in the face of interfering stimuli. Prefrontal cortex can thus serve to represent task-appropriate information, such as the most recent hiding location in the A-not-B task or the most recent rule in the card-sorting task. These representations support flexible behaviours and, via competitive interactions throughout the cortex, the representations supporting inappropriate or habitual behaviours are inhibited.

We explore the active–latent account by testing neural network models in all of the developmental tasks described above: the classic A-not-B task (Piaget, 1954), the towel-pulling task (Aguiar & Baillargeon, 2000), the card-sorting task (Zelazo et al., 1996), and the speech interpretation task (SIT; Morton & Munakata, 2002b, Morton et al., unpublished). The models provide a unified framework for understanding perseveration across a range of conditions (e.g. with hidden or visible objects, with or without explicit rules) and ages (from infancy through childhood). The models also lead to novel behavioural predictions. As outlined above, this unified approach to perseveration has much in common with existing approaches; however, the active–latent account contrasts with other theories, as we elaborate in the Discussion section.

A-not-B

This simulation (Munakata, 1998) explored infants' perseveration in searching for hidden objects. According to the active–latent account, after infants repeatedly attend to a hiding location and reach there, they lay down latent traces biasing them toward that location, making them more likely to reach there in the future. To overcome that tendency, and reach to a new location, infants must maintain active memory traces for the most recent hiding location of an object. The full simulation evaluated many variants of the A-not-B task not covered here, so we simplify the presentation of the network architecture and environment to include only those elements covered in the simulations described in this section.

Architecture and environment.   The network comprised two input layers that encoded information about the location and identity of objects, an internal representation layer, and two output layers for gaze/expectation and reach (Figure 3.1). The gaze/expectation layer responded (i.e. updated the activity of its units) to every input during the A-not-B task, while the reaching layer responded only to inputs corresponding to a stimulus within

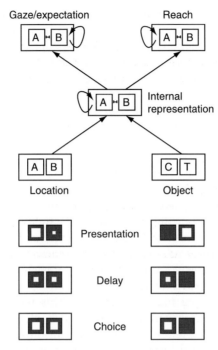

Figure 3.1. Simplified version of the A-not-B network and the elements of an *A* trial (adapted from Munakata, 1998): The activation level of the input units for the three segments of the trial is shown by the size of the white boxes. The "Object" input indicated whether a cover (C) or toy (T) was visible. Copyright © 1998 Blackwell Publishing, Oxford. Reprinted with permission.

"reaching distance". This updating constraint was meant to capture the fact that infants' reaching is permitted at only one point during each A-not-B trial, when the apparatus is moved to within the infant's reach, whereas nothing prevents infants from forming expectations (which may underlie longer looking to impossible events) throughout each trial.[2]

The network's feedforward connectivity included an initial bias to respond appropriately to location information, and also developed further biases based on the network's experience during the A-not-B task. The initial bias

---

[2] The model simplifies over nuances in infants' gazing and reaching. For example, infants' gaze is sometimes restricted during A-not-B experiments so that they cannot gaze continuously at a recent hiding location, whereas the model gazes continuously. And, infants may plan or imagine reaching movements before the point when they can reach to the A-not-B apparatus, so that they may activate brain areas relevant for reaching to some degree prior to the actual reach, whereas the model cannot activate its reaching units until the actual reach. Nevertheless, the model captures an essential difference between gaze/expectation and reach in the A-not-B task—infants have many more opportunities to gaze and to form expectations than to execute reaching responses.

allowed the network, for example, to look to location *A* if something were presented there. Infants enter A-not-B experiments with such biases, so this manipulation may be viewed as a proxy for experience prior to the A-not-B study. The network's feedforward weights changed based on its experience during the study according to a Hebbian learning rule, such that connections between units that were simultaneously active tended to be relatively strong. The network's latent memory thus took the form of these feedforward weights; they reflected the network's prior experiences and influenced its subsequent processing.

Each unit in the hidden and output layers had a self-recurrent excitatory connection back to itself. These recurrent connections were largely responsible for the network's ability to maintain representations of a recent hiding location; units that are active tend to remain active when they receive their own activity as input through sufficiently large weights. The network's active memory thus took the form of maintained representations on the network's hidden and output layers, as supported by its recurrent connections. To simulate gradual improvements with age in the network's active memory, the strength of the network's recurrent connections was manipulated, with "older" networks having higher recurrence. This manipulation might be viewed as a proxy for experience-based weight changes that have been explored elsewhere (Munakata, McClelland, Johnson, & Siegler, 1997).

The simulated A-not-B task consisted of four pretrials (corresponding to the "practice" trials typically provided at the start of an experiment to induce infants to reach to *A*), two *A* trials, and one *B* trial. Each trial consisted primarily of three segments: the presentation of a toy at the *A* or *B* location, a delay period, and a choice period (Figure 3.1). During each segment, patterns of activity were presented to the input units corresponding to the visible aspects of the stimulus event. The levels of input activity represented the salience of aspects of the stimulus, with more salient aspects producing more activity. For example, the levels of input activity for the *A* and *B* locations were higher during choice than during delay, to reflect the increased salience of the stimulus when it was presented for a response.

Performance and internal representations.   For all analyses of the network's performance, the network's percentage correct response was computed as the activation of the appropriate output unit divided by the sum of activation over all possible output units. For example, the network's percentage correct reaching on *A* trials was computed as the activity of *A* divided by ($A + B$) for the reaching layer. The model simulated the A-not-B error (successful reaching on *A* trials with perseverative reaching on *B* trials), and improvements with age (Figure 3.2). The model also showed earlier sensitivity on *B* trials in its gaze/expectation than in its reach, a finding that we will return to later.

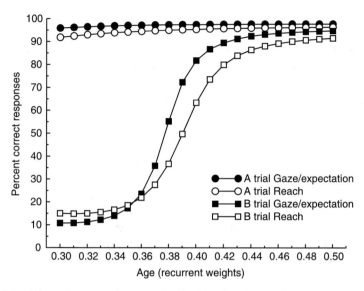

Figure 3.2.   Percentage correct responses as a function of age: On *A* trials, the network is accurate across all levels of recurrence shown. On *B* trials, the network responds nonperseveratively only as the recurrent weights get stronger.

The network performed well on *A* trials at all ages because latent changes to the feedforward weights, built up over previous trials in which the network represented and responded to *A*, favoured *A* over *B*. These latent memories thus supported enough activity at *A* that the network's ability to maintain activity at *A* had little effect on performance. The internal representations of a relatively young network during an *A* trial (Figure 3.3) showed that even with relatively weak recurrent weights to support the active maintenance of the most recent hiding location, the network was able to strongly represent *A* during all three segments of the trial. Thus, the latent memories in the network's weights, biasing it towards *A*, allowed it to respond correctly towards *A* even with only a weak ability to actively hold the most recent hiding location in mind.

In contrast, the network's ability to maintain activity for the most recent hiding location was critical to its performance on *B* trials, because the network had to maintain a representation of *B* in the face of the latent bias to respond to *A*. The activity of the units of the young network during a *B* trial (Figure 3.4) indicated that the network represented and responded appropriately to *B* in gaze/expectation during the presentation of the toy at *B*, when the *B* input unit was strongly activated. Infants in the A-not-B task similarly look to *B* when an object is hidden there. However, the memory for *B* faded during the delay, when the *A* and *B* input units were equally activated, so that the internal representation activity showed little evidence of which location

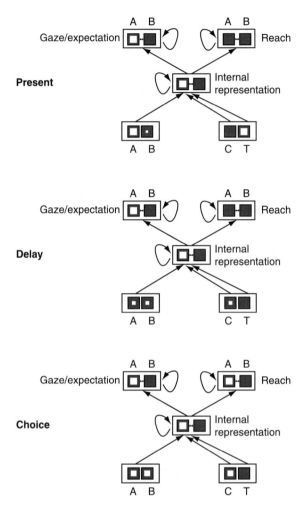

Figure 3.3. A young network's representations during an *A* trial (adapted from Munakata, 1998): Only the strongest of the feedforward weights are shown; these reflect the network's latent bias towards *A* that developed during the practice trials. The network responds correctly to *A* in gaze/expectation and in reach. Copyright © 1998 Blackwell Publishing, Oxford. Reprinted with permission.

was recently attended. If judged at that time on the basis of active traces alone, the network showed little memory of prior events. However, the network showed strong evidence of memory for the previous trials by making the A-not-B error at choice, indicating the influence of latent traces. In particular, the network's connection weights had learned to favour activity at *A* over *B*, based on the preceding pretrials and *A* trials. Thus, by repeatedly attending and responding to one location, the network became increasingly

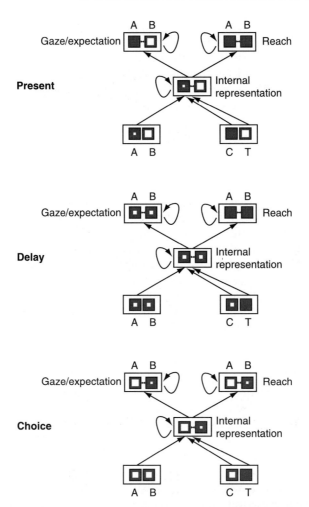

Figure 3.4. A young network's representations during a *B* trial (adapted from Munakata, 1998): Again, only the strongest of the feedforward weights are shown. The weaker weights (not shown) that support a correct response to *B* allow the network to represent and gaze at *B* when a toy is presented there (as infants do). However, after the toy is hidden, the network's weak ability to maintain an active representation of *B* cannot compete against the network's latent bias towards *A* (reflected in the strong feedforward weights shown). The network thus responds persevera-tively to *A* in gaze/expectation and in reach. Copyright © 1998 Blackwell Publishing, Oxford. Reprinted with permission.

likely to attend and respond there. Stronger recurrent weights allowed an older network to maintain an active memory of *B* during the delay. That is, the older network was better able to hold information about a recent hiding location in mind, rather than simply falling back to its biases for previous locations.

Predictions.   The A-not-B model led to the novel prediction that infants may show a U-shaped pattern of performance in their perseveration, at first showing worse performance with increasing age and then better performance. That is, networks at the youngest ages (weakest recurrent weights) in Figure 3.2 showed *more* perseveration than slightly younger networks (not shown in the figure). This prediction of U-shaped performance has since been supported (Clearfield & Thelen, 2000).

The patterns of network activity during *A* and *B* trials reveal how increases in recurrence can hurt network performance. The representations of very young networks are so weak that they fade quickly over even *A* trial delays, leading to weak prepotent responses to *A*. As these representations become stronger, they fade less quickly over *A* trial delays, leading to stronger prepotent responses to *A*. In effect, the more the network keeps *A* in mind (as recurrence increases), the more biased the network becomes to respond to *A*. Becoming increasingly able to keep something in mind helps only if *B* can be kept in mind long enough to sustain the delay; otherwise—if the system must perseverate—it is better off the less it keeps things in mind. Longer delay periods make the U-shape more prominent, because the recurrent weights influence the network's activity most during delay; the longer their period of influence, the more evident their contribution.

Towel-pulling

This simulation (Stedron et al., 2002) explored infants' perseveration when retrieving visible objects. As described earlier, infants presented with two towels, one with a distant toy on it and one with a toy behind it, will pull the correct towel to retrieve the toy, but perseverate and pull the incorrect towel (with the toy behind it) when the toy's location is switched (Aguiar & Baillargeon, 2000). Infants also perseverate in other tasks with fully visible objects. For instance, when presented with a toy inside a transparent box, infants will perseveratively attempt to reach the toy through the closed top of the box, rather than through an open side (Diamond, 1981). Perhaps counterintuitively, a competition between active and latent memory traces can also account for such perseverative behaviours with visible objects. Latent memory traces result from repeated behaviours (e.g. pulling the initially correct towel) or prepotent tendencies (e.g. to reach directly for visible objects). Active memory traces represent currently relevant information (e.g. which towel should be pulled, how the toy in the transparent box can be retrieved). When latent memory traces are stronger than the active memory traces, infants perseverate.

Why is active memory helpful with fully visible objects? Active memory can bolster representations of fully visible information, allowing one to attend to the critical features of the environment (De Fockert, Rees, Frith, &

Lavie, 2001). For example, an adult may not normally attend to the colour of a companion's shirt, but active memory may help the adult attend to that feature if he or she is trying to follow the companion through a large crowd. Similarly, in the towel-pulling task, active memory can help infants attend to which towel currently holds the toy. The stronger the representation of this critical information, the more likely active memory will prevail over latent memory, enabling the infant to reach to the correct towel. We explore these ideas in a simulation of infant behaviour in the towel-pulling task.

Architecture and environment. The network was comprised of two input layers that encoded information about the location, identity and placement (e.g. toy on towel) of the objects, and three layers that represented the two locations of the objects: an internal representation layer (hidden layer), a prefrontal cortex (PFC) layer, and an output layer for reaching (Figure 3.5). Feedforward connections linked the network's input layers to the hidden

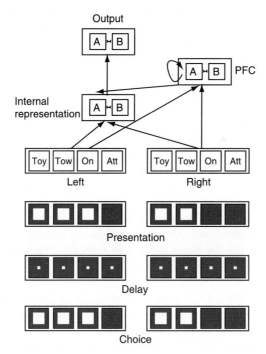

Figure 3.5. The towel-pulling network and the elements of an *A* trial: The input units encoded information about the identity of objects (toy and towel; Tow) and their placement (on and attached; Att). A toy sitting behind a towel would activate the toy and towel units only (as on the right side of the trial shown). A toy sitting on a towel would activate the toy, towel, and on units (as on the left side of the trial shown). A toy that attached to its supporting towel would activate the toy, towel, on, and attached units; this condition is discussed in the Decalage section.

and PFC layers, and the hidden layer to the output layer. This feedforward connectivity included an initial bias to accurately encode the location of various aspects of the display. For example, the weight from the left "on" input unit was strongly connected to the left hidden unit and the left PFC unit, and the weight from the left hidden unit was strongly connected to the left output unit. This initial bias allowed the network to represent and respond to the location of a toy on a towel preferentially over a toy behind a towel. Infants appear to bring such a bias into the towel-pulling task. Like the A-not-B model, the network developed a bias (latent traces in the form of stronger feedforward weights) for the towel location that originally supported the toy based on its experience with the task, according to a Hebbian learning rule.

Each prefrontal unit had a self-recurrent excitatory connection back to itself, and an excitatory connection to the corresponding hidden unit. These recurrent connections were largely responsible for the network's ability to maintain an active representation of the current (and visible) location of the towel supporting the toy. This model and subsequent ones thus elaborated the A-not-B model architecture by incorporating a separate prefrontal layer for this active memory function, rather than simply using self-recurrent connections on the hidden layer as a proxy. Again, the network's ageing was simulated by strengthening the recurrent connections.

The towel-pulling task consisted of four A trials, in which the same towel (at location A) supported the toy, and one B trial, in which the other towel (at location B) supported the toy. Each trial consisted of three segments: (1) the presentation of the toys placed on (or behind) the towels at the A and B locations; (2) a short delay in which reach was prevented (simulating a brief period in the behavioural studies when a screen was placed between the infant and the towels to prevent immediate reach); and (3) a choice period when the towels and toys were again visible (Figure 3.5). During each segment, patterns of activity were presented to the input units corresponding to the visible aspects of the stimulus event. Activity was low and equally distributed across all input units during the delay period, to reflect the lack of any particular visual input due to the occluding screen.

Performance and internal representations. As in the A-not-B model, the network's correct response was computed as the activation of the appropriate output unit divided by the sum of activation over both output units (i.e. A divided by $(A + B)$ on A trials). The model simulated infants' correct towel-pulling on A trials, their perseverative towel-pulling on B trials, and improvements with age.

The network performed well on A trials at all ages because of the network's initial bias to reach to the towel supporting the toy. Because the network responded to the same towel supporting the toy throughout the four

A trials, an initial bias for the towel supporting the toy at the *A* location was strengthened as a result of latent changes to the feedforward weights.

During the *B* trials, this latent bias to respond to the old towel competed with the network's ability to strongly represent information about the new towel supporting the toy. As with infants, the information about the two towel choices was fully visible to the network. The total input activation on the correct side was greater than the activation on the previous side, because the "on" unit was active only on the correct side. The recurrent connections were necessary for amplifying this greater activation for the correct side, thus more strongly influencing the activation of the hidden units. In younger networks with weaker recurrent weights, the latent bias for the old location was stronger than the activation for the correct location provided by the PFC layer, leading to perseveration. In older networks with stronger recurrent weights, the stronger PFC representation of the correct location provided stronger input to the hidden layer, and stronger competition against the latent bias for the old towel, leading the network to reach to the correct towel.

Predictions.   The towel-pulling model led to the novel prediction that infants at different points in development may show an interesting pattern in how quickly they pull the towel on *B* trials. In the model, reaction time is measured in terms of processing cycles required before the model settles on a stable response. The network produced a developmental inverted U-shaped reaction time curve in its performance, responding most quickly when it was very young and perseverating, and when it was very old and succeeding. In contrast, the network responded slowly at a transitional age, just prior to its first success and just after its first success. These differences in reaction time resulted from differences in the degree of competition between the active representation for the current location of the towel supporting the toy and the latent bias for the old location. Specifically, the more imbalanced this competition, the faster the competition was resolved, and the faster the reach. These results suggest that infants should be fastest when they are either really perseverating or really succeeding (i.e. when they are far from the transition period from perseveration to success), and they should be slowest in the transition period. Thus, the model makes clear developmental predictions about reaction times that we are now testing.

Card-sorting and speech-interpretation tasks

These simulations (Morton & Munakata, 2002a) explored children's perseveration in using prior rules rather than current rules for sorting cards (Zelazo et al., 1996) and judging the emotion of a speaker (Morton & Munakata, 2002b; Morton et al., unpublished). According to the active–latent account, children need to maintain a strong active representation of the current (postswitch) rule to overcome latent biases that are established or strengthened by use of the prior (preswitch) rule. Failure to do so results in perseveration.

The networks for the two tasks had virtually equivalent architectures, differing only in the strength of initial biases and the labelling of units. Consequently, the underlying causes of perseveration and dissociation were identical for both models. To simplify the presentation, we focus on the results from the card-sort model, and save a discussion of the differences between the models for the Decalage section.

Architecture and environment. The networks consisted of three input layers, an internal representation layer, a PFC rule layer, and an output layer (Figures 3.6 and 3.7). In the card-sorting network, the input layers encoded

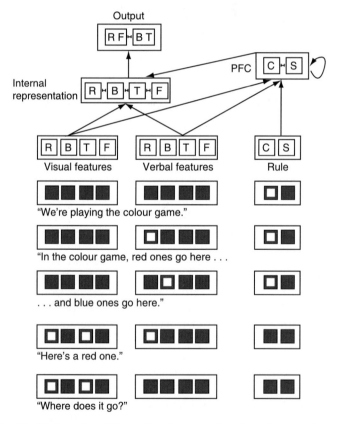

Figure 3.6. Simplified version of the card-sorting network and the elements of a trial. In the inputs with "go here", the corresponding output unit was activated for the network to indicate where the card should go. B, blue; C, colour; F, flower; PFC, prefrontal cortex; R, red; S, shape; T, truck.

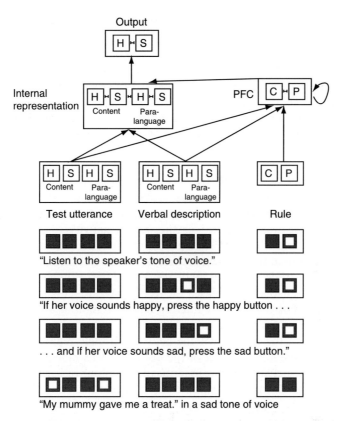

Figure 3.7. Simplified version of the speech-interpretation network and the elements of a trial. In the inputs with "press the . . . button," the corresponding output unit was activated for the network to indicate which button should be pushed. C, content; H, happy; P, paralanguage; PFC, prefrontal cortex; S, sad.

the shape and colour of the test cards, verbal descriptions of these features, and the sorting rule. The two output units represented the sorting trays in which children place the test cards, and were labelled red/flower and blue/truck, respectively.

The network's feedforward connectivity included an initial bias to respond appropriately to colour and shape information, and also developed further biases based on the network's experience during the card-sorting task. The "Red" hidden unit, for example, became active when either the "Red" visual features or the "Red" verbal features units were active, and the "Red/Flower" output became active when either the "Red" or the "Flower" hidden units were active. Children appear to bring such biases with them into the card-sorting task. As in the A-not-B and towel-pulling models, these connections changed with experience according to a Hebbian learning rule, such that the network's latent memory took the form of stronger connections between units. And as in those models, the network's ageing was simulated by strengthening the recurrent connections supporting the network's active representations.

The simulated card-sorting task consisted of two demonstrations of the preswitch rule, six trials with the preswitch rule, and six trials with the post-switch rule. Each simulated trial of the card-sort task included a statement of the rules followed by a presentation of a test card (Figure 3.6).

Performance and internal representations. We measured the network's percentage correct response as the activation of the appropriate output unit divided by the sum of activation over both output units. For example, the network's percentage correct response on a trial with a red flower (RF) in the colour game was computed as the output activity of RF divided by ($RF + BT$). The network simulated good preswitch performance at all ages, and perseveration in the postswitch trials with age-related improvements.

In preswitch trials, networks at all ages sorted correctly because the demonstration trials had slightly biased the feedforward weights in favour of the preswitch rule. For example, the internal representation of a young network presented with a blue flower showed that, even in the absence of a strong representation of the colour rule, the network strongly represented the blue aspect but not the flower aspect of the test card in its hidden layer. This, in turn, caused the network to sort in terms of the colour rather than the shape of the test card. Continued experience of correctly sorting the test cards further strengthened the feedforward weights in favour of the preswitch rule.

The network's age (strength of recurrent connections) played a larger role in performance on the postswitch trials. Young networks were unable to maintain a strong active representation of the shape rule for the full duration of a trial, and therefore were unable to overcome the latent bias to internally represent the colour rather than the shape of the test cards. Consequently, young networks responded to colour and not shape. In contrast, older networks had stronger recurrent connections that allowed them to maintain a strong active representation of the shape rule. This active representation strengthened the representation of shape in the hidden layer, allowing older networks to overcome the latent bias to represent colour.

Predictions. According to the active–latent account, children's ability to switch rules rapidly in response to verbal instructions depends on variations in the strength of active memory. This leads to the prediction that increasing the delay between the delivery of a new rule and testing should compromise children's ability to switch. A longer delay would give more opportunity for the active representation of the new rule to decay, making it more difficult to overcome a latent bias for using the old rule. Conversely, repeating the new rule more frequently might facilitate switching, due to a strengthening of the active representation of the new rule.

In addition, the model suggests a more effective method than direct instruction for helping perseverating children switch to a new rule. The model predicts that children may be more likely to switch to a new rule (e.g. sorting cards by colour after sorting them by shape), if they could gain some experience with the new rule that would strengthen latent memories for it. For example, after sorting cards by shape, children could easily sort cards by colour if the cards were completely blue or red, without any shapes on them to conflict with the colour cues. According to the model, this experience would strengthen children's latent representations for the new colour rule, making them more likely to switch to colour when presented with the original cards (e.g. red trucks and blue flowers). In contrast, direct instructions to switch to a new rule would be less effective, if children could not maintain active representations of the new rule. We are currently testing these predictions.

DISSOCIATIONS

The preceding simulations demonstrate how improvements in active memory can reduce perseveration across a range of conditions (e.g. with hidden objects, fully visible objects, and explicit rules). However, as discussed earlier, infants and children sometimes show dissociations in their behaviour, perseverating despite seeming to demonstrate that they know what they should do. How can the problem then be one of active memory? For example, if children can answer questions about the correct card-sorting rule, and infants can look at the correct hiding location in the A-not-B task, how could their incorrect perseverative responses reflect limitations in remembering the rule or the hiding location?

This type of challenge builds on the assumption that memory is an all-or-nothing construct—either present or absent. From this standpoint, if individuals succeed on one memory test (e.g. by answering a question about a rule), their memory must be fine, so perseveration must be attributed to other factors. By contrast, if one allows that various capacities may be graded in nature rather than all or nothing, memory limitations can in fact explain perseveration and dissociations in behaviour (reviewed in Munakata, 2001a). That is, memories, perceptions, rules, and so on may vary in their strength rather than simply being present or absent (Farah, O'Reilly, & Vecera, 1993; Mathis & Mozer, 1996; McClelland, Rumelhart, & PDP Research Group, 1986). Strength might be instantiated by the number of neurons contributing to a particular representation and the firing rates and coherence of those neurons. Weak representations might suffice for some tasks but not others, leading to dissociations in behaviour. For example, some degree of memory for a card-sorting rule might support the ability to answer questions about the rule, but not to correctly sort a card when faced with the conflicting features present in it. When children perseverate with an old rule (e.g. sorting a red truck by its shape rather than by its colour) despite appearing to know the new rule (by correctly answering the question, "Where do red things go in the colour game?"), the sorting measure requires resolving a conflict between rules (i.e. deciding where to place an object that is both red and a truck) whereas the knowledge question does not. A weak memory for the colour rule might allow children to correctly answer nonconflict questions, but not to respond correctly when presented with the conflict inherent in the sorting task.

Thus, if one allows that memory may be graded in nature, with weaker representations sufficing for some tasks but not others, behavioural dissociations can be understood in terms of memory limitations. We use neural network simulations to explore the role of graded representations in dissociations observed across perseverative tasks.

A-not-B

As shown in Figure 3.2, the A-not-B model, like infants, showed earlier sensitivity on *B* trials in its gaze/expectation than in its reaching (Munakata, 1998). This dissociation can be understood by considering a network slightly older than the one shown in Figures 3.3 and 3.4. (The younger networks perseverated in both gaze/expectation and reaching.) With stronger recurrent weights, the slightly older network was better able to hold in mind information about a recent location (Figure 3.8). The gaze/expectation system was able to take advantage of this information with its constant updating, showing correct responding during presentation and delay, which carried over to choice. In contrast, the reach system was able to respond only at choice. Because the network's active memory for the most recent location faded with time, by the choice point the network's internal representation reflected more of the network's latent memory of *A*. The gaze/expectation system was thus able to make better use of relatively weak active representations of the recent hiding location.

Similarly, infants may show earlier success in gaze/expectation variants of the A-not-B task because they can constantly update their gazing and their expectations. As a result, they can counter perseverative tendencies on *B* trials by gazing at *B* and forming expectations about *B* during the presentation, delay, and choice trial periods. In contrast, infants can only reach at the choice point, by which time their memories have become more susceptible to perseverative biases.

Unexpectedly, very young networks showed slightly more perseveration in gaze/expectation than in reach (Figure 3.2). The basis for this difference was

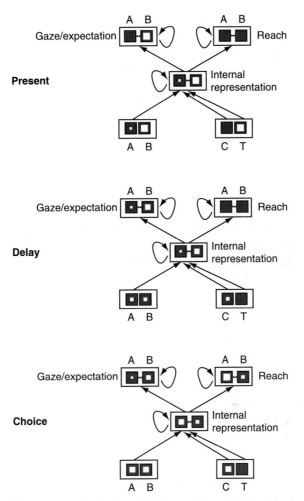

Figure 3.8. A slightly older network's representations during a *B* trial (adapted from Munakata, 1998): The network responds correctly to *B* in gaze/expectation, but reaches perseveratively to *A*. Copyright © 1998 Blackwell Publishing, Oxford. Reprinted with permission.

again the different rates of updating in the two output systems. Networks with relatively weak recurrent weights tended to default to the prepotent response, in which case the continual updating of the gaze/expectation system led it to show more of this prepotent response than the reach system. In effect, when recurrence was high enough to keep the right location (*B*) in mind, then "repeating" it, as the gaze/expectation system did, helped performance; in contrast, when recurrence was low so that the wrong, prepotent location (*A*) came to mind, then repeating hurt performance. In other words, if infants can hold *B* in mind to some degree, they can show more sensitivity to this information in their continually updating gaze/expectation systems than in their reaching. However, if infants cannot hold this new location in mind (and in fact switch to representing *A* based on their latent biases), they will show less sensitivity to the correct location in their continually updating gaze/expectation systems, which are now updating more frequently than the reach system on incorrect information. The simulation thus yielded the novel empirical prediction that infants may perseverate more in gaze/expectation than in reaching early in development, a prediction that we are now testing.

Card-sorting and speech-interpretation tasks

Like 3-year-olds, young models (both card-sorting and SIT models) correctly answer simple questions about the postswitch rules, but fail to sort cards according to these rules in the postswitch trials. These behaviours can be understood by considering the degree of conflict that must be resolved in the two tasks. Sorting involves a high degree of conflict, because both previously and currently relevant sorting dimensions are presented (e.g. an object to be sorted is both a truck and blue). Under these circumstances, a weak representation of the postswitch dimension does not lead to a correct response because this representation cannot compete against a strong representation of the preswitch dimension. In contrast, answering simple knowledge questions (e.g. "Where do the trucks go in the shape game?") involves no conflict, because only information about the postswitch dimension is presented. Under these circumstances, a weak representation of the postswitch dimension can support correct performance because there are no other competing representations.

This account led to the prediction that children would no longer show an advantage on knowledge questions relative to sorting if the knowledge questions contained the same amount of conflict as test cards. This prediction was confirmed. When knowledge questions contained information about both the pre- and the postswitch dimensions (e.g. "Where do the blue trucks go in the shape game?"), 3-year-olds' knowledge of the postswitch rules no longer outstripped their sorting behaviour (Munakata & Yerys, 2001). This pattern of findings has also been observed with 6-year-olds in the speech interpretation task (Morton & Munakata, 2002b).

Finally, the model suggests that active representations are required in complex tasks involving conflict, whereas latent representations can suffice in simple tasks that contain little or no conflict. For example, networks needed to maintain a strong active representation of the shape rule to switch from sorting by colour to sorting by shape, and to correctly answer conflict knowledge questions. However, weak latent representations sufficed for answering simple questions that contained no conflict. Indeed, networks continued to

answer simple knowledge questions correctly even if active memory was eliminated altogether by setting the weight of the recurrent connections to 0. This
may imply that with development, representations become stronger both
quantitatively and qualitatively. Early in development, performance in certain
tasks may be supported almost exclusively by latent representations. These
latent representations may become stronger with development, and may additionally benefit from an increasing contribution from active memory. Thus,
developmental changes in the strength of representations may comprise both
quantitative and qualitative changes.

DECALAGE

The preceding simulations demonstrate how graded representations might
lead infants and children to show dissociations in their behaviour, succeeding
on one task (e.g. looking to a hidden object, answering a question about a
rule) while failing another task meant to measure the same knowledge (e.g.
reaching for the hidden object, sorting cards based on the rule). This section
explores a related phenomenon: Why do infants and children master formally
similar tasks at different ages? This phenomenon of decalage (Piaget, 1941,
1967) poses a challenge to many theories of development. Most theories
attribute infants' or children's success in a task to the development of a
certain ability or collection of abilities. However, if a putative ability is operative in one task at an early age, why does the same ability not appear to be
operative in a formally similar task until later in development?[3]

In this section, we consider two instances of decalage in perseverative
tasks: one within variants of the towel-pulling task, the other across the card-
sort and speech-interpretation tasks. Infants show a decalage in variations of
the towel-pulling task from 7 to 11 months. Infants at all of these ages pull
the correct towel on *A* trials (i.e. the towel that will yield the toy), but succeed
or fail on *B* trials depending on the task variant. Nine-month-old infants
succeed on *B* trials if they are shown that the toy is attached to the towel
during presentation but they perseverate on *B* trials if the toy is simply placed
(unattached) on the towel; 11-month-old infants succeed in both versions of
the towel pulling task while 7-month-old infants perseverate in both versions.
The attached and unattached versions of the task are formally equivalent
(choose a towel on the *B* trials based on the same features used to make the
decision on the *A* trials, rather than perseverating to location), but infants
show a decalage in when they succeed on these tasks.

---

[3] Dissociations might be viewed as a broad class of discrepancies in behaviour (any cases
where one measure shows success, and another measure, meant to tap the same knowledge,
shows failure), with instances of decalage as a particular type of dissociation (i.e. behavioural
discrepancies across tasks that are formally similar).

The towel-pulling model simulated this decalage naturally, based on the strength of active representations and their ability to compete with latent representations of previous behaviours. Specifically, the network had stronger representations for a toy *attached* to a towel than for a toy *on* a towel, allowing younger networks to successfully overcome prepotent responses. The network's input units represented the stimuli by encoding the presence of the towel, the toy, whether the toy was on the towel, and whether the toy was attached to the towel (Figure 3.5). Thus, the "toy", "towel", and "on" units were activated on the correct side for both variants of the task, but the "attached" unit provided additional activity on the correct side for the attached condition only. With midrange recurrent weights (reflecting 9-month-olds) this additional input was sufficient to override the prepotent response supported by the latent representations. However, when the toy merely sat on the towel, the resulting lower level of input activity was not sufficient for the network's active representations to override the prepotent response. At younger ages (lower recurrent levels), the additional input provided by the "attached" unit could not be maintained enough to overcome the latent bias. At older ages (higher recurrent levels), the network could maintain activation for the correct side to overcome the latent bias, regardless of the additional input provided by the attached unit.

According to this account, infants with some active memory abilities may overcome perseverative tendencies, if their developing active memories are bolstered by strong input from the environment supporting correct responding. That is, infants can better maintain a representation of the correct choice if that choice is made more salient. When a toy is attached to a towel, this provides such environmental support for the correct choice. Nine-month-old infants can use this additional information to strengthen their active representation of the correct choice, to succeed with attached toys while perseverating with toys that are simply on towels. Younger infants' active memory abilities are too weak to benefit from the greater input for the correct choice, and older infants' active memory abilities are too strong to see benefits from this greater input.

The card-sorting and speech-interpretation tasks provide another interesting example of decalage. These tasks are formally equivalent (switch from one dimension to a conflicting dimension for classifying stimuli), but most 4-year-olds pass the card-sorting task while most 6-year-olds fail the speech-interpretation task. The card-sorting and speech-interpretation models simulated this decalage naturally, based on the strength of latent representations underlying prepotent responses. Specifically, the network had stronger latent representations to override for the speech-interpretation task than for the card-sorting task. At the outset of the simulations, feedforward connections were stronger for content than paralanguage in the speech-interpretation task, whereas they were equal in strength for shape and colour in the card-sorting model. This manipulation reflected the fact that children come into the speech-interpretation task with a strong pre-existing bias to respond to content, a bias that is stronger than any bias that children bring to the card-sorting task. As a result of these stronger latent representations, the model required stronger recurrent connections to overcome the prepotent response in the speech-interpretation task than in the card-sorting task (see also Cohen & Servan-Schreiber, 1992). That is, the model showed a decalage, by succeeding in these formally similar tasks at different ages.

In this way, our active–latent account provides a natural framework for understanding why infants and children show decalages in their mastery of formally similar tasks. Tasks may have the same formal demands, but differ in how much support they provide for active representations of the correct response (as in the "on" and "attached" versions of the towel-pulling task), or in how strong the latent representations are that must be overcome (as in the card-sorting and speech-interpretation tasks). Infants, children, and net-works may thus succeed or fail on formally similar tasks depending on the competitive dynamic between latent representations underlying perseverative responses and active representations supporting currently relevant information.

DISCUSSION

Our active–latent account of perseveration, dissociation, and decalage shares much with existing approaches (Cohen & Servan-Schreiber, 1992; Dehaene & Changeux, 1991; Goldman-Rakic, 1987; Thelen et al., 2001). We discuss the relation between our active–latent account and these similar theories else-where (Morton & Munakata, 2002a; Munakata, 1998; Munakata, Sahni, & Yerys, 2001; Stedron et al., 2002). Our active–latent account contrasts with several other theories. We discuss three such alternatives here: working memory and inhibition, miscategorisation, and reflective consciousness.

Working memory and inhibition

Our account of perseveration and the prefrontal cortex has focused on the primary construct of active memory, a component of working memory. In this view, prefrontal cortex does not serve specifically to inhibit prepotent responses; instead inhibition falls out of the more basic mechanism of working memory (Cohen & Servan-Schreiber, 1992; Goldman-Rakic, 1987; Kimberg & Farah, 1993; Miller & Cohen, 2001; O'Reilly et al., 1999; Roberts et al., 1994). In contrast, other accounts have focused on working memory and inhibition as separate mechanisms subserved by prefrontal cortex (Diamond, 1991, 1998; Fuster, 1989).

The critical difference between the working memory and inhibition accounts is whether a separate mechanism of inhibition needs to be attributed to prefrontal cortex. Our simulations serve as an existence proof that working memory alone may be sufficient, because perseveration is reduced solely by changes to the working memory system. Two additional types of evidence further suggest that inhibition may fall out of the more basic mechanism of working memory, rather than being a separate construct. First, impairing working memory impairs inhibitory abilities. For example, adults have more difficulty inhibiting inappropriate eye movements in the antisaccade task when simultaneously engaging in a working memory task (Roberts et al., 1994). Such data suggest that the same mechanisms may contribute to working memory and inhibition. Second, the nature of cortical connectivity suggests that inhibition is not a function localised to one region (i.e. prefrontal cortex) that inhibits other regions. Instead, inhibitory interneurons show very diffuse patterns of connectivity within circumscribed regions of cortex, and long-range intracortical connections are excitatory (Shepherd, 1992; White, 1989). This evidence supports the idea that the inhibition of prepotent responses arises from the use of working memory, dependent on prefrontal cortex, to support appropriate behaviours; the inhibition of inappropriate behaviours falls out of competitive interactions dependent on inhibitory interneurons throughout the cortex.

Miscategorisation

The miscategorisation account proposes that infants (and adults) perseverate because they fail to encode relevant information when the task changes (Aguiar & Baillargeon, 2000; Baillargeon & Wang, 2002). According to this account, they would succeed if they only attended to the relevant information, but their miscategorisation of the task as old leads them to ignore the task changes and rely on prior solutions. For example, after repeatedly searching in the correct hiding location or pulling the correct towel, infants miscategorise a new trial (with a new location for the hidden toy or for the correct towel for retrieving a toy) as old; they perseverate to the same location because they fail to notice that the toy has moved. Similarly, after repeatedly sorting cards by colour or making judgements about emotion based on content, children might perseverate with these rules because they fail to notice that the experimenter has specified a new set of rules. Thus, the miscategorisation account focuses on what infants and children encode, whereas the active memory account focuses on what infants and children can maintain in memory.

Miscategorisation may contribute to perseveration in some tasks but does not appear to explain all perseverative behaviour. For example, children do much better at switching to a new rule in the card-sorting task if negative feedback is provided when they perseverate (Yerys & Munakata, 2001). The negative feedback may change children's assumption that the task is the same as the previously mastered task (with the old sorting rule), thus enabling them to encode and act on the new rule. However, even with negative feedback, some children still sort perseveratively, suggesting that miscategorisation cannot be their only difficulty. In addition, infants who perseverate in the A-not-B task receive similar negative feedback (the location they search in is empty and they do not get to play with the toy), yet they often continue to perseverate in subsequent trials (Butterworth, 1977).

The miscategorisation and active memory accounts may lead to different predictions about infants' reaction times, which would help to address the role of these factors in perseveration (Stedron et al., 2002). As described earlier, the active memory model predicts an inverted U-shaped reaction time curve across development: infants will have the slowest reaction times just before and after they succeed at the task, whereas much younger (perseverating) infants and much older (nonperseverating) infants will be much faster. In contrast, the miscategorisation model of this task may not predict a significant change in reaction time for infants who are first succeeding and older infants, because both can encode and remember changes to the task, and so should perform similarly.

Reflective consciousness

Cognitive complexity and control (CCC) theory (Zelazo & Frye, 1997) and the related levels of consciousness framework (Zelazo, 2000), emphasise the role of reflection and higher-order representations in the development of executive control. For example, according to the levels of consciousness framework, reflective consciousness allows infants to maintain representations of hidden objects in working memory. In the absence of reflection, awareness of an object is confined to the present, and unrecoverable if the object is removed from view. As a result, infants fall prey to prepotent responses when searching for hidden toys. Similarly, according to CCC theory, 3-year-olds in the card-sorting task fail to use postswitch rules they evidently know because they are unable to reflect on these rules and subordinate them to a higher-order rule. In sum, age-related advances in reflective consciousness allow increasingly complex representations to govern action. This account has been explored through a neural network model (Marcovitch & Zelazo, 2000) using the cascade correlation learning algorithm (Fahlman & Lebiere, 1990), according to which networks recruit additional units as they are needed to solve tasks.

Accounts that emphasise the role of reflective consciousness contrast with our active–latent account in several ways. For example, the levels of consciousness framework argues that infants must be able to reflect on representations to maintain them in working memory. In contrast, our active–latent account focuses on the more basic mechanism of recurrence for understanding infants' abilities to maintain active memories. Further, CCC theory argues that the difficulty of a task is related to its formal complexity: Tasks that require the use of embedded rules are more difficult than tasks that involve the use of simple rules. However, as described earlier, children show a decalage in performance across tasks with equivalent formal complexity (card sorting and speech interpretation). It appears that this decalage may not be easily interpretable within the basic CCC framework. In contrast, our active–latent account naturally accounts for this decalage in terms of the strength of latent biases that need to be overcome.

In addition, whereas CCC theory argues that knowledge–action dissociations occur because children are unable to reflect on their knowledge, our active–latent account maintains knowledge–action dissociations are more apparent than real. Knowledge appears to outstrip action only when they are measured under different conditions. When knowledge and action are measured under more equivalent conditions, systematic dissociations disappear (Morton & Munakata, 2002b; Munakata & Yerys, 2001).

CONCLUSION

Our neural network explorations suggest the following answers to the questions that guided this chapter:

- *How* does prefrontal development reduce perseveration?

    The development of prefrontal cortex can support the strengthening of active representations—of hidden toys, towels to pull, or rules for sorting cards or judging utterances. Stronger active representations can compete better against latent representations that build over repeated experience and support perseverative behaviours.
- *Why* are dissociations observed in perseveration?

    The strengthening of active representations is not an all-or-nothing process; these representations are graded in nature. Weak representations may allow infants and children to succeed in some tasks (e.g. those that require less effort or involve little conflict) but not others (e.g. those that require more effort or involve greater conflict).
- *Why* do children show the remarkable decalage in their flexibility, overcoming perseveration at such different ages across various tasks?

    The strength of active and latent representations influences when infants and children can pass a task. One version of a task may support stronger active representations (e.g. for a toy that is attached to a towel in addition to being on it) than those of a formally similar task (e.g. for a toy that is simply on a towel); younger infants may succeed only in the task that supports stronger active representations. In addition, stronger latent representations (e.g. representing a bias to speech content after years of processing speech) require stronger active representations to overcome them than do relatively weak latent representations (e.g. those established during a few trials in a card-sorting experiment).

In exploring each of these questions, we have found neural network models to be particularly useful tools, for specifying our theories in working models, for testing the abilities of the models to simulate the developmental time course of behaviours observed in infants and children, and for generating testable empirical predictions that may help to distinguish our theories from alternative theories. For all of these reasons, neural network models provide a useful tool for understanding cognitive development more generally (Elman, Bates, Johnson, Karmiloff-Smith, Parisi, & Plunkett, 1996; Munakata & Stedron, 2001).

ACKNOWLEDGEMENTS

Preparation of this chapter was supported by research grants from NICHD (1R29 HD37163-01) and NSF (IBN-9873492).

REFERENCES

Aguiar, A., & Baillargeon, R. (2000). Perseveration and problem solving in infancy. In H. Reese (Ed.), *Advances in child development and behavior* (Vol. 27, pp. 135–180). New York: Academic Press.

Ahmed, A., & Ruffman, T. (1998). Why do infants make A not B errors in a search task, yet show memory for the location of hidden objects in a non-search task? *Developmental Psychology, 34*, 441–453.

Baillargeon, R., & Wang, S.-H. (2002). Event categorization in infancy. *Trends in Cognitive Sciences, 6*, 85–93.

Bell, M., & Fox, N. A. (1992). The relations between frontal brain electrical activity and cognitive development during infancy. *Child Development, 63*, 1142–63.

Berthier, N., DeBlois, S., Poirier, C., Novak, M., & Clifton, R. (2000). Where's the ball? Two- and three-year-olds reason about unseen events. *Developmental Psychology, 36*, 394–401.

Butterworth, G. (1977). Object disappearance and error in Piaget's stage IV task. *Journal of Experimental Child Psychology, 23*, 391–401.

Clearfield, M. W., & Thelen, E. (2000). *Reaching really matters: The development of infants' perseverative reaching*. Talk presented at the 2000 meeting of the International Conference on Infant Studies, Brighton, UK.

Cohen, J. D., Perlstein, W. M., Braver, T. S., Nystrom, L. E., Noll, D. C., Jonides, J., & Smith, E. E. (1997). Temporal dynamics of brain activation during a working memory task. *Nature, 386*, 604–608.

Cohen, J. D., & Servan-Schreiber, D. (1992). Context, cortex, and dopamine: A connectionist approach to behavior and biology in schizophrenia. *Psychological Review, 99*, 45–77.

De Fockert, J., Rees, G., Frith, C., & Lavie, N. (2001). The role of working memory in visual selective attention. *Science, 291*, 1803–1806.

Dehaene, S., & Changeux, J.-P. (1989). A simple model of prefrontal cortex function in delayed-response tasks. *Journal of Cognitive Neuroscience, 1,* 244–261.

Dehaene, S., & Changeux, J.-P. (1991). The Wisconsin Card Sorting Test: Theoretical analysis and modeling in a neuronal network. *Cerebral Cortex, 1,* 62–79.

Diamond, A. (1981). Retrieval of an object from an open box: The development of visual–tactile control of reaching in the first year of life. *Society for Research in Child Development Abstracts, 3,* 78.

Diamond, A. (1985). Development of the ability to use recall to guide action, as indicated by infants' performance on *AB. Child Development, 56,* 868–883.

Diamond, A. (1991). Neuropsychological insights into the meaning of object concept development. In S. Carey & R. Gelman (Eds.), *The epigenesis of mind* (pp. 67–110). Hillsdale, NJ: Lawrence Erlbaum Associates, Inc.

Diamond, A. (1998). Understanding the A-not-B error: Working memory vs. reinforced response, or active trace vs. latent trace. *Developmental Science, 1,* 185–189.

Diamond, A. (2002). A model system for studying the role of dopamine in prefrontal cortex during early development in humans: Early and continuously treated phenylketonuria (PKU). In M. H. Johnson, Y. Munakata, & R. O. Gilmore (Eds.), *Brain development and cognition: A reader.* (Chapter 22, pp. 441–493). Oxford: Blackwell.

Diamond, A., & Goldman-Rakic, P. S. (1986). Comparative development in human infants and infant rhesus monkeys of cognitive functions that depend on prefrontal cortex. *Neuroscience Abstracts, 12,* 742.

Diamond, A., & Goldman-Rakic, P. S. (1989). Comparison of human infants and rhesus monkeys on Piaget's *AB* task: Evidence for dependence on dorsolateral prefrontal cortex. *Experimental Brain Research, 74,* 24–40.

Elman, J. L., Bates, E. A., Johnson, M. H., Karmiloff-Smith, A., Parisi, D., & Plunkett, K. (1996). *Rethinking innateness: A connectionist perspective on development.* Cambridge, MA: MIT Press.

Fahlman, S. E., & Lebiere, C. (1990). The cascade-correlation learning architecture. In D. S. Touretzky (Ed.), *Advances in neural information processing systems 2* (pp. 524–534). San Mateo, CA: Morgan Kaufmann.

Farah, M. J., O'Reilly, R. C., & Vecera, S. P. (1993). Dissociated overt and covert recognition as an emergent property of a lesioned neural network. *Psychological Review, 100,* 571–588.

Flavell, J. H. (1963). *The developmental psychology of Jean Piaget.* New York: D. Van Nostrand Company, Inc.

Fuster, J. (1989). *The prefrontal cortex* (2nd ed.). New York: Raven Press.

Goldman-Rakic, P. S. (1987). Circuitry of primate prefrontal cortex and regulation of behavior by representational memory. In F. Plum & V. Mountcastle (Eds.), *Handbook of physiology: The nervous system V* (pp. 373–417). Bethesda, MD: American Physiological Society.

Harris, P. L. (1986). Bringing order to the A-not-B error: Commentary on Wellman, Cross, and Bartsch (1986). *Monographs of the Society for Research in Child Development, 51* (3, Serial No. 214).

Hofstadter, M. C., & Reznick, J. S. (1996). Response modality affects human infant delayed-response performance. *Child Development, 67,* 646–658.

Hood, B., & Willatts, P. (1986). Reaching in the dark to an object's remembered position: Evidence for object permanence in 5-month-old infants. *British Journal of Developmental Psychology, 4,* 57–65.

Kimberg, D. Y., & Farah, M. J. (1993). A unified account of cognitive impairments following frontal lobe damage: The role of working memory in complex, organized behavior. *Journal of Experimental Psychology: General, 122,* 411–428.

Lhermitte, F. (1986). Human autonomy and the frontal lobes: Part II. Patient behavior in complex and social situations: The "environmental dependency syndrome". *Annals of Neurology, 19*, 335–343.

Marcovitch, S., & Zelazo, P. D. (2000). A generative connectionist model of the development of rule use in children. *Proceedings of the Twenty-second Annual Conference of the Cognitive Science Society* (pp. 334–339). Mahwah, NJ: Lawrence Erlbaum Associates, Inc.

Mathis, D. A., & Mozer, M. C. (1996). Conscious and unconscious perception: A computational theory. In G. Cottrell (Ed.), *Proceedings of the 18th Annual Conference of the Cognitive Science Society* (pp. 324–328). Mahwah, NJ: Lawrence Erlbaum Associates, Inc.

McClelland, J. L., Rumelhart, D. E., & PDP Research Group (Eds.). (1986). *Parallel distributed processing. Volume 2: Psychological and biological models.* Cambridge, MA: MIT Press.

Miller, E. K., & Cohen, J. D. (2001). An integrative theory of prefrontal cortex function. *Annual Review of Neuroscience, 24*, 167–202.

Miller, E. K., & Desimone, R. (1994). Parallel neuronal mechanisms for short-term memory. *Science, 263*, 520–522.

Miller, E. K., Erickson, C. A., & Desimone, R. (1996). Neural mechanisms of visual working memory in prefrontal cortex of the macaque. *Journal of Neuroscience, 16*, 5154–5167.

Milner, B. (1963). Effects of different brain lesions on card sorting. *Archives of Neurology, 9*, 90–100.

Miyake, A., & Shah, P. (Eds.). (1999). *Models of working memory: Mechanisms of active maintenance and executive control.* New York: Cambridge University Press.

Morton, J. B., & Munakata, Y. (2002a). Active versus latent representations: A neural network model of perseveration and dissociation in early childhood. *Developmental Psychobiology.*

Morton, J. B., & Munakata, Y. (2002b). Are you listening? Exploring a knowledge action dissociation in a speech interpretation task. *Developmental Science 5*, 435–440.

Morton, J. B., & Trehub, S. E. (2001). Children's understanding of emotion in speech. *Child Development, 72*, 834–843.

Morton, J. B., Trehub, S. E., & Zelazo, P. D. (unpublished). *Representational inflexibility in 6-year-olds' understanding of emotion in speech.*

Munakata, Y. (1998). Infant perseveration and implications for object permanence theories: A PDP model of the *AB* task. *Developmental Science, 1*, 161–184.

Munakata, Y. (2001a). Graded representations in behavioral dissociations. *Trends in Cognitive Sciences, 5*, 309–315.

Munakata, Y. (2001b). Task-dependency in infant behavior: Toward an understanding of the processes underlying cognitive development. In F. Lacerda, C. V. Hofsten, & M. Heimann (Eds.), *Emerging cognitive abilities in early infancy* (pp. 29–52). Mahwah, NJ: Lawrence Erlbaum Associates, Inc.

Munakata, Y., McClelland, J. L., Johnson, M. H., & Siegler, R. (1997). Rethinking infant knowledge: Toward an adaptive process account of successes and failures in object permanence tasks. *Psychological Review, 104*, 686–713.

Munakata, Y., Sahni, S. D., & Yerys, B. E. (2001). An embodied theory in search of a body: Challenges for a dynamic systems model of infant perseveration. *Behavioral and Brain Sciences, 24*, 56–57.

Munakata, Y., & Stedron, J. M. (2001). Neural network models of cognitive development. In C. Nelson, & M. Luciana (Eds.), *Handbook of developmental cognitive neuroscience* (pp. 159–171). Cambridge, MA: MIT Press.

Munakata, Y., & Stedron, J. M. (2002). Memory for hidden objects in early infancy. In J. W. Fagen & H. Hayne (Eds.), *Advances in infancy research* (Vol. 14, Chapter 2, pp. 25–70). Norwood, NJ: Ablex Publishing Corporation.

Munakata, Y., & Yerys, B. E. (2001). All together now: When dissociations between knowledge and action disappear. *Psychological Science, 12*, 335–337.

O'Reilly, R. C., Braver, T. S., & Cohen, J. D. (1999). A biologically based computational model of working memory. In A. Miyake & P. Shah (Eds.), *Models of working memory: Mechanisms of active maintenance and executive control* (pp. 375–411). New York: Cambridge University Press.

Petrides, M. (1989). Frontal lobes and memory. In F. Boller & J. Grafman (Eds.), *Handbook of neuropsychology* (Vol. 2, pp. 75–90). New York: Elsevier.

Piaget, J. (1941). Le méchanisme du développement mental et les lois du groupement des opération. *Archives de Psychologie, Genève, 28*, 215–285.

Piaget, J. (1952). *The origins of intelligence in childhood.* New York: International Universities Press.

Piaget, J. (1954). *The construction of reality in the child.* New York: Basic Books.

Piaget, J. (1967). *Six psychological studies.* New York: Random House.

Roberts, R., Hager, L., & Heron, C. (1994). Prefrontal cognitive processes: Working memory and inhibition in the antisaccade task. *Journal of Experimental Psychology: General, 123*, 374–393.

Roberts, R. J., & Pennington, B. F. (1996). An interactive framework for examining prefrontal cognitive processes. *Developmental Neuropsychology, 12*, 105–126.

Shepherd, G. M. (1992). *Foundations of the neuron doctrine.* New York: Oxford University Press.

Spelke, E., Breinlinger, K., Macomber, J., & Jacobson, K. (1992). Origins of knowledge. *Psychological Review, 99*, 605–632.

Stedron, J., Munakata, Y., & Sahni, S. D. (2002). *In plain sight: Simulating the role of memory in perseveration with visible solutions.* Unpublished manuscript.

Steinmetz, M., Connor, C., Constantinidis, C., & McLaughlin, J. (1994). Covert attention suppresses neuronal responses in area 7a of the posterior parietal cortex. *Journal of Neurophysiology, 72*, 1020–1023.

Stuss, D., & Benson, D. (1984). Neuropsychological studies of the frontal lobes. *Psychological Bulletin, 95*, 3–28.

Thelen, E., Schoner, G., Scheier, C., & Smith, L. B. (2001). The dynamics of embodiment: A field theory of infant perseverative reaching. *Behavioral and Brain Sciences, 24*, 1–86.

Wellman, H. M., Cross, D., & Bartsch, K. (1986). Infant search and object permanence: A meta-analysis of the A-Not-B error. *Monographs of the Society for Research in Child Development, 51* (3, Serial No. 214).

White, H. (1989). Learning in artificial neural networks: A statistical perspective. *Neural Computation, 1*, 425–464.

Yerys, B. E., & Munakata, Y. (2001). *Feedback improves children's flexibility: Rethinking perseveration in a card sorting task.* Manuscript in preparation.

Zelazo, P. D. (2000). Self-reflection and the development of consciously controlled processing. In P. Mitchell & K. Riggs (Eds.), *Children's reasoning and the mind* (pp. 169–189). Hove: Psychology Press.

Zelazo, P. D., & Frye, D. (1997). Cognitive complexity and control: A theory of the development of deliberate reasoning and intentional action. In M. Stamenov (Ed.), *Language structure, discourse, and the access to consciousness* (pp. 113–153). Amsterdam: John Benjamins.

Zelazo, P. D., Frye, D., & Rapus, T. (1996). An age-related dissociation between knowing rules and using them. *Cognitive Development, 11*, 37–63.

CHAPTER FOUR

Language acquisition in a self-organising neural network model

Ping Li
Department of Psychology, University of Richmond, Virginia, USA

INTRODUCTION

One crucial aspect of human language learning is the learner's ability to generalise existing patterns to novel instances. This ability often leads to various erroneous generalisations in learning. "Overgeneralisation" is one such type of error, characterised by the learner's use of a linguistic pattern that is broader in scope than the corresponding adult uses (Bowerman, 1982; Brown, 1973; Clark, 1987; Pinker, 1989). Perhaps the best-known example of overgeneralisation is the acquisition of the English past tense: children generalise *-ed* to irregular verbs, producing errors like *falled*, *breaked*, and *comed* (Brown, 1973; Kuczaj, 1977). But just what leads to children's overgeneralisations has been under intensive debate. Using the acquisition of the English past tense as an example, researchers have debated whether language acquisition should be characterised as a symbolic, rule-based learning process or as a connectionist, statistical learning process. Symbolic theorists assume that overgeneralisation errors result from the child's internalisation and application of linguistic rules (Ling & Marinov, 1993; Marcus, Pinker, Ullman, Hollander, Rosen & Xu, 1992; Pinker, 1991, 1999; Pinker & Prince, 1988), whereas connectionists argue that overgeneralisations reflect the child's ability to extract statistical regularities from the input (Mac-Whinney & Leinbach, 1991; Plunkett & Marchman, 1991, 1993; Rumelhart & McClelland, 1986; Seidenberg, 1997).

In contrast to the well-known overgeneralisation patterns, learners sometimes also exhibit "undergeneralisation"—generalisations that are narrower in scope than the corresponding adult usage. A typical example of undergeneralisation is one in which young children initially restrict tense-aspect morphology to specific semantic categories of verbs. For example, early on, English-speaking children use the progressive marker *-ing* only with atelic verbs that indicate durative processes (e.g. *walk*, *swim*, and *play*), whereas they use the past-perfective marker *-ed* only with telic verbs that indicate actions with clear endpoints or end result (e.g. *spill*, *break*, and *fall*). Capitalising on these patterns in early child language, some investigators hypothesise that children have innate semantic categories that bias them towards certain grammatical distinctions as expressed by contrasting morphological markers (Bickerton, 1981, 1984). Other researchers disagree with such hypotheses, arguing that the undergeneralisation patterns reflect learners' statistical analyses of the distributional properties of verbs and morphology in the input language (see Li & Shirai, 2000, for a summary).

In this chapter, I present a self-organising neural network that attempts to model both overgeneralisations and undergeneralisations in language acquisition, without making strong assumptions about the innateness of semantic categories or the symbolic nature of categorical representation. In particular, I will examine: (1) the acquisition of the English reversive prefixes that has been discussed by Whorf (1956) and Bowerman (1982) in the context of morphological overgeneralisation; and (2) the acquisition of grammatical suffixes that has been discussed by Brown (1973), Bloom, Lifter, and Hafitz (1980), and, Li and Shirai (2000), in the context of morphological undergeneralisation. I take the following observations as a starting point for the current study:

- Most previous connectionist models of language acquisition have been concerned with the phonological properties that govern the use of verb forms, for example, in the acquisition of the English past tense (see Klahr & MacWhinney, 2000, for an overview). Few studies have paid attention to the meaning structure of words, perhaps because of the level of difficulty in representing meaning faithfully in connectionist networks (but see Burgess & Lund, 1997, and Li, Burgess, & Lund, 2000). Reversive prefixes and aspect suffixes in English provide ideal cases where the use of grammatical morphology is governed primarily by semantic rather than phonological properties of lexical items. Our model addresses the relationship between the acquisition of lexical semantics and the learner's ability to generalise morphological devices.

- Most previous models have used artificially generated input representations that are in many cases isolated from realistic language uses. In addition, these input patterns are in most cases "handcrafted" *ad hoc* by the modeller. Representations of linguistic information constructed in this way are often subject to the criticism that the network works precisely because of the use of certain features in the representation (Lachter & Bever, 1988). To overcome potential problems associated with such approaches to linguistic representations, we attempt to use phonological and semantic representations that more closely approximate the reality of language use. Moreover, we rely on corpus-based linguistic data to establish the sequence as well as the structure of the input data.

- Most previous models have used supervised learning, in particular, the back-propagation learning algorithm as their basis of network training. Although significant progress has been made with these types of networks, there are serious problems concerning the biological and psychological plausibility of such networks. In particular, "back-propagation networks" are known to suffer from catastrophic forgetting (inability to remember old information with new learning), scalability (inability to handle realistic, large-scale problems), and above all, an error-driven learning process that adjusts weights according to the error signals from the discrepancy between desired and actual outputs. In the context of language acquisition, these problems become more transparent. In particular, it would be a very strong argument that the feedback process used in back-propagation resembles realistic processes of child language learning. Such considerations lead us to self-organising neural networks, in particular, the self-organising feature maps, in which learning proceeds in an "unsupervised" fashion, without explicit teaching signals as in back-propagation nets.

This chapter is organised as follows. First, I briefly discuss the two linguistic problems—the use of reversive prefixes in connection with covert semantic categories and the use of grammatical suffixes in connection with aspectual semantic categories. I then describe the acquisition of the reversive prefixes and aspectual suffixes and the corresponding overgeneralisation and undergeneralisation patterns. Next, I present a self-organising neural network model that captures the processes underlying overgeneralisation and undergeneralisation. Finally, I conclude with general remarks on the significance of self-organising neural networks in unravelling the computational and psycholinguistic mechanisms of language acquisition.

THE INTERACTION BETWEEN VERB SEMANTICS AND MORPHOLOGY

Prefixes, suffixes, and verbs

Language is an interactive system. In contrast to early conceptions about systems of language (Chomsky, 1957), linguists and cognitive scientists now accept that linguistic components interact across levels: between syntax and semantics, between syntax and phonology, and between semantics and morphology, and so on. In this chapter, I focus on the interaction between semantics and morphology, one that can be best illustrated with examples from the use of the English reversive prefixes such as *un-* and *dis-* and the use of aspectual suffixes like *-ed* and *-ing*. The centrepiece of grammatical morphology in a sentence is the verb, and thus the study of verbs along with prefixes and suffixes is the main focus of our present research.

In one of the classic papers of early cognitive linguistics, Whorf (1956) presented the following puzzle on prefixation. In English, the reversive prefix *un-* can be used productively with many verbs to indicate the reversal of an action, for example, as in *undress*, *unfasten*, *unlock*, or *untie*. Similar reversal meanings can also be expressed by other prefixes such as *dis-* or *de-*. However, English prevents the use of *un-*, *dis-*, or *de-* in many seemingly parallel forms, such as the ill-formed **undry*, **unkick*, or **unmove*. Why? Whorf proposed that there is an underlying semantic category that governs the use of *un-*: a "cryptotype" or covert semantic category. According to Whorf, cryptotypes only make their presence known by the restrictions that they place on the possible combinations of overt forms. When the overt prefix *un-* is combined with the overt verb *tie*, there is a covert cryptotype that licenses the combination *untie*. This same cryptotype also prohibits combinations such as **unkick*. To Whorf, the deep puzzle is that while the use of the prefix *un-* is a productive morphological device, the cryptotype that governs its productivity is elusive: "we have no single word in the language which can give us a proper clue to its meaning or into which we can compress this meaning; hence the meaning is subtle, intangible, as is typical of cryptotypic meanings."

Whorf did propose the "covering, enclosing, and surface-attaching meaning" as a core meaning for the cryptotype of *un-*. However, it is not clear whether we should view this cryptotype as a single unit, three separate meanings, or a cluster of related meanings. Nor is it clear whether these notions of attachment and covering fully exhaust the subcomponents of the cryptotype; for example, Marchand (1969) and Clark, Carpenter, & Deutsch (1995) argue that verbs that license *un-* all involve a change of state, usually expressing a transitive action that leads to some end state or result, as encoded by telic verbs. When the meaning of a verb does not involve a change of state or telicity, the verb cannot take *un-*, thus the ill-formedness of verbs like **unswim*, **unplay*, and **unsnore*.

An alternative prefix, *dis-*, shows many similar properties with *un-*, although Whorf did not discuss this prefix in the context of cryptotype. For example, the base verbs in *disassemble, disconnect, disengage, disentangle*, and *dismantle* all fit Whorf's cryptotypic meanings of binding, covering, and attaching. As a result, many *dis-* and *un-* verbs are competitors, for example, *disconnect* versus *unlink*, or *disengage* versus *uncouple*. These two suffixes, however, do not overlap completely: *dis-* is used for many abstract mental verbs to which *un-* does not apply (e.g. *disassociate, disengage*, and *disentangle*) and, overall, *un-* is much more productive than is *dis-* in modern English.

An equally interesting domain as the above where semantics meets morphology is the use of inflectional suffixes that mark aspectual contrasts, for example, between perfective and imperfective. According to Comrie (1976), imperfective aspect presents a situation with an internal point of view, often as ongoing (progressive) or enduring (continuous), whereas perfective aspect presents a situation with an external perspective, often as completed. In English, the imperfective–perfective contrast is realised in the difference between the progressive *-ing* and the past-perfective *-ed*.[1] Thus, *-ing* marks the progressive aspect—an ongoing event (e.g. "John is walk*ing*"), *-ed* marks the perfective aspect—a completed event (e.g. "John has walk*ed* for an hour"), and *-s* marks the habitual aspect—a routinely performed action or an enduring state (e.g. "John walk*s* for an hour everyday"). In contrast to the grammatical aspect expressed by suffixes, linguists also recognise the importance of "lexical aspect" or "inherent aspect": the temporal properties of a verb's meaning, for example, whether the verb encodes an inherent endpoint or end result of a situation. There are various linguistic descriptions of lexical aspect, but we adopt here a three-way classification (Mourelatos, 1981; Parsons, 1990): (1) *processes*—verbs that encode situations with no inherent endpoint (e.g. *walk*); (2) *events*—verbs that encode situations with inherent endpoint or end result (e.g. *break*); and (3) *states*—verbs that encode situations as homogeneous involving no dynamic or successive phases (e.g. *know*).

The complex relationship between grammatical aspect and lexical aspect is another clear case where morphology interacts with semantics. Like the derivational prefixes *un-* and *dis-*, uses of the inflectional suffixes *-ed, -ing* and *-s* are also in many cases constrained. For example, in English, *-ing* rarely occurs with state verbs; thus, while "John knows the story" is good, "John is knowing the story" sounds odd (Smith, 1983). There are also combinatorial constraints between *-ing* and event verbs; for example, "John is noticing a friend" is distinctly odd. These kinds of constraints are sometimes referred to as

---

[1] Note that *-ed* marks both past tense and perfective aspect in English, just as *-s* marks both present tense and habitual aspect. In other languages, separate affixes are often used for expressing tense and aspect.

"naturalness of combination" (Comrie, 1976) between verbs and morphology, which may ultimately reflect the intricate relationships between language use and event characteristics. For example, many events with an end result last for such a brief period of time that any comment on them is likely to occur only after the event has ended, for example, situations denoted by verbs like *drop*, *fall*, and *crash* (cf. Brown, 1973). Thus, it is rare for speakers to describe the "ongoing-ness" of such events with *-ing* but more natural to describe them using past-perfective forms. In some languages the less natural combinations may be prohibited altogether from the grammar (see Li & Shirai, 2000).

The prediction that we can derive from these kinds of constraints is that natural speech will exhibit strong associations between given types of verbs and given types of morphology (for example, the perfective-to-event associations). A further, perhaps more important, prediction is that children are able to explore the statistical relationships that exist between verb semantics and morphology in language acquisition. I will return to these predictions when considering empirical and modelling studies of acquisition.

The acquisition of lexicon and morphology

The above discussion demonstrates the close interactions between verb semantics and grammatical morphology in adult language. How do children acquire such interactions?

Bowerman (1982) was among the first to point out the important role of lexical semantics in children's morphological acquisition. In particular, she argued that the onset of lexical or morphological errors signals a change or reorganisation in the child's mental lexicon: Words that are not initially recognised as related are later on grouped together. Thus, we should pay attention not only to the acquisition of morphology *per se*, but also to the developing semantic structure in the child's lexicon. Bowerman illustrated the point with the acquisition of *un-*. Her data suggest that children follow a U-shaped learning curve in learning *un-*, a pattern also found in other areas of morphological acquisition (e.g. the acquisition of the English past tense). At the initial stage, children produce *un-* verbs in appropriate contexts, treating *un-* and its base verb as an unanalysed whole. This initial stage of rote control is analogous to the child's saying *went* without realising that it is the past tense of *go*. At the second stage (from about age 3), children produce overgeneralisation errors like **unarrange*, **unbreak*, **unblow*, **unbury*, **unget*, **unhang*, **unhate*, **unopen*, **unpress*, **unspill*, **unsqueeze*, and **untake* (Bowerman, 1982, 1983; see also Clark et al., 1995 for similar errors in naturalistic and experimental settings). At the final stage of this U-shaped learning, children recover from these errors and overgeneralisations cease.

Bowerman (1982, 1983) proposed that Whorf's notion of cryptotype might play an important role in children's acquisition of *un-*. Cryptotype might influence acquisition at either the second stage or the final stage of the U-shape: (1) "generalisation via cryptotype"—recognition of the cryptotype leads to overly general uses (overgeneralisations); e.g. *tighten* fits the crypto-type just as *tie* does, so the child says **untighten*; or (2) "recovery via cryp-totype"—children use the cryptotype to recover from overgeneralisation errors; e.g. *hate* does not fit the cryptotype meaning, and given that only verbs in the cryptotype can take *un-* the child stops saying **unhate*. Both of these possibilities have some empirical evidence in Bowerman's data. How-ever, there is an important question unanswered: How could the child extract the cryptotype and use it as a basis for morphological generalisation or recovery, if the cryptotype is intangible even to linguists like Whorf? (See Whorf's comment on the elusiveness of cryptotype, p. 118.)

In an earlier connectionist model (Li, 1993; Li & MacWhinney, 1996), we hypothesised that cryptotypes seemed intangible because of the limita-tions of traditional symbolic methods for analysing complex semantic structures. The meanings of a cryptotype constitute a complex semantic network, in which words in a cryptotype can vary in: (1) how many seman-tic features are relevant to each word; (2) how strongly each feature is activated in the representation of the word; and (3) how features overlap with each other across members in the cryptotype. For example, the verb *screw* in *unscrew* may be viewed as having both the "circular movement" and the "locking" meaning; circular movement is an essential part of the meaning for *screw*, but less so for *wrap*. These complex structural relation-ships in lexical semantics make a rule-based analysis less effective, if not impossible, but lend themselves naturally to distributed representations and nonlinear processes in neural networks. In this chapter, I further argue that a self-organising neural network can derive cryptotype representations by identifying the complex nonlinear structure from high-dimensional space of language use.

Turning to the acquisition of suffixes, the major empirical findings are that young children show strong patterns of association between verb semantics and morphology in the acquisition of aspect, that is, undergeneralisations in which children restrict morphology to specific categories of verbs. In particu-lar, English-speaking children tend to use the progressive marker *-ing* with process verbs only, whereas they associate the past-perfective marker *-ed* with event verbs. These associations are very strong initially, but weaken over time. Cross-linguistic data suggest similar patterns in children's acquisition of other languages (Li & Shirai, 2000). These patterns prompted some researchers to argue for the existence of innate or prelinguistic categories. In particular, Bickerton (1984) argued strongly that the patterns reflect the func-tioning of a language bioprogram, in which certain semantic distinctions, for example, distinctions between state and process and between punctual and nonpunctual categories, are hardwired, and that the learner simply needs to find out how they are instantiated in the target language. For example, Brown (1973) observed that English-speaking children do not use the progressive -*ing* with state verbs. To Bickerton, this is strong evidence for the state–process distinction: Children's early use of morphology is to mark bioprogrammed semantic distinctions, not grammatical distinctions.[2]

Thus, the key developmental issue here is whether the empirical patterns reflect innate biases originating from predetermined semantic categories. In this chapter, I present an alternative proposal that rejects the strong version of the nativist argument on innate semantic categories. Earlier discussions (p. 120) have predicted that, in parental input, there are strong associations between verb semantics (lexical aspect) and morphological categories (grammatical suffixes). A further prediction is that children are able to explore the statistical relationships between verbs and morphology in language acquisition. Li and Bowerman (1998) propose that the initial verb–suffix associations could arise as a result of the learner's analyses of the semantics–morphology co-occurrence probabilities in the linguistic input. In the following, I present a connectionist model that implements this proposal. The goal is to demonstrate that a neural network model that draws on realistic linguistic corpus can capture complex semantic structures that are often difficult for symbolic analyses. Through modelling, we can identify more clearly how semantic representations emerge as a function of learning rather than innate hardwiring.

SELF-ORGANISING NEURAL NETWORK AND LANGUAGE ACQUISITION

Modelling semantics in connectionist networks

As mentioned earlier, most previous connectionist models have explored only the formal characteristics, particularly the phonological properties of words. It is relatively straightforward to represent such formal properties, for example, by using acoustic or articulatory features of phonemes (Li & MacWhinney, 2002; MacWhinney & Leinbach, 1991; Miikkulainen, 1997).

---

[2] A somewhat different, but related view is advocated by Slobin (1985). He suggested the examination of the morphology–semantics mapping by identifying what are "basic" to the learner—constructs that are "prelinguistic" or "privileged" in the initial stages of language acquisition. Slobin's basic child grammar contains a prestructured "semantic space" with universal semantic notions or categories, such as *process* and *result* for the acquisition of tense and aspect. However, because the issue of innateness is less fundamental to the basic child grammar than to the language bioprogram hypothesis, we do not consider it as a nativist theory in this debate. See Li and Shirai (2000) for an analysis of Slobin's perspectives in the context of the nativist–functionalist debate in language acquisition.

It is much more difficult to represent the meaning of words, and thus the modelling of lexical semantics represents a challenge to connectionist language research.

In previous connectionist models involving semantics, researchers have generally constructed semantic representations for a specific set of words on the basis of their own linguistic analyses (Li, 1993; Li & MacWhinney, 1996; MacWhinney, 1998; Ritter & Kohonen, 1989). Alternatively, they use a localist coding to approximate semantics (Cottrell & Plunkett, 1994; Joanisse & Seidenberg, 1999). For example, in our model of the acquisition of prefix, we constructed 20 semantic features for the *un-* verbs, including the general characteristics of actions, relationships between objects, and joint properties of objects that were designed to capture the semantic range of the verbs that can be prefixed with or without *un-* (Li, 1993; Li & MacWhinney, 1996). We presented these features to native speakers of English, and asked them to rate the extent to which a given feature applies to a given verb. A feature-by-verb matrix was derived for each rater, and the mean ratings for each verb became our semantic vectors.

In our modelling, these feature vectors were submitted as input to a feed-forward network with back-propagation learning, and the network's task was to predict which verb could take *un-*, its competitor *dis-*, or no prefix. Two major results were found in our simulations. First, our network formed internal representations of semantic categories that captured Whorf's semantic cryptotypes, on the basis of learning the 20 semantic features. The cryptotype emerged as a function of the network's identification of the relationship that holds between *un-* and the multiple weighted features shared by the *un-* verbs. Our results suggest that in learning of the use of *un-*, the child, like our network, may be computing the combinatorial constraints on the co-occurrences between the prefix, the verb forms, and the semantic features of verbs. Such a process allowed the system to extract a meaningful representation of the *un-* verbs. Second, our network produced overgeneralisation errors similar to those reported in empirical research, for example, *unpress*, *unfill*, and *unsqueeze*. More interestingly, these overgeneralisations were all based on the cryptotype representations that the network developed, indicating clearly that semantic representations served to trigger morphological generalisation. They provided support for Bowerman's (1982) "generalisation-via-cryptotype" hypothesis, but showed no evidence for the "recovery-via-cryptotype" hypothesis.

Although results from these initial simulations are encouraging, the way that semantic features were derived in our model, as in many connectionist models, is subject to the criticism that the network worked precisely because of the use of the "right" features (cf. Lachter & Bever, 1988). It can be argued, for example, that in coding the features the modeller preprocesses the meaning, and what the network receives is very different from what the learner is exposed to in a realistic learning situation. Consideration of this problem led us to look for semantic representations whose actual features are blind to the modeller. High-dimensional space models figure prominently in our search, especially the hyperspace analogue to language (HAL) model of Burgess and Lund (1997, 1999). Li (1999) used HAL semantic representations based on lexical co-occurrence analyses. In HAL, the meaning and function of a given word are determined by lexical co-occurrence constraints in large-scale speech corpora. HAL focuses on global rather than local lexical co-occurrences: A word is anchored with reference not only to other words immediately preceding or following it, but also to words that are further away from it in a variable co-occurrence window, with each slot in the window (occurrence of a word) acting as a constraint to define the meaning of the target word. Global lexical co-occurrence is a measure of a word's total contextual history—what words occur before and after a given word, and how frequently. In this perspective, the semantics of a word can be represented as a vector that encodes the global lexical constraints in a high-dimensional space of language use. Figure 4.1 presents a schematic representation of such vectors: each of the 25-dimension vectors represents the semantics of a word, with each unit representing the degree of a given lexical co-occurrence constraint.

To verify if HAL can be used successfully to capture the acquisition of word meaning, Li, Burgess, and Lund (2000) analysed 3.8 million word tokens from parental speech in the CHILDES English database (MacWhinney, 2000). We found that the HAL method can derive accurate lexical semantic representations, given a reasonable size of speech such as our CHILDES parental speech (rather than a huge amount of speech such as the Usenet data for the original HAL model). The implication of our study is that young children can acquire word meanings if they exploit the considerable amount of contextual information in the linguistic input by computing multiple lexical co-occurrence constraints. The limitation of the study is that no learning was involved in the representation of word meanings, as it was based purely on extraction of statistical information. I will return to this

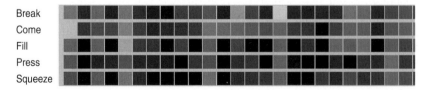

Figure 4.1. A grey-scale representation of HAL vectors for five words. Each dimension of the 25-unit vector represents the degree of a given lexical co-occurrence constraint. A high degree of constraint is represented as white or grey, and a low degree of constraint as dark or black (on a continuous scale from 0 = all black, to 1 = all white).

point in the Conclusions section, where I suggest a developmental learning model of the HAL type.

Self-organising feature maps and language representation

Like most previous connectionist models of language acquisition, the model of Li (1993) and Li and MacWhinney (1996) was based on the standard back-propagation learning algorithm. Although significant progress has been made with models based on back-propagation, there are some known limitations associated with these models (see the Introduction section). Some of these problems become most transparent when considered in the context of language acquisition. For example, a strong assumption has been made that the language learner can be considered as a "hypothesis generator": each time the learner hears some linguistic information, he or she will compare it with existing knowledge and make a guess as to what should be correct in the target language (Plunkett & Juola, 1999). However, there is so far no psychological evidence that the language learner is a hypothesis generator of this nature (i.e. as a back-propagation machine). Children do not receive constant feedback about what is incorrect in their speech, or the kind of error corrections on a word-by-word basis as provided to the network (consider the "no negative evidence problem" in language acquisition; see Baker, 1979; Bowerman, 1988). The gradient descent mechanism used in back-propagation also leads to other problems, for example, local minima, the problem that the network is entrapped into a local landscape and unable to move to the global error minimum (Hertz, Krogh, & Palmer, 1991).

Consideration of these problems led us to look for models that bear more biological and psychological plausibility. We turned to a class of self-organising neural networks, the self-organising feature maps (SOFMs). SOFMs belong to the class of "unsupervised" neural networks, because learning in these networks does not require the presence of a supervisor or an explicit teacher; learning is achieved by the system's self-organisation in response to the input. During learning, the self-organising process extracts an efficient and compressed internal representation from the high-dimensional input space and projects this new representation onto a two-dimensional space (Kohonen, 1982, 1989, 1995). Several important properties of SOFMs and related features make them particularly well suited to the study of language acquisition. We briefly discuss three of them here and their implications for language acquisition.

(1) *Self-organisation.* Self-organisation in these networks typically occurs in a two-dimensional topological map, where each unit (or "neuron") is a location on the map that can uniquely represent one or several input

patterns. At the beginning of learning, an input pattern randomly activates one of the many units on the map, according to how similar by chance the input pattern is to the weight vectors of the units. Once a unit becomes active in response to a given input, the weight vectors of that unit and its neighbouring units are adjusted so that they become more similar to the input and will therefore respond to the same or similar inputs more strongly the next time. In this way, every time an input is presented, an area of units will become activated on the map (the so-called activity "bubbles"), and the maximally active units are taken to represent the input. Initially activation occurs in large areas of the map, but gradually learning becomes focused so that only the maximally responding unit or units are active. This process continues until all the inputs have found some maximally responding units.

(2) *Representation.* As a result of this self-organising process, the statistical structures implicit in the high-dimensional input space are represented as topological structures on the two-dimensional space. In this new representation, similar inputs will end up activating the same units in nearby regions, yielding meaningful activity bubbles that can be visualised on the map. The self-organising process and its representation have clear implications for language acquisition: The formation of activity bubbles may capture critical processes for the emergence of semantic categories in children's acquisition of the lexicon. In particular, the network organises information first in large areas of the map and gradually zeros in onto smaller areas; this zeroing-in is a process from diffuse to focused patterns, as a function of the network's continuous adaptation to the input structure. This process allows us to model the emergence of semantic categories as a gradual process of lexical development. It naturally explains many generalisation errors reported in the child language literature: for example, substitutions errors (e.g. *put* for *give*, *fall* for *drop*; Bowerman, 1978) often reflect the child's initial recognition of diffuse similarities but not fine-grained distinctions between the words. It also explains language disorders that result from the breakdown of focused activation or the inability to form focused representations (Miikkulainen, 1997; Spitzer, 1999).

(3) *Hebbian learning.* Hebbian learning is not an intrinsic feature of a SOFM, but several SOFMs can be connected via Hebbian learning, such as in the multiple feature-map model of Miikkulainen (1993, 1997). Hebbian learning is a well-established biologically plausible learning principle, according to which the associative strength between two neurons is increased if the neurons are both active at the same time (Hebb, 1949). The amount of increase may be proportional to the level of activation of the two neurons. In a multiple SOFM model, all units on one map are initially connected to all units on the other map. As self-organisation takes place, the associations

become more focused, such that in the end only the maximally active units on the corresponding maps are associated. Hebbian learning combined with SOFMs has strong implications for language acquisition: It can account for the process of how the learner establishes relationships between word forms, lexical semantics, and grammatical morphology, on the basis of how often they co-occur and how strongly they are co-activated in the representation.

Thus, models based on the above properties: (1) allow us to track the development of the lexicon clearly as an emergent property in the network's self-organisation (from diffuse to focused patterns or from incomplete to complete associative links); (2) allow us to model one-to-many or many-to-many associations between forms and meanings in the development of the lexicon and morphology; and (3) provide us with a set of biologically plausible and computationally relevant principles to study language acquisition without relying on negative evidence to learn. They are biologically plausible because the human cerebral cortex can be considered as essentially a self-organising map (or multiple maps) that compresses information on a two-dimensional space (Kohonen, 1989; Spitzer, 1999), and computationally relevant because language acquisition in the natural setting (especially organisation and reorganisation of the lexicon) is largely a self-organising process that proceeds without explicit teaching (MacWhinney, 1998, 2001).

A number of studies have employed SOFMs for language research. An earlier attempt was made by Ritter and Kohonen (1989), who constructed a network that takes semantic features of animals (e.g. *small-size*, *has hair*, *can fly*) and organises them on a feature map. In the input, each animal was represented as a combination of these features in a feature vector and, after 2000 epochs of self-organisation, the network developed meaningful representations of types of animals. Wild predators (e.g. *tiger*, *lion*, *wolf*) were grouped together on one area of the map, whereas birds (e.g. *hawk*, *owl*, *goose*) were grouped nearby on another area. Within each group, similar animals were closer to each other than were dissimilar ones. Although Ritter and Kohonen's model used only a dozen or so animal words with a highly idealised feature representation, their results showed that interesting semantic structures could develop from the network's self-organisation of relevant features, and that the new representations in a SOFM can correspond closely to the hierarchical structure of human conceptual relationships.

Miikkulainen's (1993) research represents another important step in using SOFMs for language research. He proposed an integrated model of memory and natural language processing, in which multiple SOFMs dedicated to different levels of information are connected. A subcomponent of this model is DISLEX (Miikkulainen, 1997), a SOFM model of the lexicon. In DISLEX, different maps correspond to different linguistic information (orthography, phonology, or semantics) and are connected through associative links via Hebbian learning. During learning, an input pattern activates a unit or a group of units on one of the maps, and the resulting bubble of activity propagates through the associative links and causes an activity bubble to form in the other map. The activation of co-occurring form–meaning representations leads to adaptive formations of the associative connections between the maps. DISLEX successfully models the mental lexicon in normal and disordered language processing. Miikkulainen showed that in a lesioned SOFM, behaviours of dyslexia (e.g. producing *dog* in reading *sheep*) can result from partial damage to the semantic representation. The network also displayed behaviour of surface dyslexia (e.g. producing *ball* in reading *doll*), which results from partial damage to the form representations.

MacWhinney (2001) further considered the use of SOFMs in the domain of lexical acquisition. A normal English-speaking child, starting from the age of 2, learns an average of nine words per day, ending up with an active vocabulary of about 14,000 words by age 6 (Carey, 1978). Apparently, this size of lexicon exceeds the capacity of most current connectionist models (the "scalability" problem in connectionism). To answer this challenge, MacWhinney trained two feature maps to associate with each other, one representing lexical semantics, and the other phonological features. In a simplified scheme, the phonology or semantics of an input was represented by four units with random values. The two maps were associated through Hebbian learning, as in the DISLEX model. It was found that a network with 10,000 nodes was able to learn the form–meaning associations of up to 6000 words, with an average error of less than 1 per cent. MacWhinney suggested that it would be possible to increase the size of the feature map to learn more words and that given the enormous number of cells in the human brain, the size of the feature map is not an important limiting constraint on lexical acquisition by children.

The above studies all attest to the utility and importance of self-organising neural networks in language research. However, they suffer from the same problems we discussed earlier, either because the semantic representations were too simplified, or because the target lexicon of the model was too small and unrealistic, or both. In considering these problems, Li (1999, 2000) explored SOFMs as a feasible model of language acquisition in the context of lexicon and morphology. In what follows, I will present a sketch of the model and its implications for language acquisition; for details, see Li (1999, 2000), and Li and Shirai (2000, Chapter 7).

A SOFM MODEL OF LEXICAL AND MORPHOLOGICAL ACQUISITION

On the basis of the discussions above, I present two modelling studies: (1) the acquisition of semantic cryptotypes of verbs in the context of derivational prefixes; and (2) the acquisition of lexical aspect of verbs in the context of inflectional suffixes. In each case, the model simulates the development of the lexicon and morphology in young children. The goal is to show: (1) how a SOFM model can capture processes of semantic organisation that lead to distinct semantic categories, categories that have been claimed to be either intangible (e.g. cryptotypes) or innate (e.g. state and result); and (2) how such a model can derive semantic–morphological associations as observed in child language, on the basis of analysing distributional information in realistic linguistic data. Evidence from such a model should provide insights into psycholinguistic mechanisms underlying lexical and morphological acquisition.

The model consisted of two SOFMs, each of the size of 25 × 25 units, one for the organisation of lexical form, including the phonology of verb stems and affixes (the lexical map), and the other for the organisation of semantic information (the semantic map). Because the simulation of suffixes involved twice as many verbs as the simulation of prefixes, the size of the maps for the suffix model was correspondingly expanded (50 × 50 units). Figure 4.2 illustrates the model diagrammatically.

Method

Input and representation.   As we model the acquisition of prefixes and suffixes, the input data to our network consist mainly of lexical representations of verbs with which the affixes co-occur. In the case of prefixes, we selected 228 verbs according to the *Webster's New Collegiate Dictionary* and the Francis and Kucera (1982) corpus. The 228 verbs for prefixes include 49 *un-* verbs, 19 *dis-* verbs, and 160 verb stems with no prefixes. In the case of suffixes, we selected 562 verbs from the CHILDES parental corpus (see Li & Shirai, 2000) with the following criterion: A verb was included in our training

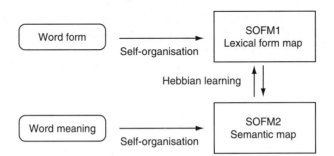

Figure 4.2.   A SOFM model of lexical and morphological acquisition. The model consisted of two SOFMs: one self-organises on lexical form (the lexical map), and the other self-organises on word meaning (the semantic map). The associations between the two maps are trained via Hebbian learning.

data if it occurred in the parental corpus for five or more times at a given age period (see the Stages of training section below).

To represent the phonology of the verbs, we used a syllable-based template coding developed by MacWhinney and Leinbach (1991). This coding scheme has the advantage over traditional phonemic representations in that it can more accurately capture phonological similarities of multisyllabic words. A word's representation is made up by combinations of syllables in a metrical grid, and the slots in each grid are made up by bundles of features that correspond to phonemes, Cs (consonants) and Vs (vowel). For example, the 18-slot template $CCCVV\ CCCVV\ CCCVV\ CCC$ represents a full trisyllabic structure in which each $CCCVV$ is a syllable (the last CCC represents the consonant endings). Each C is represented by 10 feature units, and each V by 8 feature units, making a total of 168 units for each phonological vector (see Li & MacWhinney, 2002, for a more recent version of this representation).

The semantic representations of verbs to our network were based on lexical co-occurrence analyses in the HAL model (Burgess & Lund, 1997). As discussed earlier, HAL measures the semantics of a word by its total contextual history, encoded as a vector that represents multiple lexical co-occurrence constraints from large-scale corpora. Of course, not all lexical constraints contribute equally to the representation, so we extracted 100 components that have the greatest contextual diversity as the appropriate vector dimensions (see Lund & Burgess, 1996, for details). Thus, each semantic representation is formed by a 100-unit vector.

Task and procedure.   Upon training of the network, a phonological representation of a verb was input to the network and, simultaneously, the semantic representation of the same verb was also presented to the network. By way of self-organisation, the network formed an activity on the phonological map in response to the phonological input, and an activity on the semantic map in response to the semantic input. Depending on whether the verb is compatible with a given affix in the language (prefix) or in the input speech (suffix), the phonological representation of the affix was also coactivated with the phonological and the semantic representations of the verb stem. As the network received input and continued to self-organise, it simultaneously learned associations between maps through Hebbian learning: Initially, all the units on one map were fully connected to all the units on the other map; as learning continued, only the units that were coactivated in response to the input were associated. If the direction of the associative propagation goes from phonology to semantics, *comprehension* is modelled; if it goes from semantics to phonology, *production* is modelled. As the goal of learning, the network should create new representations in the corresponding maps for all the inputs and link the semantic properties of a verb to its phonological shape and morphological pattern. All simulations were conducted with the DISLEX simulator (Miikkulainen, 1999).

Stages of training. To observe effects of the interaction between lexicon and morphology in learning, we designed four stages to train the network. In the case of prefixes, a given verb is paired with *un-*, *dis-*, or zero-marking according to whether the prefixation is allowed in the adult language. In the case of suffixes, a given verb is paired with *-ing*, *-ed*, *-s*, or zero-marking according to whether the verb co-occurs with the suffix in the parental speech.

For prefixes, the four stages were: (1) the phonological representation of a verb stem was coactivated with its semantic representation on a one-to-one basis in the input. This was done to model the whole-word learning stage—a stage at which children have not analysed morphological devices as separate entities from the verb stems (Bowerman, 1982); (2) phonological and semantic representations of verb stems (e.g. *tie*, *connect*), prefixed verbs (*untie*, *disconnect*), and the prefixes themselves (*un-*, *dis-*) were all coactivated in the input; (3) 25 novel verbs were introduced to the network to test whether generalisations would occur in our network as in children's speech. These were verbs on which previous studies have reported children's generalisations (Bowerman, 1982; Clark et al., 1995). Generalisation was tested by inputting the verbs to the network without having the network self-organise or learn the phonological–semantic associations; (4) self-organisation and Hebbian learning resumed for the novel verbs introduced at stage 3 to test if the network could recover from generalisations.

For suffixes, the four stages were based on the age groups of the input data (i.e. the age of the child for which adult input was available in our corpus—the input age). The four stages were: (1) input age 1;6 (13–18 months). Relatively few uses of suffixes occur in the CHILDES parental data before the child is 13 months old. For the period of 13–18 months, a total of 186 verbs fit our selection criteria (i.e. occurred five or more times); (2) input age 2;0 (19–24 months) included 324 verbs; (3) input age 2;6 (25–30 months) included 419 verbs; and (4) input age 3 (31–36 months) included 562 verbs. These stages reflect an incremental growth of vocabulary, and the verbs at a later stage always included verbs at the previous stage. It also reflected a coarse frequency coding: a verb or a suffix was presented to the network for the number of times it occurred across the four stages.

In the following sections, I report two sets of simulation results, one for prefixes, and the other for suffixes. However, the acquisition patterns are comparable for both types of morphology, to which we will return in the Conclusions section.

Results and discussion: Prefix simulations

In this section, I focus on three levels of analysis on the prefix simulations: the network's representation of the cryptotype, its patterns of overgeneralisation, and its ability to recover from the generalisation errors.

Representation of cryptotype. One of the major motivations for this study was whether neural networks can develop structured representation as a function of its self-organisation on verb semantics. In particular, I wanted to see how the patterns of activity formed in the semantic map can capture Whorf's covert, "intangible", category of cryptotype.

In Li and MacWhinney (1996) we suggested that there are several "mini-cryptotypes" that work collaboratively as interactive "gangs" (McClelland & Rumelhart, 1981) to support the formation of a larger cryptotype. For example, "enclosing" verbs, such as *coil, curl, fold, ravel, roll, screw, twist*, and *wind*, all seem to share a meaning of circular movement; another set of verbs such as *cover, dress, mask, pack, veil*, and *wrap* form the "covering" mini-cryptotype, and so on. Members in these mini-cryptotypes are closely related by overlapping semantic features. Previously, we have used hierarchical cluster analyses to identify the existence of mini-cryptotypes in our network, by analysing the hidden-unit activation patterns. In the current study, these mini-cryptotypes can be seen more clearly in the emerging structure of the SOFM's two-dimensional layout as activity bubbles. In our network, the self-organisation process extracted semantic structures from the input and projected the new representations on the semantic map. Figure 4.3 presents a snapshot of the network's representation after it was trained on 120 verbs for 600 epochs at stage 1.

A close examination of the semantic map shows that the network developed clear representations that correspond to the cryptotype which Whorf believed governs the use of *un-*. Our network, without using *ad hoc* semantic features, mapped members in mini-cryptotypes onto nearby regions of the SOFM. For example, towards the lower right-hand corner, verbs like *lock, clasp, latch, lease*, and *button* were mapped to the same region, and these verbs all share the "binding/locking" meaning. Similarly, "attachment" verbs like *snap, mantle, tangle, ravel, tie*, and *bolt* occurred towards the lower left-hand corner, and verbs of perceptions and audition like *hear, say, speak, see*, and *tell* can be found in the upper left-hand corner. One can also observe that *embark, engage, integrate, assemble*, and *unite* are being mapped towards the upper right-hand corner of the map, which all seem to share the "connecting" or "putting-together" meaning and, interestingly, these are the verbs that can take the prefix *dis-*. Of course, the network's representation at this point is still incomplete, as self-organisation is moving from diffuse to more focused patterns of activity; for example, the verb *show*, which shares similarity with

```
Assoc weights: CLASP                    LEXICAL MAP
SCRE         SNAP   FREE   KEEP   more     REEL   RAVE          TANG   MANT   MOUN   MASK   more
    STRI     STOP
    SLIP            SAY                    REAC   FIND          TELL   MELT   WAIT   PAY
SPLI         ZIP    SPEA SEE  TIE          LATC   STAN   HELP          VEIL   BRAI   PLAY
    SIT      GIVE   LIKE                   LOCK   STAR   SOLV                 PLAC
    THIS            LIVE   LEAS            LOOK                 CHAI   ASK            CLEN
DETA         LIFT                                        ARM
DELE                LOOS          LINK            TURN          TRUS   DRES   CLOS   CLOG   PLUG
RELE         REVE                                 LEAR                              BRIN
BEGI         BELI   REMO   DEPR   CURL            WORK          CORK          CLEA   PROV
BECO                APPR          AGRE            COME          HEAR          PULL           MOVE
BUTT         AFFI   APPE                                       HITC   HOOK   PUT    DO       TALK
                    COVE          EMBA                                        GO
FAST         SEPA   CONF          INVI    INFE                 USE    LOAD   SHOW   WALK
STRA  SETT                        ENGA                  EXPE          UNIT                  CALL
                                                                      POSS          POSE
SPRI SCRA    BAND   CONT          INTE    ASSE   AFFE          ALLO   OBEY          more

Source unit: clasp                      SEMANTIC MAP
agre  findhear  spea     tell    writ   pay      conf   more   obey   more   embadepr
beli   say   see         put     use    go       reac   make   brin   stra   enga   expe
invi   do    ask   wait  sit     give          more   keep          fast   inte   asse
      live         stan  come                   help   play                        unit
like         trus  come  poss    cont   allo   infe    clen          loos   remo
look   call  walk  appr        affe    beco    work    turn    scre   pull          begi
affi         pose        appe   clea   clos   curl    move   dele   star   deta
      wrap   clog         clea   clos   spli   scra   load   moun         fold
spri                roll         free   slip   dres   plug   hook   lift         cove
snap   reve  stri  tie          reel          link   brai   hitc   lock   show   rele
mant         twis  bolt   cork         link          sepa   band         latc
tang   rave        mask          chai   zip    sepa          leas   arm    butt
```

Figure 4.3. The representation of semantic cryptotypes in a SOFM. The upper panel is the lexical map, and the lower panel the semantic map. The phonological representations of words are in capitals, and the semantic representations in lower case. Words longer than four letters are truncated.

none of the above, is grouped with the binding/locking verbs. What is crucial, however, is that these clusters form the semantic basis for the overall cryptotype of the *un-* verbs. As shown in Figure 4.3, the network has mapped most verbs in the cryptotype to the bottom layer of the semantic map, and importantly, these are the verbs that can take the prefix *un-*.

These results from our model offer a tangible solution to the "intangible" aspects of Whorf's cryptotype. Connectionist learning provides us with a natural way of capturing Whorf's insights of cryptotype as well as its acquisition in a formal mechanism. It gives a precise account of how the *un-* cryptotype emerges from learning in a distributed representation: The formation of a cryptotype is supported by mini-cryptotypes that interact collaboratively, which are in turn supported by multiple weighted features shared by all the *un-* verbs through summed activation.

Representation and overgeneralisation. Connectionist networks can generalise learned patterns to novel instances, but do they show the same types of generalisation as children do? And on what basis do they generalise?

In our network, as discussed earlier, the two SOFMs can be connected via Hebbian learning: the phonological and semantic representations of a verb are coactivated in different maps, along with the corresponding prefixes that the verb can take in the language. Hebbian learning determines how strong the connections between the phonology, the meaning, and the affix should be during each stage of the learning. At the same time, the two maps also self-organise. In this way, Hebbian learning and self-organisation provide the network with focused pathways from form to meaning and from meaning to form. Thus, when the network receives a new input, it can readily "comprehend" the input (from form to meaning) or "produce" the input (from meaning to form) using its existing, learned pathways between the feature maps. This procedure also allows us to test the network's generalisation ability when meaningful representations have emerged from the maps.

The simulation results indicate that our network was not only able to capture the elusive cryptotype by way of self-organisation, but also able to generalise on the basis of this representation. For example, when tested for generalisation at stage 3, the network produced overgeneralisation errors (e.g. *unbreak, *uncapture, *unconnect, *ungrip, *unpeel, *unplant, *unpress, *unspill, *untighten) that match up with empirical data. These overgeneralisations were based both on the network's established structure of semantic representations and on the associative connections that it formed in learning the meaning–form mappings. Several observations can be made on the network's overgeneralisations.

First, most of these overgeneralisations involve verbs that fall within the Whorfian cryptotype (e.g. *connect, grip, peel, plant, press, spill,* and *tighten*). Earlier, we pointed out two hypotheses regarding the role of the cryptotype in children's acquisition of *un-* according to Bowerman: "generalisation via cryptotype" and "recovery via cryptotype". Our results here are consistent with the first hypothesis, that is, the representation of cryptotype leads to overly general uses of *un-*. Consistent with our previous simulations, we found no violations of the cryptotype in the network's overgeneralisations such as *unhate or *untake (as found in Bowerman's data); hence there was no evidence for the hypothesis that the learner can use the cryptotype representation to recover from overgeneralisations.

Second, the associative pathways between the two maps formed via Hebbian learning provide the basis for the production of overgeneralisations. For example, the semantic properties of *tighten* and *clench* are similar and they were mapped onto nearby regions of the semantic map. During learning, the semantics of *clench* and *unclench* were coactivated, and the phonology of *clench, unclench,* and *un-* were also coactivated. When the semantics and the phonology of these items were associated through Hebbian learning, the network can associate the semantics of *tighten* with the phonology of *un-* because of *clench*, even though the network learned only the association of *un-clench* and not *un-tighten* (i.e. at an earlier stage *tighten* was withheld from the training). This associative process of correlating semantic features, lexical forms, and morphological devices simulates the process of learning and generalisation in children's language acquisition, and shows that overgeneralisations can arise naturally from structured semantic representations (a result of self-organisation) and from associative learning of meanings and forms.

Finally, overgeneralisations were not limited to morphological generalisations. There were lexical generalisations similar to those reported by Bowerman (1982) and Miikkulainen (1997). For example, the network produced *see* in response to *say*, *detach* in response to *delete*, *begin* in response to *become*, due to its representation of these pairs of words in the same region on the phonological map. These generalisations resemble lexical errors in surface dyslexia. Similarly, the network comprehended *see* as *speak*, *arm* as *clasp*, and *unscrew* as *hook*, due to its representation of these pairs of words in nearby regions in the semantic map, and these errors resemble lexical errors in deep dyslexia in reading comprehension. They demonstrate further the intimate relationship between semantic representation and generalisation. Again, self-organisation and Hebbian learning account for the origin of this type of generalisation errors.

Mechanisms of recovery from generalisations. Can our self-organising network recover from generalisations as children do? If so, what computational mechanisms permit its recovery?

Our network displayed significant ability to recover from overgeneralisations. When tested for generalisations at stage 3, no learning took place in the network for self-organisation or associative connection. When tested for recovery at stage 4, self-organisation and Hebbian learning resumed. Within 200 epochs of new learning during the last stage, the network recovered from the majority of the overgeneralisations tested at stage 3. Recovery in this case is a process of restructuring the mapping between phonological, semantic, and morphological patterns, and this restructuring is based on the network's ability to reconfigure the associative pathways through Hebbian learning, in our case, the ability to form new associations between prefixes and verbs and the ability to eliminate old associations that were the basis of erroneous overgeneralisations. When a given phonological unit and a given semantic unit have fewer chances to become coactivated, Hebbian learning decreases the strengths of their associative links. For example, *un-* and *tighten* were coactivated because of *un-* and *clench* at stage 3; at stage 4 *un-* and *clench* continue to be coactivated, but *un-* and *tighten* are not coactivated. Hebbian learning determines that the associative connection between *un-* and *clench* continues to increase as learning progresses, but that between *un-* and *tighten* gets decreased and eventually eliminated, thereby simulating what happens at the final phase of U-shaped learning. This result models the process in which children's overgeneralisations are gradually eliminated when there is no auditory support in the input about specific co-occurrences that they expect (MacWhinney, 2001). In the realistic learning situation, the strength of the connection between *un-* and inappropriate verbs may also be reduced by a competing form such as *loosen* that functions to express the meaning of *untighten*. This type of process is often discussed in the literature as the pre-emption mechanism (Clark, 1987) or the competition mechanism (Bates & MacWhinney, 1987; MacWhinney, 1987). Our model has not yet incorporated this type of mechanism.

Hebbian learning coupled with self-organisation provides a simple but powerful computational principle to account for the recovery process. Restructuring of associative links often goes hand-in-hand with the reorganisation of the maps. For example, at stage 4, the network developed finer representations for verbs such as *clench* and *tighten*: As the associative strengths of these verbs to *un-* varied, their representations also became more distinct. This process in our simulation is consistent with the proposal that children recover from generalisations by recognising fine and subtle semantic and phonological properties of verbs (Pinker, 1989). Interestingly, in cases where it did not recover from overgeneralisations, the network had difficulty making fine semantic distinctions. For example, because it was unable to separate word pairs like *press* and *zip* in the semantic map, it continued to produce erroneous forms like *unpress*.

An additional parameter that we considered in the SOFM's error recovery was the size of the feature map (i.e. the number of units available for learning). The inability to further distinguish semantically similar words might be due to resource limitations. To verify this hypothesis, in a separate but otherwise identical simulation, we doubled the size of both maps (from 25×25 units to 50×50 units). In this new simulation, at stage 3 we continued to observe the same type of overgeneralisations as in the original simulations, but at stage 4 the network recovered completely from all the overgeneralisations. Thus, there is reason to believe that enough learning resource is needed for the network to further reorganise confused items that are due to great similarity. For the child, it is likely that the increasing capacity of memory and other cognitive abilities make resource limitation a nonproblem. We could model this type of resource increase with an architecture in which the number of neurons dynamically grows in response to the learning task (see Farkas & Li, 2002, for a recent implementation). This type of dynamic growth of SOFMs could be compared to the cascade correlation mechanism in back-propagation learning (Fahlman & Lebiere, 1990).

Results and discussion: Suffix simulations

The simulation procedures for the suffixes were similar to those for the prefixes except the training materials and stages. We also used larger maps (50 × 50 units) given the resource problem considered above and given that twice as many verbs were involved in the suffix simulations as in the prefix simulations. Below, I focus on three levels of analysis for the suffix simulations: the role of input, the emergence of lexical aspect categories, and the formation and relaxation of strong associations between lexical semantic categories and grammatical suffixes.

Role of input. One important rationale behind the current modelling effort is the understanding of the role of linguistic input in guiding children's acquisition of lexical and grammatical aspect. The relationship between patterns observed in children's speech and those in parental speech with respect to the interaction between verb semantics and aspect suffixes has been emphasized elsewhere (Li & Bowerman, 1998; Li & Shirai, 2000) but a simple correlation between children's and adults' patterns tells us only that the child is sensitive to the linguistic environment and is able to incorporate information from that environment into his or her own speech. It does not tell us how the child actually does the analysis, or what mechanisms allow the child to do the analysis. Thus, we need to test if a connectionist network—endowed with self-organisation and Hebbian learning principles—is able to display learning patterns as found in child language. If so, we can conclude that self-organisation and Hebbian learning may provide the necessary kinds of mechanisms that allow for the formation of patterns in language acquisition. In this way, our modelling enterprise provides insights into the mechanisms underlying the learning process.

Table 4.1 presents a summary of the major patterns from the network's learning according to the tense-aspect suffixes it produced at the different learning stages. It shows the results of the network's production of three suffixes, *-ing*, *-ed*, and *-s* with three types of verbs, processes, events, and states. The results are based on the unit activations on the phonological map that each verb in the semantic map activated, after the network had been trained for 200 epochs at each stage.

The results in this table are highly consistent with empirical patterns observed in early child language: the use of the progressive aspect (marked by *-ing* in English) is closely associated with process verbs that indicate ongoing processes, while the use of past-perfective aspect (marked by *-ed* in English) is closely associated with event verbs that indicate endpoints or end results. Some studies also suggest a strong association between the habitual *-s* and state verbs (Clark, 1996). Our network, having received input patterns based on parental data, behaved in the same way as children do. For example, at

TABLE 4.1

Percentage of use of tense-aspect suffixes with different verb types across input age groups in the network's production and in the parental input data[*]

| | Tense-aspect suffixes | | | | | | | | | | | |
| | Age 1;6 | | | Age 2;0 | | | Age 2;6 | | | Age 3;0 | | |
Verbs	-ing	-ed	-s	-ing	-ed	-s	-ing	-ed	-s	-ing	-ed	-s
Network production												
Processes	75	18	0	66	16	0	64	26	0	52	9	10
Events	25	82	0	28	84	0	31	74	0	44	77	10
States	0	0	100	0	0	100	0	0	100	4	14	80
Item totals[**]	40	11	3	71	19	9	89	19	7	70	22	10
Parental input data												
Processes	69	22	0	74	15	17	67	23	20	67	23	23
Events	28	77	33	24	77	0	25	69	20	31	65	8
States	3	0	67	2	8	83	8	8	60	2	12	69
Item totals	29	3	9	54	13	12	40	13	10	60	26	13

* The table includes only verbs that could be uniquely assigned to one or the other suffixation pattern and does not include instances for which the network produced a given verb with multiple suffixes. See Table 4.2 for the latter.
** These are the total number of verbs that occurred with the given suffix. Note that the percentages within a given column do not always add up to 100, reflecting that some verbs could not be easily classified into one or the other category. This is also true for Table 4.2.

input age 1;6, the network produced -*ing* predominantly with process verbs (75 per cent), -*ed* overwhelmingly with event verbs (82 per cent), and -*s* exclusively with state verbs (100 per cent). Such associations remained strong at input age 2 but gradually became weaker (although still transparent) at later stages.

Interestingly, when we analysed the actual input to our network (based on parental speech), we found similar patterns. Table 4.1 also presents the percentages of the use of suffixes with different verb types in the input data. The degree to which the network's production matches up with the input patterns (Table 4.1) indicates that our network was able to learn on the basis of the information of the co-occurrences between lexical aspect (verb types) and grammatical aspect (use of suffixes). This learning ability was due to the network's use of Hebbian associative learning in computing: (1) when the semantic, phonological, and morphological properties of a verb co-occur; and (2) how often they do so.

The results in Table 4.1 also match up nicely with several empirical studies that have examined the correspondence between children's speech and adult input in the acquisition of tense–aspect suffixes, in English (Shirai & Andersen, 1995), Japanese (Shirai, 1998), modern Greek (Stephany, 1981), and Turkish (Aksu-Koç, 1998). Note that the patterns in the input, as discussed by Li and Shirai (2000), are usually less absolute or restrictive than in children's early productions, showing that adults are more flexible in associating various types of grammatical morphology with various types of verbs. Indeed, the patterns in Table 4.1 show that the associations between verb types and suffixes are weaker in the input to the network than they were in the network's production. This is important, because if the learner—child and network alike—simply mimicked what is in the input, the learner would have no productive control over the relevant linguistic problem and would simply produce the patterns verbatim. The modelling results further confirm the hypothesis that a probabilistic pattern in the input can lead to more absolute patterns in the learner's output, because the learner initially capitalises on the prototypical representations of the verb–suffix association (see Li & Shirai, 2000, for the role of input in inducing prototypes).

Emergence of semantic categories of lexical aspect.   Figure 4.4 presents a snapshot of the network's self-organisation of the semantic representations of verbs at input age 1;6 (from the semantic map). The network clearly developed structured semantic representations that correspond to categories of lexical aspect such as processes, events, and states. For example, towards the lower right-hand corner, state verbs like *feel, know, think, remember, won-der, love,* and *like* were mapped onto the same region of the map. Event verbs can be found in the middle-to-left portion of the map, including verbs like *catch, fix, break, knock, grab,* and *throw,* all of which indicate actions that lead to clear end results. Process verbs can be found spanning the upper end of the map, including (from left to right) *rub, scrub, sleep, shout, laugh, drink, walk, kiss, cry, swim, dance,* and so on.

The above patterns of semantic neighbourhood bear close similarity with the formation of mini-cryptotypes in the case of prefixes. As discussed earlier, the formation of semantic categories goes hand-in-hand with the acquisition of grammatical morphology. On the one hand, similar verbs form concen-trated patterns of activity, providing the basis for semantic categories, and on the other hand, they also form focused associative pathways to the phono-logical and morphological representations of verbs in the other map. When concentrated activities occur both horizontally (within a two-dimensional map) and vertically (across the maps), the semantic categories of lexical aspect will behave like magnets to connect the lexicon to morphology. Thus, when a new input has semantic overlap with verbs of an existing lexical category and resembles members of that category, its mapping to correspond-ing morphemes will be readily done through the existing associative pathways going from verb semantics to suffixes; that is, no additional learning will be needed for the new mapping. This analysis provides a mechanistic account for

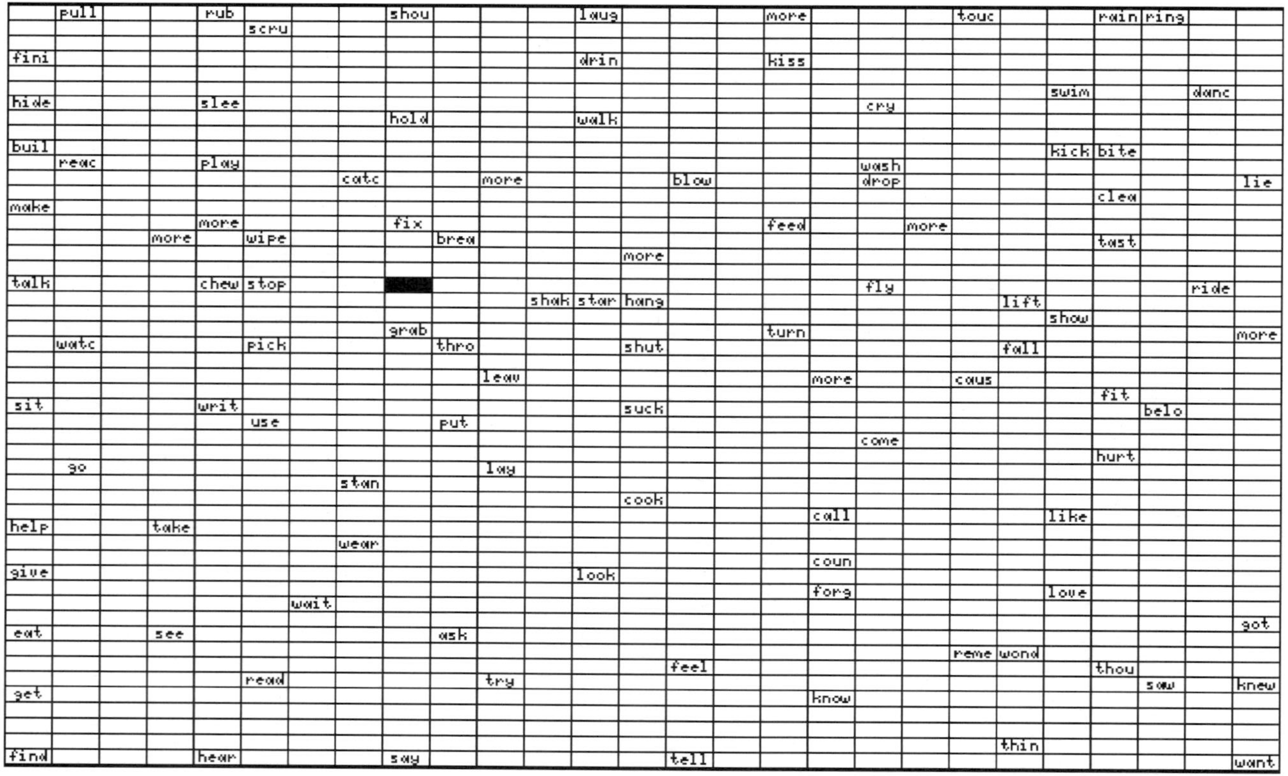

Figure 4.4. The representation of verb categories in a SOFM (semantic map only). Only the left portion of the complete map is shown due to space limit. Words longer than four letters are truncated.

Slobin's (1985) basic child grammar hypothesis that the initial semantic categories act as magnets to attract grammatical mappings in the input language.

From strong associations to diverse mappings..   As with the prefix simulations, the associative pathways between forms and meanings are established
via Hebbian learning across learning stages. Depending on how often forms
and meanings co-occur, Hebbian learning establishes either stronger or
weaker associations. Thus, when the network has a focused pathway, for
example, between -s on the lexical map and state verbs on the semantic map,
it can readily "comprehend" new state verbs at no additional learning, pro-
moting an even stronger state-to-s association (a prototypical association).
However, as learning progresses, -s may be used more diversely with other
verb types in the input, so that the prototypical association weakens over
time. The fact that a given suffix occurs with multiple verbs, and a given
verb occurs with multiple suffixes in the input tells the system that it should
no longer be restricted to the prototypical associations, but develop new
nonprototypical mappings between lexicon and morphology.

Table 4.2 presents the same simulation results as in Table 4.1, except that
multiple suffixation patterns are included here—a given verb was counted for
multiple number of times in the table depending on the number of suffixes
with which it co-occurred (Table 4.1 included only verbs that could be
uniquely assigned to one suffixation pattern; see Li & Shirai, 2000, for the
rationale behind this treatment).

A comparison of this table with Table 4.1 reveals that, for the early stages
(1;6 and 2;0), the two tables are very similar; for the later stages, however, they
become more distinct, mainly with respect to the uses of *-ed* and *-s*. Detailed
analyses show that over 50 per cent of all suffixed verbs had more than one

TABLE 4.2

Percentage of use of tense-aspect suffixes with different verb types across input age
groups in the network's production (multiple suffixations)[*]

	Tense-aspect suffixes											
	Age 1;6			*Age 2;0*			*Age 2;6*			*Age 3;0*		
Verbs	-*ing*	-*ed*	-*s*	-*ing*	-*ed*	-*s*	-*ing*	-*ed*	-*s*	-*ing*	-*ed*	-*s*
Processes	72	16	0	62	29	6	64	40	44	52	38	30
Events	28	75	0	32	66	31	32	60	12	43	53	26
States	0	8	100	0	4	63	0	0	44	5	9	44
Item totals[*]	43	12	5	81	24	16	114	35	16	121	64	27

* Because the same verb could occur in more than one column, the sum of the item totals across
columns does not equal the total word types. This differs from the interpretation of item totals in
Table 4.1.

suffix at input age 3;0, compared with only 5 per cent at input age 1;6. These results suggest that multiple suffixations might be the driving force for the learner to break from the strong associations to more diverse mappings. There was relatively little change with the -*ing* verbs, because the majority of the early verbs were process verbs that take -*ing*. Overall, these results indicate that increasing associative links between verbs and suffixes (along with incremental vocabulary growth) lead to diverse mappings, first with some words and then spreading to others, thus accounting for how the strong associations weaken over time in children's language.

Our simulation results also shed some light on the acquisition of the English past tense. First, given that children's early use of -*ed* is restricted to specific lexical meanings, overgeneralisations of -*ed* would not occur across the board for all types of verbs but will rather be restricted to event verbs initially. Second, overgeneralisations of -*ed* not only may be semantically restricted, but also sometimes semantically motivated. In our network, semantic pathways formed via Hebbian learning provide the basis for the production of overgeneralisation errors. For example, *knock* and *break* share semantic similarities and were mapped onto nearby regions in the semantic map. During learning, the semantics of *knock* and *knocked* were coactivated, and the phonological forms of *knock*, *knocked*, and -*ed* were also coactivated. When the semantics and the phonology of these items were associated via Hebbian learning, the network would connect the semantics of *break* with the phonology of -*ed* because of *knock*, even though it learned only the association for *knock-ed* and not *break-ed* (i.e. when *break* was withheld from training initially). This result parallels the overgeneralisation errors on prefixes such as **un-tighten* (due to *un-clench*) that we discussed earlier.

CONCLUSIONS

In this chapter, I started by reviewing some of the problems in previous connectionist models of language acquisition. I pointed out that previous models have been largely restricted to the examination of phonological patterns (in contrast to semantic structures), to the use of artificially generated input (in contrast to realistic linguistic data), and to the use of supervised learning algorithms (in contrast to unsupervised learning). I proposed a new connectionist model of language acquisition that is based on the examination of the acquisition of semantics, with exposure to realistic child-directed parental data, and in self-organising networks with unsupervised learning. I showed how SOFMs can be used successfully to model the acquisition of lexicon and morphology. In particular, I applied SOFMs to examine two linguistic domains where the development of lexicon and morphology is crucial: (1) the acquisition of derivational prefixes with respect to semantic cryptotypes of verbs; and (2) the acquisition of inflectional suffixes with respect to grammatical and lexical aspect of verbs. The new model sheds light on issues of semantic representation, morphological overgeneralisation and undergeneralisation, and recovery from erroneous generalisations in humans and networks. I argue that self-organising neural networks coupled with Hebbian learning provide computationally relevant and psychologically plausible principles for modelling language development.

One of our major tasks in modelling the acquisition of semantics is to see how structured semantic representations could emerge from the network's self-organisation of lexical features of verbs. This task is designed to answer two challenges: (1) how can neural networks capture the formation of covert semantic categories, categories that have been traditionally thought elusive, subtle, or even intangible (e.g. the Whorfian cryptotype)? and (2) how can neural networks capture the emergence of lexical aspect categories, categories that have been believed to be innate or otherwise universal (e.g. Bickerton's bioprogram or Slobin's semantic space)? Our SOFM network, through the self-organisation of multiple semantic features, develops concentrated patterns of activity that correspond to cryptotypes (in the case of prefix acquisition) and verb categories (in the case of suffix acquisition). Note that the actual identity of each of the semantic features is unknown to the modeller, because the features encode lexical co-occurrence constraints in a high-dimensional space (see the discussion of input representations on pp. 129–130; see also p. 124). This contrasts with traditional hand-crafted or *ad hoc* features. Our simulation results suggest that connectionist mechanisms as implemented in our model can indeed capture critical aspects of semantic organisation and category formation in language acquisition, without making *a priori* assumptions about the intangibility or the innate nature of lexical semantics.

One might argue that our input representations already contain a rich set of semantic information (as in the HAL semantic vectors), and so it is misleading to claim that the network is acquiring semantic categories. This argument should be considered in at least two perspectives. First, our network takes in only individual verbs as input, in no structured order, but with each verb having information of lexical co-occurrences. What the network needs to do is to re-represent the lexical co-occurrence information in such a way that the resulting two-dimensional map can maximally preserve the similarity of verbs in the original high-dimensional space. This is a process in which the network attempts to discover the underlying structure or organisation for all the verbs in question. None of this structural or organisational information is labelled in the individual verbs, but derived only by the statistical procedure of the network.

A second, and perhaps more important perspective, is to consider that the learner has two simultaneous processes, one that organises the lexical co-occurrence information into meaningful structures (as in SOFMs), and another that extracts the co-occurrence information from the corpus (part of the language experience). In fact, we have recently built a model that does just that. In Farkas and Li (2001, 2002), we developed a connectionist model that acquires lexical knowledge from the learning of distributional characteristics of words. The model consists of two subnetworks: one learns word transitional probabilities in sentence contexts, and the other—a SOFM—reads these probabilities as distributed representations and self-organises them. We applied the model to a CHILDES parental data set and found that the model is able to acquire grammatical and semantic categories through learning in the corpus. In addition, the network demonstrates ability to develop rather accurate representations even with sparse training data, contrary to what is commonly expected of large-scale statistical learning models that typically compute tens or hundreds of millions of lexical items in the corpus.

Thus, the argument here is that the linguistic input to the learner contains very rich distributional information, and our network as well as the child can explore and extract from the input the necessary semantic categories (see Rohde & Plaut, 1999, and Seidenberg & MacDonald, 1999, for similar arguments in the case of grammar induction). Instead of assuming that certain semantic categories are available ahead of time for the child, we need only to make a few simple assumptions about what the child can do: (1) the child has the ability to track continuous speech with some limitation on working memory; and (2) the child is sensitive to lexical co-occurrence probabilities during language comprehension. Such statistical abilities seem to be readily available to the child at a very early age, as studies of statistical learning in infants have revealed (Saffran, Aslin, & Newport, 1996; Saffran et al., 1997). Note that such assumptions differ from the empiricist *tabula rasa* approach to the learning problem, as illustrated clearly by Elman, Bates, Johnson, Karmiloff-Smith, Parisi, and Plunkett (1996) on connectionist learning. Along the arguments of Elman et al., I suggest that specific linguistic categories (e.g. semantic categories discussed here) are not innate; rather, the learner has available a set of statistical mechanisms (which can be operationalised as connectionist principles), and these mechanisms, when applied onto the linguistic input, can yield relevant semantic or grammatical categories. Our modelling results show exactly how such categories can emerge naturally from connectionist learning of the statistical properties of lexical and morphological uses.

Finally, our modelling endeavour has also attempted to make a connection between structured semantic representations and the acquisition of morphology. Our SOFM network, when coupled with Hebbian learning, produces developmental patterns of both overgeneralisation (in prefix acquisition) and undergeneralisation (in suffix acquisition) that mirror empirical data in child language. Our analyses of the simulations indicate that these generalisation errors naturally result from the structure of the network's semantic representations (a result of self-organisation) and from the focused associative pathways in the mappings between semantic features, lexical forms, and morphological markers (a result of Hebbian learning). Further analyses also show that our network is able to recover from the generalisation errors as learning progresses, achieved by the readjustment of the associative weights between forms and meanings via Hebbian learning. These analyses suggest that the learning of a morphological affix is not simply the learning of a rule (leaving alone the fact that it is unclear what the rule is, as per Whorf on the use of *un*-), but the accumulation of associative strengths that hold between a particular affix and a complex set of semantic features distributed across verbs. This learning process can be best described as a statistical process in which the learner implicitly tallies and registers the frequency of co-occurrences (strengthening what goes with what) and identifies the co-occurrence constraints (inhibiting what does not go with what) among the semantic features, lexical forms, and morphological markers.

To conclude, our self-organising neural network model of language acquisition provides significant insights into the mechanisms and processes of language acquisition. It may also serve to stimulate further empirical research, because the model often generates detailed patterns that are not yet available from empirical studies. Future research in our laboratory involves the development of models that tie even more closely to realistic language learning, for example, in the dynamic growth of networks' processing resources, automatic extraction of contextual constraints, and the dynamic representation of lexical–semantic information.

ACKNOWLEDGEMENTS

This research was supported by a grant from the National Science Foundation (#BCS-9975249). I am very grateful to Brian MacWhinney and Risto Miikkulainen for their comments and discussions at various stages of the project. I would also like to thank Curt Burgess and Kevin Lund for making the HAL vectors available. The simulations were run on a SUN Sparc, using the DISLEX code configured by Miikkulainen (1999). Some of the preliminary results are reported in Li (1999), Li (2000), and Li and Shirai (2000).

REFERENCES

Aksu-Koç, A. (1998). The role of input vs. universal predispositions in the emergence of tense-aspect morphology: Evidence from Turkish. *First Language, 18*, 255–280.

Baker, C. (1979). Syntactic theory and the projection problem. *Linguistic Inquiry, 10*, 533–581.

Bates, E., & MacWhinney, B. (1987). Competition, variation, and language learning. In B. MacWhinney (Ed.), *Mechanisms of language acquisition* (pp. 157–193). Hillsdale, NJ: Lawrence Erlbaum Associates, Inc.

Bickerton, D. (1981). *Roots of language*. Ann Arbor, MI: Karoma.

Bickerton, D. (1984). The language bioprogram hypothesis. *Behavioral and Brain Sciences, 7*, 173–188.

Bloom, L., Lifter, K., & Hafitz, J. (1980). Semantics of verbs and the development of verb inflection in child language. *Language, 56*, 386–412.

Bowerman, M. (1978). Systematising semantic knowledge: Changes over time in the child's organisation of word meaning. *Child Development, 49*, 977–987.

Bowerman, M. (1982). Reorganisational processes in lexical and syntactic development. In E. Wanner & L. Gleitman (Eds.), *Language acquisition: The state of the art* (pp. 319–346). Cambridge: Cambridge University Press.

Bowerman, M. (1983). Hidden meanings: The role of covert conceptual structures in children's development of language. In D. Rogers & J. Sloboda (Eds.), *The acquisition of symbolic skills* (pp. 445–470). New York: Plenum.

Bowerman, M. (1988). The "no negative evidence" problem: How do children avoid constructing an overly general grammar? In J. Hawkins (Ed.), *Explaining language universals* (pp. 73–101). New York: Blackwell.

Brown, R. (1973). *A first language*. Cambridge, MA: Harvard University Press.

Burgess, C., & Lund, K. (1997). Modelling parsing constraints with high-dimensional context space. *Language and Cognitive Processes, 12*, 1–34.

Burgess, C., & Lund, K. (1999). The dynamics of meaning in memory. In E. Dietrich & A. Markman (Eds.), *Cognitive dynamics: Conceptual and representational change in humans and machines* (pp. 17–56). Mahwah, NJ: Lawrence Erlbaum Associates, Inc.

Carey, S. (1978). The child as word learner. In M. Halle, G. Miller, & J. Bresnan (Eds.), *Linguistic theory and psychological reality* (pp. 264–293). Cambridge, MA: MIT Press.

Chomsky, N. (1957). *Syntactic structures*. The Hague, North Holland: Mouton.

Clark, E. V. (1987). The principle of contrast: A constraint on language acquisition. In B. MacWhinney (Ed.), *Mechanisms of language acquisition* (pp. 1–34). Hillsdale, NJ: Lawrence Erlbaum Associates, Inc.

Clark, E. V. (1996). Early verbs, event-types, and inflections. In C. E. Johnson & J. H. V. Gilbert (Eds.), *Children's language, 9*. Hillsdale, NJ: Lawrence Erlbaum Associates, Inc.

Clark, E. V., Carpenter, K., & Deutsch, W. (1995). Reference states and reversals: Undoing actions with verbs. *Journal of Child Language, 22*, 633–662.

Comrie, B. (1976). *Aspect: An introduction to the study of verbal aspect and related problems*. Cambridge: Cambridge University Press.

Cottrell, G., & Plunkett, K. (1994). Acquiring the mapping from meaning to sounds. *Connection Science, 6*, 379–412.

Elman, J., Bates, A., Johnson, M. H., Karmiloff-Smith, A., Parisi, D., & Plunkett, K. (1996). *Rethinking innateness: A connectionist perspective on development*. Cambridge, MA: MIT Press.

Fahlman, S., & Lebiere, C. (1990) The cascade-correlation learning architecture. In D. S. Touretzky (Ed.), *Advances in neural information processing systems 2* (pp. 524–532). Los Altos, CA: Morgan Kaufmann Publishers.

Farkas, I., & Li, P. (2001). A self-organising neural network model of the acquisition of word meaning. In E. M. Altmann, A. Cleeremans, C. D. Schunn, & W. D. Gray (Eds.), *Proceedings of the Fourth International Conference on Cognitive Modeling* (pp. 67–72). Mahwah, NJ: Lawrence Erlbaum Associates, Inc.

Farkas, I., & Li, P. (2002). Modeling the development of lexicon with a growing self-organising map. In H. J. Caulfield et al. (Eds.), *Proceedings of the Sixth Joint Conference on Information Science* (pp. 553–556). Association for Intelligent Machinery, Inc.

Francis, W., & Kucera, H. (1982). *Frequency analysis of English usage: Lexicon and grammar*. Boston, MA: Houghton Mifflin.

Hebb, D. (1949). *The organisation of behavior: A neuropsychological theory*. New York: Wiley.

Hertz, J., Krogh, A., & Palmer, R. (1991). *Introduction to the theory of neural computation.* Redwood City, CA: Addison-Wesley.

Joanisse, M., & Seidenberg, M. (1999). Impairments in verb morphology after brain injury: A connectionist model. *Proceedings of the National Academy of Sciences, 96*, 7592–7597.

Klahr, D., & MacWhinney, B. (2000). Information processing. In D. Kuhn, R. S. Siegler, & W. Damon (Eds.), *Handbook of child psychology: Vol. 2. Cognition, perception, and language* (pp. 631–678). New York: Wiley.

Kohonen, T. (1982). Self-organized formation of topologically correct feature maps. *Biological Cybernetics, 43*, 59–69.

Kohonen, T. (1989). *Self-organisation and associative memory.* Heidelberg: Springer-Verlag.

Kohonen, T. (1995). *Self-organising maps.* Heidelberg: Springer-Verlag.

Kuczaj, S. (1977). The acquisition of regular and irregular past tense forms. *Journal of Verbal Learning and Verbal Behavior, 16*, 589–600.

Lachter, J., & Bever, T. (1988). The relation between linguistic structure and associative theories of language learning: A constructive critique of some connectionist learning models. *Cognition, 28*, 195–247.

Li, P. (1993). Cryptotypes, form-meaning mappings, and overgeneralisations. In E. V. Clark (Ed.), *The Proceedings of the 24th Child Language Research Forum* (pp. 162–178). Center for the Study of Language and Information, Stanford University, CA.

Li, P. (1999). Generalisation, representation, and recovery in a self-organising feature-map model of language acquisition. In M. Hahn & S. C. Stoness (Eds.), *Proceedings of the 21st Annual Conference of the Cognitive Science Society* (pp. 308–313). Mahwah, NJ: Lawrence Erlbaum Associates, Inc.

Li, P. (2000). The acquisition of lexical and grammatical aspect in a self-organising feature-map model. In L. Gleitman & Aravind K. Joshi (Eds.), *Proceedings of the 22nd Annual Conference of the Cognitive Science Society* (pp. 304–309). Mahwah, NJ: Lawrence Erlbaum Associates, Inc.

Li, P., & Bowerman, M. (1998). The acquisition of lexical and grammatical aspect in Chinese. *First Language, 18*, 311–350.

Li, P., Burgess, C., & Lund, K. (2000). The acquisition of word meaning through global lexical co-occurrences. In E. V. Clark (Ed.), *Proceedings of the 30th Child Language Research Forum* (pp. 167–178). Center for the Study of Language and Information, Stanford University, CA.

Li, P., & MacWhinney, B. (1996). Cryptotype, overgeneralisation, and competition: A connectionist model of the learning of English reversive prefixes. *Connection Science, 8*, 3–30.

Li, P., & MacWhinney, B. (2002). PatPho: A phonological pattern generator for neural networks. *Behavior Research Methods, Instruments and Computers, 34*, 408–415.

Li, P., & Shirai, Y. (2000). *The acquisition of lexical and grammatical aspect.* Berlin: Mouton de Gruyter.

Ling, C., & Marinov, M. (1993). Answering the connectionist challenge. *Cognition, 49*, 267–290.

Lund, K., & Burgess, C. (1996). Producing high-dimensional semantic spaces from lexical co-occurrence. *Behavior Research Methods, Instruments, and Computers, 28*, 203–208.

MacWhinney, B. (1987). The competition model. In B. MacWhinney (Ed.), *Mechanisms of language acquisition* (pp. 249–308). Hillsdale, NJ: Lawrence Erlbaum Associates, Inc.

MacWhinney, B. (1998). Models of the emergence of language. *Annual Review of Psychology, 49*, 199–227.

MacWhinney, B. (2000). *The CHILDES project: Tools for analysing talk* (3rd ed). Hillsdale, NJ: Lawrence Erlbaum Associates, Inc.

MacWhinney, B. (2001). Lexicalist connectionism. In P. Broeder & J. M. Murre (Eds.), *Models of language acquisition: Inductive and deductive approaches* (pp. 9–32). Oxford: Oxford University Press.

MacWhinney, B., & Leinbach, J. (1991). Implementations are not conceptualisations: Revising the verb learning model. *Cognition, 40*, 121–157.

Marchand, H. (1969). *The categories and types of present-day English word-formation: A synchronic–diachronic approach*. Munich: C. H. Beck'sche Verlagsbuchhandlung.

Marcus, G., Pinker, S., Ullman, M., Hollander, M., Rosen, T., & Xu, F. (1992). Overregularisation in language acquisition. *Monographs of the Society for Research in Child Development, 57* (Serial No. 228).

McClelland, J., & Rumelhart, D. (1981). An interactive activation model of context effects in letter perception: Part 1. An account of the basic findings. *Psychological Review, 88,* 375–402.

Miikkulainen, R. (1993). *Subsymbolic natural language processing: An integrated model of scripts, lexicon, and memory*. Cambridge, MA: MIT Press.

Miikkulainen, R. (1997). Dyslexic and category-specific aphasic impairments in a self-organising feature map model of the lexicon. *Brain and Language, 59,* 334–366.

Miikkulainen, R. (1999). The DISLEX simulator (new version). Available online at http://www.cs.utexas.edu/users/nn/pages/software/dislex.2.1.tar.Z/

Mourelatos, A. (1981). Events, processes, and states. In P. Tedeschi & A. Zaenen (Eds.), *Syntax and semantics: Vol. 14. Tense and aspect*. New York: Academic Press.

Parsons, T. (1990). *Events in the semantics of English: A study in subatomic semantics*. Cambridge, MA: MIT Press.

Pinker, S. (1989). *Learnability and cognition: The acquisition of argument structure*. Cambridge, MA: MIT Press.

Pinker, S. (1991). Rules of language. *Science, 253,* 530–535.

Pinker, S. (1999). Out of the minds of babes. *Science, 283,* 40–41.

Pinker, S., & Prince, A. (1988). On language and connectionism: Analysis of a parallel distributed processing model of language acquisition. *Cognition, 28,* 73–193.

Plunkett, K., & Juola, P. (1999). A connectionist model of English past tense and plural morphology. *Cognitive Science*, 23, 463–490.

Plunkett, K., & Marchman, V. (1991). U-shaped learning and frequency effects in a multi-layered perceptron: Implications for child language acquisition. *Cognition, 38,* 43–102.

Plunkett, K., & Marchman, V. (1993). From rote learning to system building: Acquiring verb morphology in children and connectionist nets. *Cognition, 48,* 21–69.

Ritter, H., & Kohonen, T. (1989). Self-organising semantic maps. *Biological Cybernetics, 61,* 241–254.

Rohde, D., & Plaut, D. (1999). Language acquisition in the absence of explicit negative evidence: How important is starting small? *Cognition, 72,* 67–109.

Rumelhart, D., & McClelland, J. (1986). On learning the past tenses of English verbs. In J. McClelland, D. Rumelhart, and the PDP research group (Eds.), *Parallel distributed processing: Explorations in the microstructure of cognition* (Vol. II, pp. 216–271). Cambridge, MA: MIT Press.

Saffran, J., Aslin, R., & Newport, E. (1996). Statistical learning by 8-month-old infants. *Science, 274,* 1926–1928.

Saffran, J., Newport, E., Aslin, R., Tunick, R., & Barrueco, S. (1997). Incidental language learning: Listening (and learning) out of the corner of your ear. *Psychological Science, 8,* 101–105.

Seidenberg, M. (1997). Language acquisition and use: Learning and applying probabilistic constraints. *Science, 275,* 1599–1603.

Seidenberg, M., & MacDonald, M. (1999). A probabilistic constraints approach to language acquisition and processing. *Cognitive Science, 23,* 569–588.

Shirai, Y. (1998). The emergence of tense-aspect morphology in Japanese: Universal predisposition? *First Language, 18,* 281–309.

Shirai, Y., & Andersen, R. (1995). The acquisition of tense-aspect morphology: A prototype account. *Language, 71,* 743–762.

Slobin, D. (1985). Crosslinguistic evidence for the language-making capacity. In D. Slobin (Ed.),

The crosslinguistic study of language acquisition (Vol. 2, pp. 1157–1249). Hillsdale, NJ: Lawrence Erlbaum Associates, Inc.

Smith, C. (1983). A theory of aspectual choice. *Language, 59*, 479–501.

Spitzer, M. (1999). *The mind within the net: Models of learning, thinking, and acting*. Cambridge, MA: MIT Press.

Stephany, U. (1981). Verbal grammar in modern Greek early child language. In P. S. Dale & D. Ingram (Eds.), *Child language: An international perspective*. Baltimore, MD: University Park Press.

Whorf, B. (1956). A linguistic consideration of thinking in primitive communities. In J. B. Carroll (Ed.), *Language, thought, and reality* (pp. 65–86). Cambridge, MA: MIT Press.

CHAPTER FIVE

Connectionist modelling of lexical segmentation and vocabulary acquisition

Matt H. Davis
MRC Cognition and Brain Sciences Unit, Cambridge, UK

Words are the building blocks of language. Native speakers typically know tens of thousands of words, which they combine into sentences to communicate an indefinite number of possible messages. A significant question in understanding how infants learn language is therefore to understand how they acquire words. This chapter focuses on two of the obstacles facing children learning words—first, how they discover which sequences of speech sounds cohere to form words (lexical segmentation), and second, how they learn to associate sound sequences with meanings (vocabulary acquisition). The connectionist simulations presented in this chapter provide a modelling framework for these two aspects of language acquisition. Although the simulations fall short of the scale and complexity of the learning task faced by infants, they provide an explicit account of some of the sources of information that are available to infants and how this information might be deployed in learning.

Adults typically hear sentences in their native language as a sequence of separate words. We might assume that words in speech are physically separated in the way that they are perceived. However, when listening to an unfamiliar language we no longer experience sequences of discrete words, but rather hear a continuous stream of speech with boundaries separating individual sentences or utterances. Examination of the physical form of speech confirms the impression given by listening to foreign languages. Speech does not contain gaps or other unambiguous markers of word boundaries—there is no auditory analogue of the spaces between words in printed text (Lehiste,

1960). Thus the perceptual experience of native speakers reflects language-specific knowledge of ways in which to divide speech into words. An important set of questions, therefore, concerns the sources of information that are used for segmentation and how the need to segment the speech stream affects infants learning their first words.

The continuous nature of speech might not be a problem for infants learning language if they were "spoon-fed" with single-word utterances. However, while infant-directed speech contains exaggerations of many aspects of adult speech (e.g. distinctive intonation patterns; Fernald et al., 1989), child-directed speech does not primarily contain single word utterances. For instance in the Korman corpus (1984) less than a quarter of all utterances are single words. Furthermore, parents who are asked to teach their children new words, do not simply repeat single words to them (Aslin, Woodward, La Mendola, & Bever, 1996). Even if infants were taught isolated words, this would be poor preparation for perceiving connected speech where words are produced more quickly and with greater acoustic variation than in isolation (Barry, 1981). For these reasons, infants learning their first words must first learn to segment a stream of connected speech into smaller units that communicate meaning.

Theories of how adult listeners segment the speech stream into words emphasise the role that knowledge of individual words plays in the segmentation of speech. Most current models of spoken word recognition in adults propose that segmentation arises through the identification of words in connected speech. Either by using the recognition of words to predict the location of word boundaries (Cole & Jakimik, 1980; Marslen-Wilson & Welsh, 1978) or through processes of lexical competition which ensure that only words that make up a consistent segmentation of the speech stream are activated (McClelland & Elman, 1986; Norris, 1994).

However, since words cannot be learnt until the speech stream can be segmented, it seems unlikely that infants will be able to use word recognition to segment connected speech. For this reason, researchers have proposed a variety of strategies and cues that infants could use to identify word boundaries without being able to recognise the words that these boundaries delimit. This chapter describes some computational simulations proposing ways in which these cues and strategies for the acquisition of lexical segmentation can be integrated with the infants' acquisition of the meanings of words. The simulations reported here describe simple computational mechanisms and knowledge sources that may support these different aspects of language acquisition.

Modelling language acquisition

In creating computational models of language acquisition, a variety of approaches have been taken. As with the other chapters in the current volume, this chapter focuses on theories that have been implemented using artificial neural networks (connectionist models). The ability of neural networks to extract structure from noisy and probabilistic input suggests that these models provide a plausible account of learning processes that are at the heart of cognitive development. Although there has been some debate on whether learning algorithms such as back-propagation can be neurally instantiated in the brain (see, for example, Crick, 1989; O'Reilly, 1996) it is clear that "gradient-descent" learning algorithms provide more neurally plausible accounts of learning than accounts that propose symbolic systems (see Elman, Bates, Johnson, Karmiloff-Smith, Parisi, & Plunkett, 1996 for further discussion).

An important aspect of the computational modelling of psychological processes is to provide an account of the behavioural profile of language learners. Recent years have seen rapid advances in experimental methods for investigating the abilities of prelinguistic infants. These empirical data provide informative constraints on computational models of lexical segmentation and vocabulary acquisition and will be reviewed in the chapter. We begin by describing the pre-existing cognitive abilities that infants bring to these domains.

Prerequisites for language acquisition

By the age of 6 months, infants have begun to acquire knowledge that is specific to their native language. Although it has been shown that newborn infants are able to discriminate between utterances that differ by a single phoneme (Eimas, Siqueland, Jusczyk, & Vigorito, 1971), it is only at around 6 months of age that infants organise their phonetic categories in an adult-like manner. For instance, infants start to lose sensitivity to phonemic contrasts that are not used in their native language (Kuhl, Williams, Lacerda, Stevens, & Lindblom, 1992; Werker & Tees, 1984; and see Jusczyk, 1997, for a review). The ability to detect phonemic differences while ignoring other, noncontrastive differences provides an important first step towards language acquisition. Infants will be able to focus on those aspects of the speech signal that have the potential to convey meaning in their (soon-to-be) native language.

Similarly, children's knowledge of objects in the world around them shows rapid development during the first 6 months of life. By this age, infants have acquired knowledge of the physical properties of objects and their interactions, as shown by their performance on tests of object permanence and their correct predictions concerning the fate of colliding and occluded objects (Baillargeon, 1995; Mareschal, 2000 and Chapter 2).

A key problem in language acquisition can then be framed by asking how infants pair the sounds of their native language with objects and actions in the outside world.[1] This problem can be divided into two distinct aspects: (1) lexical segmentation, that is, how infants chunk speech into words; and (2) vocabulary acquisition, that is, how infants map those words onto objects and meanings. We will review experimental evidence and computational models relating to these aspects of the language acquisition problem.

THE ACQUISITION OF LEXICAL SEGMENTATION

In investigating the acquisition of lexical segmentation, researchers have focused on what knowledge infants have acquired about the structure of words in their native language. Two aspects of word structure that have been of primary interest are knowledge of frequently and infrequently occurring sequences of phonemes (phonotactics) and knowledge of the rhythmic alteration of stressed and unstressed syllables in words (metrical information). Both phonotactics and metrical stress have been invoked as cues that infants may use in beginning to segment the speech stream.[2]

Experimental investigations

Experimenters have used a head-turn preference procedure (Fernald, 1985) to evaluate infants knowledge of higher-level structure in spoken language. This procedure allows experimenters to compare the amount of time that infants remain interested in two sets of speech stimuli, as indicated by the duration of head-turns towards either of a pair of loudspeakers that present the stimuli. This measure of infants' preferences for a given speech stimulus can be used to infer that the infants tested are sensitive to differences that exist between the two sets of stimuli.

For example, Jusczyk, Cutler, and Redanz (1993a) showed that 9-month-old infants prefer listening to lists of bisyllabic words in which the two syllables of the word were stressed then unstressed (strong/weak words such as "butter" and "ardour") rather than words that followed the reverse pattern (weak/strong words like "between" or "arouse"). This preference is of

---

[1] Not all words in speech are content words; infants must also learn the role played by articles, prepositions and other function words in speech. However, for the purposes of the current chapter we will focus our attention solely on how infants learn their first words—typically concrete nouns.

[2] Our discussion of the use of metrical stress and phonotactic information focuses on cues that support word-boundary detection in English. One strength of the statistical mechanisms proposed here is that they may be sufficiently flexible to account for segmentation in other languages in which different phonotactic and metrical cues operate. For reasons of space, the current chapter will concentrate on lexical segmentation and vocabulary acquisition in English.

interest, since in "stress-timed" languages such as English, the majority of nouns start with a strong syllable (Cutler & Carter, 1987). Thus 9-month-old infants show a consistent preference for words with the more frequent strong/weak pattern. Since this pattern was not observed in 6-month-olds, it suggests that, between 6 and 9 months, infants learn something of the metrical structure of words in their native language.

A similar preference for more commonly occurring patterns has also been observed for phonotactic regularities—sequences of phonemes that are permitted or not permitted in a language. For instance, in English, the sequence of phonemes /br/ can occur at the start of a word like "bread" or "brief" but is not permitted at the end of word. Conversely, the sequence /nt/ can occur at the end of a word ("want", "tent") but not at the beginning of a word. These constraints are in many cases unique to a particular language, for instance, English does not permit the sequence /vl/ at the start of a word, whereas this sequence is commonly found at the start of words in Dutch or Russian.

Preferential listening experiments suggested that infants may use these phonotactic constraints to distinguish between languages. For instance, Jusczyk, Friederici, Wessels, Svenkerud and Jusczyk (1993b) demonstrated that 9-month-old infants prefer to listen to words in their native language (although this pattern was not shown at 6 months). Although both the Dutch and the English nouns used in this experiment typically have a strong/weak stress pattern, they have different constraints on legal and illegal phoneme sequences. These results therefore suggest that, by the age of 9 months, infants may be aware of the phonotactic properties of words in their native language. Further evidence for this proposal comes from Jusczyk, Luce, and Charles-Luce (1994), who observed that 9-month-old infants prefer to listen to lists of monosyllabic nonwords that contain high-frequency phoneme sequences (e.g. "chun") than to lists containing low-probability sequences (e.g. "yush").

Thus, by the age of 9 months, infants have acquired knowledge of the typical sound patterns (both metrical and phonotactic) of words in their native language. These findings indicate that infants have acquired some knowledge of words in their native language, and are significant for our understanding of lexical segmentation; both metrical stress and phonotactic information have been proposed as cues that could be used to break the speech stream into words. Research has therefore focused on whether infants can use this knowledge in segmenting words from longer utterances.

An extension to the head-turn preference procedure has allowed investigations of infants' abilities to segment words from connected speech (Jusczyk & Aslin, 1995; see Jusczyk, 1999, for a review). Infants are first familiarised with multiple repetitions of a word (either in a list of isolated words or as a word that is found in several unrelated sentences). In a subsequent test phase, infants are then presented with lists or sentences (whichever was not presented previously) containing the same or different words as the familiar-isation phase. The duration of head-turns towards the loudspeakers used to present each test stimulus provides a measure of familiarity. Any significant difference in listening times between the two stimuli provides evidence that infants retain knowledge of the familiarised word forms.

For instance, Jusczyk and Aslin (1995) showed that 7.5-month-old infants familiarised with repetitions of the word "cup" listen longer to sentences that contain "cup" than to sentences that do not contain this word. Similar results were also obtained when infants are tested with words when familiarised with sentences. In a follow-up experiment it was shown that infants at this age did not show an equivalent preference when familiarised with near neighbours of the test word (e.g. training on "tup" did not produce a listening preference for "cup"). Thus, infants of 7.5 months (but not 6-month-olds) are able to retain a detailed representation of the sound patterns of words in order to detect those same words subsequently. Further investigations have shown that infants retain some memory of these familiarised words in testing sessions 2 weeks after the initial familiarisation (Jusczyk & Hohne, 1997).

These findings demonstrate that infants are able to segment word forms from connected speech. An experiment carried out by Saffran and colleagues (Saffran, Aslin, & Newport, 1996) suggests one cue that appears to be used by infants to divide the speech stream into words. In this study, infants were presented with 2-minute sequences of synthetic speech composed of continu-ous repetitions of four different trisyllabic words (e.g. "tibudo" or "pabiku"). Since each syllable occurred in more than one word, infants would have to learn the order of syllables (as well as their identity) if they were to segment words from this continuous stream. Nonetheless, after only a few minutes of training, 8-month-old infants preferred to listen to words from the training set than words generated by combining the last syllable of one word with the first two syllables of another (e.g. "dopabi" or "kutibu"). Since the only information available to infants during training concerned which syllables followed others, Saffran and colleagues conclude that this information alone (transitional probabilities) was sufficient for infants to segment words from continuous sequences of speech.

Further evidence of the cues used by infants in detecting words in con-nected speech comes from experiments investigating infants familiarised with bisyllabic words with different stress patterns (Jusczyk, Houston, & New-some, 1999). A series of experiments demonstrated that 7.5-month-old infants were able to segment strong/weak bisyllables ("kingdom" or "ham-let") from sentences (showing a familiarity preference for these words but not related items like "king" or "ham"). However, infants at this age were still liable to mis-segment words with a weak/strong stress pattern; for example detecting the words "tar" and "vice" following familiarisation with words like "guitar" and "device". Furthermore, when these weak/strong items were followed by a consistent syllable (for example, if the word "guitar" always followed by "is" to make the weak/strong/weak sequence "guitaris") then the infants would tend to treat the strong/weak unit ("taris") as familiar rather than the word "guitar". These results indicate that sequential constraints on syllable sequences are combined with a strong bias towards assuming that metrically stressed syllables mark the start of a word.

Computational simulations of lexical segmentation

These experimental studies illustrate two forms of knowledge acquired during the first year of life that contribute to infants' ability to segment words from connected speech. Interpretations of these experimental findings have been enhanced by neural network models designed to simulate the means by which knowledge of phonotactics and metrical stress contributes to lexical segmentation.

For both metrical and phonotactic cues, simple models can be proposed in which the occurrence of a particular pattern of input can inform the placement of word boundaries. For instance, a sequence of phonemes like /mgl/ is unlikely to occur within a word in English, but can occur between words (such as in the sequence "same glove"). Knowledge of sequences of sounds that are unlikely to occur within a word therefore provides a cue that can be used to propose word boundaries in an otherwise unsegmented speech stream (Harrington, Watson, & Cooper, 1989). Similarly, since content words typically begin with a strong syllable placing a word boundary before fully stressed syllables would correctly segment many words in connected speech (Cutler & Carter, 1987; Cutler & Norris, 1988).

However, although these models can detect word boundaries in a stream of connected speech, neither will suffice as an account of how infants learn to use metrical or phonotactic cues. Since infants do not hear substantial numbers of single words in parental speech, computational accounts of the acquisition of lexical segmentation are faced with a bootstrapping problem. How could a system learn these or other cues to segmentation *without* prior knowledge of the location of word boundaries? Connectionist models of the acquisition of lexical segmentation have described two strategies that could be used to learn cues to the location of word boundaries without explicitly marked boundaries being present in the input.

Learning from utterance boundaries

One account of how infants' learn to segment connected speech is that they learn the metrical and phonotactic properties of word boundaries by generalising from the properties of boundaries between utterances (Aslin et al., 1996). Since there are consistent acoustic cues (e.g. pauses and changes in pitch) to indicate boundaries between utterances, infants can use these cues to identify word boundaries that fall at utterance boundaries. Infants can then use the metrical and phonotactic properties of utterance boundaries for the segmentation of words within utterances.

Aslin et al. (1996) presented a connectionist model that implemented this segmentation strategy. They trained a three-layer, feedforward neural network to map from phoneme trigrams to an output unit that was activated at boundaries between utterances. Input to the network was provided by a three-segment window that stepped through a corpus of child-directed speech one segment at a time. When exposed to a test corpus, the network activated the output unit not only at utterance boundaries but also at many word boundaries. With an appropriate threshold on the output, the network identified over half of the word boundaries in the test corpus. This network therefore learns to lexically segment connected speech by detecting trigrams that typically straddle boundaries between utterances.

The task of identifying utterance boundaries provides a psychologically plausible means by which infants could learn a trigram-based segmentation strategy similar to that proposed by Harrington et al. (1989). A system such as this could therefore account for results suggesting that infants are sensitive to phonotactic constraints on sequences that occur at the start and end of words (cf. Jusczyk et al., 1993b) by learning sequences that occur before or after an utterance boundary. However, other results in the experimental literature might prove more problematic for this model. For instance, Saffran et al. (1996) report that infants are able to detect words in a stream of speech that is presented without pauses or utterance boundaries.

Distributional accounts of segmentation

An alternative computational mechanism for acquiring segmentation operates by dividing the speech stream into frequently occurring sequences. It is assumed that these high-frequency sequences will form meaningful units or words, while infrequent phoneme sequences are likely to straddle a word boundary. Thus, the frequency and distribution of sound sequences can be used for lexical segmentation without requiring that word boundaries are explicitly marked in the input. This technique for dividing utterances into words was originally proposed as a technique for linguistic analysis by Harris (1955). More recently, this idea has been proposed as an account of how infants divide speech into words—under the catch-all term "distributional regularity" (Brent, 1999; Brent & Cartwright, 1996; Wolff, 1977).

As suggested above, these distributional approaches encompass two distinct but related strategies—grouping frequently occurring sequences to form words (a "synthetic" approach), and placing boundaries at infrequent transitions to break longer utterances into words (an "analytic" approach).

In symbolic computational systems, these distinct approaches could be implemented separately using different computational mechanisms (see Brent, 1999, for further discussion). However, recent connectionist simulations suggest that both approaches may be served by a single computational mechanism—the prediction of upcoming input.

One interesting implementation of this distributional approach involves training a neural network to predict subsequent phonemes based on the current and previous input. This prediction task is made easier if the next phoneme occurs within the same word as previous phonemes. For instance, following the sequence of phonemes /trɛs/, there are only two likely segments that could continue this sequence as a single word (/p/ in "trespass" or /l/ in "trestle"). However, if this same sequence of sounds occurred before a word boundary (for instance, at the end of the word "actress") then the following segments will be much less constrained. Thus, segment prediction will be much more accurate during a word than immediately before a word boundary.

One influential demonstration of this approach was reported by Elman (1990). A simple recurrent network was trained on this segment prediction task using a small artificial language, presented a segment at a time without word boundaries. Elman observed two properties of the network's output error on test sequences. First, the network's prediction error decreased later on in a word—as the current input matched fewer and fewer words in the network's vocabulary, future segments in the word could be predicted with greater accuracy. The network therefore acquired some knowledge of words in its training vocabulary. Elman's second observation was that prediction error increased sharply at the end of a word, as a result of the greater variety of phonemes that can occur after a word boundary. The predictability of segments therefore provides a metric not only for grouping segments into words but also for detecting word boundaries.

Models that include the prediction task have been suggested as an account of the experimental results of Saffran et al. (1996). In these experiments, infants became familiar with words from training sequences that are presented without boundaries between words or utterances. Infants learn that the sequences include groups of predictable syllables. Test sequences which contain whole words from the training set will therefore be more predictable (and hence more familiar) than sequences which combine parts of different words. Recurrent network simulations using similar materials have shown that models using the prediction task are able to simulate these experimental results (Allen & Christiansen, 1996).

Simulations reported by Cairns, Shillcock, Chater, and Levy (1997) extend these recurrent network prediction systems to a large corpus of phonologically transcribed conversations; scaling up the Elman (1990) simulations to a realistic input. Consistent with these earlier simulations they showed that error peaks in segment-prediction can be used to detect word boundaries in a test corpus. However, even when carefully optimised this system only detects 21 per cent of word boundaries. Although this is superior to chance performance it still falls short of the level of performance that would be required for word identification, especially as the network placed boundaries within many words (a hit:false-alarm ratio of 1.5:1). In describing the performance of their network, Cairns and colleagues suggested that boundaries were placed between phonotactically well-formed syllables rather than between words. Thus the lexical knowledge that was acquired in Elman's small-scale simulations may not scale-up to larger training sets.

Combining multiple cues for segmentation and identification

One way to improve the performance of segmentation systems is to incorporate more than one strategy for the detection of word boundaries (Christiansen, Allen, & Seidenberg, 1998). Christiansen et al. described simulations in which a simple recurrent network was trained with three cues that have been proposed for segmentation–utterance boundaries (cf. Aslin et al., 1996), phoneme prediction (cf. Elman, 1990), and metrical stress (cf. Cutler & Carter, 1987). These cues were presented to different networks either singly or in combination. Interestingly, the performance of networks trained on all three cues exceeded the performance of networks trained on single cues or pairs of cues. This combined system also out-performed the systems reported by Aslin et al. (1996), or Cairns et al. (1997), detecting 74 per cent of word boundaries, with a hit:false-alarm ratio of 2.3:1. Christiansen and colleagues propose that combining multiple cues is a particularly productive strategy for language acquisition in general and lexical segmentation in particular. Segmentations that are predicted by a single cue may be unreliable, whereas segmentations supported by multiple cues are more likely to correspond to true word boundaries in the input.

Nonetheless, this combined approach still falls short of segmenting all words in the speech stream. As might be expected, a system that detects less than three quarters of word boundaries still fails to segment half of all words from connected speech. Furthermore, the lexical effects observed for small vocabulary recurrent network models (Elman, 1990) were still not observed. Christiansen et al., (1998) reported that the prediction error reflected knowledge of phonological clusters that occurred in many words in the training set, and did not capture specific phoneme sequences that occurred in any single lexical item.

Thus, despite the potential for systems trained on prediction tasks to learn sequences corresponding to individual lexical items, it is clear that for realistically sized vocabularies these systems do not segment the speech stream by storing chunks of speech as familiar words. It is possible that the prediction task does not place sufficient demands on these networks to retain information from early time-points (since local information may be sufficient to predict subsequent segments). Alternatively, some more fundamental limitations on the memory capacity of recurrent neural networks for learning long-distance dependencies provide the limiting factor on the performance of these systems (see, for instance, Maskara & Noetzel, 1993; Servan-Schrieber, Cleeremans, & McClelland, 1991; and Chapter 6 for further discussion).

In view of these limitations, computational models of how infants begin to acquire and store word forms have mostly proposed symbolic systems that determine the most likely (i.e. maximum probability) set of words in an utterance (Brent, 1999; Brent & Cartwright, 1996). Sections of speech that have been hypothesised to be words are stored and reused to segment subsequent utterances. Although this approach successfully simulates how infants discover words in connected speech, unrealistic assumptions are made regarding the computational resources available to infants. In particular these algorithms require: (1) an unbounded and undecaying memory for storing potential vocabulary items; (2) pre-existing mechanisms to compensate for the noise and variability that exists in all speech; and, in some cases (3) built-in knowledge of phonotactic constraints on viable and nonviable segmentations. The increased effectiveness of these models therefore comes at some cost to their psychological plausibility.

One goal of the computational account developed here is to explore the potential for recurrent neural networks to not only simulate the development of lexical segmentation but also to account for the identification of lexical items and the acquisition of the mapping from spoken word forms to meaning. These simulations allow us to explore whether the failure to observe lexical effects in recurrent networks reflects an intrinsic limitation of the processing capacities of these neural network models or, simply, that alternative cues or learning strategies are required. Given this interest in vocabulary acquisition we will review the developmental literature concerning how infants learn to map from word forms to meaning.

VOCABULARY ACQUISITION

Infants face a number of difficult problems in learning how words are paired with meaning. From a philosophical perspective, a single new word could denote a potential infinity of referents (Quine, 1960). For instance, a child learning the pairing between the word "rabbit" and a furry stuffed toy may be unclear whether the word refers to the whole animal, a part of the animal, or indeed some entity that is not present in the current scene. A variety of strategies have been proposed to account for infants' ability to learn language in spite of this seemingly intractable problem—for instance, cues that help infants determine the likely referents of words that they hear.

For example, experiments on how infants categorise objects that are accompanied by novel words suggest a bias towards assuming that new words refer to whole, bounded objects rather than to other possible referents such as parts of these objects, the materials from which they are made, their colour, and so on (Waxman & Markow, 1996). It is unclear whether this bias reflects the operation of a constraint that is specifically tuned to detecting those aspects of the environment that have been labelled linguistically, or whether infants share with adults a more general bias towards treating objects in the world as salient (Bloom, 1994). Nonetheless, since many of the earliest words that are learnt by infants refer to concrete nouns (Fenson et al., 1994) this bias is apparent in early language acquisition even if the precise cause remains unclear.

Another source of constraint that infants could use to help determine the possible referents of words in connected speech is to pay attention to nonverbal cues. For instance, by observing the direction of gaze of the speaker or other forms of "pointing" behaviour infants are provided with cues to the referents of an utterance even in the absence of any comprehension of the linguistic label. Infants appear to use this cue from an early age in determining the objects to which words in speech refer (Baldwin, 1991, 1993).

Mapping from speech to meaning

These and other strategies assist the infant in determining the meanings of unknown words and will therefore reduce the number of possible target meanings for the words that they hear. However, learning the speech-to-meaning mapping cannot be reduced to a simple one-to-one association. On any occasion on which more than one word is spoken (i.e. for the majority of the utterances heard by infants) there will be more than one word that can be learnt and therefore more than one target referent for the words in that utterance. For instance, infants' experience of the word "cat" may arise from multiple-word utterances like "look at the fat cat", "that cat is sitting on the fence again", "does the cat need feeding?" A one-to-one mapping between the sounds of words and their meanings is not specified in the learning environment, but must be discovered by infants. An important question therefore remains: how is it that children discover the one-to-one correspondence that exists between sequences of sounds and their referents to associate the word /kæt/ with the furry animal to which this word commonly refers?

One proposal concerning how infants discover these one-to-one correspondences is that they will analyse multiple utterances and make use of the word–meaning pairings that these different utterances have in common. This very general idea of "cross-situational learning" has been proposed by many authors, including Pinker (1989) and Gleitman (1994). Symbolic models of vocabulary acquisition have included a more formal description of algorithms that permit these cross-situational inferences (Siskind, 1996). However, connectionist models of early vocabulary acquisition have so far not considered the problems that are involved in discovering word form to meaning mappings. Existing connectionist models of early vocabulary acquisition (such as Plaut & Kello, 1998; Plunkett, Sinha, Møller, & Strandsby, 1992) have focused on other issues and have therefore used training sets in which word forms and word meanings are paired on a one-to-one basis. The simulations conducted here investigate the acquisition of one-to-one mappings between words and meanings without requiring that these correspondences are explicitly specified in the training set.

Experimental investigations of early vocabulary acquisition

In specifying mechanisms for learning the mapping from words to meaning, it might be expected that infants build on their pre-existing linguistic knowledge. As reviewed previously, a variety of sources of evidence have demonstrated infants' acquisition of language-specific knowledge during the second half of their first year of life. In particular, evidence has suggested that, at the age of 7.5 months, infants are first able to isolate and recognise single words from connected speech (Jusczyk & Aslin, 1995). The age at which infants develop the ability to relate words to meanings is largely consistent with the assumption that vocabulary acquisition begins after infants are able to segment words from connected speech.

Investigators have used preferential looking procedures to derive evidence of infants' earliest comprehension of the meanings of words. Typically, infants are presented with an array of two or more objects and their tendency to fixate a particular object if an appropriate name is produced is compared with fixations following a novel or unfamiliar word (Oviatt, 1980; Thomas, Campos, Shucard, Ramsay, & Shucard, 1981). This method has shown comprehension of words for concrete objects in infants as young as 13 months. However, as this method is susceptible to biases arising from infants' visual preferences (e.g. a preference for fixating objects for which a name is known; Schafer, Plunkett, & Harris, 1999) only cautious conclusions should be drawn from these comparisons. More robust evidence is obtained from experiments comparing preferences for looking at appropriate versus inappropriate objects where names for both objects are known. With this more careful procedure, the age of earliest comprehension is raised to approximately 15 months (Golinkoff, Hirsh-Pasek, Cauley, & Gordon, 1987). These results are consistent with the earliest estimates of when infants can be shown to learn novel pairings between words and objects (Schafer & Plunkett, 1998).

Such demonstrations require that infants are taught two novel names for two novel objects (avoiding confounding effects of pre-existing familiarity with either words or concepts and hence confounding biases). Under these tightly controlled conditions, 15-month-old infants show learning of new names such as "bard" and "sarl" for photographs of two novel objects after only 12 pairings of the word and the concept.

One important issue for investigations of spoken word recognition concerns how word forms are represented and how those representations are activated during comprehension. It has been suggested that infants' representations of their first words are not structured in an adult-like, segmental fashion, but may comprise holistic, whole-word representations (Walley, 1993). Infants may only structure their word representations using individual phonemes (e.g. storing "cat" as /kæt/) when their vocabulary has reached a sufficient size for other neighbouring words such as "rat", "kit", and "cap" to be known (Charles-Luce & Luce, 1995).

Experimental evidence concerning the time course of word identification in children, however, has cast doubt on the holistic representations proposed by Walley (1993). Investigations of the timing of eye movements towards the referents of heard words (Fernald, Pinto, Swingley, Weinberg, & McRoberts, 1998) have demonstrated that during the second year of life, infants become increasingly skilled at mapping the sounds of speech onto their meanings. Between 15 and 24 months infants' fixations of pictures referred to by spoken words become increasingly rapid—despite little evidence of developmental changes in the speed with which saccadic eye movements can be programmed and executed. Fernald and colleagues (1998) have shown that, by 24 months of age, infants can initiate a saccade towards the appropriate picture before the acoustic offset of a word. This finding suggests that infants, like adults, can identify words at the earliest point at which sufficient information becomes available in the speech stream (see Marslen-Wilson, 1984, for a discussion).

This theory is further supported by experiments reported by Swingley, Pinto, and Fernald (1999) showing that this rapid and efficient word processing is accompanied by an adult-like time course of identification. In 24-month-old infants, fixations to target pictures are delayed for stimuli in which two competing items share their initial sound (e.g. "tree" and "truck"), exactly as predicted by accounts of spoken recognition in which speech processing keeps track with the speech stream. Even with the small receptive vocabularies typical of infants at this age, these results suggest that word representations during early stages of acquisition are organised as sequences of phonemes and processed incrementally—consistent with the sequential processes observed in adult listeners (Marslen-Wilson & Welsh, 1978).

The goal of the simulations reported here is to investigate connectionist networks that can account for the developmental profile that has been observed in the literature on lexical segmentation and vocabulary acquisition. Any psychologically plausible account must fit two primary requirements: (1) the system must simulate the behavioural profile that has been observed in infants; and (2) the model must make realistic assumptions concerning the processing mechanisms and sources of information that are available to infants.

Computational models of spoken word identification

The task of recognising words in connected speech can be described as a mapping from sequences of input representing the sounds of speech to a lexical/semantic representation of the word or words contained in the speech stream. Recurrent network models of this mapping (Gaskell & Marslen-Wilson, 1997; Norris, 1990) simulate the time course of word iden-tification for adult listeners as a continuous process in which the activation of lexical representations responds immediately to incoming information in the speech signal. In training these recurrent networks, the target represen-tation is specified throughout the word, irrespective of whether sufficient information is available in the input at that time. Thus the network is fre-quently given an impossible task—to identify words from only their initial segments. The effect of this time pressure, however, is to ensure that in testing the network the appropriate lexical representation is activated as soon as sufficient information becomes available. Input sequences that are consistent with more than one word lead the network to activate multiple lexical representations in proportion to the probability that they represent the current word in the speech stream. For example, in response to the sequence of sounds /kæptɪ/, lexical representations for "captain" and "cap-tive" will be partially activated. At the offset of /kæptɪn/, when the input matches only a single word, the appropriate lexical representation is fully activated.

An important limitation of these simulations was revealed by Norris (1990, 1994). Specifically, these networks have problems in recognising short words embedded at the start of longer words (such as the word "cap" that is embedded in "captain"). At the offset of the syllable /kæp/, the network will activate short words and longer competitors equally. For a sequence like "cap fits", in which a longer word can be ruled out, the network uses the following context to identify the subsequent word (activating lexical items that begin with /f/ such as "fits", "feels", etc.), but is unable to use this input to revise its interpretation of the syllable /kæp/. Thus onset-embedded words like "cap" remain ambiguous and cannot be identified by the network.

One solution to this problem is to allow speech input arriving after the offset of a word to play a role in the identification of previous words in the speech stream. In models such as TRACE (McClelland & Elman, 1986) or Shortlist (Norris, 1994) this is achieved by incorporating inhibitory connections between lexical candidates, such that information arriving later on in the speech stream can affect the lexical activation of earlier words. However, these inhibitory connections are hard-wired in TRACE or dynamically rewired in Shortlist. It is at present unclear how this additional competition mechanism can be incorporated into a network trained by back-propagation or some other gradient-descent algorithm.

A further limitation of these recurrent network models as an account of development is that the training procedure assumes that a one-to-one correspondence between speech stream and lexical/semantic representations is available in the learning environment. The network is provided with a target representation that, at every time-step in the input, specifies the appropriate lexical/semantic representation for the current word. This training regime requires not only that word boundaries are specified beforehand but also, and more importantly, that a target lexical representation can be assigned to each word in the speech stream. The assumption that is implicit in this training procedure is that infants are supplied with the one-to-one relationship between words and meanings prior to vocabulary acquisition. This is exactly analogous to the one-to-one pairings that we described as unrealistic in some connectionist models of vocabulary acquisition (Plaut & Kello, 1998; Plunkett et al., 1992). These models all assume that words are learnt by a process of ostensive definition by which infants hear a single-word utterance and are directed to the meaning of that word. As we described previously, this situation does not capture crucial aspects of the learning problem faced by infants.

The recurrent network simulations that are explored here demonstrate that a very simple change to the training assumptions of the model provides a solution to both of these limitations of previous recurrent network simulations. Providing a recurrent network with a more developmentally plausible training set (i.e. not including one-to-one correspondences between speech and meaning) results in a system that is able to identify all the words in the training set, including onset-embedded words. To compensate for the increased complexity produced by removing these one-to-one correspondences we make an extreme, simplifying assumption that the meaning of each word in a sequence can be represented by a single, lexical node. Although this assumption is clearly false—the meanings of individual words vary considerably depending on context and therefore cannot be represented by a single, fixed representation—this assumption can in part be justified by suggesting that for the names of concrete objects (which form the heart of infants' early vocabularies), a categorical representation of certain classes of concrete concepts may be available to infants prior to vocabulary acquisition (see, for example, Quinn, Eimas, & Rosenkrantz, 1993).

SIMULATION 1: LEARNING TO IDENTIFY WORDS IN CONNECTED SPEECH

This simulation explores the effect of altering the training task for a recurrent network model of spoken word identification. Whereas previous models (e.g. Gaskell & Marslen-Wilson, 1997; Norris, 1990) were trained to activate a representation of the current word in the input, the networks presented here are trained to activate a representation of an entire sequence of words. The network must maintain an active representation of all the words that have been heard until the end of an utterance. By extending the network's task so that it must continue to activate an identified word after its acoustic offset, we can ensure that the system can resolve the temporary ambiguities created by onset-embedded words.

Since the network is trained using a fixed target representation for an entire sequence of words this training regime no longer includes a one-to-one pairing of words and their meanings. Instead, the network is exposed to a variety of word sequences paired with a target representation in which all the words in each sequence are activated. The task of the network is to uncover the set of one-to-relationships that best captures the contribution of each input word to the target representation (cf. Goldowsky & Newport, 1993; Roy & Pentland, 2002; Siskind, 1996). This training assumption is analogous to the cross-situational learning proposed by Pinker (1989) and Gleitman (1994).

A similar approach to language comprehension is described by St John and McClelland (1990) for a model in which the goal of the comprehension system is to activate a "sentence gestalt" capturing the meaning and thematic relationships between words in sentences. The output representation used in the current simulations is simpler than that used by St John and McClelland (1990) because it employs localist units, each representing the meaning of a single word in the network's vocabulary. Although structured as discrete lexical units, this aspect of the model is intended as a computational convenience rather than as an integral part of the account. Distributed output representations would provide a more realistic account since the network would then be forced to extract a consistent lexical/semantic representation from the noisy and contextually variable meanings of words in different sequences. However, this change to the model would greatly increase the amount of computer time required to train the networks without substantially altering the behavioural profile of the simulation, except for circumstances in which multiple items were very weakly activated (see Gaskell & Marslen-Wilson, 1999, for illustrative simulations and further discussion).

A further advantage of the localist output representations used here is that they avoid the binding problem that is incurred in combining existing representations of single words to produce a distributed representations of a sequence (see Page, 2000; Sougné, 1998, for further discussion). More complex representation schemes such as temporal binding (Shastri & Ajjanagadde, 1993) or tensor-product binding (Smolensky, 1990) have been proposed to allow the use of distributed representations that can represent multiple words simultaneously without interference. However, these more complex output representation would further increase the size and complexity of the simulations. The networks presented here provide a simple demonstrations of the computational properties of recurrent networks without requiring a solution to this contentious issue. However, these simulations must therefore come with the caveat that scaling-up to more realistic semantic representations may present additional problems.

Method

A simple recurrent network (Elman, 1990) was used for these simulations. The network was trained with back-propagation to map from sequences of distributed representations of phonemes (as sets of binary phonetic features) to an unordered localist representation of all the words in each sequence. This training target remains static throughout each sequence of words so that the network is not provided with any information about the location of word boundaries, nor which segments in the input map onto individual lexical items. The network must extract the one-to-one correspondences between speech and lexical items from this many-to-many mapping.

The training sequences for the network were generated from an artificial language with 7 consonants and 3 vowels placed in CVC syllables. This language contained 20 lexical items (14 monosyllables and 6 bisyllables), which varied in the segment at which they became unique from other words. This word set included "cohort" pairs (such as "lick" and "lid" that shared onsets), onset-embedded words ("cap" and "captain") and offset-embedded words ("lock" and "padlock"). Words were selected at random (without replacement) to create sequences between 2 and 4 words in length. Individual sequences were separated by a boundary marker (an input and output vector of zeros). Ten networks were trained from different sets of random initial weights and with different random sequences using back-propagation of error ($r = .02$, no momentum, cross-entropy output error; see Davis, Gaskell, & Marslen-Wilson, 1997, for more details) until output error stabilised (500,000 training sequences). The architecture of the network and a snapshot of activations during training is shown in Figure 5.1.

Results

Figure 5.2 shows the activation of lexical units for an illustrative test sequence averaged over 10 fully trained networks. The network activates words as their constituent segments are presented at the input. Lexical units

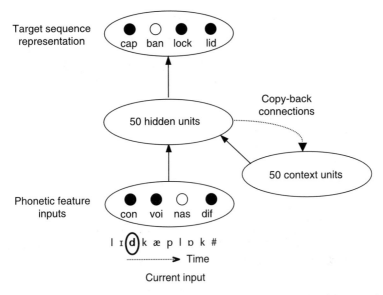

Figure 5.1.   Simple recurrent network architecture used for simulation 1, showing a snapshot of training activations during the segment /d/ in the sequence "*lid cap lock*". Throughout each training sequence, the target for the network is to activate a representation of all the words in the sequence, not just the current word. Solid arrows show trainable connections, the dotted arrow shows fixed one-to-one connections that store a copy of the hidden-unit activations at the previous time-step.

are partially activated in cases of ambiguity (for example "lick" is partially activated by the onset of "lid"), with the output activation approximating the conditional probability of each word being present in the input sequence. Full activation is consequently only observed when words are uniquely speci-fied in the input. In contrast to previous recurrent network simulations the network is also able to identify onset-embedded words, by using segments in the onset of the following word to rule out longer competitors. For example, in Figure 5.2 the word "cap" is identified only when information in the onset of the following syllable (/l/ from "lock") rules out the longer word "captain". Thus the network can resolve the temporary ambiguity created by onset-embedded words (see Davis, Gaskell, & Marslen-Wilson, 1997; Davis, Marslen-Wilson, & Gaskell, 2002, for further discussion).

Since this model is intended to account for the development of spoken-word identification in infants, it is important that the developmental profile is assessed. The performance of each network was therefore tested after every 5000 training sequences; measuring the network's ability to recognise indi-vidual words in test sequences. A word was considered to be "recognised" if at some point during the input sequence, the network activated the

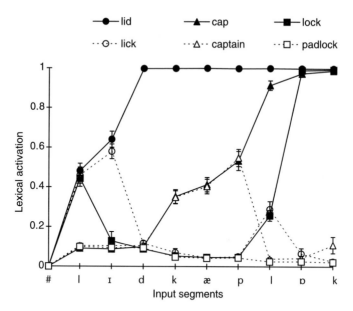

Figure 5.2. Lexical activation for target words and competitors during the sequence "*lid cap lock*" averaged over 10 fully trained networks from simulation 1. Error bars show ±1 standard error.

appropriate output unit to a value 0.5 higher than all other competitors.[3] To simplify the test procedure, only responses to the first word in a sequence were considered in this analysis. Results were averaged over every possible two-word sequence (19 sequences for each word) in each of the 10 networks.

The network's recognition performance throughout training is shown in Figure 5.3. As can be seen, it shows a rapid growth in recognition performance. This vocabulary spurt (as in other acquisition models, e.g. Plunkett et al., 1992) may be analogous to the rapid increase in the number of words that infants comprehend that is typically observed during the second year of life (Fenson, Dale, Reznick, Bates, Thal, & Perthick, 1994).

A more interesting question is whether the network shows the same gains in the speed of word identification as shown in eye-movement data by Fernald et al. (1998). Although these gains in performance may appear unsurprising—after all, infants show improvements on a range of tasks as they get older—this increased speed of identification is accompanied by an increase in the number of similar sounding words that infants know. Word identification will therefore require more fine-grained discriminations for

---

[3] This value provides a suitable threshold to ensure that only correct identifications are made. Results showed a similar pattern (when false identifications were excluded) with a lower threshold.

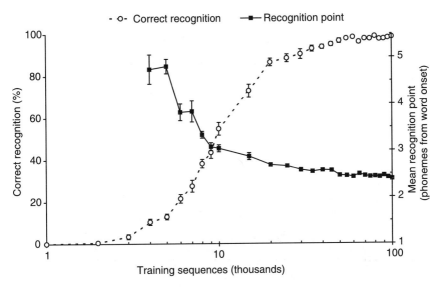

Figure 5.3.   Correct recognition (left axis) and recognition point (right axis) throughout training. Results averaged over 10 networks from simulation 1. Error bars show ±1 standard error.

older infants with larger vocabularies. The activation of lexical competitors has been shown to delay word identification in adults (see Monsell & Hirsh, 1998, for relevant experimental data and further discussion); it is therefore of interest to observe whether the network also shows improvements in the speed of word identification when rapid increases in vocabulary size are seen.

A measure was therefore taken of the time at which individual words are identified by the network. These recognition points were calculated as the exact number of phonemes (starting from word onset) at which an activation threshold was achieved (output activation should be 0.5 greater for the target word than for competitors). As in Gaskell and Marslen-Wilson (1997), we used linear interpolation between activations at successive segments to improve the accuracy of identification points, although near-identical results were obtained without interpolation. The mean recognition point throughout the training of 10 networks is shown in Figure 5.3. As can be seen, the networks show marked changes in the speed with which words can be identified throughout vocabulary acquisition. Recognition points become substantially earlier with increased training, consistent with the experimental data reported by Fernald et al. (1998) and despite increases in the size of the networks' receptive vocabulary (i.e. improved recognition performance).

Recognition points were also computed for two subsets of the items in the network that had different lexical environments. As shown in Figure 5.4, cohort competitors (pairs that share their initial CV, like "lick" and "lid") are identified at a later phoneme than words that have an equivalent phonemic

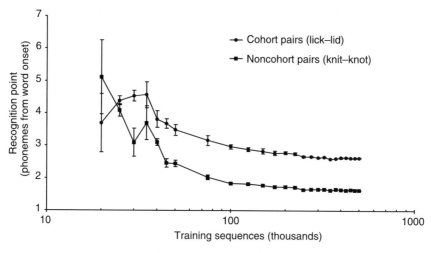

Figure 5.4.   Recognition point for items with cohort competitors (sharing consonant and vowel, e.g. *lick–lid*) and items without cohort competitors (e.g. *knit–knot*) in simulation 1. Results averaged over 10 networks. Error bars show ±1 standard error.

overlap, but do not share an initial CV (e.g. "bat" and "cat"). This result is consistent with the experimental data presented by Swingley, Pinto & Fernald (1999) in which identification of pairs like "truck" and "tree" that share an onset is delayed in comparison with rhyming pairs like "duck" and "truck".

Interestingly, the advantage for noncohort pairs is not observed at the earliest time points at which these items are recognised (i.e. before approximately 40,000 training sequences—a point at which only around 30 per cent of words are correctly identified). It may be that early on in training these networks do not use sequential information to rule out mismatching items in the same way as at later stages of development when words can be identified with greater accuracy. This prediction that cohort effects only emerge once word recognition is reasonably reliable could be tested experimentally were it possible to repeat the experiments of Swingley et al. (1999) with younger infants.

Discussion

This model provides an effective simulation of the time course of identification of words in sequences—progressively updating lexical activations as more input is presented. Unlike previous recurrent network accounts (Gaskell & Marslen-Wilson, 1997; Norris, 1990) the model is able to resolve temporarily ambiguous input for sequences in which post-offset information is required—as is the case for onset-embedded words like "cap" in "captain". The developmental profile shown by this model is suggestively similar to the profile shown by infants during vocabulary acquisition. The network shows gains in the speed of word processing during a period of rapid learning, consistent with the advances shown by infants during the second year of life.

One important difference between these simulations and previous recurrent network accounts of spoken word recognition is the use of a training set in which the input is not segmented into words and in which the output representation does not have prespecified correspondences with the speech input. In these simulations the target representation provides only the identity of the words contained in an utterance; the networks are not provided with information on the order in which words occur or the location of boundaries between words. By generalising from experience of different input sequences and activated output units, the network learns the set of one-to-one correspondences between the speech stream and lexical representations. At least for the artificial language investigated here, input–output correspondences (analogous to regularities in the mapping from word form to word meaning) provide a cue that the network can use to segment and identify words in connected speech.

Although the networks in simulation 1 learn to segment the speech input into lexical items by detecting these input–output correspondences, this is clearly not the only means by which the speech stream can be divided into words. These networks come to the task of vocabulary acquisition without any knowledge of words and word boundaries in connected speech—an assumption that is unlikely to be true for the developing infant. A range of evidence has already been reviewed suggesting that, by the end of the first year of life, infants have considerable knowledge of their native language at their disposal (e.g. phonotactics, metrical stress) that they can use as cues to identify the boundaries between words. This evidence questions one of the assumptions made in simulation 1—namely, that the speech input is unsegmented prior to lexical acquisition. Further simulations were therefore carried out to explore how infants' abilities to segment the speech stream may contribute to vocabulary acquisition in this model.

SIMULATION 2: COMBINING PHONOLOGICAL LEARNING AND VOCABULARY ACQUISITION

The success of the distributional accounts of lexical segmentation that were reviewed previously suggests that simple, statistical mechanisms play an important role in discovering the boundaries between words. Two developmentally plausible mechanisms were described which allow connectionist networks to discover the location of word boundaries—generalising from the properties of utterance boundaries (Aslin et al., 1996) and using prediction error to determine sections of the speech stream that cohere as words or are likely to contain a word boundary (Cairns et al., 1997; Elman, 1990).

Simulations have also shown that the combination of these two strategies produces more accurate segmentation than either approach alone (Christiansen et al., 1998).

Given the success of these statistical mechanisms in detecting the boundaries between words, and the segmentation abilities of infants in their first year of life (before vocabulary acquisition), it is of interest to investigate whether similar computational mechanisms might benefit the connectionist model of vocabulary acquisition presented here. It is likely that a system provided with information concerning the location of word boundaries would be more successful at learning associated speech and meaning than a system without this information. However, the second set of simulations asked a different question—namely, whether providing the network with *mechanisms* previously shown to support the learning of cues to word boundaries will assist the acquisition of word–meaning correspondences.

Method

The approach taken here was to retrain the networks from simulation 1, adding an additional set of output units that predict future input segments and utterance boundaries. By comparing the developmental profile of networks trained with this prediction task with the results of simulation 1, the role of distributional analysis in vocabulary acquisition can be explored. Ten networks were therefore trained using the same network architecture, learning parameters, and randomly generated training sets as the 10 previous simulations. Those weights common to the two sets of networks (i.e. connections from input to hidden units, recurrent hidden-unit connections and connections linking the hidden units to the output) were initialised to the same random values. The one change to the network was to add a set of output units that were trained to activate a representation of the input segment or utterance boundary (an output vector of zeros) that would be presented at the next time-step. The only difference between the two sets of simulations was the presence of the additional prediction output in simulation 2. A depiction of the network during training is shown in Figure 5.5.

Results and discussion

Inspection of the lexical output of 10 fully trained networks that used the prediction task showed an identical behavioural profile to that reported for simulation 1 and illustrated in Figure 5.2. The network identifies words in speech as they are presented in the input and those lexical items remain active until the end of the current utterance. More interesting results, however, are obtained in the comparison of the network's profile during training. The analysis of the network's recognition performance was again conducted after

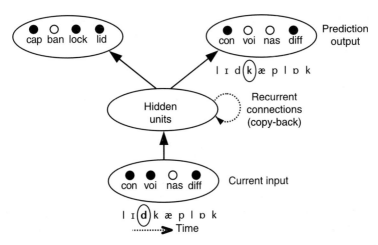

Figure 5.5. Simple recurrent network architecture used for simulation 2, showing a snapshot of training activations during the segment /d/ in the sequence "*lid cap lock*". The network is identical to simulation 1 (Figure 5.1) except for the addition of output units trained to predict the input at the next time step.

every 5000 training sequences, and performance was compared with results from simulation 1. Figure 5.6 shows the average performance of 10 networks trained with and without the prediction task, comparing percentage correct recognition (Figure 5.6(a)) and recognition points (Figure 5.6(b)).

As can be seen in Figure 5.6(a), the addition of the prediction task significantly speeds lexical acquisition. Comparing the results of simulations 1 and 2 shows that networks trained with the prediction task recognise more words than networks that receive the same amount of training without the prediction task. Thus, vocabulary acquisition in the network is significantly speeded by the addition of the prediction task. Furthermore, comparison of the recognition points depicted in Figure 5.6(b) indicates that networks trained with the prediction task not only recognise more words, but also recognise them more rapidly than the equivalent network trained in simulation 1.

Both sets of output units in simulation 2 (prediction task and lexical identification) are trained concurrently, using the same set of hidden units, learning algorithm and parameters. However, the network may not be learning the two tasks at the same rate. To compare the networks' learning profile on each of these tasks, root mean square (RMS) output error (normalised for the number of units in each portion of the output) was measured at each set of output units for a test set presented every 5000 sequences during training (Figure 5.7).

Root mean square error measures for networks in simulation 2 suggest that the prediction task is learnt more rapidly than the lexical task. Learning in the prediction task is mostly complete after 10,000 sequences, and reaches

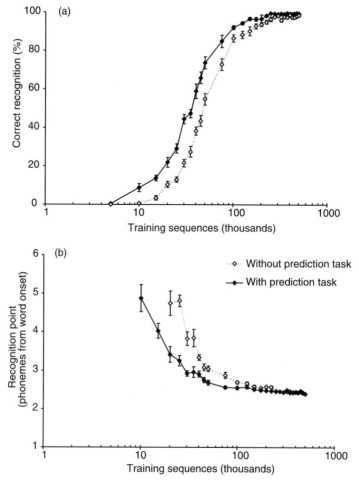

Figure 5.6. (a) Correct recognition and (b) recognition point for networks trained with (simulation 2) and without (simulation 1) the prediction task. Results averaged over 10 networks in each simulation. Error bars show ±1 standard error.

asymptote at around 25,000 sequences, whereas lexical learning continues until later in training. The network's performance on the prediction task provides evidence that it has learnt something of the structure of the artificial speech input before being able to map the speech input onto the correct lexical output.

This time course of acquisition is similar to the pattern observed in the developmental literature. As described previously, infants become sensitive to statistical aspects of speech input during the first year of life. By the age of 9 months, infants prefer listening to stimuli that follow the typical sound

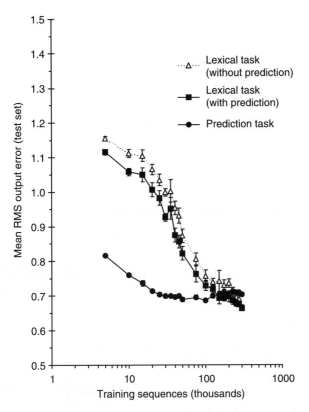

Figure 5.7. Root mean square (RMS) output error for the both output tasks from simulation 2 (lexical task with prediction task and prediction task) compared to output error for simulation 1 (lexical task). Results averaged over 10 networks. Error bars show ±1 standard error.

pattern of words in their native language (e.g. words containing high-frequency phonotactic sequences or a strong/weak stress pattern). It is exactly these forms of knowledge that are encoded by networks performing the prediction task (cf. Cairns et al., 1997). Therefore, learning the prediction task may be sufficient for the network to account for infants' knowledge of phonotactics and metrical stress. However, despite early acquisition of the form of words in their native language, it is only during the second year that infants readily associate words with the objects to which they refer. In these simulations it is proposed that vocabulary acquisition is modelled by the lexical output task. Thus the developmental profile observed in these combined simulations is broadly consistent with that observed in infants; lexical learning continues on from earlier phonological learning.

An important question concerns how it is that the addition of the prediction task assists the network in learning to recognise words. To pursue this issue, hidden-unit representations developed by networks trained with and without the prediction task were compared. One informative measure is the amount that hidden-unit activations change between successive segments in the input, that is the distance that the hidden-unit representations change at each time-step. The Euclidean distance between hidden-unit representations for successive input segments was calculated for the set of 10 networks trained with and without the prediction task. These distance measures were averaged for two types of segment position in the input: (1) between segments that occur within the same word; and (2) between segments that cross a word boundary. These results, averaged over the 10 networks trained in simulations 1 and 2 are shown in Figure 5.8.

Results indicate that, throughout training, networks with the additional prediction task made larger steps through hidden-unit space in processing the input. Furthermore, for those networks trained with the prediction task, hidden-unit representations changed more within words than across word boundaries. This effect of segment position on movement through the networks' hidden-unit space is particular apparent at the beginning of training. Even at the earliest test phase, networks trained with the prediction task process sections of the input that occur within words differently from sections that cross word boundaries (i.e. they show signs of having lexically segmented the input sequences). Networks from simulation 1 that were trained only on the lexical task did not show an equivalent difference in processing input within and between words.

Thus the inclusion of the prediction task enables the networks to develop

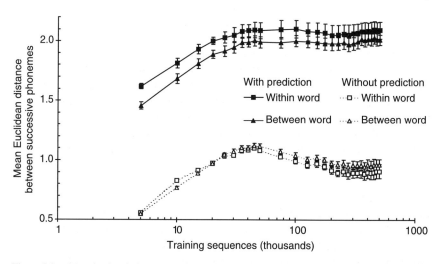

Figure 5.8. Magnitude of change (Euclidean distance) in hidden-unit states within words and between words for networks trained without the prediction task (simulation 1) and with a prediction task (simulation 2). Results averaged over 10 networks. Error bars show ±1 standard error.

a more structured internal representations of the speech input. Phonological learning provided by the prediction task serves to "bootstrap" lexical acquisition by chunking the speech input into units that potentially correspond to units in the output representation.

GENERAL DISCUSSION

The computational simulations that have been presented here illustrate two convergent aspects of the modelling of spoken word identification in recurrent network models. First, these simulations show that training a network to preserve the activation of previous words produces an appropriate activation profile for the identification of words in connected speech—in particular, for words that are embedded at the start of longer competitors. Second, these networks provide a plausible simulation of the developmental profile of word recognition in infants. The networks are trained without the one-to-one correspondences between speech and meaning that have been provided previously. In discovering the appropriate mapping between the speech input and lexical/conceptual representations, these networks show a realistic developmental profile since the speed and accuracy of word identification increases throughout training, consistent with experimental data from infants.

Interestingly, a single novel assumption appears to be responsible for both of these successes. The developmental plausibility of these simulations is enhanced by being trained to map entire sequences of words to a representation of an entire utterance. Similarly, the success of the networks at identifying onset-embedded words arises as a direct consequence of being trained to preserve the activation of lexical representations over an entire utterance.

As was discussed, before, one aspect of simulation 1 is unrealistic by comparison with the developmental literature. These networks were presented with an unsegmented sequence of words in the input. As reviewed in the introductory section there is substantial evidence to suggest that infants are able to segment the speech stream into word-sized chunks before beginning to acquire the mapping from speech to meaning.

The ability of infants to use distributional information to segment connected speech was explicitly incorporated in simulation 2. However, rather than supplying these networks with presegmented sequences, they were provided with an additional mechanism to assist in segmenting the speech input. The networks in simulation 2 were required to activate an additional prediction output trained in parallel with the lexical output. Prior simulations have shown that this prediction task allows a network to identify a substantial proportion of word boundaries (Cairns et al., 1997; Christiansen et al., 1998). An important finding from these simulations was that the addition of the prediction task significantly improved the speed with which the network learnt the task of recognising words in connected speech. Interpretations of the effect of this additional task in assisting lexical acquisition will be discussed in more detail.

Bootstrapping vocabulary acquisition

The simulations reported here demonstrated that an additional, input-prediction task assists learning in a network model of vocabulary acquisition. Such a result may appear counterintuitive—it might have been expected that giving a network an additional task to perform would reduce the processing resources available for lexical acquisition. Connectionist simulations of other domains have shown that training a network to perform multiple tasks with a single set of hidden units can impair performance by comparison with networks that are provided with separate hidden-unit modules for each task (e.g. for recognising stems and affixes of morphologically complex words, see Gasser, 1994; for the what and where vision task, see Rueckl, Cave, & Kosslyn, 1989; but see also Bullinaria, 2001). However, in the simulations reported here, forcing two tasks to share the same internal representation assists acquisition.

In the current simulation, both the prediction and lexical acquisition tasks were imposed on the network from the beginning of training. Nonetheless, the network showed more rapid learning of segment prediction than lexical acquisition (see Figure 5.7). Several properties of the two mappings may be relevant in this respect. For instance, the prediction task may be more easily solved using the input available at the current time-step, while the lexical task depends on representations of preceding segments. Alternatively, this result may reflect greater input–output similarity in the prediction task, since the same distributed representations are used at the input and at the prediction output. In either case, since the prediction task is learnt first, it seems that it is this task (and not lexical identification) that provides an early influence on the structure of the networks' representations of the input sequences. This is evident in the marked differences between the networks' hidden representations when trained with and without the prediction task (see Figure 5.8).

This finding helps explain the benefit that is provided by simultaneously training a network with both the lexical identification and the prediction task. By reusing the hidden-unit representations that develop to perform the prediction task, the network gains a substantial head-start on lexical acquisition. As indicated in Figure 5.8, the hidden-unit representations resulting from the prediction task provide an initial segmentation of the speech stream into lexical units which benefits lexical acquisition. This simulation therefore provides an explicit demonstration of how learning the statistical and distributional structure of the speech stream may serve to bootstrap vocabulary acquisition.

This simulation demonstrates the benefits of statistical learning as a starting point for the acquisition of higher-level mappings. This finding has obvious similarities with physiologically inspired simulations in which the computational properties of the system force a similar development from learning first-order statistics to developing more abstract representations of the input either through change to the number of hidden units in the network (Fahlman & Lebiere, 1990), through changes to the timing of weight changes in different regions of the network (Shrager & Johnson, 1996) or through changes to the memory capacity of the network (Elman, 1993)—see Chapters 6 and 9 for further discussion. What is particularly striking in the simulations reported here is that no changes to the processing properties of the network are required to ensure that the network learns simple statistical properties of the input first. Whether this is a consequence of the particular tasks and training sets used or is a more general property of recurrent networks is unclear. Other authors have demonstrated that additional tasks assist in training recurrent networks (Maskara & Noetzel, 1993), it is therefore at least possible that this demonstration reflects a general property of recurrent neural networks.

Puzzles and contradictions in vocabulary acquisition

The simulations that have been presented here are largely consistent with developmental evidence concerning the acquisition of lexical segmentation and vocabulary acquisition. The simple assumption that has been made in relating these simulations to the developmental time course in infancy is that the prediction output accounts for infants' knowledge of the statistical structure of the speech input during the first year of life and that the performance of the lexical output simulates the acquisition of mappings from speech to meaning early in the second year. This interpretation is consistent with a role for the prediction task in developing structured representations that support subsequent lexical acquisition.

While the work presented here falls short of providing a detailed account of any single set of experimental data, it seems likely that much of the existing experimental literature can be accounted for within this framework. However, there are some results in the experimental literature that appear to be inconsistent with this framework. One well-publicised result concerns the ability of infants to learn regularities that supposedly cannot be learnt by recurrent network (Marcus, Vijayan, Bandi Rao, & Vishton, 1999; although various authors have subsequently demonstrated neural network accounts of exactly this data, e.g. Dominey & Ramus, 2000; Sirois, Buckingham, & Shultz, 2000; see also Chapter 7). This discussion will instead focus on results that suggest a developmental dissociation between word-form learning and the properties of the systems that map from speech to meaning. These dissociations challenge the account proposed here in which vocabulary acquisition reuses representations that arise from the acquisition of word forms.

The first result that might challenge the account presented here was reported by Stager and Werker (1997). They observed that infants in the early stages of vocabulary acquisition (at around 14 months), are unable to learn that phonological neighbours such as "bih" and "dih" refer to two distinct objects. Infants did not pay increased attention to trials in which the word–object association was switched for these two highly similar names, although they did show a novelty preference for trials that involved switching two phonologically distinct words such as "lif" and "neem". This result is surprising because it is inconsistent with a finding first reported by Jusczyk and Aslin (1995)—and replicated by Stager and Werker (1997)—that, even at 9 months, infants who are familiarised with word forms in connected speech can readily distinguish between minimal pairs like "bih" and "dih".

At face value these results suggest that the processes involved in mapping speech to meaning do not have access to as detailed a representation of the speech stream as the system involved in learning word forms. Such a result may be difficult to reconcile within the model presented here, in which both mappings make use of the same internal representation of the speech input. One tempting conclusion might be to assume that the systems involved in learning word forms and mapping to meaning operate on separate representations of the speech input. However, such a conclusion appears to condemn much of the research on early word-form learning as being irrelevant to vocabulary acquisition. It is unclear what function a system for representing word forms might serve if it does not assist in acquiring the mapping from speech to meaning. Stager and Werker themselves suggest that ignoring the full detail of speech in mapping to meaning may somehow assist the infant in learning language. However, if this "less-is-more" interpretation is to be convincing it must be backed up by detailed simulations that illustrate the advantage that can be gained by ignoring potentially informative detail in one learning situation but not in another. Further experimental investigations of the abilities of infants at different ages may be enlightening in this respect.

A further empirical challenge to the account that has been developed here focuses on the abilities of 6-month-olds who have yet to master the segmentation of words from connected speech. By the account that has been proposed here, it would not be expected that these infants could map from speech to meaning since they do not yet have fully formed representations of word forms. However, results reported by Tincoff and Jusczyk (1999) demonstrate that 6-month-olds show precocious knowledge of the meaning of two particular words—"mummy" and "daddy"[4]—indicated by increased looking

---

[4] Infants were actually tested on the form of these two words that parents reported as being most frequently used around them. These are assumed to be "mummy" and "daddy" for clarity.

time towards a video of the named parent (though not to images of an unfamiliar male or female). Although "mummy" and "daddy" are clearly exceptional words because of their extremely high frequency in infant-directed speech and the salience of parents in the lives of infants, this result clearly challenges any simple account in which word forms can only be attached to meaning after they have been segmented from connected speech.

It remains to be seen whether the model presented here could account for the early acquisition of words like "mummy" that are of high frequency and salience to infants. If these results do reflect the operation of the same system that maps word forms to meaning in older infants, then these precociously learned words may provide a valuable insight into the functioning of the immature system. Further investigations of the infants responses to these words (e.g. sensitivity to noisy or mispronounced tokens) may be especially valuable.

At face value, therefore, the results reported by Stager and Werker (1997) and Tincoff and Jusczyk (1999) suggest some separation of the processes that allow word forms to be mapped to meaning and systems that are involved in discovering words in the speech stream. It is unclear at present whether the modelling framework presented here could account for these apparent dissociations. Further simulations to explore these seemingly contradictory aspects of the behavioural literature should be carried out.

In conclusion, the work that we have presented here provides a modelling framework within which to explore a variety of important issues in lexical segmentation and vocabulary acquisition. While these simulations fall short of capturing the scale and complexity of the acquisition problem faced by infants, the mechanisms proposed appear to be sufficiently general to merit further investigation. Further simulations that include the specific tasks and materials used in the developmental literature would be valuable.

ACKNOWLEDGEMENTS

This work was supported by EPSRC research studentship number 94700590 and by an MRC Programme Grant to William Marslen-Wilson and Lorraine Tyler. I would like to thank Gareth Gaskell and William Marslen-Wilson for advice and encouragement throughout. I would also like to thank Gary Cottrell, Morten Christiansen, Tom Loucas, Billi Randall, and Ingrid Johnsrude for comments and suggestions on this work and Julian Pine and Philip Quinlan for useful feedback on a previous draft of this manuscript. All simulations were carried out using the Tlearn simulator developed by Jeff Elman of the Centre for Research in Language, University of California, San Diego. Finally, I would like to thank my niece Isobel for providing such a concrete illustration of the wonderful abilities of infants during the first 2 years.

REFERENCES

Allen, J., & Christiansen, M. H. (1996). Integrating multiple cues in word segmentation: A connectionist model using hints. In G. W. Cottrell (Ed.), *Proceedings of the 18th Annual Cognitive Science Society Conference* (pp. 370–375). Mahwah, NJ: Lawrence Erlbaum Associates, Inc.

Aslin, R. N., Woodward, J. Z., La Mendola, N. P., & Bever, T. G. (1996). Models of word segmentation in fluent speech to infants. In J. L. Morgan & K. Demuth (Eds.), *Signal to syntax: Bootstrapping from speech to grammar in early acquisition* (pp. 117–134). Mahwah, NJ, Lawrence Erlbaum Associates, Inc.

Baillargeon. R. (1995). Physical reasoning in infancy. In M. S. Gazzaniga (Ed.), *The cognitive neurosciences* (pp. 181–204). Cambridge, MA: MIT Press.

Baldwin, D. A. (1991). Infants' contribution to the achievement of joint reference. *Child Development, 62*, 875–890.

Baldwin, D. A. (1993). Infants' ability to consult the speaker for clues to word reference. *Journal of Child Language, 20*, 395–418.

Barry, W. J. (1981). Internal juncture and speech communication. In W. J. Barry & K. J. Kohler (Eds.), *Beitrage zur experimentalen und angewandten phonetik* (pp. 231–288). Kiel, Germany: AIPUK.

Bloom, P. (1994). Possible names: The role of syntax–semantics mappings in the acquisition of nominals. *Lingua, 92*, 297–329.

Brent, M. R. (1999). Speech segmentation and word discovery: A computational perspective. *Trends in Cognitive Sciences, 3*, 294–301.

Brent, M. R., & Cartwright, T. A. (1996). Distributional regularity and phonotactic constraints are useful for segmentation. *Cognition, 61*, 93–125.

Bullinaria, J. A. (2001). Simulating the evolution of modular neural systems. In J. D. Moore & K. Stenning (Eds.), *Proceedings of the Twenty-third Annual Conference of the Cognitive Science Society* (pp. 146–153). Mahwah, NJ: Lawrence Erlbaum Associates, Inc.

Cairns, P., Shillcock, R., Chater, N., & Levy, J. (1997). Bootstrapping word boundaries: A bottom-up corpus based approach to speech segmentation. *Cognitive Psychology, 33*, 111–153.

Charles-Luce, J., & Luce, P. A. (1995). An examination of similarity neighbourhoods in young children's receptive vocabularies. *Journal of Child Language, 22*, 727–735.

Christiansen, M. H., Allen, J., & Seidenberg, M. S. (1998). Learning to segment speech using multiple cues: A connectionist model. *Language and Cognitive Processes, 13*, 221–268.

Cole, R. A., & Jakimik, J. (1980). A model of speech perception. In R. A. Cole (Ed.), *Perception and production of fluent speech* (pp. 130–163). Hillsdale, NJ: Lawrence Erlbaum Associates, Inc.

Crick, F. H. C. (1989). The recent excitement about neural networks. *Nature, 337*, 129–132.

Cutler, A., & Carter, D. M. (1987). The predominance of strong initial syllables in the English vocabulary. *Computer Speech and Language, 2*, 133–142.

Cutler, A., & Norris, D. (1988). The role of strong syllables in segmentation for lexical access. *Journal of Experimental Psychology: Human Perception and Performance, 14*, 113–121.

Davis, M. H., Gaskell, M. G., & Marslen-Wilson, W. D. (1997). Recognising embedded words in connected speech: Context and competition. In J. Bullinaria, D. Glasspool, & G. Houghton (Eds.), *Proceedings of the Fourth Neural Computation in Psychology Workshop* (pp. 254–266). London: Springer-Verlag.

Davis, M. H., Marslen-Wilson, W. D., & Gaskell, M. G. (2002). Leading up the lexical garden-path: Segmentation and ambiguity in spoken word recognition. *Journal of Experimental Psychology: Human Perception and Performance, 28*, 218–244.

Dominey, P. F., & Ramus, F. (2000). Neural network processing of natural language: I. Sensitivity to serial, temporal and abstract structure of language in the infant. *Language and Cognitive Processes, 15*, 87–127

Eimas, P. D., Siqueland, E. R., Jusczyk, P., & Vigorito, J. (1971). Speech perception in early infancy. *Science, 171*, 304–306.

Elman, J. L. (1990). Finding structure in time. *Cognitive Science, 14*, 179–211.

Elman, J. L. (1993). Learning and development in neural networks: The importance of starting small. *Cognition, 48*, 71–99.

Elman, J., Bates, E. A., Johnson, M. H., Karmiloff-Smith, A., Parisi, D., & Plunkett, K. (1996). *Rethinking innateness.* Cambridge, MA: MIT Press.

Fahlman, S. E., & Lebiere, C. (1990). The cascade correlation learning architecture. In D. Touretzky (Ed.), *Advances in neural information processing, 2* (pp. 524–532). Los Altos, CA: Morgan-Kaufman.

Fenson, L., Dale, P. S., Reznick, J. S., Bates, E., Thal, D. J., & Perthick, S. J. (1994). Variability in early communicative development. *Monographs of the Society for Research in Child Development, 59* (serial 242).

Fernald, A. (1985). Four month old infants prefer to listen to motherese. *Infant Behaviour and Development, 8*, 181–195.

Fernald, A., Pinto, J. P., Swingley, D., Weinberg, A., & McRoberts, G. W. (1998). Rapid gains in speed of verbal processing by infants in the second year. *Psychological Science, 9*, 228–231.

Fernald, A., Taeschner, T., Dunn, J., Papousek, M., de Boysson-Bardies, B., & Fukui, I. (1989). A cross-language study of prosodic modifications in mothers' and fathers' speech to preverbal infants. *Journal of Child Language, 16*, 477–501.

Gaskell, M. G., & Marslen-Wilson, W. D. (1997). Integrating form and meaning: A distributed model of speech perception. *Language and Cognitive Processes, 12*, 613–656.

Gaskell, M. G., & Marslen-Wilson, W. D. (1999). Ambiguity, competition and blending in spoken word recognition. *Cognitive Science, 23*, 439–462.

Gasser, M. (1994). Modularity in a connectionist model of morphology acquisition. In *Proceedings of the International Conference on Computational Linguistics, 15* (pp. 214–220) Kyoto, Japan: COLING.

Gleitman, L. R. (1994). Words, words, words. *Philosophical Transactions of the Royal Society of London. Series B, 346*, 71–77.

Goldowsky, B. N., & Newport, E. L. (1993). Modeling the effects of processing limitations on the acquisition of morphology: The less is more hypothesis. In E. V. Clark (Ed.), *Proceedings of the 24th Annual Child Language Forum* (pp. 124–138). Stanford, CA: CSLI.

Golinkoff, R. M., Hirsh-Pasek, K., Cauley, K. M., & Gordon, L. (1987). The eyes have it: Lexical and syntactic comprehension in a new paradigm. *Journal of Child Language, 14*, 23–45.

Harrington, J., Watson, G., & Cooper, M. (1989). Word boundary detection in broad class and phoneme strings. *Computer Speech and Language, 3*, 367–382.

Harris, Z. S. (1955). From phoneme to morpheme. *Language, 31*, 190–222.

Jusczyk, P. W. (1997). *The discovery of spoken language.* Cambridge, MA, MIT Press.

Jusczyk, P. W. (1999). How infants begin to extract words from speech. *Trends in Cognitive Science, 3*, 323–328.

Jusczyk, P. W., & Aslin, R. N. (1995). Infants' detection of the sound patterns of words in fluent speech. *Cognitive Psychology, 29*, 1–23.

Jusczyk, P. W., Cutler, A., & Redanz, N. (1993a). Preference for the predominant stress patterns of English words. *Child Development, 64*, 675–687.

Jusczyk, P. W., Friederici, A. D., Wessels, J. M., Svenkerud, V. Y., & Jusczyk, A. M. (1993b). Infants' sensitivity to the sound patterns of native language words. *Journal of Memory and Language, 32*, 402–420.

Jusczyk, P. W., & Hohne, E. A. (1997). Infants' memory for spoken words. *Science, 277*, 1984–1985.

Jusczyk, P. W., Houston, D. M., & Newsome, M. (1999). The beginnings of word segmentation in English-learning infants. *Cognitive Psychology, 39*, 159–207.

Jusczyk, P. W., Luce, P. A., & Charles-Luce, J. (1994). Infants' sensitivity to phonotactic patterns in the native language. *Journal of Memory and Language, 33*(5), 630–645.

Korman, M. (1984). Adaptive aspects of maternal vocalizations in differing contexts at ten weeks. *First Language, 5,* 44–45.

Kuhl, P. K., Williams, K. A., Lacerda, F., Stevens, K. N., & Lindblom, B. (1992). Linguistic experience alters phonetic perception in infants by 6 months of age. *Science, 255,* 606–608.

Lehiste, I. (1960). An acoustic–phonetic study of internal open juncture. *Phonetica, 5* (Supplement), 5–54.

Marcus, G. F., Vijayan, S., Bandi Rao, S., Vishton, P. M. (1999). Rule learning by seven-month-old infants. *Science, 283,* 77–80.

Mareschal, D. (2000). Object knowledge in infancy: Current controversies and approaches. *Trends in Cognitive Science, 4,* 408–416.

Marslen-Wilson, W. D. (1984). Function and processing in spoken word recognition: A tutorial review. In H. Bouma & D. G. Bouwhuis (Eds.), *Attention and performance X: Control of language processing* (pp. 125–150). Hillsdale NJ: Lawrence Erlbaum Associates, Inc.

Marslen-Wilson, W. D., & Welsh, A. (1978). Processing interactions and lexical access during word recognition in continuous speech. *Cognitive Psychology, 10,* 29–63.

Maskara, A., & Noetzel, W. (1993). Sequence recognition with recurrent neural networks. *Connection Science, 5,* 139–152.

McClelland, J. L., & Elman, J. L. (1986). The TRACE model of speech perception. *Cognitive Psychology, 18,* 1–86.

Monsell, S., & Hirsh, K. W. (1998). Competitor priming in spoken word recognition. *Journal of Experimental Psychology: Learning, Memory and Cognition, 24,* 1495–1520.

Norris, D. (1990). A dynamic-net model of human speech recognition. In G. T. M. Altmann (Ed.), *Cognitive models of speech processing.* Cambridge, MA: MIT Press.

Norris, D. (1994). Shortlist: A connectionist model of continuous speech recognition. *Cognition, 52,* 189–234.

O'Reilly, R. C. (1996). Biologically plausible error-driven learning using local activation differences: The generalized recirculation algorithm. *Neural Computation, 8,* 895–938.

Oviatt, S. L. (1980). The emerging ability to comprehend language: An experimental approach. *Child Development, 51,* 97–106.

Page, M. (2000). Connectionist modelling in psychology: A localist manifesto. *Behavioural and Brain Sciences, 23,* 443–512.

Pinker, S. (1989). *Learnability and cognition.* Cambridge, MA: MIT Press.

Plaut, D. C., & Kello, C. T. (1998). The emergence of phonology from the interplay of speech comprehension and production: A distributed connectionist approach. In B. MacWhinney (Ed.), *The emergence of language* (pp. 381–415). Mahwah, NJ: Lawrence Erlbaum Associates, Inc.

Plunkett, K., Sinha, C., Møller, M. F., & Strandsby, O. (1992). Symbol grounding or the emergence of symbols? Vocabulary growth in children and a connectionist net. *Connection Science, 4,* 293–312.

Quine, W. V. O. (1960). *Word and object.* Cambridge, MA: MIT Press.

Quinn, P., Eimas, P., & Rosenkrantz, S. (1993). Evidence for representations of perceptually similar natural categories by 3- and 4-month-old infants. *Perception, 22,* 463–475.

Roy, D. K., & Pentland, A. P. (2002). Learning words from sights and sounds: A computational model. *Cognitive Science, 26,* 113–146.

Rueckl, J. G., Cave, K. R., & Kosslyn, S. M. (1989). Why are "what" and "where" processed by separate cortical visual systems? A computational investigation. *Journal of Cognitive Neuroscience, 1,* 171–186.

Saffran, J. R., Aslin, R. N., & Newport, E. L. (1996). Statistical language learning by 8 month olds. *Science, 274,* 1926–1928.

Schafer, G., & Plunkett, K. (1998). Rapid word-learning by 15 month olds under tightly-controlled conditions. *Child Development, 69*, 309–320.

Schafer, G., Plunkett, K., & Harris, P. L. (1999). What's in a name? Lexical knowledge drives infants' visual preferences in the absence of referent input. *Developmental Science, 2*, 187–194.

Servan-Schrieber, D., Cleeremans, A., & McClelland, J. L. (1991). Graded state machines: The representation of temporal contingencies in simple recurrent networks. *Machine Learning, 7*, 161–193.

Shastri, L., & Ajjanagadde, V. (1993). From simple associations to systematic reasoning: A connectionist representation of rules, variables and dynamic bindings using temporal synchrony. *Behavioural and Brain Sciences, 16*, 417–494.

Shrager, J., & Johnson, M. H. (1996). Dynamic plasticity influences the emergence of function in a simple cortical array. *Neural Networks, 9*, 1119–1129.

Sirois, S., Buckingham, D., & Shultz, T. R. (2000). Artificial grammar learning by infants: An auto-associator perspective. *Developmental Science, 4*, 442–456.

Siskind, J. M. (1996). A computational study of cross-situational techniques for learning word-to-meaning mappings. *Cognition, 61*, 39–91.

Smolensky, P. (1990). Tensor product variable binding and the representation of symbolic structures in connectionist systems. *Artificial Intelligence, 46*, 159–216.

Sougné, J. (1998). Connectionism and the problem of multiple instantiation. *Trends in Cognitive Science, 2*, 183–189.

St John, M. F., & McClelland, J. L. (1990). Learning and applying contextual constraints in sentence comprehension. *Artificial Intelligence, 46*, 217–257.

Stager, C. L., & Werker, J. F. (1997). Infants listen for more phonetic detailed in speech perception than in word-learning tasks. *Nature, 388*, 381–382.

Swingley, D., Pinto, J. P., & Fernald, A. (1999). Continuous processing in word recognition at 24 months. *Cognition, 71*, 73–108.

Thomas D. G., Campos J. J., Shucard D. W., Ramsay D. S., & Shucard, J. (1981). Semantic comprehension in infancy: A signal detection analysis. *Child Development, 52*, 798–903.

Tincoff, R., & Jusczyk, P. W. (1999). Some beginnings of word comprehension in 6-month-olds. *Psychological Science, 10*, 172–175.

Walley, A. (1993). The role of vocabulary development in children's spoken word recognition and segmentation ability. *Developmental Review, 13*, 286–350.

Waxman, S., & Markow, D. (1996). Words as an invitation to form categories: Evidence from 12- to 13-month-olds. *Cognitive Psychology, 29*, 257–302.

Werker, J. R., & Tees, R. C. (1984). Cross-language speech perception: Evidence for perceptual reorganisation during the first year of life. *Infant Behaviour and Development, 7*, 49–63.

Wolff, J. G. (1977). The discovery of segmentation in natural language. *British Journal of Psychology, 68*, 97–106.

CHAPTER SIX

Less is less in language acquisition

Douglas L. T. Rohde
Massachusetts Institute of Technology, Cambridge, USA

David C. Plaut
Carnegie Mellon University and the Center for the Neural Basis of Cognition, Pittsburgh, USA

A principal observation in the study of language acquisition is that people exposed to a language as children are more likely to achieve fluency in that language than those first exposed to it as adults, giving rise to the popular notion of a critical period for language learning (Lenneberg, 1967; Long, 1990). This is perhaps surprising because children have been found to be inferior to adults in most tests of other cognitive abilities.

Various explanations have been put forward to account for the benefit of early language learning. Possibly the most prevalent view is that children possess a specific "language acquisition device" that is programmatically deactivated prior to or during adolescence (Chomsky, 1965; McNeill, 1970). Important to this view is that knowledge or processes necessary for effective language learning are available for only a limited period of time. But this theory has trouble accounting for continued effects of age of acquisition after adolescence (Bialystok & Hakuta, 1999) and evidence that some adult second language learners are still able to reach fluency (Birdsong, 1999).

An alternative account is provided by Newport's (1990) "less-is-more" hypothesis. Rather than attributing the early language advantage to a specific language learning device, this theory postulates that children's language acquisition may be aided rather than hindered by their limited cognitive resources. According to this view, the ability to learn a language declines over time as a result of an increase in cognitive abilities. The reasoning behind this suggestion is that a child's limited perception and memory may force the child to focus on smaller linguistic units, which form the fundamental components of language, as opposed to memorising larger units, which are less amenable to recombination. While this is an attractive explanation, for such a theory to be plausible, the potential benefit of limited resources must be demonstrated both computationally and empirically.

The strongest evidence for Newport's theory comes from computational simulations and empirical findings of Elman (1991, 1993), Goldowsky and Newport (1993), Kareev, Lieberman, and Lev (1997), Cochran, McDonald, and Parault (1999), and Kersten and Earles (2001). In the current chapter, we consider these studies in detail and, in each case, find serious cause to doubt their intended support for the less-is-more hypothesis.

- Elman (1991, 1993) found that simple recurrent connectionist networks could learn the structure of an English-like artificial grammar only when "starting small"—when either the training corpus or the network's memory was limited initially and only gradually made more sophisticated. We show, to the contrary, that language learning by recurrent networks does not depend on starting small; in fact, such restrictions hinder acquisition as the languages are made more realistic by introducing graded semantic constraints (Rohde & Plaut, 1999).
- We discuss the simple learning task introduced by Goldowsky and Newport (1993) as a clear demonstration of the advantage of memory limitations. But we show that their filtering mechanism actually constitutes a severe impairment to learning in both a simple statistical model and a neural network model.
- Kareev et al. (1997) argued that small sample sizes, possibly resulting from weak short-term memory, have the effect of enhancing correlations between two observable variables. But we demonstrate that the chance that a learner is able to detect a correlation actually improves with sample size and that a simple prediction model indeed performs better when it relies on larger samples.
- Cochran et al. (1999) taught participants American Sign Language (ASL) verbs with and without additional cognitive loads and found apparently better generalisation performance for participants in the load condition. But we argue that the learning task actually provided no support for the expected generalisation and that the no-load participants simply learned the more reasonable generalisation much better.
- Finally, we consider the Kersten and Earles (2001) findings to provide little support for the less-is-more hypothesis because the task learned by participants in their experiment is unlike natural language learning in some important and relevant aspects and the critical manipulation in their experiment involved staged input, rather than cognitive limitations.

In the final section, we consider some general principles of learning language-like tasks in recurrent neural networks and what the implications for human learning might be. We then briefly discuss an alternative account for the language-learning superiority of children.

ELMAN (1991, 1993)

Elman (1990, 1991) set out to provide an explicit formulation of how a general connectionist system might learn the grammatical structure of a language. Rather than comprehension or overt parsing, Elman chose to train the networks to perform word prediction. Although word prediction is a far cry from language comprehension, it can be viewed as a useful component of language processing, given that the network can make accurate predictions only by learning the structure of the grammar. Elman trained a simple recurrent network—sometimes termed an "Elman" network—to predict the next word in sentences generated by an artificial grammar exhibiting number agreement, variable verb argument structure, and embedded clauses. He found that the network was unable to learn the prediction task— and hence the underlying grammar—when presented from the outset with sentences generated by the full grammar. However, the network was able to learn if it was trained first on only simple sentences (i.e. those without embeddings) and only later exposed to an increasing proportion of complex sentences.

It thus seems reasonable to conclude that staged input enabled the network to focus early on simple and important features, such as the relationship between nouns and verbs. By "starting small", the network had a better foundation for learning the more difficult grammatical relationships which span potentially long and uninformative embeddings. Recognising the parallel between this finding and the less-is-more hypothesis, Elman (1993) decided to investigate a more direct test of Newport's (1990) theory. Rather than staging the input presentation, Elman initially interfered with the network's memory span and then allowed it to gradually improve. Again, he found successful learning in this memory limited condition, providing much stronger support for the hypothesis.

Rohde and Plaut (1999) simulation 1: Progressive input

Rohde and Plaut (1999) investigated how the need for starting small in learning a pseudonatural language would be affected if the language incorporated more of the constraints of natural languages. A salient feature of the grammar used by Elman is that it is purely syntactic, in the sense that all words of a particular class, such as the singular nouns, were identical in usage. A consequence of this is that embedded material modifying a head noun provides relatively little information about the subsequent corresponding verb. Earlier work by Cleeremans, Servan-Schreiber, and McClelland (1989), however, had demonstrated that simple recurrent networks were better able to learn long-distance dependencies in finite-state grammars when intervening sequences were partially informative of (i.e. correlated with) the distant prediction. The intuition behind this finding is that the network's ability to represent and maintain information about an important word, such as the head noun, is reinforced by the advantage this information provides in predicting words within embedded phrases. As a result, the noun can more effectively aid in the prediction of the corresponding verb following the intervening material.

One source of such correlations in natural language is distributional biases, due to semantic factors, on which nouns typically co-occur with verbs. For example, suppose dogs often chase cats. Over the course of training, the network has encountered *chased* more often after processing sentences beginning *The dog who* . . . than after sentences beginning with other noun phrases. The network can, therefore, reduce prediction error within the embedded clause by retaining specific information about *dog* (beyond it being a singular noun). As a result, information on dog becomes available to support further predictions in the sentence as it continues (e.g. *The dog who chased the cat barked*). These considerations led us to believe that languages similar to Elman's but involving weak semantic constraints might result in less of an advantage for starting small in child language acquisition. We began by examining the effects of an incremental training corpus, without manipulating the network's memory. The methods we used were very similar, but not identical, to those used by Elman (1991, 1993).

Grammar. Our pseudonatural language was based on the grammar shown in Table 6.1, which generates simple noun-verb and noun-verb-noun sentences with the possibility of relative clause modification of most nouns. Relative clauses could be either subject-extracted or object-extracted. Although this language is quite simple, in comparison to natural language, it is nonetheless of interest because, to make accurate predictions, a network must learn to form representations of potentially complex syntactic structures and remember information, such as whether the subject was singular or plural, over lengthy embeddings. The grammar used by Elman was nearly identical, except that it had one fewer mixed transitivity verb in singular and plural form, and the two proper nouns, *Mary* and *John*, could not be modified.

In our simulation, several additional constraints were applied on top of the grammar in Table 6.1. Primary among these was that individual nouns could engage only in certain actions, and that transitive verbs could act only on certain objects (Table 6.2). Another restriction in the language was that

TABLE 6.1
The grammar used in simulation 1

S	→ NP VI . | NP VT NP .
NP	→ N | N RC
RC	→ who VI | who VT NP | who NP VT
N	→ boy | girl | cat | dog | Mary | John | boys | girls | cats | dogs
VI	→ barks | sings | walks | bites | eats | bark | sing | walk | bite | eat
VT	→ chases | feeds | walks | bites | eats | chase | feed | walk | bite | eat

Transition probabilities are specified and additional constraints are applied on top of this framework.

TABLE 6.2
Semantic constraints on verb usage

Verb	Intransitive subjects	Transitive subjects	Objects if transitive
chase	–	any	any
feed	–	human	animal
bite	animal	animal	any
walk	any	human	only dog
eat	any	animal	human
bark	only dog	–	–
sing	human or cat	–	–

Columns indicate legal subject nouns when verbs are used intransitively or transitively and legal object nouns when transitive.

proper nouns could not act on themselves. Finally, constructions which repeat an intransitive verb, such as *Boys who walk walk*, were disallowed because of redundancy. These so-called semantic constraints always applied within the main clause of the sentence as well as within any subclauses. Although number agreement affected all nouns and verbs, the degree to which the semantic constraints applied between a noun and its modifying phrase was controlled by specifying the probability that the relevant constraints would be enforced for a given phrase. In this way, effects of the correlation between a noun and its modifying phrase, or of the level of information the phrase contained about the identity of the noun, could be investigated.

Network architecture.   The simple recurrent network used in both Elman's simulations and in the current work is shown in Figure 6.1. Inputs were represented as localist patterns or basis vectors: Each word was

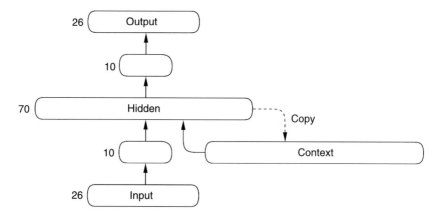

Figure 6.1.   The architecture of the network used in the simulations. Each solid arrow represents full connectivity between layers, with numbers of units next to each layer. Hidden unit states are copied to corresponding context units (dashed arrow) after each word is processed.

represented by a single unit with activity 1.0, all other units having activity 0.0. This representation was chosen to deprive the network of any similarity structure among the words that might provide indirect clues to their grammatical properties. The same 1-of-n representation was also used for outputs, as it has the convenient property that the relative activations of multiple words can be represented independently.

On each time step, a new word was presented by fixing the activations of the input layer. The activity in the main hidden layer from the previous time step was copied to the context layer. Activation then propagated through the network, as in a feedforward model, such that each unit's activation was a smooth, nonlinear (logistic, or sigmoid) function of its summed weighted input from other units. The resulting activations over the output units were then compared with their target activations, generating an error signal. In a simple recurrent network, errors are not back-propagated through time (cf. Rumelhart, Hinton, & Williams, 1986) but only through the current time step, although this includes the connections from the context units to the hidden units. These connections allow information about past inputs—as encoded in the prior hidden representation copied onto the context units—to influence current performance.

Although the target output used during training was the encoding for the actual next word, a number of words were typically possible at any given point in the sentence. Therefore, to perform optimally the network must generate, or predict, a probability distribution over the word units indicating the likelihood that each word would occur next. Averaged across the entire corpus, this distribution will generally result in the lowest performance error.

Corpora. Elman's complex training regimen involved training a network on a corpus of 10,000 sentences, 75 per cent of which were "complex" in that they contained at least one relative clause. In his simple regimen, the network was first trained exclusively on simple sentences and then on an increasing proportion of complex sentences. Inputs were arranged in four corpora, each consisting of 10,000 sentences. The first corpus was entirely simple, the second 25 per cent complex, the third 50 per cent complex, and the final corpus was 75 per cent complex—identical to the initial corpus that the network had failed to learn when it alone was presented during training. An additional 75 per cent complex corpus, generated in the same way as the last training corpus, was used for testing the network.

To study the effect of varying levels of information in embedded clauses, we constructed five grammar classes. In class A, semantic constraints did not apply between a clause and its subclause, only between nouns and verbs explicitly present in each individual clause. In class B, 25 per cent of the subclauses respected the semantic constraints of their parent clause. In such cases, the modified noun must be a semantically valid subject of the verb for a subject-relative or object of the verb for an object-relative. In class C, 50 per cent of the subclauses respected this constraint, 75 per cent in class D, and 100 per cent in class E. Therefore, in class A, which was most like Elman's grammar, the contents of a relative clause provided no information about the noun being modified other than whether it was singular or plural, whereas class E produced sentences that were the most English-like. We should emphasise that, in this simulation, semantic constraints always applied within a clause, including the main clause. This is because we were interested primarily in the ability of the network to perform the difficult main verb prediction, which relied not only on the number of the subject, but on its semantic properties as well. In a second simulation, we investigate a case in which all the semantic constraints were eliminated to produce a grammar essentially identical to Elman's.

As in Elman's work, four versions of each class were created to produce languages of increasing complexity. Grammars A_0, A_{25}, A_{50}, and A_{75}, for example, produce 0 per cent, 25 per cent, 50 per cent, and 75 per cent complex sentences, respectively. In addition, for each level of complexity, the probability of relative clause modification was adjusted to match the average sentence length in Elman's corpora, with the exception that the 25 per cent and 50 per cent complex corpora involved slightly longer sentences to provide a more even progression, reducing the large difference between the 50 per cent and 75 per cent complex conditions apparent in Elman's corpora. Specifically, grammars with complexity 0 per cent, 25 per cent, 50 per cent, and 75 per cent respectively had 0 per cent, 10 per cent, 20 per cent, and 30 per cent modification probability for each noun.

For each of the 20 grammars (five levels of semantic constraints crossed with four percentages of complex sentences), two corpora of 10,000 sentences were generated, one for training and the other for testing. Corpora of this size are quite representative of the statistics of the full language for all but the longest sentences, which are relatively infrequent. Sentences longer than 16 words were discarded in generating the corpora, but these were so rare (<0.2 per cent) that their loss should have had negligible effects. To perform well, a network of this size couldn't possibly "memorise" the training corpus but must learn the structure of the language.

Training and testing procedures.   In the condition Elman referred to as "starting small", he trained his network for five epochs (complete presentations) of each of the four corpora, in increasing order of complexity. During training, weights were adjusted to minimise the summed squared error between the network's prediction and the actual next word, using the back-propagation learning procedure (Rumelhart et al., 1986) with a learning rate of 0.1, reduced gradually to 0.06. No momentum was used and weights were updated after each word presentation. Weights were initialised to random values sampled uniformly between ±0.001.

For each of the five language classes, we trained the network shown in Figure 6.1 using both incremental and nonincremental training schemes. In the complex regimen, the network was trained on the most complex corpus (75 per cent complex) for 25 epochs with a fixed learning rate. The learning rate was then reduced for a final pass through the corpus. In the simple regimen, the network was trained for five epochs on each of the first three corpora in increasing order of complexity. It was then trained on the fourth corpus for 10 epochs, followed by a final epoch at the reduced learning rate. The six extra epochs of training on the fourth corpus—not included in Elman's design—were intended to allow performance with the simple regimen to approach asymptote.

Because we were interested primarily in the performance level possible under optimal conditions, we searched a wide range of training parameters to determine a set which consistently achieved the best performance overall.[1] We trained our network with back-propagation using momentum of 0.9, a learning rate of 0.004 reduced to 0.0003 for the final epoch, a batch size of 100 words per weight update, and initial weights sampled uniformly between ±1.0 (cf. ±0.001 for Elman's network). Network performance for both training and testing was measured in terms of divergence and network outputs were normalised using Luce ratios (Luce, 1986), also known as softmax constraints (see Rohde & Plaut, 1999).

Because our grammars were in standard stochastic, context-free form, it

---

[1] The effects of changes to some of these parameter values—in particular, the magnitude of initial random weights—are evaluated in a second simulation.

was possible to evaluate the network by comparing its predictions to the theoretically correct next-word distributions given the sentence context (Rohde, 1999). By contrast, it was not possible to generate such optimal predictions based on Elman's grammar. To form an approximation to optimal predictions, Elman trained an empirical language model on sentences generated in the same way as the testing corpus. Predictions by this model were based on the observed next-word statistics given every sentence context to which it was exposed.

Results and discussion. Elman did not provide numerical results for the complex condition but he did report that his network was unable to learn the task when trained on the most complex corpus from the start. However, learning was effective in the simple regimen, in which the network was exposed to increasingly complex input. In this condition, Elman found that the mean cosine[2] of the angle between the network's prediction vectors and those of the empirical model was 0.852 (SD = 0.259), where 1.0 is optimal.

Figure 6.2 shows, for each training condition, the mean divergence error per word on the testing corpora of our network when evaluated against the theoretically optimal predictions given the grammar. To reduce the effect of outliers, and because we were interested in the best possible performance, results were averaged over only the best 16 of 20 trials. Somewhat surprisingly, rather than an advantage for starting small, the data reveal a significant advantage for the complex training regimen; $F(1, 150) = 53.8$, $p < .001$. Under no condition did the simple training regimen outperform the complex training. Moreover, the advantage in starting complex increased with the proportion of fully constrained relative clauses. Thus, when the 16 simple and 16 complex training regimen networks for each grammar were paired with one another in order of increasing overall performance, there was a strong positive correlation, $r = .76$, $p < .001$, between the order of the grammars from A to E and the difference in error between the simple versus complex training regimes.[3] This is consistent with the idea that starting small is most effective when important dependencies span uninformative clauses. Nevertheless, against expectations, starting small failed to improve performance even for class A, in which relative clauses did not conform to semantic constraints imposed by the preceding noun.

In summary, starting with simple inputs proved to be of no benefit, and was actually a significant hindrance when semantic constraints applied across

---

[2] The cosine of the angle between two vectors of equal dimensionality can be computed as the dot product (or sum of the pairwise products of the vector elements) divided by the product of the lengths of the two vectors.

[3] The correlation with grammar class is also significant, $r = .65$, $p < .001$, when using the ratio of the simple to complex regimen error rates for each pair of networks, rather than their difference.

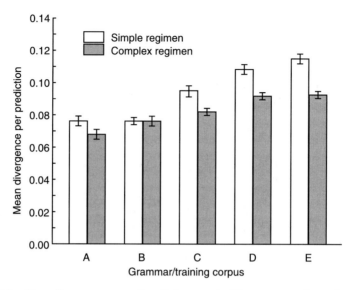

Figure 6.2.   Mean divergence per word prediction over the 75 per cent complex testing corpora generated from grammar classes A to E (increasing in the extent of semantic constraints) for the simple and complex training regimes. Note that lower values correspond to better performance. Means and standard errors were computed over the best 16 of 20 trials in each condition.

clauses. The networks were able to learn the grammars quite well even in the complex training regimen, as evidenced by additional analyses reported in Rohde and Plaut (1999). Moreover, the advantage for training on the fully complex corpus increased as the language was made more English-like by enforcing greater degrees of semantic constraints. While it has been shown previously that beginning with a reduced training set can be detrimental in classification tasks such as exclusive-OR (Elman, 1993), it appears that beginning with a simplified grammar can also produce significant interference on a more language-like prediction task. At the very least, starting small does not appear to be of general benefit in all language learning environments.

Rohde and Plaut (1999) simulation 2: Replication of Elman (1993)

Our failure to find an advantage for starting small in our initial work led us to ask what differences between that study and Elman's were responsible for the discrepant results. All of the grammars in the first set of simulations differed from Elman's grammar in that the language retained full semantic constraints within the main clause. It is possible that within-clause dependencies were in some way responsible for aiding learning in the complex training regimen. Therefore, we produced a language, labelled R for replication, which was identical to Elman's in all known respects, thus ruling out all but the most subtle differences in language as the potential source of our disparate results.

Methods.   Like Elman's grammar, grammar R uses just 12 verbs: two pairs each of transitive, intransitive, and mixed transitivity. In addition, as in Elman's grammar, the proper nouns Mary and John could not be modified by a relative clause and the only additional constraints involved number agreement. We should note that, although our grammar and Elman's produce the same set of strings to the best of our knowledge, the probability distributions over the strings in the languages may differ somewhat. As before, corpora with four levels of complexity were produced. In this case they very closely matched Elman's corpora in terms of average sentence length.

Networks were trained on this language both with our own methods and parameters and with those as close as possible to the ones Elman used. In the former case, we used normalised output units with a divergence error measure, momentum of 0.9, eleven epochs of training on the final corpus, a batch size of 10 words, a learning rate of 0.004 reduced to 0.0003 for the last epoch, and initial weights between ±1. In the latter case, we used logistic output units, squared error, no momentum, five epochs of training on the fourth corpus, online weight updating (after every word), a learning rate of 0.1 reduced to 0.06 in equal steps with each corpus change, and initial weights between ±0.001.

Results and discussion.   Even when training on sentences from a grammar with no semantic constraints, our learning parameters resulted in an advantage for the complex regimen. Over the best 12 of 15 trials, the network achieved an average divergence of 0.025 under the complex condition compared with 0.036 for the simple condition; $F(1, 22) = 34.8$, $p < .001$. Aside from the learning parameters, one important difference between our training method and Elman's was that we added six extra epochs of training on the final corpus to both conditions. This extended training did not, however, disproportionately benefit the complex condition. Between epoch 20 and 25, the average divergence error under the simple regimen dropped from 0.085 to 0.061, or 28 per cent. During the same period, the error under the complex regimen only fell 8 per cent, from 0.051 to 0.047.[4]

When the network was trained using parameters similar to those chosen by Elman, it failed to learn adequately, settling into bad local minima. The network consistently reached a divergence error of 1.03 under the simple

---

[4] The further drop of these error values, 0.047 and 0.061, to the reported final values of 0.025 and 0.036 resulted from the use of a reduced learning rate for epoch 26. Ending with a bit of training with a very low learning rate is particularly useful when doing online, or small batch size, learning.

training regimen and 1.20 under the complex regimen. In terms of city-block distance, these minima fall at 1.13 and 1.32 respectively—much worse than the results reported by Elman. We did, however, obtain successful learning by using the same parameters but simply increasing the weight initialisation range from ±0.001 to ±1.0, although performance under these conditions was not quite as good as with all of our parameters and methods. Even so, we again found a significant advantage for the complex regimen over the simple regimen in terms of mean divergence error (means of 0.122 versus 0.298, respectively; $F(1, 22) = 121.8, p < .001$).

Given that the strength of initial weights appears to be a key factor in successful learning, we conducted a few additional runs of the network to examine the role of this factor in more detail. The networks were trained on 25 epochs of exposure to corpus R_{75} under the complex regimen using parameters similar to Elman's, although with a fixed learning rate of 1.0 (i.e. without annealing). Figure 6.3 shows the sum squared error on the testing corpus over the course of training, as a function of the range of the initial random weights. It is apparent that larger initial weights help the network break through the plateau which lies at an error value of 0.221.

The dependence of learning on the magnitudes of initial weights can be understood in light of properties of the logistic activation function, the back-propagation learning procedure, and the operation of simple recurrent networks. It is generally thought that small random weights aid error-correcting

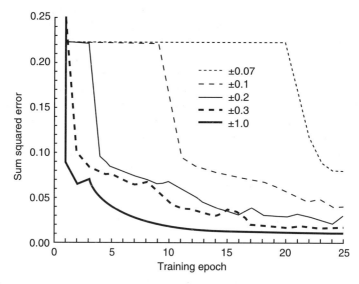

Figure 6.3. Sum squared error produced by the network on the testing set at each epoch of training on corpus R_{75} under the complex regimen, as a function of the range of initial random weights.

learning in connectionist networks because they place unit activations within the linear range of the logistic function where error derivatives, and hence weight changes, will be largest. However, the error derivatives that are back-propagated to hidden units are scaled by their outgoing weights; feedback to the rest of the network is effectively eliminated if these weights are too small. Moreover, with very small initial weights, the summed inputs of units in the network are all almost zero, yielding activations very close to 0.5 regardless of the input presented to the network. This is particularly problematic in a simple recurrent network because it leads to context representations (copied from previous hidden activations) that contain little if any usable information about previous inputs. Consequently, considerably extended training may be required to accumulate sufficient weight changes to begin to differentiate even the simplest differences in context (see Figure 6.3). By contrast, starting with relatively large initial weights not only preserves the back-propagated error derivatives but also allows each input to have a distinct and immediate impact on hidden representations and, hence, on context representations. Although the resulting patterns may not be particularly good representations for solving the task (because the weights are random), they at least provide an effective starting point for beginning to learn temporal dependencies.

In summary, on a grammar essentially identical to that used by Elman (1991, 1993), we found a robust advantage for training with the full complexity of the language from the outset. Although we cannot directly compare the performance of our network to that of Elman's network, it appears likely that the current network learned the task considerably better than the empirical model that we used for evaluation. By contrast, the network was unable to learn the language in either the simple or the complex condition when we used parameters similar to those employed by Elman. However, increasing the range of the initial connection weights allowed the network to learn quite well, although in this case we again found a strong advantage for starting with the full grammar. It was possible to eliminate this advantage by removing all dependencies between main clauses and their subclauses, and even to reverse it by, in addition, training exclusively on complex sentences. But these training corpora bear far less resemblance to the actual structure of natural language than do those that produce a clear advantage for training on the full complexity of the language from the beginning.

Rohde and Plaut (1999) simulation 3: Progressive memory

Elman (1993) argued that his finding that initially simplified inputs were necessary for effective language learning was not directly relevant to child language acquisition because, in his view, there was little evidence that adults modify the grammatical structure of their speech when interacting with children (although we would disagree, see, for example, Gallaway & Richards, 1994; Snow, 1995; Sokolov, 1993). As an alternative, Elman suggested that the same constraint could be satisfied if the network itself, rather than the training corpus, was initially limited in its complexity. Following Newport's less-is-more hypothesis (Goldowsky & Newport, 1993; Newport, 1990), Elman proposed that the gradual maturation of children's memory and attentional abilities could actually aid language learning.

To test this proposal, Elman (1993) conducted additional simulations in which the memory of a simple recurrent network (i.e. the process of copying hidden activations onto the context units) was initially hindered and then allowed to gradually improve over the course of training. When trained on the full complexity of the grammar from the outset, but with progressively improving memory, the network was again successful at learning the structure of the language that it had failed to learn when using fully mature memory throughout training. In this way, Elman's computational findings dovetailed perfectly with Newport's empirical findings to provide what seemed like compelling evidence for the importance of maturational constraints on language acquisition (see Elman et al., 1996, for further discussion).

Given that the primary computational support for the less-is-more hypothesis comes from Elman's simulations with limited memory rather than those with incremental training corpora, it is important to verify that our contradictory findings of an advantage for the complex regimen in simulations 1 and 2 also hold by comparison with training under progressively improving memory. Accordingly, we conducted simulations similar to those of Elman, in which a network with gradually improving memory was trained on the full semantically constrained grammar, E, as well as on the replication grammar, R, using both Elman's and our own training parameters.

Methods.   In his limited-memory simulation, Elman (1993) trained a network exclusively on the complex corpus,[5] which he had previously found to be unlearnable. As a model of limited memory span, the recurrent feedback provided by the context layer was eliminated periodically during processing by setting the activations at this layer to 0.5. For the first 12 epochs of training, this was done randomly after 3–4 words had been processed, without regard to sentence boundaries. For the next 5 epochs the memory window was increased to 4–5 words, then to 5–6, 6–7, and finally, in the last stage of training, the memory was not interfered with at all.

In the current simulation, the training corpus consisted of 75 per cent complex sentences, although Elman's may have extended to 100 per cent complexity. Like Elman, we extended the first period of training, which used

---

[5] It is unclear from the text whether Elman (1993) used the corpus with 75 per cent or 100 per cent complex sentences in the progressive memory experiments.

a memory window of 3–4 words, from 5 epochs to 12 epochs. We then trained for 5 epochs each with windows of 4–5 and 5–7 words. The length of the final period of unrestricted memory depended on the training methods. When using our own methods (see simulation 2), as when training on the final corpus in the simple regimen, this period consisted of 10 epochs followed by one more with the reduced learning rate. When training with our approximation of Elman's methods on grammar R, this final period was simply 5 epochs long. Therefore, under both conditions, the memory-limited network was allowed to train for a total of 7 epochs more than the corresponding full-memory network in simulations 1 and 2. When using our methods, learning rate was held fixed until the last epoch, as in simulation 1. With Elman's method, we reduced the learning rate with each change in memory limit.

Results and discussion.   Although he did not provide numerical results, Elman (1993) reported that the final performance was as good as in the prior simulation involving progressive inputs. Again, this was deemed a success relative to the complex, full-memory condition which was reportedly unable to learn the task.

Using our training methods on language R, the limited-memory condition resulted in equivalent performance to that of the full-memory condition, in terms of divergence error (means of 0.027 versus 0.025, respectively; $F(1, 22) = 2.12$, $p > .15$). Limited memory did, however, provide a significant advantage over the corresponding progressive-inputs condition from simulation 2 (mean 0.036; $F(1, 22) = 24.4$, $p < .001$). Similarly, for language E, the limited-memory condition was equivalent to the full-memory condition (mean of 0.093 for both; $F < 1$) but better than the progressive-inputs condition from Simulation 2 (mean of 0.115; $F(1, 22) = 31.5$, $p < .001$).

With Elman's training methods on grammar R, the network with limited memory consistently settled into the same local minimum, with a divergence of 1.20, as did the network with full memory (see simulation 2). Using the same parameters but with initial connection weights in the range ±1.0, the limited-memory network again performed almost equivalently to the network with full memory (means of 0.130 versus 0.122, respectively; $F(1, 22) = 2.39$, $p > 0.10$), and significantly better than the full-memory network trained with progressive inputs (mean of 0.298; $F(1, 22) = 109.1$, $p < .001$).

To summarise, in contrast with Elman's findings, when training on the fully complex grammar from the outset, initially limiting the memory of a simple recurrent network provided no advantage over training with full memory, despite the fact that the limited-memory regimen involved seven more epochs of exposure to the training corpus. On the other hand, in all of the successful conditions, limited memory did provide a significant advantage over gradually increasing the complexity of the training corpus.

204 ROHDE AND PLAUT

Summary

Contrary to the results of Elman (1991, 1993), Rohde and Plaut (1999) found that it is possible for a standard simple recurrent network to gain reasonable proficiency in a language roughly similar to that designed by Elman without staged inputs or memory. In fact, there was a significant advantage for starting with the full language and this advantage increased as languages were made more natural by increasing the proportion of clauses that obeyed semantic constraints. There may, of course, be other training methods that would yield even better performance. However, at the very least, it appears that the advantage of staged input is not a robust phenomenon in simple recurrent networks.

To identify the factors that led to the disadvantage for starting small, we returned to a more direct replication of Elman's work in simulation 2. Using Elman's parameters, we did find what seemed to be an advantage for starting small, but the network failed to sufficiently master the task in this condition. We do not yet understand what led Elman to succeed in this condition where we failed. One observation made in the course of these simulations was that larger initial random connection weights in the network were crucial for learning. We therefore reapplied Elman's training methods but increased the range of the initial weights from ±0.001 to ±1.0. Both this condition and our own training parameters revealed a strong advantage for starting with the full language.

Finally, in simulation 3 we examined the effect of progressive memory manipulations similar to those performed by Elman (1993). It was found that, despite increased training time, limited memory failed to provide an advantage over full memory in any condition. Interestingly, training with initially limited memory was generally less of a hindrance to learning than training with initially simplified input. In all cases, though, successful learning again required the use of sufficiently large initial weights.

Certainly there are situations in which starting with simplified inputs is necessary for effective learning of a prediction task by a recurrent network. For example, Bengio, Simard, and Frasconi (1994) (see also Lin, Horne, & Giles, 1996) report such results for tasks requiring a network to learn contingencies that span 10–60 entirely unrelated inputs. However, such tasks are quite unlike the learning of natural language. It may also be possible that starting with a high proportion of simple sentences is of significant benefit in learning other language processing tasks, such as comprehension. A child's discovery of the mapping between form and meaning will likely be facilitated if he or she experiences propositionally simple utterances whose meaning is apparent or is clarified by the accompanying actions of the parent. However, the real question in addressing the less-is-more hypothesis is whether limited cognitive capacity will substantially aid this process.

Having failed to replicate Elman's results, it seems appropriate to turn a critical eye on the other major sources of evidence for the less-is-more hypothesis. Aside from Elman's findings, four main studies have been characterised as providing support for the advantage of learning with limited resources. Goldowsky and Newport (1993) presented evidence of the noise-reducing power of random filtering in a statistical learning model of a simple morphological system. Kareev et al. (1997) offered a statistical argument in favour of the correlation-enhancing power of small samples and performed two empirical studies purported to confirm this. The other two studies are more purely empirical. Cochran et al. (1999) taught participants ASL verbs with and without the presence of a simultaneous cognitive load and with practice on the full signs or on individual morphemes. Finally, Kersten and Earles (2001) taught participants a simple novel language with and without sequential input. We discuss each of the four papers here in some detail.

GOLDOWSKY AND NEWPORT (1993)

Goldowsky and Newport (1993) proposed a simple learning task, and one form of learning model that might be used to solve the task. Training examples consisted of pairings of forms and meanings. A form had three parts, A, B, and C. For each part there were three possible values: A_1, A_2, A_3, B_1, B_2, etc. Meanings were also composed of three parts, M, N, and O, each with three values. There was a very simple mapping from forms to meanings: A_1, A_2, and A_3 corresponded to M_1, M_2, and M_3, respectively, B_1, B_2, and B_3 corresponded to N_1, N_2, and N_3, and so forth.[6] Thus, the form $A_2B_1C_3$ had the meaning $M_2N_1O_3$. The task was, apparently, to learn this simple underlying mapping.

Goldowsky and Newport suggested that one way to solve the task might be to gather a table with counts of all form and meaning correspondences across some observed data. If the form $A_2B_1C_3$ and the meaning $M_2N_1O_3$ were observed, the model would increment values of cells in the table corresponding to the pairing of each of the eight subsets of the form symbols with each subset of the three meaning symbols. If trained on all 27 possible examples, the model would have a value of 9 for each of the cells correctly pairing individual elements of the form to individual elements of the meaning (e.g. A_1 to M_1 and B_3 to N_3). The next largest, incorrectly paired, cells would have a value of 3 and the rest of the cells would have a value of 1.

Goldowsky and Newport suggested that there is too much noise in such a table because of the many values representing incorrect or overly complex

---

[6] The mapping used in the Goldowsky and Newport (1993) paper actually included one exception—that form $A_4B_4C_4$ has meaning $M_3N_3O_3$. Because the introduction of this did not seem to strengthen their case for starting small, it is eliminated here for simplicity.

pairings. They then introduced a filtering scheme meant to simulate the effect of poor working memory on a child's experiences. Before a form/meaning pair is entered into the table, some of its information is lost at random. Half of the time one of the three elements of the form is retained and half of the time two elements are retained. Likewise for the meaning. The authors argued that this improves learning because it produces a table with a higher signal-to-noise ratio. Therefore, they concluded, having limited memory can be helpful because it can help the learner focus on the simple, often important, details of a mapping.

But we should examine this learning situation a bit more carefully. First of all, in what sense is the signal-to-noise ratio improving as a result of filtering? The ratio between the correct, largest values in the table in the adult (unfiltered) case and the next largest competitors was 3:1. In the child (filtered) case, the expected ratio remains 3:1. Although some of the competitors will become proportionately less likely, others will not. What is eliminated by the filtering is the large number of very unlikely mappings. So the signal-to-noise ratio is improving if it is taken to be the ratio of the correct value to the sum of all other values. If taken to be the ratio of the correct value to the nearest incorrect value, there is no improvement. Furthermore, the child learner must experience many more form/meaning pairings than the adult learner before it can adequately fill its co-occurrence table.

To see the implications of these points, we need to make the task somewhat more explicit. Goldowsky and Newport (1993) presented a model that counts statistics, but not one that actually solves the form/meaning mapping. To complete the story, we will need to generate a model that is capable of taking a form and producing its best guess for the appropriate meaning. Two potential solutions to this problem immediately come to mind. In the first, arguably simpler, method, the model looks down the column of values under the given form and chooses the meaning corresponding to the largest value. If two meanings have the same strength, the model is counted wrong. This will be referred to as the *Plurality* method.

In the second method, the model draws at random from the distribution of values, such that the probability of selecting a meaning is proportional to the value associated with that meaning. This *Sampling* method seems to be more in line with what Goldowsky and Newport implied might be going on, judging from their use of the term signal-to-noise ratio. The Plurality method fails only if the nearest competitor is as strong as the correct answer. By contrast, the Sampling method is wrong in proportion to the total strength of competitors. Both of these methods were implemented and tested experimentally with and without random filtering. The models were judged by their ability to provide the correct meaning for each of the nine forms involving a single element. The results, averaged over 100 trials in each condition, are shown in Figure 6.4.

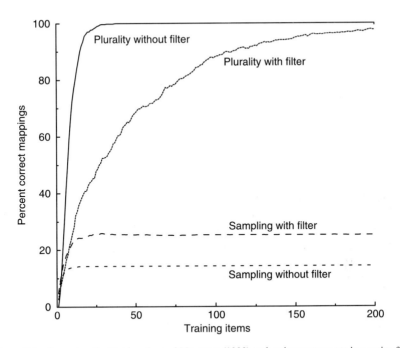

Figure 6.4. Learning the Goldowsky and Newport (1993) task using raw counts in a noise-free environment.

As Goldowsky and Newport (1993) suggested, their filtering mechanism is indeed beneficial when used with the Sampling method, achieving a score of about 25.2 per cent versus 14.3 per cent without filtering. However, sampling overall performs quite poorly. The Plurality method is much more effective. But in that case, filtering is harmful, and slows learning down considerably. Even after 200 trials, the filtered model is able to solve the task completely only about 80 per cent of the time.

Now, one might reasonably make the argument that this isn't a fair comparison. Perhaps the Plurality method is much more susceptible to noise and the benefit of the filter isn't apparent in such perfect conditions. After all, it is probably unreasonable to expect that a human learner is able to perfectly notice and store all available information. To test this possibility, a source of noise was added to the simulations; 50 per cent of the time, the operation of incrementing a value in the table failed. Thus, half of the data was lost at random. As shown in Figure 6.5, this manipulation had almost no effect on the Sampling method, but did have some effect on the Plurality method. However, the Plurality method remained significantly better without the filter.

A final consideration is that the bubble diagrams used to represent the form/meaning co-occurrence table in the Goldowsky and Newport (1993)

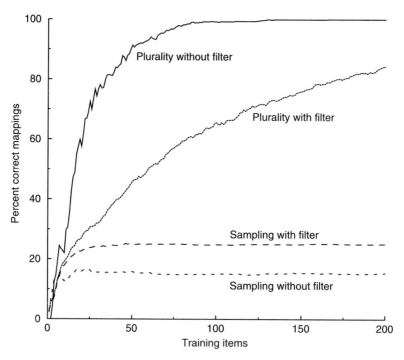

Figure 6.5.   Learning the Goldowsky and Newport (1993) task using raw counts with random loss of 50 per cent of the data.

paper did not directly reflect raw co-occurrence counts. The radius of the bubbles was proportional to the ratio of the co-occurrence count to the square root of the product of the overall number of occurrences of the form and the overall number of occurrences of the meaning. This was termed the "consistency of co-occurrence". So, one might ask, how well do the two proposed models perform if they work with co-occurrence consistency values rather than raw counts? As shown in Figure 6.6, performance declines slightly for the Sampling method and improves slightly for the Plurality method with filtering; but overall the results are qualitatively similar.

Thus, with the much more effective Plurality method of determining form/ meaning pairs from co-occurrence data, the filtering mechanism was a serious hindrance. But it seems that building a large table may not be at all similar to the way the human brain might solve this mapping task. Perhaps a better model is that of a connectionist network. Could such a model learn the underlying regularity and would it benefit from the same filtering method proposed by Goldowsky and Newport? To answer this question, we performed some simulation experiments.

First a simple one-layer network was constructed, with a nine-unit input

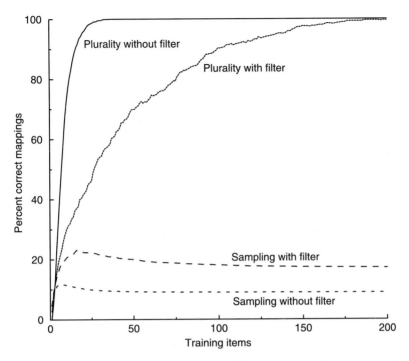

Figure 6.6. Learning the Goldowsky and Newport (1993) task using correlation values with no noise.

layer fully connected to a nine-unit output layer. The nine input units corresponded to the nine possible elements of the form. One of the first three units was turned on to represent the *A* element, one of the second set of three units was turned on to represent the *B* element, and so forth. Similarly, the nine units in the output representation corresponded to the nine possible elements of the meaning, with three of the nine units normally having targets of 1, and the rest having targets of 0. If an element of the form was eliminated by the filtering mechanism, the corresponding three units of the input were all turned off. If an element of the meaning was eliminated, the corresponding three units of the output had no target values. The network was tested by presenting it with a single element of the form as an input. Although the network may never have been trained to perform this particular mapping, the desired response is that it will output just the corresponding element of the meaning. A response was considered correct if the activations of all nine output units were on the correct side of 0.5.

To argue that filtering is or is not beneficial, one cannot simply rely on performance under a single set of training parameters. It is possible that the benefit of filtering could be masked by a poor choice of parameters.

TABLE 6.3

Final performance levels with a 9-9 network under various conditions. The left value in each pair is the performance without filtering and the right value is the performance with filtering

Weight decay	Momentum	Initial weights	Learning rate							
			0.05		0.1		0.2		0.4	
0	0	±0.1	100.0	98.9	100.0	98.4	100.0	76.7	100.0	44.9
0	0	±1.0	85.6	77.3	96.9	88.7	98.7	75.6	100.0	45.6
0	0.9	±0.1	100.0	33.3	100.0	16.7	100.0	4.4	100.0	3.3
0	0.9	±1.0	100.0	32.2	100.0	15.8	100.0	4.4	100.0	3.3
0.0001	0	±0.1	100.0	99.6	100.0	97.6	100.0	78.0	100.0	44.4
0.0001	0	±1.0	88.9	79.6	97.1	89.3	100.0	76.0	100.0	46.4
0.0001	0.9	±0.1	100.0	42.2	100.0	22.2	100.0	5.6	100.0	3.3
0.0001	0.9	±1.0	100.0	42.2	100.0	22.0	100.0	5.6	100.0	3.1

Therefore, we trained networks using 32 parameter sets. Four learning rates (0.05, 0.1, 0.2, 0.4) were crossed with two momentum values (0.0, 0.9), two initial weight ranges (± 0.1, ±1.0), and two weight decay values (0.0, 0.0001). Networks were trained on 1000 randomly selected examples using online learning, meaning that weight updates were performed after each example.

Performance was measured by testing the model's ability to produce the correct meaning for each of the nine isolated forms. The final performance in each condition, averaged over 50 trials, is shown in Table 6.3. Without filtering, the network learns best with small initial weights, some weight decay, momentum, and a large learning rate. With filtering, the network learns best with a small learning rate and no momentum. But under no conditions did filtering improve learning. Figure 6.7 shows the averaged learning profiles with and without filtering using training parameters with which the filtered networks performed quite well: no weight decay or momentum, initial weights ±0.1, and learning rate 0.05. Although they reach similar final performance, the networks learned much more quickly and smoothly without filtering.

One might argue that we have cheated by applying a single-layer network to the task because such a network cannot learn very complex mappings, so it doesn't need filtering to learn this simple one. Admittedly, if the task were not so simple, we would have used a larger network. To test the possibility that a larger network will fail to learn the simple rule without filtering, we trained a two-layer, 9-9-9, feedforward network using the same task and parameters.

As shown in Table 6.4, the two-layer network doesn't solve the task as easily as the one-layer network. But under several different choices of parameters, the network is able to master the task nearly all of the time without filtering. The best performance achieved with filtering, on the other hand,

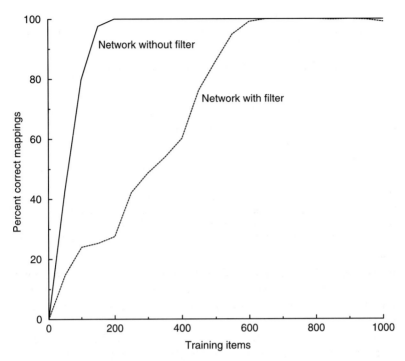

Figure 6.7. Learning the Goldowsky and Newport (1993) task using a single-layer neural network.

TABLE 6.4
Final performance levels with a 9-9-9 network under various conditions. The left value in each pair is the performance without filtering and the right value is the performance with filtering

Weight decay	Momentum	Initial weights	Learning Rate							
			0.05		0.1		0.2		0.4	
0	0	±0.1	0.0	1.1	42.0	2.2	92.9	8.9	99.1	26.9
0	0	±1.0	60.2	14.2	72.2	41.6	88.4	40.7	88.4	33.3
0	0.9	±0.1	98.7	24.9	93.8	14.4	81.1	6.4	19.6	2.4
0	0.9	±1.0	81.8	23.8	79.1	14.4	76.2	5.8	41.1	2.4
0.0001	0	±0.1	0.0	1.1	35.6	2.2	94.0	7.6	99.6	26.9
0.0001	0	±1.0	66.0	10.0	79.1	37.1	93.1	47.1	88.4	34.7
0.0001	0.9	±0.1	99.3	24.7	99.3	16.2	99.6	6.9	94.0	2.9
0.0001	0.9	±1.0	99.3	25.6	99.3	15.6	99.1	5.6	99.1	3.6

was just 47.1 per cent correct. In only two cases—with a small learning rate, small initial weights, and no momentum—did the filtered networks perform better than the unfiltered ones. But in those cases the filtered networks only reached an average performance of 1.1 per cent.

In summary, the filtering mechanism proposed by Goldowsky and Newport (1993) for this task did not improve the performance of either an effective tabulation strategy or two neural network models. Although the random filtering mechanism sometimes isolates correct one-to-one form/meaning pairs, it more frequently destroys those pairs and isolates incorrect ones. This introduces noise that outweighs the occasional benefit and that can be detrimental to learning.

KAREEV, LIEBERMAN, AND LEV (1997)

Kareev et al. (1997) began by reiterating a theoretical point about sampled distributions that was first raised in Kareev (1995). If a distribution over two correlated real-valued variables is sampled repeatedly, the expected median of the observed correlations in the samples increases as the size of the sample decreases. On the basis of this fact, Kareev et al. suggested that humans estimating correlations in observed events will be better at detecting those correlations if they have limited working memory, and thus presumably rely on smaller remembered samples in formulating their judgements.

In the first experiment, participants were given 128 envelopes, each containing a coin. Envelopes were either red or green and the coin inside was either marked with an X or an O. Participants opened envelopes one by one in random order and each time tried to predict the type of coin based on the envelope's colour. The envelopes' contents were manipulated to produce true colour/mark correlations ranging from –0.6 to 0.6. The eight participants in each condition were grouped based on the results of a single-trial digit-span test of working memory. Response correlation was computed for each participant using the matrix of envelope colours and mark predictions. Kareev et al. found that the low-span participants tended to have larger response correlations and to have more accurate overall predictions.

This is certainly an interesting result but the theoretical explanation ought to be reconsidered. To begin with, the authors stressed the fact that *median* observed correlation increases as sample size decreases. That is, with a smaller sample, observers have a higher probability of encountering a correlation that is larger than the true correlation. This is mainly an artefact of the increased noise resulting from small samples. On the basis of increasing median, Kareev et al. (1997, p. 279) concluded that, "The limited capacity of working memory increases the chances for early detection of a correlation. . . . [A] relationship, if it exists, is more likely to be detected, the smaller the sample." Thus, the authors seem to be equating median estimation with the ability to detect any correlation whatsoever. However, they do not offer an explicit account of how participants might be solving the correlation detection or coin prediction task.

The median correlation happens to be one measure computable over a series of samples.[7] But other measures might be more directly applicable to the problem of detecting a correlation, such as the *mean*, and not all measures increase in magnitude with smaller samples. The mean correlation diminishes with decreasing sample size. However, an individual participant is not encountering a series of samples, but just one sample, so the median or mean computed over multiple samples is not necessarily relevant.

So what is an appropriate model of how participants are solving the task, and how is this model affected by sample size? Signal detection theory typically assumes that human observers have a threshold above which a signal is detected. In this case, we might presume that the signal is the perceived correlation between envelope colour and coin type, and that the correlation, whether positive or negative, is detectable if its magnitude is above a participant's threshold. If participants are basing their responses in the coin prediction task on a signal detection procedure involving a fixed threshold, we must ask what is the probability that a sample of size N from a distribution with true correlation C has an observed correlation greater than a given threshold?

It seems reasonable to suppose that the typical human threshold for detecting correlations in small samples probably falls between 0.05 and 0.2, although it presumably varies based on task demands. Figure 6.8 shows the probability that a small sample has an observed correlation above 0.1 as a function of the size of the sample and the strength of the true correlation. The data in this experiment involved pairs of real-valued random variables. A desired correlation, C, was achieved by generating the values as follows:

$$a = rand(\,)$$

$$b = Ca + \sqrt{1 - C^2}\, rand(\,)$$

where *rand( )* produces a random value uniformly distributed in the range [−1,1]. One million trials were conducted for each pairing of sample size and correlation.

Clearly, for the range of parameters covered, the chance that the observed correlation is greater than threshold increases monotonically with sample size. Larger samples lead to a greater chance of detecting a correlation. One may disagree with the arbitrary choice of 0.1 for the detection threshold, but the same penalty for small samples is seen with a value of 0.2, provided the true correlation is greater than 0.2, and the effect becomes even stronger with

---

[7] The term "sample" is used here to refer to a set of observations, or examples, not just a single observation.

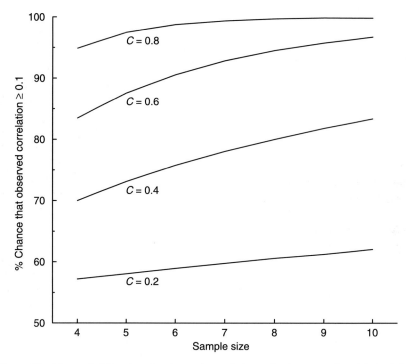

Figure 6.8. The probability that the observed correlation value is greater than 0.1 (and thus presumably detectable) as a function of sample size and true correlation (C).

thresholds below 0.1. Thus, the fact that the median observed correlation increases with small sample sizes does not bear on what is arguably a reasonable model of human correlation detection.

Another important issue is that the sampling distribution measures discussed by Kareev et al. were for pairs of real-valued variables, but the experiments they conducted involved binary variables. Do the same principles apply to small samples of binary data? Figure 6.9 shows the median observed correlation in small samples of binary data, as a function of the sample size and the true correlation. Although median correlation decreases as a function of sample size for real-valued data, median correlation doesn't seem to vary in any systematic way as a function of sample size for binary data. There is simply more variability in the small samples. But again, median correlation value is not necessarily indicative of the ease of detection. As with real-valued data, the probability that an observed correlation is greater than some small threshold tends to increase with larger samples of binary data.

But it may be possible that these statistical measures don't accurately reflect the power of small samples in a practical context. Therefore, we designed a simple model to perform the envelope/coin task using varying

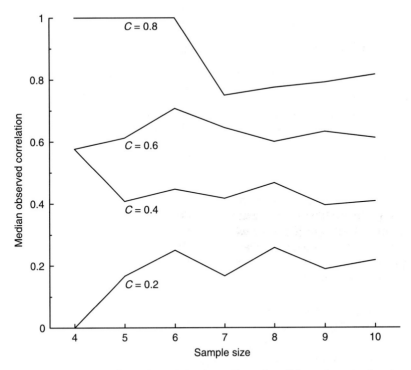

Figure 6.9. The median observed correlation in small samples of binary data, as a function of sample size and true correlation (*C*).

levels of working memory. The model was intended to reflect the manner in which Kareev et al. seem to imply humans might be solving this task. The model simply remembers the contents of the last *N* cards of each colour and chooses the coin that was more frequent in that sample. If the coins were equally frequent in the sample, the choice is random. The model was run with three sample sizes, 5, 9, and 13, meant to reflect small, medium, and large working memory capacity, and was run 1000 times on each of the 14 distributional conditions used by Kareev et al. (1997). Seven of these conditions were symmetric in that they used an equal number of Xs and Os and seven did not satisfy this constraint and were termed asymmetric. Each symmetric condition had a corresponding asymmetric one with approximately the same envelope/coin correlation. The correlation between the model's predictions and the envelope colour was computed in the same way as for the experimental participants.

Figure 6.10 shows the prediction correlation values as a function of actual correlation for the three working memory levels, with results in the corresponding symmetric and asymmetric conditions averaged. The identity

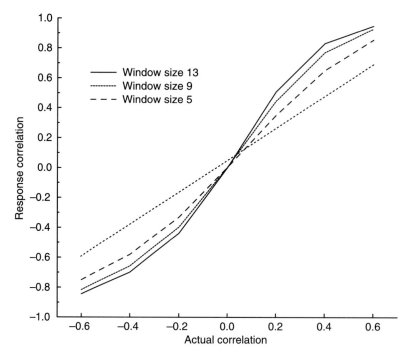

Figure 6.10. The correlation between envelope colour and the model's predictions of coin marking as a function of the actual correlation and the model's memory window size.

baseline is provided as a reference but note that optimal performance in this task has nothing to do with matching the actual correlation values. An optimal predictor will always predict the more likely coin, whether the actual correlation is 0.1 or 0.9. Contrary to Kareev et al.'s prediction, the larger sample size results in larger response correlations, not smaller ones. Figure 6.11 gives the prediction accuracy as a function of correlation and window size. Although the difference is fairly small, larger window sizes consistently outperformed the smaller ones.

Therefore, although the results of the first experiment in Kareev et al. (1997) are rather interesting and deserve replication and explanation, these results cannot be attributed to the effects of small samples on perceived correlation. The probability of observing a correlation stronger than a relatively sensitive detection threshold is lower with small sample sizes and the median observed correlation value with binary data does not change systematically with sample size. A simple prediction model that relies on samples of varying size performs better with larger samples. While it is true that this model does not appear to fully capture human performance in this task, the

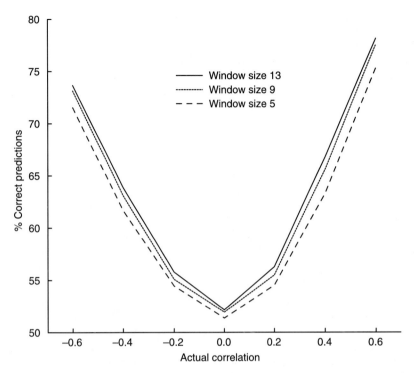

Figure 6.11. The prediction accuracy as a function of the actual correlation and the model's memory window size.

relevant point is that the effects of small sample sizes on perceived correlation do not adequately explain the empirical findings.

The second experiment reported by Kareev et al. (1997) also does not seem to fully support their theory. In this case, participants were not blocked by digit span but were given samples of varying size upon which to base a prediction. The samples were either fully visible throughout the process or were presented sequentially and were unavailable in formulating the prediction. In this case, the variables were real-valued, rather than binary. The results indicated that when samples were absent, there was better performance with the small samples than with the medium or large ones. But when the samples were present, performance increased with sample size. This latter result is inconsistent with the prediction that small samples should statistically magnify correlations. If that were true, larger samples would lead to worse performance, especially if the samples are present. The fact that participants viewing sequential samples performed better with smaller ones is indeed interesting, but cannot be explained by a statistical property of sample size itself.

COCHRAN, McDONALD, AND PARAULT (1999)

Much of the empirical support for the less-is-more hypothesis derives from the study of American Sign Language (ASL). Newport (1990) observed that late learners of ASL tend to make more morphological errors in the production of verbs than do early learners. Although interesting, it is not clear to what this finding should be attributed. The problems incurred by late learners could be due to deactivation of a language acquisition device, greater cognitive capacity, different types or degrees of exposure, or a variety of other factors. Cochran et al. (1999) sought to provide empirical evidence supporting the idea that cognitive limitations can actually lead to better learning of ASL verbs. They conducted three experiments in which participants unfamiliar with ASL were taught some sentences and then tested in their ability to produce either the same or novel ASL sentences.

In the first two experiments, participants were taught 16 verbs. Each verb was encountered in the context of a single sentence, in which either the subject was "I" and the object was "you", or vice versa. Six of the verbs used congruent agreement, in which the direction of the sign was from the verb's subject (either the signer or the addressee) to the verb's object; two of the verbs used incongruent agreement, in which the direction of the sign was from object to subject; four nonagreement verbs required a static direction of motion, which was either always away from or always towards the signer. The last four verbs had a direction of motion aligned vertically, either up or down.

Participants were exposed to each verb in a single context, with half of the verbs in each condition using the subject "I" and half using the subject "you". The 16 study sentences were observed three times in the first experiment and eight times in the second experiment. To place a load on working memory, half of the participants performed a tone-counting task during training. This was known as the load condition. Participants were then tested on the 16 familiar sentences as well as the 16 novel sentences created by reversing the subject and object.

Cochran et al. (1999) found that participants in the no-load condition produced the familiar sentences better overall and performed better on familiar and novel nonagreement verbs. However, participants in the no-load condition did not perform as well on the agreement verbs in novel sentences. They were much more likely to produce the sign in the same direction that they learned it, rather than reversing the direction in the new context. This was taken as evidence that "adults learning under normal conditions were failing to learn the internal structure of the language and were therefore limited in their ability to generalise to new contexts" (Cochran et al., 1999, p. 30).

However, an alternative reading of the data is that participants in the load condition were simply not learning as well and performed more randomly during test. Not only did load participants have more movements in the correct direction, they produced more verbs with no movement or, in the first experiment, with movement outside the axis between the signer and addressee. The fact that load condition participants happened to use the correct movement more often in novel conditions can be attributed to their generally more noisy behaviour, rather than their having learned to generalise to novel conditions.

The main problem with these experiments is that participants are expected to learn that the movement of certain verbs should agree with sentence context when there was no basis for such a generalisation in the examples to which the participants had been exposed. Each verb was seen in just one context, with just one direction of motion, and only 6 of the 16 verbs underwent congruent agreement. The evidence to which the participants were exposed fully supports the simpler hypothesis: that direction of motion is an intrinsic, noninflected part of the sign for a verb. In fact, this is the correct rule for half of the verbs used in the experiment. Given the lack of any evidence to the contrary, it seems much more reasonable for participants to surmise that ASL permits no agreement, than to surmise that some verbs have agreement, some have incongruent agreement, and some have no agreement. The results in these experiments are consistent with the hypothesis that participants in the no-load condition learned this very reasonable rule much better than did participants in the load condition.

A true test of generalisation ability must provide the learner with some support for the validity of the expected generalisation. Had participants experienced some agreement verbs used with different motions in different circumstances, they would have some basis for expecting that agreement plays a role in ASL. A second factor biasing the participants against formulating the desired generalisation was that, unlike in ASL, pronouns were explicitly produced in all training sentences. Languages with strong verb inflection, such as Spanish, often drop first- and second-person pronouns, because they convey redundant information. Because such pronoun drop was not a feature of the training sentences, learners are more likely to assume that pronominal information is not redundantly conveyed in the verb form. In summary, the first two experiments of this study essentially found that participants trained to perform one reasonable generalisation did poorly when tested on a different, more complex, generalisation.

The third experiment conducted by Cochran et al. (1999) tested the learning of ASL motion verbs, comparing participants who were taught to mimic whole signs with those who were taught to mimic just one part of each sign, either the form or the motion, at a time. During training, signs for a certain type of actor moving in a certain way were paired with a hand movement indicating the path of motion. For some verbs, the motion sign is produced at the same time as the verb, but for other verbs they are produced in sequence. During testing, all verbs were paired with all path signs.

Overall there was no difference in performance on the studied or the novel signs between the "whole" and "part" learners. There was an unexplained trade-off, in that whole learners did better if the parts of the new sign were to be performed sequentially and worse if they were to be performed simultaneously. The only other difference was the marginally significant tendency for whole-practice participants to produce more frozen signs,[8] which could be a cause or effect of the other difference. If anything, this study seems to provide strong evidence that learning individual parts of signs is not, overall, of significant benefit. Although whole-sign learners produced more frozen signs, they performed better in other respects, balancing the overall performance. Somewhat disturbingly, however, more participants were thrown out for inadequate performance or unscorable data from the part-learning group. One person in the whole-sign condition was thrown out for unscoreable data and nine people in the part-sign condition were replaced, three for bad performance and two for unscoreable data. Across the three experiments, three participants were discarded from the no-load and whole-sign conditions for performance or scoreability reasons, compared with 12 participants in the load and part-sign conditions. In experiments of this sort involving a direct comparison between training methods, eliminating participants for performance reasons during training has the clear potential to bias the average testing performance. If participants must be removed from one condition for performance reasons, an equal number of the worst performers in the other conditions should be removed as well, although this still may not fully eliminate the bias.

KERSTEN AND EARLES (2001)

Kersten and Earles (2001) conducted three language-learning experiments that compared learning in a staged input condition to learning in a full-sentence condition. In each experiment, participants viewed events in which one bug-like object moved towards or away from another, stationary, bug-like object. In the full-sentence condition, each event was paired with the auditory presentation of a three-word sentence. The first word corresponded to the appearance of the moving bug and ended in "-ju". The second word described the manner of motion—either walking with legs together or alternating—and ended in "-gop".[9] The third word described the direction of walking—towards or away from the stationary bug—and ended in "-tig".

---

[8] A frozen sign was a new sign that contained an unnecessary part of a previously studied sign.

[9] In the first experiment, some participants heard object-manner-path word order and others heard object-path-manner.

In the first two experiments, half of the participants heard complete sentences for the whole training period. The other participants initially heard just the first (object) word for a third of the trials, then the first two words, and finally all three words. In the testing period, participants were shown two events that varied on a single attribute and heard either an isolated word (corresponding to the manipulated attribute) or a sentence. They were to identify the event that correctly matched the word or sentence.

The most important finding in these experiments was significantly better performance, overall, for participants in the staged input condition. Kersten and Earles interpreted this as evidence in favour of the less-is-more hypothesis. However, one should exercise some caution in drawing conclusions from these experiments. Although there was an overall advantage for starting small, if one tests performance on object words, manner words, and path words independently, the effect is only significant for object words. Thus, the results are consistent with the hypothesis that starting small was only beneficial in learning the meanings of the object words, i.e. those words trained in isolation for the first third of the trials.

Kersten and Earles sought to rule out a slightly different, but equally viable, hypothesis—that the effect relies on the fact that the object words, as opposed to manner or path, were learned first. Therefore, in the third experiment, participants in the staged condition first heard the last (path) word, then the last two words (manner-path), and finally all three words. Again there was a significant overall advantage for the staged input condition. In this case, path words were learned better than object and manner words in both conditions. Although the overall advantage for the starting small condition reached significance, none of the tests isolating the three word types was significant. These results therefore do not rule out the hypothesis that participants in the staged input condition were only better on the words trained in isolation. Nevertheless, it is possible that these effects would reach significance with more participants.

The third experiment also added a test of the participants' sensitivity to morphology. Novel words were created by pairing an unfamiliar stem with one of the three familiar word endings (-ju, -gop, or -tig). Each word was first paired with an event that was novel in all three important dimensions. Participants were then shown a second event that differed from the first in a single dimension and were instructed to respond "Yes" if the second event was also an example of the new word. In other words, participants responded "Yes" if the two events *didn't* differ on the feature associated with the word ending. Kersten and Earles again found a significant advantage for the starting small condition.

However, there is some reason to question the results of this experiment. With the path-word ending, there was clearly no difference between the two conditions. In three of the four other conditions, participants performed

below chance levels, significantly so in one of them. The finding of significantly below chance performance leads one to suspect that participants may
have been confused by the task and that some participants may have incorrectly been responding "Yes" if the events did differ on the feature associated
with the word ending.

Even if we accept that there was an across-the-board advantage for the
staged input condition in these experiments, we should be cautious in generalising to natural language learning. The language used in this study was missing a number of important features of natural language. Word order and
morphology were entirely redundant and, more importantly, conveyed no
meaning. Words always appeared in the same position in every sentence and
were always paired with the same ending. In this simple language, there
wasn't a productive syntax or morphology, just a conventional word order.
Participants were thus free to use strategies such as ignoring word order and
morphological information, much as they learned to ignore meaningless
details of the events.

Participants in the full sentence condition were therefore at a potential
disadvantage. Any effective, general learning mechanism in a similar situation
would devote time and resources to testing the information carried in all
aspects of the events and sentences, including morphology and word order.
In this case, those features happened to convey no additional information
beyond that provided by the word stems themselves, placing participants who
paid attention to word order and morphology at a disadvantage. However,
these factors play critical roles in shaping the meaning of natural language
sentences, and devoting time and resources to learning them is useful, and
even necessary. The staged input learner, on the other hand, will have traded
off exposure to syntax for more exposure to individual words and their meanings, which is not clearly advantageous. A stronger test of the importance of
staged input would be to measure comprehension or production of whole,
novel sentences in a language with some aspects of meaning carried
exclusively by syntax and morphology.

Perhaps tellingly, some studies cited by Kersten and Earles comparing
children learning French in immersive programmes with and without prior
exposure to more traditional, elementary French-as-a-second-language
courses found either no difference or an advantage for children in the purely
immersive programme (Day & Shapson, 1988; Genesee, 1981; Shapson &
Day, 1982). Although these studies may not have adequately controlled for
age of exposure, intelligence, or motivational factors, it certainly is suggestive
that staged input may be less effective than immersion in learning natural
languages.

A final point of criticism of the Kersten and Earles (2001) paper is their
desire to equate the effects of staged input with those of internal memory
limitations. There is little reason to believe that these two factors will have

similar effects. Teaching the meanings of isolated words is bound to be help-ful, provided that it is only a supplement to exposure to complete language, is relatively noise free, and makes up a relatively small percentage of linguistic experience. However, memory limitations do not result in the same simple pairing of words and their meanings. At best, memory limitations have the effect of pairing isolated words or phrases to noisy, randomly sampled por-tions of a complex meaning. The actual part of the complex meaning con-tributed by the isolated word may be partially or completely lost and some extraneous information may be retained. Learning the correct pairings of words to meanings is no easier in this case than when faced with the full, complex meaning.

A more appropriate, although still not entirely sufficient, test of the benefit of memory limitations in the context of Kersten and Earles's design would be to test randomly selected words in the isolated word condition, rather than always the first or last word of the sentence. These should be paired with scenes with randomly selected details, such as the identity of the moving object or the location of the stationary object, obscured. Furthermore, tests should not be performed on familiar sentences but on novel ones, as the potential problem in starting with complete sentences is that adults will memorise them as wholes and will not generalise well to novel ones. It would be quite interesting if initial training of this form, which is more like the presumed effect of poor attention or working memory, was beneficial in the comprehension or production of novel sentences.

The actual claim of Newport's less-is-more hypothesis does not concern staged input. It is that memory or other internal limitations are the key factor in enabling children to learn language more effectively. Evidence for or against the benefit of staged input should be clearly distinguished from evidence concerning the effect of internal cognitive impairments.

GENERAL DISCUSSION

We believe that studying the way in which connectionist networks learn languages is particularly helpful in building an understanding of human lan-guage acquisition. The intuition behind the importance of starting with properly chosen simplified inputs is that it helps the network to focus immediately on the more basic, local properties of the language, such as lexical syntactic categories and simple noun–verb dependencies. Once these are learned, the network can more easily progress to harder sentences and further discoveries can be based on these earlier representations.

Our simulation results indicate, however, that such external manipulation of the training corpus is unnecessary for effective language learning, given appropriate training parameters. The reason, we believe, is that recurrent connectionist networks already have an inherent tendency to extract simple regularities first. A network does not begin with fully formed representations and memory; it must learn to represent and remember useful information under the pressure of performing particular tasks, such as word prediction. As a simple recurrent network learns to represent information about an input using its hidden units, that information then becomes available as context when processing the next input. If this context provides important constraints on the prediction generated by the second input, the context to hidden connections involved in retaining that information will be reinforced, leading the information to be available as context for the third input, and so on.

In this way, the network first learns short-range dependencies, starting with simple word-transition probabilities for which no deeper context is needed. At this stage, the long-range constraints effectively amount to noise, which is averaged out across a large number of sentences. As the short dependencies are learned, the relevant information becomes available for learning longer-distance dependencies. Very long-distance dependencies, such as grammatical constraints across multiple embedded clauses, still present a problem for this type of network in any training regimen. Information must be maintained across the intervening sequence to allow the network to pick up on such a dependency. However, there must be pressure to maintain that information or the hidden representations will encode more locally relevant information. Long-distance dependencies are difficult because the network will tend to discard information about the initial cue before it becomes useful. Adding semantic dependencies to embedded clauses aids learning because the network then has an incentive to continue to represent the main noun, not just for the prediction of the main verb, but for the prediction of some of the intervening material as well (see also Cleeremans et al., 1989).[10]

It might be thought that starting with simplified inputs would facilitate the acquisition of the local dependencies so that learning could progress more rapidly and effectively to handling the longer-range dependencies. There is, however, a cost to altering the network's training environment in this way. If the network is exposed only to simplified input, it may develop representations that are overly specialised for capturing only local dependencies. It then becomes difficult for the network to restructure these representations when confronted with harder problems whose dependencies are not restricted to those in the simplified input. In essence, the network is learning in an environment with a nonstationary probability distribution over inputs. In

---

[10] It should be pointed out that the bias towards learning short- before long-range dependencies is not specific to simple recurrent networks; back-propagation-through-time and fully recurrent networks also exhibit this bias. In the latter case, learning long-range dependencies is functionally equivalent to learning an input–output relationship across a larger number of intermediate processing layers (Rumelhart et al., 1986), which is more difficult than learning across fewer layers when the mapping is simple (see Bengio et al., 1994; Lin et al., 1996).

extreme form, such nonstationarity can lead to so-called catastrophic interference, in which training exclusively on a new task can dramatically impair
performance on a previously learned task that is similar to but inconsistent
with the new task (see McClelland, McNaughton, & O'Reilly, 1995;
McCloskey & Cohen, 1989).

A closely related phenomenon has been proposed by Marchman (1993) to
account for critical period effects in the impact of early brain damage on the
acquisition of English inflectional morphology. Marchman found that the
longer a connectionist system was trained on the task of generating the past
tense of verbs, the poorer it was at recovering from damage. This effect was
explained in terms of the degree of entrenchment of learned representations:
As representations become more committed to a particular solution within
the premorbid system, they become less able to adapt to relearning a new
solution after damage. More recently, McClelland (2001) and Thomas and
McClelland (1997) have used entrenchment-like effects within a Kohonen
network (Kohonen, 1984) to account for the apparent inability of non-native
speakers of a language to acquire native-level performance in phonological
skills, and why only a particular type of retraining regimen may prove
effective (see also Merzenich, Jenkins, Johnson, Schreiner, Miller, & Tallal,
1996; Tallal et al., 1996). Thus, there are a number of demonstrations
that connectionist networks may not learn as effectively when their training environment is altered significantly, as is the case in the incremental training
procedure employed by Elman (1991).

There has been much debate on the extent to which children experience
syntactically simplified language (see Richards, 1994; Snow, 1994, 1995, for a
discussion). While child-directed speech is undoubtedly marked by characteristic prosodic patterns, there is also evidence that it tends to consist of relatively short, well-formed utterances and to have fewer complex sentences and
subordinate clauses (Newport, Gleitman, & Gleitman, 1977; Pine, 1994). The
study by Newport and colleagues is instructive here, as it is often interpreted
as providing evidence that child-directed speech is not syntactically simplified. Indeed, these researchers found no indication that mothers carefully
tune their syntax to the current level of the child or that aspects of mothers'
speech styles have a discernible effect on the child's learning. Nonetheless,
it was clear that child-directed utterances, averaging 4.2 words, were quite
unlike adult-directed utterances, averaging 11.9 words. Although child-
directed speech included frequent deletions and other forms that are not
handled easily by traditional transformational grammars, whether or not
these serve as complexities to the child is debatable.

If children do, in fact, experience simplified syntax, it might seem as if our
findings suggest that such simplifications actually impede children's language
acquisition. We do not, however, believe this to be the case. The simple
recurrent network simulations have focused on the acquisition of syntactic

structure (with some semantic constraints), which is just a small part of the overall language learning process. Among other things, the child must also learn the meanings of words, phrases, and longer utterances in the language. This process is certainly facilitated by exposing the child to simple utterances with simple, well-defined meanings. We support Newport and colleagues' conclusion that the form of child-directed speech is governed by a desire to communicate with the child and not to teach syntax. However, we would predict that language acquisition would ultimately be hindered if particular syntactic or morphological constructions were avoided for extended periods in the input to either a child or adult learner.

But the main implication of the less-is-more hypothesis is not that staged input is necessary, but that the child's superior language learning ability is a consequence of the child's limitations. This might be interpreted in a variety of ways. Goldowsky and Newport (1993), Elman (1993), Kareev et al. (1997), and Cochran et al. (1999) suggest that the power of reduced memory is that it leads to information loss that can be beneficial in highlighting simple contingencies in the environment. This, it is suggested, encourages analytical processing over rote memorisation. We have argued, to the contrary, that in a range of learning procedures—from simple decision-making models to recurrent connectionist networks—such random information loss is of no benefit and may be harmful. Although it sometimes has the effect of isolating meaningful analytical units, it more often destroys those units or creates false contingencies.

Another take on the less-is-more hypothesis is that a learning system can benefit by being differentially sensitive to local information or simple input–output relationships. This we do not deny. In fact, it seems difficult to conceive of an effective learning procedure that is not better able to learn simple relationships. A related argument is that when the mapping to be learned is componential, a learning procedure specialised for learning such mappings, as opposed to one specialised for rote memorisation, is to be preferred. This, too, we support. However, we suggest that neural networks—and, by possible implication, the human brain—are naturally better at learning simple or local contingencies and regular, rather than arbitrary, mappings. But this is true of learning in experienced networks or adults, just as it is true of learning in randomised networks or children. The general architecture of the system is the key factor that enables learning of componentiality, not the child's limited working memory.

Simulating poor working memory by periodically disrupting a network's feedback during the early stages of learning has relatively little effect because, at that point, the network has not yet learned to use its memory effectively. As long as memory is interfered with less as the network develops, there will continue to be little impact on learning. In a sense, early interference with the network's memory is superfluous because the untrained network is naturally memory limited. One might say that is the very point of the less-is-more argument, but it is missing a vital component. While we accept that children have limited cognitive abilities, we don't see these limitations as a source of substantial learning advantage to the child. Both are symptoms of the fact that the child's brain is in an early stage in development at which its resources are largely uncommitted, giving it great flexibility in adapting to the particular tasks to which it is applied.

Late exposure and second languages

Elman's (1991, 1993) computational findings of the importance of starting small in language acquisition, as well as the other studies reviewed here, have been influential in part because they seemed to corroborate empirical observations that language acquisition is ultimately more successful the earlier in life it is begun (see Long, 1990). While older learners of either a first or a second language show initially faster acquisition, they tend to plateau at lower overall levels of achievement than do younger learners. The importance of early language exposure has been cited as an argument in favour of either an innate language acquisition device that operates selectively during childhood or, at least, genetically programmed maturation of the brain that facilitates language learning in childhood (Goldowsky & Newport, 1993; Johnson & Newport, 1989; Newport, 1990). It has been argued that the fact that late first- or second-language learners do not reach full fluency is strong evidence for "maturationally scheduled *language-specific* learning abilities" (Long, 1990, p. 259, emphasis in the original).

We would argue, however, that the data regarding late language exposure can be explained by principles of learning in connectionist networks without recourse to maturational changes or innate devices. Specifically, adult learners may not normally achieve fluency in a second language because their internal representations have been largely committed to solving other problems—including, in particular, comprehension and production of their native language (see Flege, 1992; Flege, Munro, & MacKay, 1995). The aspects of an adult's second language that are most difficult may be those that directly conflict with the learned properties of the native language. For example, learning the inflectional morphology of English may be particularly difficult for adult speakers of an isolating language, such as Chinese, which does not inflect number or tense.

By contrast to the adult, the child ultimately achieves a higher level of performance on a first or second language because his or her resources are initially uncommitted, allowing neurons to be more easily recruited and the response characteristics of already participating neurons to be altered. Additionally, the child is less hindered by interference from prior learned representations. This idea, which accords with Quartz and Sejnowski's (1997) theory of neural constructivism, is certainly not a new one, but is one that seems to remain largely ignored (although see Marchman, 1993; McClelland, 2001). On this view, it seems unlikely that limitations in a child's cognitive abilities are of significant benefit in language acquisition. While adults' greater memory and analytical abilities lead to faster initial learning, these properties are not themselves responsible for the lower asymptotic level of performance achieved, relative to children.

Along similar lines, the detrimental impact of delayed acquisition of a first language may not implicate a language-specific system that has shut down. Rather, it may be that, in the absence of linguistic input, those areas of the brain that normally become involved in language may have been recruited to perform other functions (see Merzenich & Jenkins, 1995, for relevant evidence and discussion). While it is still sensible to refer to a critical or sensitive period for the acquisition of language, in the sense that it is important to start learning early, the existence of a critical period need not connote language-acquisition devices or genetically prescribed maturational schedules.

Indeed, similar critical periods exist for learning to play tennis or a musical instrument. Rarely, if ever, does an individual attain masterful abilities at either of these pursuits unless he or she begins at an early age. And certainly in the case of learning the piano or violin, remarkable abilities can be achieved by late childhood and are thus not simply the result of the many years of practice afforded to those who start early. One might add that no species other than humans is capable of learning tennis or the violin. Nevertheless, we would not suppose that these abilities rely on domain-specific innate mechanisms or constraints.

While general connectionist principles may explain the overall pattern of results in late language learning, considerable work is still needed to demonstrate that this approach is sufficient to explain the range of relevant detailed findings. For example, it appears that vocabulary is more easily acquired than morphology or syntax, and that second language learners have variable success in mastering different syntactic rules (Johnson & Newport, 1989). In future work, we intend to develop simulations that include comprehension and production of more naturalistic languages, in order to extend our approach to address the empirical issues in late second-language learning and to allow us to model a wider range of aspects of language acquisition more directly.

CONCLUSION

We seem to be in agreement with most proponents of the less-is-more hypothesis in our belief that the proper account of human language learning need not invoke the existence of innate language-specific learning devices. However, we depart from them in our scepticism that limited cognitive resources are themselves of critical importance in the ultimate attainment of linguistic fluency. The simulations reported here, principally those inspired by Elman's language-learning work, call into question the proposal that staged input or limited cognitive resources are necessary, or even beneficial, for learning. We believe that the cognitive limitations of children are only advantageous for language acquisition to the extent that they are symptomatic of a system that is unorganised and inexperienced but possesses great flexibility and potential for future adaptation, growth and specialisation.

ACKNOWLEDGEMENTS

This research was supported by NIMH Program Project Grant MH47566 (J. McClelland, PI), and by an NSF Graduate Fellowship to the first author.

REFERENCES

Bengio, Y., Simard, P., & Frasconi, P. (1994). Learning long-term dependencies with gradient descent is difficult. *IEEE Transactions on Neural Networks, 5*, 157–166.

Bialystok, E., & Hakuta, K. (1999). Confounded age: Linguistic and cognitive factors in age differences for second language acquisition. In D. P. Birdsong (Ed.), *Second language acquisition and the critical period hypothesis* (pp. 161–181). Mahwah, NJ: Lawrence Erlbaum Associates, Inc.

Birdsong, D. (1999). Introduction: Whys and why nots of the critical period hypothesis for second language acquisition. In D. P. Birdsong (Ed.), *Second language acquisition and the critical period hypothesis* (pp. 1–22). Mahwah, NJ: Lawrence Erlbaum Associates, Inc.

Chomsky, N. (1965). *Aspects of the theory of syntax*. Cambridge, MA: MIT Press.

Cleeremans, A., Servan-Schreiber, D., & McClelland, J. (1989). Finite state automata and simple recurrent networks. *Neural Computation, 1*, 372–381.

Cochran, B. P., McDonald, J. L., & Parault, S. J. (1999). Too smart for their own good: The disadvantage of a superior processing capacity for adult language learners. *Journal of Memory and Language, 41*, 30–58.

Day, E. M., & Shapson, S. (1988). A comparison study of early and late French immersion programs in British Columbia. *Canadian Journal of Education, 13*, 290–305.

Elman, J. L. (1990). Finding structure in time. *Cognitive Science, 14*, 179–211.

Elman, J. L. (1991). Distributed representations, simple recurrent networks, and grammatical structure. *Machine Learning, 7*, 195–225.

Elman, J. L. (1993). Learning and development in neural networks: The important of starting small. *Cognition, 48*, 71–99.

Elman, J. L., Bates, E. A., Johnson, M. H., Karmiloff-Smith, A., Parisi, D., & Plunkett, K. (1996). *Rethinking innateness: A connectionist perspective on development*. Cambridge, MA: MIT Press.

Flege, J. E. (1992). Speech learning in a second language. In C. A. Ferguson, L. Menn, & C. Stoel-Gammon (Eds.), *Phonological development: Models, research, implications* (pp. 565–604). Timonium, MD: York Press.

Flege, J. E., Munro, M. J., & MacKay, I. R. A. (1995). Factors affecting strength of perceived foreign accent in a second language. *Journal of the Acoustical Society of America, 97*, 3125–3134.

Gallaway, C., & Richards, B. J. (Eds.). (1994). *Input and interaction in language acquisition.* London: Cambridge University Press.

Genesee, F. (1981). A comparison study of early and late second language learning. *Canadian Journal of Behavioral Sciences, 13*, 115–128.

Goldowsky, B. N., & Newport, E. L. (1993). Modeling the effects of processing limitations on the acquisition of morphology: The less is more hypothesis. In E. Clark (Ed.), *The proceedings of the 24th annual Child Language Research Forum* (pp. 124–138). Stanford, CA: Center for the Study of Language and Information.

Johnson, J. S., & Newport, E. L. (1989). Critical period effects in second language learning: The influence of maturational state on the acquisition of English as a second language. *Cognitive Psychology, 21*, 60–99.

Kareev, Y. (1995). Through a narrow window: Working memory capacity and the detection of covariation. *Cognition, 56*, 263–269.

Kareev, Y., Lieberman, I., & Lev, M. (1997). Through a narrow window: Sample size and the perception of correlation. *Journal of Experimental Psychology, 126*, 278–287.

Kersten, A. W., & Earles, J. L. (2001). Less really is more for adults learning a miniature artificial language. *Journal of Memory and Language, 44*, 250–273.

Kohonen, T. (1984). *Self-organization and associative memory.* New York: Springer-Verlag.

Lenneberg, E. H. (1967). *Biological foundations of language.* New York: Wiley.

Lin, T., Horne, B. G., & Giles, C. L. (1996). *How embedded memory in recurrent neural network architectures helps learning long-term temporal dependencies* (Tech. Rep. Nos. CS-TR-3626, UMIACS-TR-96-28). College Park, MD: University of Maryland.

Long, M. (1990). Maturational constraints on language development. *Studies in Second Language Acquisition, 12*, 251–285.

Luce, D. R. (1986). *Response times.* New York: Oxford.

Marchman, V. A. (1993). Constraints on plasticity in a connectionist model of the English past tense. *Journal of Cognitive Neuroscience, 5*, 215–234.

McClelland, J. L. (2001). Failures to learn and their remediation: A competitive, Hebbian approach. In J. L. McClelland & R. S. Siegler (Eds.), *Mechanisms of cognitive development: Behavioral and neural perspectives.* Mahwah, NJ: Lawrence Erlbaum Associates, Inc.

McClelland, J. L., McNaughton, B. L., & O'Reilly, R. C. (1995). Why there are complementary learning systems in the hippocampus and neocortex: Insights from the successes and failures of connectionist models of learning and memory. *Psychological Review, 102*, 419–457.

McCloskey, M., & Cohen, N. J. (1989). Catastrophic interference in connectionist networks: The sequential learning problem. In G. H. Bower (Ed.), *The psychology of learning and motivation* (pp. 109–165). New York: Academic Press.

McNeill, D. (1970). *The acquisition of language: The study of developmental psycholinguistics.* New York: Harper & Row.

Merzenich, M. M., & Jenkins, W. M. (1995). Cortical plasticity, learning and learning dysfunction. In B. Julesz & I. Kovacs (Eds.), *Maturational windows and adult cortical plasticity* (pp. 247–272). Reading, MA: Addison-Wesley.

Merzenich, M. M., Jenkins, W. M., Johnson, P., Schreiner, C., Miller, S. L., & Tallal, P. (1996). Temporal processing deficits of language-learning impaired children ameliorated by training. *Science, 271*, 77–81.

Newport, E. L. (1990). Maturational constraints on language learning. *Cognitive Science, 34*, 11–28.

Newport, E. L., Gleitman, H., & Gleitman, L. R. (1977). Mother, I'd rather do it myself: Some effects and non-effects of maternal speech style. In C. E. Snow & C. A. Ferguson (Eds.), *Talking to children: Language input and acquisition* (pp. 109–149). Cambridge: Cambridge University Press.

Pine, J. M. (1994). The language of primary caregivers. In C. Gallaway & B. J. Richards (Eds.),

Input and interaction in language acquisition (pp. 38–55). London: Cambridge University Press.

Quartz, S. R., & Sejnowski, T. J. (1997). The neural basis of cognitive development: A constructivist manifesto. *Behavioral and Brain Sciences, 20*, 537–596.

Richards, B. J. (1994). Child-directed speech and influences on language acquisition: Methodology and interpretation. In C. Gallaway & B. J. Richards (Eds.), *Input and interaction in language acquisition* (pp. 74–106). London: Cambridge University Press.

Rohde, D. L. T. (1999). *The simple language generator: Encoding complex languages with simple grammars* (Tech. Rep. No. CMU-CS-99-123). Pittsburgh, PA: Carnegie Mellon University, Department of Computer Science.

Rohde, D. L. T., & Plaut, D. C. (1999). Language acquisition in the absence of explicit negative evidence: How important is starting small? *Cognition, 72*, 67–109.

Rumelhart, D. E., Hinton, G. E., & Williams, R. J. (1986). Learning internal representations by error propagation. In D. E. Rumelhart, J. L. McClelland, & the PDP Research Group (Eds.), *Parallel distributed processing: Explorations in the microstructure of cognition. Volume 1: Foundations* (pp. 318–362). Cambridge, MA: MIT Press.

Shapson, S. M., & Day, E. M. (1982). A comparison of three late immersion programs. *Alberta Journal of Educational Research, 28*, 135–148.

Snow, C. E. (1994). Beginning from baby talk: Twenty years of research on input and interaction. In C. Gallaway & B. J. Richards (Eds.), *Input and interaction in language acquisition* (pp. 3–12). London: Cambridge University Press.

Snow, C. E. (1995). Issues in the study of input: Finetuning, universality, individual and developmental differences, and necessary causes. In P. Fletcher & B. MacWhinney (Eds.), *The handbook of child language* (pp. 180–193). Oxford: Blackwell.

Sokolov, J. L. (1993). A local contingency analysis of the fine-tuning hypothesis. *Developmental Psychology, 29*, 1008–1023.

Tallal, P., Miller, S. L., Bedi, G., Byma, G., Wang, X., Nagaraja, S. S., Schreiner, C., Jenkins, W. M., & Merzenich, M. M. (1996). Language comprehension in language-learning impaired children improved with acoustically modified speech. *Science, 271*, 81–84.

Thomas, A., & McClelland, J. L. (1997). How plasticity can prevent adaptation: Induction and remediation of perceptual consequences of early experience (Abstract 97.2). *Society for Neuroscience Abstracts, 23*, 234.

CHAPTER SEVEN

Pattern learning in infants and neural networks

Michael Gasser
Department of Computer Science, Indiana University, USA

Eliana Colunga
Department of Psychology, Indiana University, USA

Two recent sets of experiments have greatly expanded our understanding of the capacity of infants to detect regularities in patterns. Saffran, Aslin, and Newport (1996) conducted a set of experiments to investigate the sensitivity of infants to the statistical properties of patterns. Eight-month-old infants heard strings of syllables consisting of randomly concatenated three-syllable "words", sequences that never varied internally. Thus the transition probabilities within words were higher than between words. There were four different words consisting of 12 different syllables, and the subjects heard 180 words in all. Later the infants indicated, through differences in looking times, that they differentiated between these words and nonword three-syllable sequences, which they had either heard with less frequency than the words (because they consisted of sequences of syllables that crossed word boundaries) or not heard at all. This is taken as evidence that they had picked up the statistics in the training set. More recent experiments (Saffran, Johnson, Aslin, & Newport, 1999) have achieved similar results with patterns consisting of tones of different pitches.

Marcus, Vijayan, Bandi Rao, and Vishton (1999) conducted a set of experiments to determine whether infants could extract rules from a pattern. Seven-month-olds were presented with series of three-syllable sequences separated by gaps. Each sequence consisted of two different syllables arranged in a fixed pattern, $(x\ x\ y)$, $(x\ y\ y)$, or $(x\ y\ x)$. For example, in the $(x\ y\ y)$ condition, the presented patterns included sequences such as *le di di* and *ji je je*. During the familiarisation phase, each of 16 sequences was presented three

233

times. Later the infants were tested on sequences consisting of novel syllables, in one experiment, syllables designed so as not to overlap with the training syllables. The test sequences either obeyed the training rule, or they obeyed one of the other two rules. The infants indicated, through differences in looking times, that they differentiated the patterns that followed the training rule from those that did not. This is taken as evidence that they had in some sense picked up the rule implicit in the training patterns.

The experiments of Marcus et al. have attracted a good deal of attention because the authors, as well as Pinker (1999), have seen them as a challenge to connectionist models. Because connectionist models can respond only on the basis of similarity to training items, they apparently could not generalise to test sequences consisting of novel syllables, as the infants did. We believe that the line is not a simple one separating symbolic and connectionist models. The question is: what minimal set of mechanisms is required to achieve a behaviour, and what sorts of predictions does a model embodying these mechanisms make? In this chapter we present an account of patterns and pattern learning that brings together the two sorts of experiments in a single framework, and we propose a minimal set of mechanisms based on this account that could achieve the sort of pattern learning we see in the experiments. We also show how a connectionist implementation of these mechanisms models the results of the experiments and makes novel predictions. This is not the first connectionist model of the Marcus et al. results (see, for example, Christiansen, Conway, & Curtin, 2000; Seidenberg et al., 1999; Shultz & Bale, 2000); however, we believe that the model we propose has the advantage of simplicity and perspicuity.[1]

PATTERNS

The world is full of regularities of one sort or another, and it is to our advantage to be able to find them. Much of the regularity takes the form of what we will call patterns, in which the regularity consists of recurring relations between the elements of a sequence, presented in time or in space.

For example, say you are presented with a sequence of syllables from a language unknown to you. If you listen to such a sequence long enough, you may be able to detect certain regularities: certain syllables tend to be followed by certain other syllables or tend not to be followed by certain other syllables; certain syllables tend to be repeated; the syllables tend to group together in relatively predictable subsequences.

Now consider a static, visual example. Each morning you are served breakfast. There are always two or three food items arranged in a row in front

---

[1] It is, in fact, considerably simpler than the model we previously proposed (Gasser & Colunga, 2000).

of you. Over time you notice that the juice is always to the left of the cereal and that if there is toast, it is always on the right.

There is no question that people (and other animals) have the ability to find regularity in patterns. But there are still questions about what they can and cannot discover, as well as about what regularities are out there to be discovered. And there are even more fundamental questions about what sort of mechanism is behind the learning and processing of patterns. Figuring all this out is of great importance because of the role patterns play in our lives. Language in particular is at least to a large extent a matter of patterns. In this chapter, we consider what is involved in pattern learning, discuss two experiments with infants demonstrating pattern learning, and propose a connectionist model which accounts for the infant data.

Elements and dimensions

The processing of patterns assumes a preprocessing stage in which the input stream has already been segmented into a sequence of elements—objects all belonging to a particular general category such as syllable, musical tone, or polygon.

Before they can discover the regularities in a given pattern, we also assume that people represent the elements in terms of values on one or more dimensions such as pitch or colour. In addition, they may also be able to place the elements in one or another set of disjoint categories.

Between-element relations

The regularity within a pattern is defined in terms of relations between pattern elements. It is important to note that there may be more than one way to characterise the regularity in a given set of patterns. For human subjects, we of course do not have direct access to the manner in which they are representing the regularity, and there will normally be more than one underlying representation consistent with their performance on test patterns.

Because in the general case the relations between elements emerge out of tendencies present in multiple examples, we will speak of the relations as correlations.

Two sorts of between-element correlations can characterise patterns. In the simpler case, the relation is between specific element contents. When there are element categories, the correlation may be between specific types. For example, the syllable *ba* may tend to be followed by the syllable *gu*; the cereal may tend to be on the right of the juice. Alternatively, the correlation may be between specific values or ranges of values along element dimensions. For example, a syllable with the vowel *e* may tend to be followed by a syllable with the vowel *u*; a breakfast food item in a plastic bowl may tend to appear to the right of a hot drink. We will refer to correlations that make reference to the specific element categories or dimension values as content-specific correlations.

A second kind of correlation is more abstract; it concerns whether two elements match with respect to their category or a particular dimension. For example, in a sequence of syllables there may be a tendency for syllables to appear in same-category pairs: *bu bu go go ta ta* . . ., or adjacent syllables may tend to match on a given consonant or vowel feature such as rounding, a process known as "harmony" in phonology. At the breakfast table, the three items may tend to appear in containers of the same colour. We will refer to correlations of this type as relational correlations because their definition makes reference to the primitive relations "sameness" and "difference".

So far, the correlations we have discussed relate pairs of elements. Higher-order correlations—correlations between pairwise co-occurrences—are also possible. Examples of content-specific higher-order correlations are the following:

- when *gu* is preceded by *ba*, it tends to be followed by *li*
- when a syllable beginning with *g* is preceded by a syllable beginning with *b*, it tends to be followed by a syllable beginning with *l*.

Examples of relational higher-order correlations are the following:

- a pair of syllables of one type tends to be followed by a pair of another type
- when a syllable is preceded by another syllable beginning with the same consonant, it tends to be followed by a syllable ending in the same vowel
- when the consonants of two adjacent syllables match in one feature, they and the vowel in the syllables tend to match on all features.

Note that higher-order correlations do not presuppose that the co-occurrences they relate are actually correlations. In the first example of a content-specific correlation above, *gu* need not tend to be preceded by *ba* or tend to be followed by *li* for the correlation between these two co-occurrences to occur.

Groups and segmentation

The regularities within patterns also break the sequences of elements into subsequences that we will call groups. Groups may be distinguishable in four different ways (or some combination of these), all of which may contribute to segmentation of sequences of elements into groups:

(1) The intervals separating groups may be distinguishable from the inter-vals separating elements within groups. In the breakfast example, the distinction is obvious. The elements within a group are separated from one another spatially, whereas the groups are separated from one another temporally. In other cases, the gaps between groups may simply be longer than the gaps between elements.

(2) There may be similarity between elements in corresponding positions within groups. For example, in a sequence of tones, each group might begin on a relatively high pitch.

(3) There may be stronger correlations within groups than between groups. This appears to be a fundamental property of natural lan-guage, for example. As more and more segments of a word become available, the remainder of the word becomes more and more predict-able, but predictability across word boundaries, except in the case of idiomatic constructions, tends to be relatively low.

(4) The within-group relations between corresponding elements may be similar. For example, the first two elements in each group might be tokens of the same type.

Pattern behaviour

What does it mean to know a pattern? Two behaviours can act as measures of pattern knowledge. One is the ability to distinguish acceptable sequences of elements, those that agree with the regularities in the pattern, from unaccept-able sequences; of course, acceptability may be a matter of degree. Another is the ability to complete patterns, to fill in one part of a sequence given another. For a temporal pattern-learning task, pattern completion means prediction: given one or more of the elements in a group, one or more subsequent elements are predicted.

Pattern learning

We assume that patterns are learned through the presentation of examples to the learner. Thus, pattern learning is an unsupervised task; a learning trial consists simply of a pattern subsequence, not of an input together with a target output. At any point during learning, the learner may be tested by being presented with a test sequence and expected to judge its acceptability or with a partial sequence and expected to complete it.

Many (but not all) pattern-learning tasks are induction tasks; that is, they involve generalisation from the set of training groups of elements to a larger, "target" set of acceptable groups. The traditional characterisation of induc-tion assumes that the learner maintains a "hypothesis" about what consti-tutes the target set, updating the hypothesis when it fails to accommodate particular training items. But rating a test item for acceptability requires only that groups of elements be characterised as more or less like the training groups. Likewise, pattern completion requires no explicit hypothesis; what it requires is performance that is, to the extent possible, compatible with both the given elements and the regularities in the training set. For both behaviours, the learner takes a test item and attempts fit it into what is known of the pattern.

Even though the traditional characterisation of induction does not precisely fit pattern learning, it is still the case that the learner is often faced with items that were not in the training set. The generalisation exhibited by a model is a function of the training set, the form in which pattern elements and group positions are represented in the model, and the computational architecture and learning algorithm. We can distinguish between purely statistical learning algorithms and symbolic rule-learning algorithms.

A purely statistical learning algorithm keeps track of co-occurrences of pairs of elements or element features, or co-occurrences of such pairs. That is, it is oriented toward content-specific correlational learning. A statistical algorithm may also keep track of what tends not to occur. Such a system will tend not only to be attracted to states that resemble those it has seen but also to be repelled by states that differ from what it has seen. Note that this latter capacity represents a potential solution to the problem of the lack of negative evidence, familiar from work on language acquisition (Marcus, 1993). Negative evidence often seems to be required to constrain the learner's hypotheses about what counts as acceptable, but we are assuming that negative evidence is not available during pattern learning.

Symbolic rule-learning algorithms (Marcus, 2001) differ from statistical learning algorithms in their explicit mechanism for abstracting away from data by replacing tokens with variables. Rules for patterns are among the simplest examples. Given training items in which groups consist of three elements and the first two elements of each group always belong to the same category, a rule-learning algorithm could form a rule characterising the data of the form $(x\ x\ y)$, where x and y match any element in the element domain. That is, it could learn relational correlations. This is an instance of what Thornton (2000) calls "relational learning", contrasting with the nonrelational learning that would suffice for content-specific correlations. To work, rule-learning algorithms require a specification of what variability in the training data is required before an element is replaced by a variable in a rule and some means of determining what the element domain is (syllables, tones, polygons, etc.).

Pattern learning in infants

Now let's reconsider the experiments of Saffran et al. (1996) and Marcus et al. (1999) in terms of patterns. In the Saffran et al. experiments, infants learn about how certain specific syllables (actually syllable types) tend to be followed or preceded by certain other specific syllables. That is, this is an example of the learning of content-specific relational correlations. Although it has not been demonstrated in the experiments, the subjects may also learn content-specific higher-order correlations. For example, if the syllable sequence *pidaku* is one of the recurring words in a pattern, the subject may learn that when *da* follows *pi*, it tends to precede *ku*.

In the Marcus et al. experiments, the infants are presented with groups of syllables, segmentable on the basis of both the first and the fourth of the four grouping characteristics described above: the intervals between groups are greater than those between elements within group, and each group embodies the same sort of regularity. It is this within-group regularity that is of interest. In our terms, the infants learn within-group relational correlations; they learn about the sameness or the difference between group elements in particular positions. For example, the infants in the (x x y) condition learn about the sameness relation between the first two elements within each group and the difference relation between the second and third elements (and possibly the first and third elements) within each group. Although it has not been demonstrated in these experiments, the infants may also learn higher-order correlations within the groups. For example, the subjects in the (x x y) conditions may learn that sameness between the first two elements co-occurs with difference between the second two elements in a group.

In sum, infants apparently have the capacity to learn both content-specific and relational correlations in patterns. But what sort of learning mechanism are they equipped with that allows them to do this? And does the relational learning case require something more sophisticated than statistical learning? In the next section we attempt to answer these questions in the context of a neural network model of correlational learning.

PATTERN LEARNING IN NEURAL NETWORKS

What does it take to model the learning of patterns? In this section we describe features of the Playpen model of relational learning (Gasser, Colunga, & Smith, 2001) that are relevant for this task, specifically what is required to model the experiments of Saffran et al. and Marcus et al. In brief, the architecture is an attractor neural network with separate element units for each position in a pattern group and (for the Marcus et al. experiments) a set of hidden units representing primitive relations of sameness or difference on element dimensions in different group positions. The network is trained using a variant of Hebbian learning that punishes states which are not compatible with the pattern as well as rewarding states which are.

Architecture and learning algorithm

Our major claim is that pattern learning is correlational, and we start with the simplest architecture for correlational learning, an attractor neural network based on the continuous Hopfield model (Hopfield, 1984). An attractor network also has a natural way of implementing pattern completion and of yielding a measure of pattern goodness.

Units are joined by symmetric connections, and the network settles as unclamped units update their activations according to the familiar interactive activation update rule (McClelland & Rumelhart, 1981). A positive input moves a unit's activation towards its maximum, a negative input moves the activation towards its minimum, and a constant decay moves the activation towards a resting value. The units in the networks we describe below had a minimum activation of −0.2, a resting activation of 0.0, a maximum activation of 1.0, and a decay rate of 0.05.

There are two sorts of units, input–output units representing pattern element features or categories, and relation units, representing correlations between pattern element features or categories. Each relation unit receives input from and sends output to two input–output units. These connections, which share a single weight, are multiplicative; that is, the input into the relation unit is a function of the product of the weighted activations of the input–output units rather than the sum. Thus, in the absence of other input, a relation unit comes on only when it receives activation from both of its associated input–output units. Relation units may also be connected to one another by ordinary additive connections.

Each relation unit associates two values on an element dimension, represented by the two input–output units that it is connected to. Those associating the same value on the dimension (but in different pattern positions), sameness units, are distinguished from those associating different values on the dimension, difference units, by their pattern of connections. Sameness and difference units are illustrated in Figure 7.2 (see p. 244).

The learning algorithm is an unsupervised adaptation of contrastive Hebbian learning (Movellan, 1990), which augments simple correlational Hebbian learning with an anti-Hebbian learning phase that has the effect of punishing spurious states of the network that are not compatible with the training set. Specifically, during the positive phase of learning, a pattern is clamped on the input–output units, the hidden (relation) units are allowed to settle, and ordinary Hebbian learning is performed. That is, the weights are updated in proportion to the product of the activations of the connected units. (For the special connections joining input–output units and relation units, it is the product of the activations of all three units that is involved.) Next, in the negative phase of learning, the input–output units are unclamped, a small amount of noise is added to the activations of the units, and the network is allowed to settle again. Now anti-Hebbian learning is performed: the weights are updated in proportion to the negative of the product of the activations of the connected units. Note that if a training pattern behaves as an attractor in the network, during the negative phase the network should return to the state it was in following the positive phase (overcoming the injected noise). When this happens, the weight changes in the positive and negative phases for this pattern will cancel each other out. In other words, once the weight changes have stabilised, the network exhibits the desired behaviour.

Representation of elements and groups

As noted in the first section of this chapter, pattern elements may be represented in either a local or a distributed fashion. In the local case, a single unit is assigned to each element type. This is illustrated in Figure 7.1(a). While this has the possibly desirable effect of treating elements as computational units in and of themselves, it leaves the system with no representation of interelement similarity.

Distributed representations assign distinct sets of units to each element dimension, and each element is represented by the activation of multiple units. One possibility, then, is to turn on a single unit on each dimension for a given element. For example, say we are representing vowels. Vowels can be distinguished on several dimensions, the most important of which are (roughly) the relative height and backness of the nearest approach of the articulators in the oral cavity. With separate sets of units for each of these two dimensions, a vowel could take on the form of a pattern in which two units are activated and the others are not. Such a possibility is illustrated in Figure 7.1(b), in which a single unit is assigned to each of five possible values along each dimension. For the vowel [o], two units, representing medium height and extreme backness, are strongly activated, and the other units are off or inhibited. While this style of representation allows the system to generalise on the basis of interelement similarity, it fails to represent directly the ordering of values within dimensions. Instead, we will assume that each element activates the units associated with a particular dimension with an on-centre-off-surround pattern. That is, we are really assuming that each of the element feature units has a Gaussian receptive field over the dimension and that neighbouring units have overlapping receptive fields. It is well known that neural networks exposed to simple patterns such as activated pairs of adjacent input units can learn the weights for such receptive fields (von der Malsburg, 1973). Figure 7.1(c) illustrates this possibility for one vowel. As in

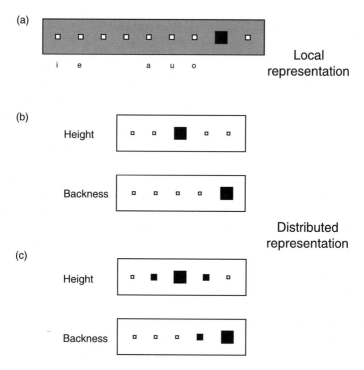

Figure 7.1.   Local (a) and distributed (b, c) representations of pattern elements, illustrated for vowels. Black squares represent positively activated units, white squares negatively activated units. The size of a square represents the magnitude of activation. For the distributed representations, there are two vowel dimensions, height and backness. Each vowel is characterised by a vowel on each of these dimensions. In b, the distributed representations are local within each dimension; in c, they are distributed within each dimension as well.

Figure 7.1(b), a single unit is assigned to each of five values on the two vowel dimensions. For the vowel [o], two units, representing medium height and extreme backness, are again strongly activated, but now the neighbours of these units are also weakly activated.

For the different positions within pattern groups, there are two possibilities. Either the elements in different positions are represented across the same set of units, or separate units are allotted to each position. The latter alternative requires multiple units representing the same element categories or features. For example, in a network that processes sequences of syllables, there would be multiple copies of the syllable dimensions, one for each of the positions that is distinguished. While this may appear expensive, it is quite similar to a solution already instantiated in natural vision systems with multiple position-specific edge and motion detectors. This alternative also has the advantage that it avoids the binding problem (Shastri & Ajjanagadde, 1993).

With distributed representations of multiple elements, this is the problem of keeping track of which activated unit goes with which object. For example, with multiple geometric figures and activated units representing CIRCLE, SQUARE, GREEN, and RED, how do we distinguish RED CIRCLE and GREEN SQUARE from GREEN CIRCLE and RED SQUARE? Or with two syllables and activated units representing FRONT, BACK, HIGH, MID on the two vowel dimensions of backness and height, how do we distinguish syllables with vowels [i] (FRONT, HIGH) and [o] (BACK, MID) from syllables with vowels [e] (FRONT, MID) and [u] (BACK, HIGH)? The problem is solved with feature units specific to particular spatial or temporal positions, for example, CIRCLE-ON-THE-LEFT, GREEN-ON-THE-RIGHT, VOWEL1:HIGH, VOWEL2:MID. That is, units associated with features of elements in a particular position are in a sense grouped together in the network. Multiple copies of feature units also solve another problem: how multiple elements with the same value on a given dimension can be represented simultaneously.

In the model we propose, then, that group positions (or relative positions within the sequence in the case of the simulation of Saffran et al.) take the form of distinct units. Relation units associate values on a given dimension across these positional groups of units. Figure 7.2 illustrates the pattern of connections. Two dimensions and two positions are shown. Within each positional copy of the dimension units, the units are arranged in the figure in the same order. That is, the first unit on the left represents the same value in the two rectangles in the first row. Sameness relation units (diamonds in the figure) associate the same value in different positions, whereas difference units (pentagons in the figure) associate different values in different positions. Other than this pattern of connectivity, the two types of relation units are identical. The dashed lines in the figure represent the multiplicative connections joining input–output units to relation units. Because the inputs to a relation unit are multiplied, it turns on (all else being equal) only when both of its input–output units are activated. This is illustrated for two sameness units and two difference unit in the figure.

Pattern behaviour

In both sets of infant experiments, the subjects made implicit judgements of the acceptability of the test items. While there is nothing in the network that corresponds directly to looking time, the network has a natural means of indicating the deviance of a particular state in the extent to which it moves away from that state during settling. Specifically we test the acceptability of an item in much the same way as the network is trained. First, the test sequence is clamped on the input–output units and the network is allowed to settle. The activations of all of the units are recorded at this point. Next, the

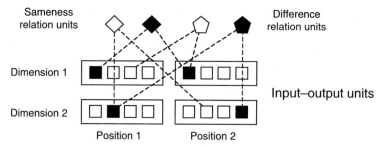

Figure 7.2. Basic architecture of the model. Input–output units represent element features (dimension values) or categories. Relation units associate input–output units along multiplicative connections (dotted lines). Separate units represent positions within pattern groups. Sameness relation units (diamonds) associate the same feature in different positions. Difference units (pentagons) associate different features in different positions. Activated units are indicated by filled figures.

input–output units are unclamped and the network is allowed to settle again (without the injection of noise as during training). We now measure the Euclidian distance between the network's state following the second settling and its state following the first settling. If the test sequence is familiar, the network should remain in roughly the same state, and the distance will be small. If the sequence is unfamiliar, the network should move toward a more familiar state, and the distance will be large.

Predictions

Simulating the experiments of Saffran et al. should be straightforward in a network of the type we have described since the differences detected by the infants are purely correlational. In fact, the network for simulating these experiments should not require hidden (relation) units because there are no higher-order correlations involved.

The major claim of this chapter is that it is also possible to simulate the learning of relational correlations, as in the experiments of Marcus et al., using simple correlational learning. What enables this in our model is distributed input representations based on overlapping receptive fields and relation units permitting higher-order relational correlations. While we can describe the patterns in these experiments with rules containing variables that are insensitive to content, the model, because it still operates by correlational learning, will always be sensitive to content. The upshot is that the network should "prefer" sequences to the extent that they resemble the training sequences. The most acceptable sequences should be those that are identical to the ones the network was trained on. At the other extreme should be sequences consisting of novel syllables that violate the training rule. In between would be sequences obeying the rule and consisting of novel syllables. Among these, acceptability should vary with the similarity of the component syllables to the training sequences. In the original experiments this range of possibilities is not tested; the test sequences consist only of very unfamiliar syllables either following or violating the training rule. We include more test sequences in our simulations to verify this aspect of the model's behaviour.

SIMULATIONS

Experiments of Saffran et al. (1996)

Architecture. In the experiments of Saffran et al. (1996), the element sequences were not presegmented for the subjects; the interval between adjacent elements within groups was the same as the interval between adjacent elements spanning group boundaries. Thus, rather than assign separate input layers to group positions, we assigned separate layers to relative positions. We used four of these positional layers, one more than the length of the groups in the patterns.

Direct connections between the pattern units were sufficient to learn the correlations in the training sequence; there was no need for a hidden layer of relation units. The connection weights were initialised at 0.0. The syllables were represented in a local fashion; we discovered that networks given distributed syllable representations alone failed to make the distinction that the subjects made. The failure of distributed representations for this task is interesting since, as we explain below, distributed representations are required to simulate the Marcus et al. experiments with the model. It may be that infants have access to both syllable categories, such as *bi* and *ku*, and syllable features, such as the voicing of the onset consonant or the height of the vowel, and they capitalise on whichever captures the correlations in the data.

The architecture of the network is shown in Figure 7.3. Each input–output position layer contains twelve units, one for each syllable category; four of these are shown in the figure. All pairs of units in different position layers are joined by trainable connections. The four position layers represent a window of four consecutive syllables which the training sequence passes over as it is presented. That is, if the first six syllables in the sequence are *pa bi ku ti bu do*, the syllables appearing on the four layers for the first three training trials are *pa bi ku ti, bi ku ti bu, ku ti bu do*. The first of these is shown in Figure 7.3.

Training. As in the original experiments, the network was presented with 180 syllables in all. The three-syllable groups ("words") appeared together with equal frequency, and no group appeared twice in succession. Because each group consisted of unique syllables, this meant that the transition probability between any two syllables within words was 1, and the transition

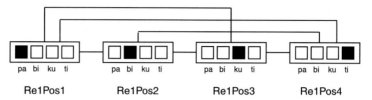

Figure 7.3. Architecture of network for simulating experiment of Saffran et al. (1996). Relative position layers consist of input–output units. Units in different layers are joined by trainable connections, indicated by the lines in the figure. Within each position layer only four of the twelve units are shown. The activated units in the figure represent the subsequence . . . *pa bi ku ti* . . . appearing somewhere within the input sequence of syllables.

probability between the last syllable of a group and the first syllable of another group was $\frac{1}{3}$. We trained three separate networks. Their behaviour was virtually identical since the only sources of differences were the order of the training trials and the order in which units were updated during settling. Not surprisingly, we also found that the negative phase of contrastive Hebbian learning is not necessary for this network with no hidden units.[2]

Testing and results.   The task in these experiments is not generalisation to novel sequences; it is to make a distinction between more and less likely sequences. Sequences constituting groups or subsequences within groups in the pattern should be more acceptable in some sense than sequences spanning groups. We used the method described above to measure acceptability (because there was no hidden layer, no initial settling was required). To simulate the presentation of three-syllable test sequences, we presented each sequence to the first three or the last three of the four layers of the trained network, starting the units in the other layer at values close to their resting activations. We then let the network settle and measured the change in activation, that is, the Euclidian distance between the states before and after settling.

The mean change in activations following the presentation of three-syllable sequences constituting words was 0.55. The mean change following three-syllable sequences spanning word boundaries was 0.88 ($t(27) = 159$, $p < 0.0001$). The network has clearly learned to distinguish within-group from between-group transitions.

---

[2] Contrastive Hebbian learning (Movellan, 1990) augments the usual Hebbian learning used to train simple attractor neural networks without hidden units (Hopfield, 1984) with the anti-Hebbian learning of the negative phase of training. The hidden units in a network represent re-encodings of the input patterns, which permit more complex mappings to be learned. However, the initial random weights to the hidden units may lead to spurious attractors. The negative phase of training is designed to eliminate these spurious attractors by effectively penalising states that do not yield appropriate input–output mappings.

Discussion.   In sum, a simple Hopfield network replicates the results of the experiments of Saffran et al. involving content-specific correlations in a pattern-learning task. These results are not particularly surprising—after all, this sort of statistical learning is what neural networks excel at—we include it mainly to clarify what the architecture requires beyond this to learn the relational correlations in the experiments of Marcus et al.

As noted in the discussion of pattern behaviour, people are capable not only of distinguishing familiar from unfamiliar patterns; they can also produce patterns that agree with the regularities they have learned. Pattern completion is a natural process in attractor neural networks such as these, and we tested the networks for this simulation to see whether they could generate portions of pattern groups given others. To do this, we clamp some of the input–output units and then let the unclamped units settle. The network should fill in the unclamped dimensions with values compatible with the clamped units and with the regularity in the training patterns.

We tested each of the four word sequences by clamping units for the first two syllables in either the first and second or second and third group layers and leaving the other layers unclamped. We then allowed the unclamped units to settle. At issue was whether the layer following the first two syllables would settle to the third syllable in the sequence, that is, whether the unit for that syllable would be more highly activated than the others in that layer. In all cases, this was what we found.

Experiments of Marcus et al. (1999)

Architecture.   In the experiments of Marcus et al. (1999), element groups were clearly delineated for the subjects by intervals longer than the interelement intervals within groups. Thus we assumed a preprocessing stage in which the group positions were assigned to distinct sets of element units. That is, there were three layers of units for the representation of syllables.

Local representations of syllables would not suffice to simulate these experiments because the network must generalise on the basis of the similarity between the syllables. We represented syllables using a minimal set of dimensions, two for consonants and two for vowels. The consonant dimensions were sonority, roughly the extent to which a consonant is vowel-like, and place of articulation, the position in the vocal tract of the narrowest contact between articulators. The vowel dimensions were height and backness of the narrowest approach between articulators. All four of these dimensions are accepted ways of characterising phonetic segments. Normally, more dimensions would be required, but these four suffice to distinguish the phones used in the third experiment of Marcus et al.: *d, j, l, w, e, i*. Each of the dimensions was represented by five units with overlapping receptive fields. Thus the presentation of an element with a given value on a dimension always activated one unit on that dimension strongly, activated its two neighbouring units (or one neighbouring unit if it was at the end of the scale) weakly, and inhibited the other units on the dimension.[3]

We discovered, to our surprise, that it was possible to train a network with no hidden units to distinguish the syllable sequences distinguished by the infants in the experiments, but this required more presentations of the patterns and the difference in the network's familiarity with the two kinds of sequences was small, not a convincing simulation of the differences in the infants' looking times.

The addition of relation units allows the network to make use of correlations of particular co-occurrences along dimensions. The most obvious of these is the nonoccurrence of both same and different values on a dimension. For example, given two successive syllables, the heights of their vowels were either the same or different. Less obvious is the tendency for sameness on one dimension to correlate with sameness on the other dimensions for a given pair of positions. This was true for the stimuli because pairs of syllables were either identical, or they were significantly different. However, it was only a tendency; sometimes the different syllables shared a vowel or a consonant (*ji, wi; ji, je*).

For every pair of units on corresponding dimensions in different positions, there was an associated relation unit. Thus there was a sameness relation unit for a sonority of 0 in group position 1 and a sonority of 0 in group position 2; this unit tended to be activated when the consonants of the first two syllables in a group both had sonority 0 (that is, when both were voiceless stops). Likewise there was a difference relation unit for a sonority of 0 in group position 1 and a sonority of 2 in group position 2. The relation units were connected to their associated input–output units with small constant weights, smaller for the difference units because there were more of these. These weights were modified during learning.

In addition to these, there were three other kinds of connection. For a given dimension and a given pair of group positions, difference and sameness units inhibited one another, reflecting the first sort of correlation discussed above. These small negative weights were not modified during learning since they presumably represent basic knowledge about the incompatibility of sameness and difference relations within a dimension which would have been learned before the experiment.

There were also connections among all of the sameness units on different dimensions for each pair of group positions. These trainable connections had initial weights of 0.0 and would permit the network to learn the second sort of correlation discussed above: correlations between sameness relations on

---

[3] In the case of *w*, there were two places of articulation, labial (0) and velar (3). Both of the corresponding units received relatively high, although not maximum, activation.

different dimensions for a given pair of group positions, for example, the tendency for sameness in vowel height to correlate with sameness in vowel backness.

Finally, there were connections permitting the learning of correlations between co-occurrences of values for different pairs of group position, for example, the tendency for sameness in vowel height between positions one and two to correlate with sameness in vowel height between positions two and three. There were actually few such correlations in the training sequences, and the inclusion of these connections made little difference in performance, but they were included for the sake of completeness. Figure 7.4 shows the architecture of the network for simulating the experiments of Marcus et al. The input–output units (white rectangles), representing position-specific syllable features, include four dimensional layers for each group position. For every pair of group positions there is a set of four dimensional layers for sameness relation units (dark grey rectangles) and four dimensional layers for difference relation units (light grey rectangles). The dashed lines summarise the multiplicative connections joining pairs of input–output units with each relation unit. Connections between relation units are not shown.

Figure 7.5 shows detail for the connections between the input–output

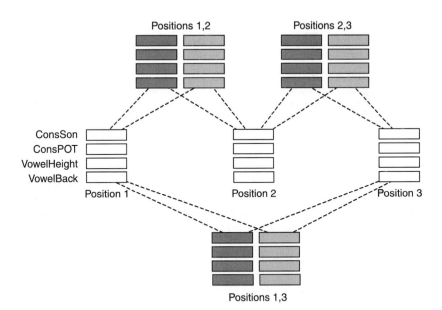

Figure 7.4. Architecture of network for simulating experiments of Marcus et al. (1999). There are input–output units (white rectangles) for each syllable dimension in each of the three group positions. Each pair of positions has associated layers of sameness (dark grey rectangles) and difference relation units (light grey rectangles). Connections between relation units are not shown.

(a)

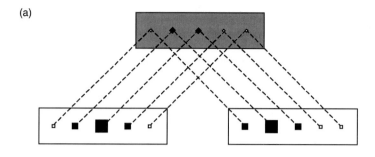

(b)

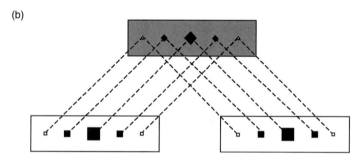

Figure 7.5. Detail of connectivity between input–output and relation unit layers. The input–output layers for one syllable dimension in two group positions and the associated layer of sameness relation units (diamonds) are shown. The response of the sameness units to two different on-centre-off-surround input patterns is shown, one in which the value on the dimension is different for the two positions (a) and one in which the value is the same (b).

units for a single dimension in two different positions and the corresponding sameness relation units. Two different input patterns are shown to illustrate how the relation units are activated in response to them. Difference units behave in the same fashion (see also Figure 7.2). However, there are more of them for each pair of position-specific dimensions, one for each combination of a value on one input layer with a different value on the other input layer, that is, 20 units for our network with 5 units per input–output dimension layer.

Training. Each network was trained on sequences obeying a particular "rule". Because the network's representations of different positions within a sequence were identical, there was no reason to train separate networks on the three rules. We will assume that the training rule is $(x\ x\ y)$. The

16 training syllable sequences were those used in Experiments 2 and 3 of Marcus et al.: *le le di, le le we, le le li, le le je, de de di, de de we, de de li, de de je, ji ji di, ji ji we, ji ji li, ji ji je, wi wi di, wi wi we, wi wi li,* and *wi wi je.*

As in the original experiments, the networks were presented with each training sequence three times during training. Contrastive Hebbian learning was used to train the network. A training sequence was clamped over the input–output units, the hidden units were allowed to settle, and Hebbian weight updates were accumulated. Then the input–output units were unclamped, a small amount of noise was added to the units' activations, and all units were allowed to settle. Finally, anti-Hebbian weight updates were accumulated.

We trained three separate networks. None of the initial weights was random and the minor variations in network performance we observed were due to the random order of training sequences and of units to update during network settling.

Testing and results.   We tested the network on the test sequences from the original experiments, made up of the syllables *ba, po, ko,* and *ga,* as well as on a set of other sequences consisting of syllables either from the training sequences or resembling those in the training sequences.

We modelled the infants' differential familiarity as described above. A test sequence was clamped on the input–output units, the hidden units were allowed to settle, and the activations of all units were recorded. Next, the input–output units were unclamped and all of the units were permitted to settle again. The state of the network was then compared to the saved state.

Figure 7.6 shows results for four categories of test sequences: training; partially familiar grammatical; unfamiliar grammatical; unfamiliar ungrammatical. "Grammatical" means following the training rule. "Partially familiar" refers to sequences containing syllables that overlap significantly with the training syllables. For example, *jo* resembles the training syllables *ji* and *je.* Each "partially familiar" syllable combined a training consonant with a test vowel or a test consonant with a training vowel. Clearly, the network exhibits the basic effect found in the experiment. Grammatical patterns consisting of unfamiliar syllables are preferred over ungrammatical patterns consisting of those same unfamiliar syllables ($t(16) = 10.8$, $p < .001$). In addition, the network makes several predictions about the extent to which subjects will generalise to novel sequences.

Discussion.   How is it that the network appears to have rule-governed behaviour when it is only learning correlations? The answer lies in the overlap between the different syllable representations and in the form that sameness takes in the network. Marcus et al. strove to define a set of training and test syllables that would not overlap at all. But *w,* one of the training consonants,

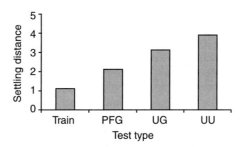

Figure 7.6. Simulation of experiment of Marcus et al. (1999). Distance between networks states before and after unclamping of IO units. Test types: Train, training; PFG, partially familiar, grammatical; UG, unfamiliar, grammatical; UU, unfamiliar, ungrammatical.

involves both bilabial (0 on our place of articulation dimension) and velar (3) articulation, so training on syllables containing this consonant in the positions where the same syllables occur exposes the model to sameness on two points along the place of articulation dimension. These happen to be the same two points that apply to the consonants in the dissimilar test syllables, that is, *p*, *b*, *k*, and *g*. Likewise, both of the training vowels, *i* and *e*, have medium height (2 on our height dimension), like one of the test vowels, *o*. The receptive fields of the input–output units, each encompassing more than one value on its dimension, also lead in general to more commonality between syllables. It is true that there is no overlap at all between the training and test syllables along the dimension of vowel backness. But given the distributed representations of syllables, there is plenty of basis for generalisation to the test syllables within the other three dimensions.

Thus the network has no abstract notion of sameness. Sameness between two sequence group positions is nothing more than a strong association (implemented in the form of a relation unit) between every pair of element features which match one another. And in the absence of exposure to examples spanning the range of values on each dimension, we can expect the learner to respond with varying commitments to sameness.

In other words, content still matters. Rather than a pristine variable which matches anything in its domain, we have a whole array of units, some readily activated, others less likely to respond. As we have seen, the model predicts different responses for sequences depending on their similarity to training sequences. We are currently performing an experiment using visual patterns and adult subjects to test this prediction. Preliminary results indicate that subjects are more accurate and faster at judging the familiarity of patterns following the training rule when their content is similar to that in the training sequences, as predicted by our model.

But in a sense, content matters for the rule-based account too. Variables are normally defined over some domain (syllables, two-dimensional figures, etc.). They match all elements within the domain equally well but fail to match elements outside the domain. In the model we are proposing, there may be no such clean lines. Just as we expect elements within the domain to match the "rule" to different degrees, there is no reason not to expect elements outside the domain to match to some extent as well. What matters is how much they overlap with the familiar elements. In fact without variables there may be no more reason to posit element domains.

There is a further sense in which symbolic models are usually all-or-none. The learner is presented with a set of training items and for some time can generalise only on the basis of similarity. Then at some point the learner "gets" the rule. But at what point? How much training and what quality of training are required for this to happen? A statistical model like the one we are proposing requires no such threshold; learning is a continuous phenomenon. Again the predictions differ; the symbolic model predicts a significant discontinuity in performance.

As we have already seen, pattern knowledge in older children and adults goes beyond the passive ability to discriminate between sequences on the basis of how well they agree with the pattern. People are also able to produce patterns of the type used in the experiments of Marcus et al. A good example of this is the ability of speakers of languages making use of productive morphological reduplication (Moravcsik, 1978) to generate the reduplicated forms of stems. In reduplication one portion of a stem is copied somewhere in the word, as in Tagalog *bibili* 'will buy' from *bili* 'buy'. As noted above, this may take the form of pattern completion, the production of some group elements given others.

As in the Saffran et al. simulations, we tested this ability in the networks using pattern completion. For the networks used in simulating the Marcus et al. experiments, the results were more negative. Having trained a network on the $(x \; x \; y)$ rule, we clamped the y syllable and one of the x syllables and allowed the units representing the other syllable to settle. For the training sequences, the network readily filled in the appropriate syllable. For the most unfamiliar syllables, those used in the test sequences in the experiments of Marcus et al., the network correctly filled in only one or two of the four syllables at best. For the intermediate case of partially familiar syllables, the correct syllable was filled in only one out of three times; more often only two or three of the four features were generated correctly.

These results do not indicate that the model cannot learn to produce patterns involving relational correlations. Pattern completion is a much more demanding task than simply ranking one sequence as more compatible with the pattern than another. The model would clearly require training on a greater variety of elements to perform this task. We do not know what it takes for a language learner to attain the ability to perform reduplication. This is an area we hope to investigate in artificial language learning experiments.

In addition to these large-scale predictions, the model makes a number of detailed predictions. For example, in the model of the Marcus et al. experiments, performance varied significantly within a category of test sequence. This was especially true for stimuli containing the partially familiar syllables, those composed of combinations of familiar and unfamiliar phones. For some reason, the sequence *la la wo* was not readily accepted by the network; in fact for these syllables all three network instantiations actually preferred the ungrammatical sequences (*la wo wo*, *la wo la*). In general, the network was less willing to accept novel vowels than novel consonants. This was probably due to the relatively small variation among the training vowels (two values for one dimension, one value for the other).

CONCLUSIONS

We began with patterns and pattern learning and described how very young children are already capable of learning the two kinds of correlations in patterns. These capacities will be fundamental in later learning, of language in particular. They will play a role in segmentation generally and in phonological development specifically. Understanding the mechanisms behind these capacities is fundamental to understanding language and cognition itself.

In struggling for this understanding, we should be aware that a given set of regularities has multiple characterisations and that the characterisation that is most obvious to us as observers of the learning process, rather than as learners, may not be the one that learners pick up on. One advantage of simple statistical learning devices that make use of distributed representations is that they can sometimes reveal these less obvious sorts of characterisations to us. Or at least thinking in terms of these models and what they can do may liberate us from thinking more abstractly than we need to.

We have shown that there is such an alternate characterisation of the artificial stimuli used in the experiments of Marcus et al. (1999), one that makes no reference to variables or formal rules. Given this sort of characterisation, building a statistical model that learns the regularities is straightforward. Other connectionist modellers have also discovered alternative ways of viewing this seemingly symbolic task. As we investigate and re-investigate the more complex tasks that make up language and higher cognition, we should keep this in mind.

REFERENCES

Christiansen, M. H., Conway, C. M., & Curtin, S. (2000). A connectionist single-mechanism account of rule-like behaviour in infancy. In *Annual Conference of the Cognitive Science Society, 22* (pp. 83–88). Mahwah, NJ: Lawrence Erlbaum Associates, Inc.

Gasser, M., & Colunga, E. (2000). Babies, variables, and relational correlations. In *Annual*

Conference of the Cognitive Science Society, 22 (pp. 160–165). Mahwah, NJ: Lawrence Erlbaum Associates, Inc.

Gasser, M., Colunga, E., & Smith, L. B. (2001). Developing relations. In E. van der Zee & U. Nikanne (Eds.), *Cognitive interfaces: Constraints on linking cognitive information* (pp. 185–214). Oxford: Oxford University Press.

Hopfield, J. (1984). Neurons with graded response have collective computational properties like those of two-state neurons. *Proceedings of the National Academy of Sciences USA, 81,* 3088–3092.

Marcus, G. F. (1993). Negative evidence in language acquisition. *Cognition, 46,* 53–85.

Marcus, G. F. (2001). *The algebraic mind: Integrating connectionism and cognitive science.* Cambridge, MA: The MIT Press.

Marcus, G. F., Vijayan, S., Bandi Rao, S., & Vishton, P. M (1999). Rule learning by seven-month-old infants. *Science, 283,* 77–80.

McClelland, J. L., & Rumelhart, D. E. (1981). An interactive activation model of context effects in letter perception: Part 1. An account of basic findings. *Psychological Review, 88,* 375–407.

Moravcsik, E. A. (1978). Reduplicative constructions. In J. H. Greenberg (Ed.), *Universals of human language: Vol. 3. Word structure* (pp. 297–334). Stanford, CA: Stanford University Press.

Movellan, J. (1990). Contrastive Hebbian learning in the continuous Hopfield model. In D. S. Touretzky, J. L., Elman, & T. J. Sejnowski (Eds.), *Proceedings of the 1990 Connectionist Models Summer School* (pp. 10–17). San Mateo, CA: Morgan Kaufmann.

Pinker, S. (1999). Out of the minds of babes. *Science, 283,* 40–41.

Saffran, J. R., Aslin, R. N., & Newport, E. L. (1996). Statistical learning by eight-month-old infants. *Science, 274,* 1926–1928.

Saffran, J. R., Johnson, E. K., Aslin, R. N., & Newport, E. L. (1999). Statistical learning of tone sequences by human infants and adults. *Cognition, 70,* 27–52.

Seidenberg, M. S., Elman, J. L., Negishi, M., Eimas, P. D., & Marcus, G. F. (1999). Do infants learn grammar with algebra or statistics? *Science, 284,* 433.

Shastri, L., & Ajjanagadde, V. (1993). From simple associations to systematic reasoning: A connectionist representation of rules, variables, and dynamic bindings using temporal synchrony. *Behavioral and Brain Sciences, 16,* 417–494.

Shultz, T. R., & Bale, A. C. (2000). Infant familiarization to artificial sentences: Rule-like behavior without explicit rules and variables. In *Annual Conference of the Cognitive Science Society, 22* (pp. 459–463). Mahwah, NJ: Lawrence Erlbaum Associates, Inc.

Thornton, C. (2000). *Truth from trash.* Cambridge, MA: The MIT Press.

von der Malsburg, C. (1973). Self-organization of orientation selective cells in the striate cortex. *Kybernetik, 14,* 85–100.

CHAPTER EIGHT

Does visual development aid visual learning?

Melissa Dominguez and Robert A. Jacobs
University of Rochester, NY, USA

Relative to adults, human infants are born with limited perceptual, motor, linguistic, and cognitive abilities. There are at least two perspectives within the field of developmental psychology regarding these limitations. The older and more popular view is that these limitations are barriers that must be overcome if a child is to achieve adult function (Piaget, 1952). That is, they are immaturities or deficiencies that serve no positive purpose. A newer view is that these apparent inadequacies are in fact helpful, and perhaps necessary, stages in development. According to this theory, limited mental abilities reflect simple neural representations, which are useful "stepping stones" or "building blocks" for the subsequent development of more complex representations (Turkewitz & Kenney, 1982).

The development of biological nervous systems is sometimes characterised in terms of this newer view. Greenough, Black, & Wallace (1987) hypothesised that asynchrony in brain development serves the useful function of "stage setting". The developmental schedule for the maturation of different brain regions is staggered such that neural systems that develop relatively early provide a suitable framework for the development of later, experience-sensitive systems. The notion of stage-setting can be generalised by considering the fact that neural events can be ordered either in time, such as temporally earlier versus later events, or in space, as in events at earlier versus later regions in a hierarchy of brain regions (e.g. lateral geniculate nucleus versus primary visual cortex).

Neuroscientific evidence consistent with the stage-setting hypothesis comes from Harwerth, Smith, Duncan, Crawford, & von Noorden (1986). These investigators performed behavioural studies of sensitive periods for visual development in monkeys. Their results suggest that these sensitive periods are organised into a hierarchy in which early visual functions requiring information processing in the peripheral portions of the visual system have shorter sensitive periods than higher-level functions requiring more central neural processing. A second example is provided by the work of Shatz (1996). Within the lateral geniculate nucleus (LGN) of adult mammals, retinal ganglion cell axons from one eye are segregated from those arising from the other eye to form a series of alternating eye-specific layers. These layers are not present initially in development. Moreover, they form during a period in which vision is not possible. Shatz argued that the development of eye-specific layers is characterised by at least two important events. First, retinal ganglion cells spontaneously show waves of activity that sweep across the retina such that activity at nearby cells is more highly correlated than at distant cells. Second, LGN cells use a Hebb-style adaptation mechanism that sorts connections based on local correlations of activity to form eye-specific layers. If this is so, then it is a clear example in which a developmental event at an earlier visual region (spontaneous waves of activity at the retina) sets the stage for an event at a later visual region (Hebb-style adaptation at the LGN).

Newport (1990) hypothesised that children use a stage-setting strategy when attempting to learn a language. Human languages are componential systems in which large linguistic structures are formed by systematically combining smaller components. According to Newport's (1990) "less is more" hypothesis, the limited attentional and memorial abilities of children are useful when learning a language because they help children segment and identify the components that comprise the language. An implementation of this general idea was studied by Elman (1993), who showed that a recurrent neural network whose memory capacity was initially limited but then gradually increased during the course of training, learned aspects of a grammar better than a network whose memory capacity was never limited (i.e. the second network's memory capacity was always equal to that of the first network at the end of training). Elman argued that this outcome supports the idea that "starting small" is a developmental property that is important to the subsequent acquisition of complex mental abilities. However, Rohde and Plaut (1999; and discussed in more detail in Chapter 6) were unable to replicate Elman's simulation results, so it is difficult to know how to interpret these results.

This chapter considers the hypothesis that systems learning aspects of visual perception may benefit from the use of suitably designed developmental progressions during training. Relative to adults, human infants are born with poor visual acuity (acuity refers to the amount of detail that can be detected or discriminated in a visual image). The acuity of newborns is about

20/400 when measured on the Snellen scale, whereas that of normal adults is 20/20. Their acuity improves approximately linearly from these low levels at birth to near adult levels by about 8 months of age (Norcia & Tyler, 1985). At the same time, infants are acquiring other visual abilities, such as the ability to detect binocular disparities (binocular disparities refer to differences in left and right visual images due to the fact that our eyes are offset from each other; these disparities carry information about the three-dimensional depth and shape of objects in the visual environment). Sensitivity to binocular disparities appears at around 4 months of age (Atkinson & Braddick, 1976; Fox, Aslin, Shea, & Dumais, 1980; Held, Birch, & Gwiazda, 1980). Is there a functional relationship between the development of visual acuity and the development of binocular disparity sensitivities? We speculate that the developments of acuity and binocular disparity sensitivity may be related in the sense that, counterintuitively, poor acuity at an early age aids the acquisition of disparity sensitivity later in life.

Unfortunately, essentially nothing is known about the psychological processes or mental representations underlying the detection and use of binocular disparities and, thus, nothing is known about how these underlying mental processes and representations change during development. Consequently, our attempt to understand the development of binocular disparity sensitivities emphasises neuroscientific variables, not psychological variables. Many (but not all) simple and complex cells in the primary visual cortex of primates are sensitive to binocular disparities, and a great deal is known about the receptive field properties of these cells from both neuroscientific and computational viewpoints.

We report the results of simulations in which three different systems were exposed to pairs of visual images, where each pair depicted an object against a background or a frontoparallel surface. The systems were trained to detect the binocular disparity of the object or of the surface, meaning the shift of the object or surface from the right-eye image to the left-eye image. Two of the systems are developmental models in the sense that the nature of their input changed during the course of training. The third system is a nondevelopmental model; its input remained constant during the course of training. The inputs to the systems were left and right retinal images filtered with binocular energy filters tuned to various spatial frequencies. Binocular energy filters are a computational tool for modelling the binocular sensitivities of simple and complex cells in primary visual cortex of primates. The training of the first system, referred to as the coarse-scale-to-multiscale model (or model C2M), included a developmental sequence such that the system was exposed only to low spatial frequency information at the start of training (i.e. coarse-scale disparity features), and information at higher spatial frequencies (mid-scale and fine-scale disparity features) was added to its input as training progressed. The training of the second system, referred to as the fine-scale-to-multiscale model (or model F2M), included an analogous developmental sequence with spatial frequency information added in the reverse order. This system received high spatial frequency information at the start of training (fine-scale disparity features); information at lower spatial frequencies (mid-scale and coarse-scale disparity features) was added as training progressed. The third system, referred to as the nondevelopmental model (or model ND), was not trained using a developmental sequence; it received information at all spatial frequencies throughout the training period.

When comparing the two developmental models with the nondevelopmental model, there are at least two reasonable predictions that one could make about the simulation results. One prediction is that the nondevelopmental model should outperform the developmental models. The nondevelopmental model received all input information throughout all stages of training, whereas the developmental models were deprived of portions of the input at certain training stages. If more information is better than less information, then the nondevelopmental model ought to perform best. This would be consistent with the traditional view of human infant development, that perceptual immaturities are barriers to be overcome.

An alternative prediction, consistent with the general approach of the "less is more" hypothesis described above, is that the developmental models would show the best performance. If it is believed that too much information could lead a learning system in its early stages of training to form poor internal representations, then the developmental models ought to have an advantage. Relative to the developmental models, the nondevelopmental model had a greater number of inputs and, thus, a greater number of modifiable weights during the early stages of training. Because learning in neural networks is a search in weight space, the nondevelopmental model needed to perform an unconstrained search in a high-dimensional weight space. Unconstrained searches frequently lead to the acquisition of poor representations. By contrast, the developmental models initially had fewer inputs and, thus, fewer modifiable weights. During early stages of training, their searches in weight space were comparatively constrained. If the constraints were appropriate, this should have facilitated the acquisition of useful representations by the developmental models.

When comparing the performances of the two developmental models, there are at least three reasonable predictions that one could make about the simulation results. One prediction is that the coarse-scale-to-multiscale model should perform best. A motivation for this prediction comes from the field of computer vision. Consider the task of aligning two images of a scene where the images differ due to a small horizontal offset in their viewpoints. Roughly, this is known as the stereo-correspondence problem. If this were something that you had never tried to do before, you might try to align fine details of each image. For example, you might pick a white dot in one image and repeatedly try aligning it with dots in the other image. If the images are highly textured, such an approach would be inefficient because there are an intractable number of potential alignments that might need to be checked before the two images are properly aligned (see panel A of Figure 8.1). If, however, the images are blurred, the fine details that were the source of so much confusion would be removed, leaving a smaller number of larger features in each image. The problem of finding a good alignment is now significantly easier because there are a smaller number of potential alignments (see panel B of Figure 8.1). After you have gained skill at aligning blurred images, you would then have a reliable foundation that you could use to learn to align clearer images. You might attempt to match the larger image features first. Subsequent analysis of fine details would seek to remove ambiguities that arise when aligning large features, instead of being a starting point for locating correspondences.

This style of processing is commonplace in the computer vision literature. For example, systems by Marr and Poggio (1979), Quam (1986), and Barnard (1987) initially search for correspondences within a pair of low-resolution images. Low-resolution images are used initially because they contain fewer image features, larger image features, and image features that are relatively robust to noise. Next, these systems refine their estimates of corresponding

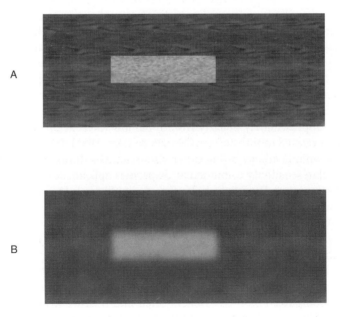

A

B

Figure 8.1. Panel A, a textured object and background. Panel B, the image from panel A blurred so as to remove the fine details. (From Dominguez & Jacobs, 2003.) Copyright © 2003 MIT Press. Reprinted with permission.

image features using information from one or more higher-resolution pairs of images. The usefulness of a coarse-to-fine processing strategy when searching for stereo correspondences suggests that a coarse-scale-to-multiscale developmental strategy might be useful for learning to detect binocular disparities. Before adopting this hypothesis, however, it is important to keep in mind the differences between these two strategies. Computer vision researchers use a coarse-to-fine strategy when searching for correspondences in individual pairs of images. In contrast, we used the coarse-scale-to-multiscale developmental sequence while training a learning system to detect binocular disparities using many pairs of images. It is not obvious that lessons from one situation can be applied to the other situation. Nonetheless, it may be the case that the use of a coarse-scale-to-multiscale developmental sequence biases a learning system so that it initially develops an approximate solution based on coarse-scale information and then subsequently learns to refine this solution using fine-scale information. If so, then the style of processing learned by this system at the end of training may resemble that of a nonadaptive system that is designed to use a coarse-to-fine processing style.

If we assume that human intelligence provides a guide to creating machine intelligence, then a second motivation for the prediction that the coarse-scale-to-multiscale developmental model should perform best is the fact that human infants show a related developmental progression. Visual acuity is often measured using a grating, which is a visual pattern whose luminance values are sinusoidally modulated. Acuity is characterised by the highest-frequency grating that is distinguishable from a solid grey pattern. Using this method, it has been found that newborns' visual acuity is extremely poor. Whereas adults with normal vision (so-called 20/20 vision) can discriminate approximately 30 cycles per degree of arc, newborns can only discriminate 1–2 cycles per degree giving them a visual acuity of about 20/400. Acuity improves approximately linearly from these low levels at birth to near adult levels by around 8 months of age (Norcia & Tyler, 1985). Importantly for our purposes, infants are acquiring other visual abilities during this time period; in particular, sensitivity to binocular disparities appears at around 4 months of age (Atkinson & Braddick, 1976; Fox, Aslin, Shea, & Dumais, 1980; Held, Birch, & Gwiazda, 1980; Petrig, Julesz, Kropfl, Baumgartner, & Anliker, 1981). We speculate that the developments of visual acuity and binocular disparity sensitivity can be related in the sense that poor acuity at an early age aids in the acquisition of disparity sensitivity later in life.

An alternative prediction is that the fine-scale-to-multiscale developmental model should perform best. A motivation for this prediction is the fact that computer vision researchers often find it easier to solve the stereo-correspondence problem by first extracting edge information from left and right images, a form of high-frequency band-pass filtering, and then searching for a good alignment of the images based on this information. This strategy is useful because edges can be sparse, large, and robust to noise relative to other image features. Analogous to the initial use of high-frequency information by computer vision systems, the fine-scale-to-multiscale model is initially trained solely with information extracted from high-frequency band-pass filters. If we are willing to assume that computer vision methods for finding stereo correspondences can provide lessons for how learning systems can learn to detect binocular disparities, as discussed above, then we might predict that model F2M has an advantage.

A second motivation for the prediction that model F2M should perform best is the seemingly counterintuitive result that neural networks trained with input patterns that have been corrupted by noise frequently show better generalisation than equivalent networks trained with input patterns that have not been corrupted (Sietsma & Dow, 1991). Training with noisy inputs has been shown analytically to be equivalent to a form of regularisation (Bishop, 1995; Matsuoka, 1992; Webb, 1994). In other words, the learning process of networks trained with noisy inputs is more constrained than that of similar networks whose inputs are not corrupted by noise. If the retinal images contain noise, and if the coarse-scale-to-multiscale model tends to filter out the noise during early stages of training, then this model will not obtain the benefits of training with noisy inputs. We would, therefore, expect the fine-scale-to-multiscale model to perform best.

Finally, another possible prediction is that the coarse-scale-to-multiscale model and the fine-scale-to-multiscale model perform about equally well. If the relative advantages of model C2M (being able to use fewer image features, larger image features, and more noise-resistant image features at the start of training) and the relative advantages of model F2M (initial exposure to high-frequency band-pass information, being able to obtain the benefits of training with noisy inputs) are roughly balanced, then neither model would be expected to show superior performance. Furthermore, we outlined above the logic of computer vision researchers who advocate a coarse-to-fine processing strategy when analysing stereo correspondences, and we tentatively speculated that the usefulness of this strategy suggests that the seemingly related coarse-scale-to-multiscale developmental strategy might be useful for learning to detect binocular disparities. If, however, we again make the assumption that human intelligence provides a guide to creating machine intelligence, then it is worth noting that psychologists have discovered that humans often do not use a coarse-to-fine strategy when analysing stereo correspondences. Mallot, Gillner, and Arndt (1996) found that unambiguous information at a coarse scale is not always used by observers to disambiguate finer-scale information, and found that observers can use unambiguous fine-scale information to disambiguate coarse-scale information, meaning that observers are using a fine-to-coarse processing strategy in these circumstances. Related findings have been reported by several other researchers (McKee &

Mitchison, 1988; Mowforth, Mayhew, & Frisby, 1981; Smallman, 1995). Because human observers neither exclusively use a coarse-to-fine strategy nor a fine-to-coarse strategy, we might not expect the exclusive use of a coarse-scale-to-multiscale developmental strategy or the exclusive use of a fine-scale-to-multiscale developmental strategy to yield a relative performance advantage.

This chapter reports the results of computer simulations comparing the learning performances of developmental and nondevelopmental models on the task of estimating binocular disparities of objects against backgrounds or of frontoparallel surfaces in novel pairs of images. Three results are highlighted. First, developmental models C2M and F2M consistently outperformed the nondevelopmental model ND. Second, models C2M and F2M outperformed a random developmental model that was also trained in stages, but the inputs to this model were randomly selected at each stage. Finally, models C2M and F2M outperformed developmental models whose inputs did not progress in an orderly fashion from one resolution scale to a neighbouring scale during the course of development. Additional details and analyses regarding these results can be found in Dominguez and Jacobs (2003). The fact that models C2M and F2M outperformed the nondevelopmental model is important because this demonstrates that models that undergo a developmental maturation can acquire a more advanced perceptual ability than one that does not. The fact that models C2M and F2M outperformed the random developmental model is important because this demonstrates that not all developmental sequences can be expected to provide performance benefits. On the contrary, only sequences whose characteristics are matched to the task should lead to superior performance. Our findings suggest that the most successful models are those that are exposed to visual inputs at a single scale early in training, and for which the resolution of their inputs progresses in an orderly fashion from one scale to a neighbouring scale during the course of training. On the basis of these results, we conclude that developmental sequences can be useful to systems learning to detect binocular disparities, and that the general idea that visual development can aid visual learning is a viable hypothesis in need of future study.

DEVELOPMENTAL AND NONDEVELOPMENTAL MODELS

The structure of the developmental and nondevelopmental models is illustrated in Figure 8.2. This structure is based on a similar architecture studied by Gray, Pouget, Zemel, Nowlan, & Sejnowski (1998). The retinal layer consisted of two one-dimensional arrays 62 pixels in length for the left and right eye images. Each retina was treated as if it were shaped like a circle; the leftmost and rightmost pixels were regarded as neighbours. This wraparound of the left and right edges was done to avoid edge artefacts. Although one-dimensional retinas are a simplification, their use is justified by the fact that the models were only concerned with horizontal disparities as these are the ones that provide information about the three-dimensional configuration of the visual environment (vertical disparities provide information about viewing distance and angle of gaze, but not about the three-dimensional nature of the environment). The retinal inputs were filtered using binocular energy filters

Based on neurophysiological studies, Ohzawa, DeAngelis, and Freeman (1990) proposed binocular energy filters as a way of modelling the binocular

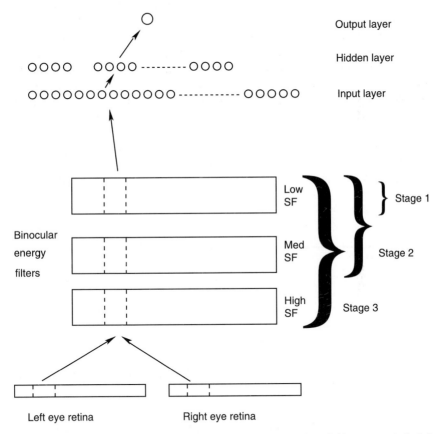

Figure 8.2. All models shared a common structure. The first portion of this structure is the left and right retinal images. These images are then filtered by binocular energy filters tuned to low, medium, and high spatial frequencies (SF), which simulate the binocular sensitivities of simple and complex cells in primary visual cortex. The outputs of these filters are the inputs to an artificial neural network that is trained to estimate the disparity present in the images. The model illustrated here is the coarse-scale-to-multiscale model in which low spatial frequency information was received during early stages of training, and information at higher frequencies was added as training progressed. (From Dominguez & Jacobs, 2003.) Copyright © 2003 The MIT Press. Reprinted with permission.

sensitivities of simple and complex cells in primary visual cortex. These filters are a modification of motion energy filters proposed by Adelson and Bergen (1985). Intuitively, these filters may be understood as follows. When tested with light patterns presented to a single eye, simple cells are often found to have a receptive-field profile that is accurately modelled by a mathematical function known as a Gabor function. Consider the Gabor function shown in the upper-left corner of Figure 8.3. The horizontal axis in this graph gives retinal position (along an axis perpendicular to the preferred orientation of the neuron), and the vertical axis represents sensitivity to a luminance increment such that upward and downward deflections of the curve correspond to ON and OFF subregions of the neuron's receptive field, respectively. Based on the receptive-field profile in the upper-left corner of this figure, the simple cell would tend to increase its activity in response to a luminance increment in the centre of its receptive field, and to decrease its activity in response to luminance increments away from its receptive-field centre.

We need to consider both its left-eye and right-eye receptive-field profiles in order to understand this cell's sensitivity to binocular disparities. The top row of Figure 8.3 illustrates these profiles for a hypothetical cell. The left-eye and right-eye profiles are identical in shape in this example. Note that this cell will have its largest response when there are luminance increments in the

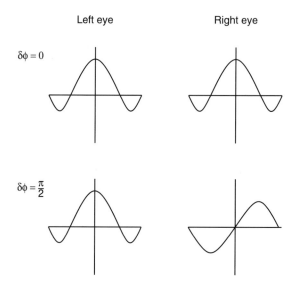

Figure 8.3.   Illustrations of left-eye and right-eye receptive-field profiles. The simple cell whose profiles are illustrated in the top row is sensitive to zero disparities (no shift between left-eye and right-eye images), whereas the cell whose profiles are illustrated in the bottom row is sensitive to nonzero disparities (a shift of a certain direction and magnitude between left-eye and right-eye images).

centre of the receptive fields of both eyes. Now consider the receptive-field profiles illustrated in the bottom row of Figure 8.3. The left-eye and right-eye profiles have different shapes in this case. This cell will have its largest response when there is a luminance increment in the centre of its left-eye receptive field and an increment towards the right of its right-eye receptive field. In other words, this cell will have its largest response when a luminance increment in the left-eye image has shifted to the right in the right-eye image. Whereas the neuron illustrated in the top row is sensitive to zero disparities (no shift between left-eye and right-eye images), the neuron illustrated in the bottom row is sensitive to a nonzero disparity (a shift of a certain direction and magnitude between left-eye and right-eye images).

Although not illustrated in Figure 8.3, complex cells are hypothesised to sum the outputs of appropriate sets of simple cells so that their responses are phase-invariant, meaning that the responses do not depend on the exact position of a disparity within the cell's receptive field. The output of a binocular energy filter is meant to model the output of a complex cell. Our simulations used filters with different phase offsets between the left-eye and right-eye receptive-field profiles (these different filters were sensitive to disparities of different sizes), and different spatial frequency scales (these different filters were sensitive to disparity features at different image resolutions, ranging from coarse, or low-resolution, disparity features to fine, or high-resolution, disparity features). When considering the simulation results discussed below, it is important to keep in mind that complex cells (and binocular energy filters) indicate the disparities present in (local) image patches, and do not indicate the (global) disparity of an object against a background or of a frontoparallel surface.

Mathematically, binocular energy filters are characterised as follows. A simple cell receives input from a pair of subunits, one for each retina. The receptive field profiles of the subunits can be described mathematically as Gabor functions:

$$g_L(x,\phi) = \frac{1}{\sqrt{2\pi}\sigma} \exp\left(-\frac{x^2}{2\sigma^2}\right) \sin\left(2\pi\omega x + \phi\right) \qquad (8.1)$$

$$g_R(x,\phi) = \frac{1}{\sqrt{2\pi}\sigma} \exp\left(-\frac{x^2}{2\sigma^2}\right) \sin\left(2\pi\omega x + \phi + \delta\phi\right) \qquad (8.2)$$

Each function is a sinusoid multiplied by a Gaussian envelope. The parameter x is the distance to the centre of the Gaussian, σ^2 is the variance of the Gaussian, ω is the frequency of the sinusoid, and ϕ and $\delta\phi$ are referred to as the base phase and phase offset of the sinusoid. The Gabor functions associated with the left and right retinal subunits differ in that the phase of one is offset from the phase of the other (a nonzero phase offset accounts for the left-eye and right-eye receptive-field profiles having a different shape).

The output of a simple cell is formed in two stages: First, the convolution of the left retinal image with the left subunit Gabor is added to the convolution of the right retinal image with the right subunit Gabor; next, this sum is half-wave rectified and squared (a negative sum is mapped to zero; a positive sum is mapped to its square). The magnitude of a simple cell's output is related to the presence of a binocular disparity of a particular size in the retinal input. Simple cells formed from subunits with different phase offsets are sensitive to disparities of different sizes (Fleet, Wagner, & Heeger, 1996; Qian, 1994). The output of a complex cell is the sum of the outputs of four simple cells. Because the base phases of these simple cells form quadrature pairs (the base phases are 0, $\frac{\pi}{2}$, π, and $\frac{3\pi}{2}$), the complex cell's output is relatively insensitive to the exact position of a disparity within its receptive field.

In our simulations, there were 35 receptive-field locations which received input from overlapping regions of the retina. At each of these locations, there were 30 complex cells corresponding to three spatial frequencies and 10 phase offsets at each frequency. The three spatial frequencies were each separated by an octave: 0.25, 0.125, and 0.0625 cycles per pixel. The standard deviations of the Gabor functions were set to be inversely proportional to the frequency: 1.0 for 0.25 cycles/pixel, 2.0 for 0.125 cycles/pixel, and 4.0 for 0.0625 cycles/ pixel. The ten phase offsets were equally spaced over a range from 0 to $\frac{\pi}{2}$.

The outputs of the complex cells were normalised using a softmax nonlinearity:

$$\hat{E}_i(x) = \frac{e^{E_i(x)/\tau}}{\sum_j e^{E_j(x)/\tau}} \tag{8.3}$$

where $E_i(x)$ was the initial output of the complex cell, $\hat{E}_i(x)$ was the normalised output, τ is a scaling parameter known as a temperature parameter (its value was set to 0.25), and j indexed the 10 complex cells with different phase offsets at a receptive-field location within a single frequency band. As a result of this normalisation, complex cells tended to respond to relative contrast in an image, rather than absolute contrast.

The normalised outputs of the complex cells were the inputs to an artificial neural network. As illustrated in Figure 8.4, the network had 1050 input units (the complex cells had 35 receptive-field locations and there were 30 cells at each location). The hidden layer of the network contained 32 units, which were organised into eight groups of 4 units each. The connectivity to the hidden units was set so that each group had a limited receptive field; a group of hidden units received inputs from seven receptive-field locations at the complex cell level. The hidden units used a logistic activation function.

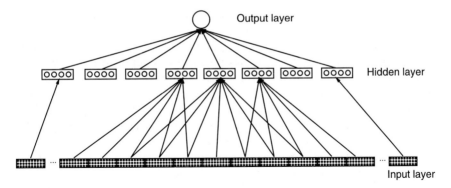

Figure 8.4. The structure of the artificial neural network portion of the developmental and nondevelopmental models.

The output layer consisted of a single linear unit; this unit's output was an estimate of the object or surface disparity present in the right and left retinal images.

The weights of an artificial neural network were initialised to small random values, and were adjusted during the course of training to minimise a sum of squared error cost function using a conjugate gradient optimisation procedure (Press, Teukolsky, Vetterling, & Flannery, 1992). This procedure was used because it tends to converge quickly and because it has no free parameters (e.g. no learning rate or momentum parameters). Weight sharing was implemented at the hidden-unit level so that corresponding units within each group of hidden units had the same incoming and outgoing weight values, and so that a hidden unit had the same set of weight values from each receptive-field location at the complex unit level. This provided the network with a degree of translation invariance, and also dramatically decreased the number of modifiable weight values in the network. It therefore decreased the number of data items needed to train the network, and the amount of time needed to train the network.

Models were trained and tested using separate sets of training and test data items. Training sets contained 250 randomly generated data items; test sets contained 122 data items that were generated so as to uniformly cover the range of possible binocular disparities. Training was terminated after 35 iterations through the training set in order to minimise over-fitting of the training data. The results reported below are based on the data items from the test set.

Model C2M was trained using a coarse-scale-to-multiscale developmental sequence. This was implemented as follows. The training period was divided into three stages where the first and second stages were each 10 iterations and the third stage was 15 iterations. During the first stage, the neural network portion of the model only received the outputs of complex cells tuned to low spatial frequencies (low-resolution disparity features). The outputs of the other complex cells were set to zero. During the second stage, the network received the outputs of complex cells tuned to low and medium spatial frequencies (low- and mid-resolution disparity features); it received the outputs of all complex cells during the third stage (low-, mid-, and high-resolution disparity features). The training of model F2M was identical to that of model C2M except that its training used a fine-scale-to-multiscale developmental sequence. During the first stage of training, its network received the outputs of complex cells tuned to high spatial frequencies. This network received the outputs of complex cells tuned to high and medium frequencies during the second stage, and received the outputs of all complex cells during the third stage. In contrast, the training period for the nondevelopmental model was not divided into separate stages; its neural network received the outputs of all complex cells throughout the training period.

DATA SETS AND SIMULATION RESULTS

The performances of the three models were evaluated on three data sets. The data sets were based on related data sets used by Gray et al. (1998). In all cases the images were grey scale with luminance values between 0 and 1, and disparities with values between 0 and 3 pixels. Ten simulations of each model on each data set were conducted.

In the solid object data set, images consisted of a single light or dark object on a grey background. The object's grey-scale value was either between 0.0 and 0.1 or between 0.9 and 1.0, whereas the grey-scale value of the background was always 0.5. The location of the object was randomly chosen to be a real-valued location on the retina. The object's disparity was randomly chosen to be a real value between 0 and 3 pixels (i.e. in going from the right-eye image to the left-eye image the position of the object was shifted by 0–3 pixels). The object's size was randomly chosen to be a real value between 10 and 25 pixels. Since the object's size, location, and disparity were all real numbers, the ends of the object could fall at a real-valued location within a pixel. In these (common) cases the value of the partially covered pixel was interpolated between the grey-scale value of the object and that of the background in proportion to the amount of the pixel covered by the object and background. An example of a right and a left image is shown in the top panel of Figure 8.5. Given the right and left images, the task of a model was to estimate the object's disparity.

The leftmost graph of Figure 8.6 illustrates the results. The horizontal axis gives the model, and the vertical axis gives the root mean squared error (RMSE) at the end of training on the data items from the test set. On average, developmental model C2M had a 16.5 per cent smaller generalisation error

Solid object

Noisy object

Planar

Figure 8.5. Examples of right and left images (top and bottom rows in each panel) from the solid object, noisy object, and planar data sets. Top panel: in going from the top to the bottom images, the dark object is shifted to the right. Middle panel: the noisy object is towards the left edge of the images. In going from the top to the bottom images, the noisy object is shifted by two pixels to the right. Bottom panel: the entire top image is shifted by two pixels to the right to form the bottom image. (From Dominguez & Jacobs, 2003.) Copyright © 2003 The MIT Press. Reprinted with permission.

than the nondevelopmental model (the difference between the mean error rates is statistically significant; $t(18) = 3.77$, $p < .002$, using a two-tailed t-test. Developmental model F2M had a 12.2 per cent smaller error than the non-developmental model, $t(18) = 23.74$, $p < .001$). Clearly, the two developmental models outperformed the nondevelopmental model. A statistical comparison between the developmental models C2M and F2M shows that their perform-ances were not significantly different.

The images in the second data set, referred to as the noisy object data set, were meant to resemble random-dot stereograms frequently used in behaviour-al experiments. Images contained a noisy object against a noisy background. The grey-scale values of the object pixels and the background pixels were set to random numbers between 0 and 1. The location of the object was randomly chosen to be a real-valued location on the retina. The object's size was random-ly chosen to be a real value between 10 and 25 pixels. The object's disparity was a randomly chosen integer between 0 and 3 pixels. As before, the task was to map the left and right images to an estimate of the object's disparity. An example of a left and a right image is shown in the middle panel of Figure 8.5.

The results are shown in the middle graph of Figure 8.6. As before, the developmental models consistently performed better than the nondevel-opmental model. On average, model C2M had a 7.1 per cent smaller gen-eralisation error than model ND, and model F2M had a 4.3 per cent smaller error than model ND. Comparing the two developmental models, model C2M had a 2.85 per cent smaller error than model F2M. (All the differ-ences in the mean error rates are statistically significant; C2M versus ND: $t(18) = 10.33$, $p < .001$; F2M versus ND: $t(18) = 15.08$, $p < .001$; C2M versus F2M: $t(18) = 3.68$, $p < .002$).

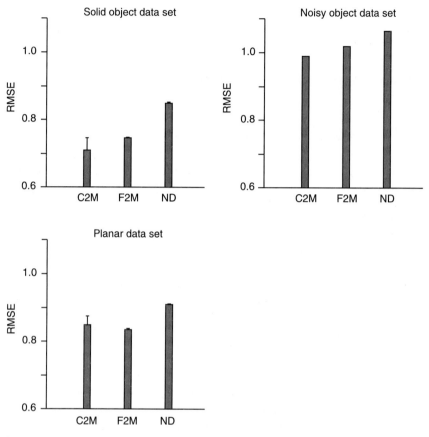

Figure 8.6.   The three models' root mean squared errors (RMSE) on the test set data items after training on the three data sets (the error bars give the standard error of the mean). (From Dominguez & Jacobs, 2003.) Copyright © 2003 The MIT Press. Reprinted with permission.

The last data set, the planar data set, was different from the first two data sets. Instead of an object in front of a background, the images depicted a frontoparallel plane. The values of the left-image pixels were randomly chosen to be either 0 or 1. The right image was generated by applying an integer shift to the left image of 0, 1, 2, or 3 pixels. Given the left and right images, the task was to estimate the size of the shift. An example of a left and a right image is shown in the bottom panel of Figure 8.5.

The results are shown in the rightmost graph of Figure 8.6. Again, the developmental models outperformed the nondevelopmental model. Model C2M had a 6.7 per cent smaller generalisation error than model ND, $t(18) = 2.27$, $p < .05$, and model F2M had an 8.3 per cent smaller error than model

ND, $t(18) = 16.84$, $p < .001$. The performances of models C2M and F2M were not statistically different.

Overall, the results show that the developmental models C2M and F2M consistently outperformed the nondevelopmental model ND. However, the results do not suggest why the developmental models showed superior performance. To obtain a better understanding of this outcome, we conducted two additional sets of simulations.

A possible reason for why the developmental models showed superior performance is that they had relatively few inputs during the initial stages of training. In other words, it might be that the exact nature of the developmental progression is irrelevant. Instead, what matters is that the input size of a system starts small and gradually grows during the course of training. To check this possibility, we simulated a random developmental model, referred to as model RD. This system was similar to models C2M and F2M in the sense that its training included a developmental sequence. However, whereas the inputs received by models C2M and F2M at each developmental stage were organised by spatial frequency content, the inputs received by model RD at each stage were randomly selected. The collection of complex cells was randomly partitioned into three equal-sized subsets with the constraint that each subset included all phase offsets at all receptive-field locations. During the first stage of training, the neural network portion of the model only received the outputs of the complex cells in the first random subset. It received the outputs of the cells in the first and second random subsets during the second stage of training, and received the outputs of all complex cells during the third stage.

The results of training and testing the developmental models C2M, F2M, and RD, and the nondevelopmental model ND on the solid object data set are shown in Figure 8.7. Model C2M had a 19.3 per cent smaller generalisation error than model RD, $t(18) = 4.60$, $p < .001$, and model F2M had a 15.2 per cent smaller error than the random developmental model, $t(18) = 49.01$, $p < .001$. This result clearly indicates that the superior performances of models C2M and F2M were not due to limitations on their input sizes. Model RD had the same limitations but its performance was relatively poor. Instead, it seems that there is something important about the exact nature of the developmental progressions that accounts for their superior performances.

We speculate that two important features of the developmental progressions of models C2M and F2M account for their superior performance. First, these models were exposed to visual inputs at a single scale or resolution early in training. Model C2M received only coarse-scale information at the start of training; model F2M received only fine-scale information. In contrast, models RD and ND received information at all spatial scales at all stages of training. We conjecture that it might be advantageous for a learning system to receive inputs at a single scale early in training because this allows

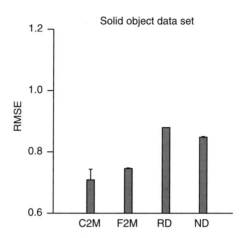

Figure 8.7.   The root mean squared errors (RMSE) of developmental models C2M, F2M, and RD, and the developmental model ND on the test items from the solid object data set.

the system to combine and compare input features without the need to compensate for the fact that these features could be at different spatial scales.

Second, models C2M and F2M might be at an advantage because the spatial scale of their inputs progressed in an orderly fashion from one scale to a neighbouring scale. Consequently, when these models received inputs at a new spatial scale, this new scale was close to a scale with which the models were already familiar. If it is the case that this second feature of models C2M and F2M is important, then this leads to an interesting prediction. We predict that developmental models whose progressions do not proceed in an orderly manner from one scale to a neighbouring scale ought to show poor performance.

To test this prediction, two additional models were created and tested on the solid object data set. These models had developmental stages based on spatial frequency content (like models C2M and F2M) but the addition of new frequency bands to their inputs at each stage did not proceed in an orderly manner. The first new model is referred to as model C-CF-CMF. It received the outputs of complex cells tuned to a low spatial frequency (coarse disparity features) early in training. In stage two it received the outputs of complex cells tuned to low and high frequencies (coarse and fine disparity features), and it received the outputs of cells tuned to low, medium, and high frequencies (coarse, medium, and fine disparity features) in stage three. The second new model, referred to as model F-CF-CMF, was similar to model C-CF-CMF but it started with high frequency information. That is, it received the outputs of complex cells tuned to a high spatial frequency early in training. It received the outputs of cells tuned to low and high frequencies in stage two, and the outputs of all complex cells in stage three.

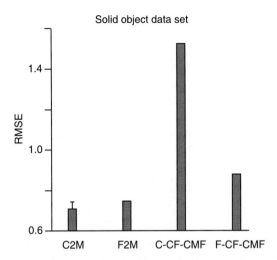

Figure 8.8.   The root mean squared errors (RMSE) of models C2M, F2M, C-CF-CMF, and F-CF-CMF on the test items from the solid object data set. (From Dominguez & Jacobs, 2003.) Copyright © 2003 The MIT Press. Reprinted with permission.

Figure 8.8 shows the performances of models C2M, F2M, C-CF-CMF, and F-CF-CMF at the end of training on the solid object data set. In accord with our prediction, models C-CF-CMF and F-CF-CMF showed very poor performance. This data is consistent with the conjecture discussed above that it is advantageous to a developmental system for the spatial scale of its inputs to progress in an orderly fashion from one scale to a neighbouring scale.

CONCLUDING REMARKS

We have considered the hypothesis that systems learning aspects of visual perception may benefit from the use of suitably designed developmental progressions during training. In particular, we have speculated that there is a functional relationship between the development of visual acuity and the development of binocular disparity sensitivities; namely, that poor acuity at an early age aids the acquisition of disparity sensitivity later in life. To evaluate this hypothesis, we simulated a number of developmental and non-developmental learning systems. Overall, the results suggest that the most successful systems at learning to detect the binocular disparities of solid or noisy objects against backgrounds or of planar surfaces are systems that are exposed to visual inputs at a single scale early in training, and for which the resolution of their inputs progresses in an orderly fashion from one scale to a neighbouring scale during the course of training. Given that human infants show a coarse-to-multiscale progression in their visual acuity, it is surprising that we found that the coarse-scale-to-multiscale and fine-scale-to-multiscale models showed similar levels of performance. It may be that there are other reasons as to why evolution has preferred a coarse-scale-to-multiscale progression in biological organisms.

With relatively few exceptions, the relationships between development and learning have largely been ignored by the neural computation community. We believe that this is unfortunate. As discussed at the beginning of this chapter, developmental cognitive neuroscientists are in the early phases of formulating a stage-setting theory of neural development. This theory postulates that early events set the stage for later events, meaning that early events are "building blocks" or "stepping stones" for later events. The research project described here highlights the fact that learning and developmental events can be coordinated such that early events provide important functional benefits to later events. In our simulations, we found that orderly changes in scale or resolution in an early computational region, the binocular energy filters, made it easier for a later region, the artificial neural network, to learn to estimate the object and surface disparities present in pairs of visual images. We believe that developmental neurobiologists should not only study individual neural events, but that they should also seek to characterise the functional relationships among these events. Computational neuroscientists have an important role to play in this endeavour.

ACKNOWLEDGEMENTS

This work was supported by NSF Graduate Fellowship DGE9616170 and by NIH research grant R01-EY13149.

REFERENCES

Adelson, E. H., & Bergen, J. R. (1985). Spatiotemporal energy models for the perception of motion. *Journal of the Optical Society of America A, 2*, 284–299.
Atkinson, J., & Braddick, O. (1976). Stereoscopic discrimination in infants. *Perception, 5*, 29–38.
Barnard, S. T. (1987). *Stereo matching by hierarchical, microcanonical annealing* (Technical Report 414). Menlo Park, CA: Artificial Intelligence Center, SRI International.
Bishop, C. M. (1995). Training with noise is equivalent to Tikhonov regularization. *Neural Computation, 7*, 108–116.
Dominguez, M., & Jacobs, R. A. (2003). Developmental constraints aid the acquisition of binocular disparity sensitivities. *Neural Computation, 15*(1), 161–182.
Elman, J. L. (1993). Learning and development in neural networks: The importance of starting small. *Cognition, 43*, 71–99.
Fleet, D. J., Wagner, H., & Heeger, D. J. (1996). Neural encoding of binocular disparity: Energy models, position shifts, and phase shifts. *Vision Research, 36*, 1839–1857.
Fox, R., Aslin, R. N., Shea, S. L., & Dumais, S. T. (1980). Stereopsis in human infants. *Science, 207*, 323–324.
Gray, M. S., Pouget, A., Zemel, R. S., Nowlan, S. J., & Sejnowski, T. J. (1998). Reliable disparity estimation through selective integration. *Visual Neuroscience, 15*, 511–528.

Greenough, W. T., Black, J. E., & Wallace, C. S. (1987). Experience and brain development. *Child Development, 58*, 539–559.

Harwerth, R. S., Smith III, E. L., Duncan, G. C., Crawford, M. L. J., & von Noorden, G. K. (1986). Multiple sensitive periods in the development of the primate visual system. *Science, 232*, 235–238.

Held, R., Birch, E., & Gwiazda, J. (1980). Stereoacuity in human infants. *Proceedings of the National Academy of Sciences USA, 77*, 5572–5574.

Mallot, H. A., Gillner, S., & Arndt, P. A. (1996). Is correspondence search in human stereo vision a coarse-to-fine process? *Biological Cybernetics, 74*, 95–106.

Marr, D., & Poggio, T. (1979). A computational theory of human stereo vision. *Proceedings of the Royal Society of London B, 204*, 301–328.

Matsuoka, K. (1992). Noise injection into inputs in back-propagation learning. *IEEE Transactions on Systems, Man, and Cybernetics, 22*, 436–440.

McKee, S. P., & Mitchison, G. J. (1988). The role of retinal correspondence in stereoscopic matching. *Vision Research, 28*, 1001–1012.

Mowforth, P., Mayhew, J. E. W., & Frisby, J. P. (1981). Vergence eye movements made in response to spatial-frequency-filtered random-dot stereograms. *Perception, 10*, 299–304.

Newport, E. L. (1990). Maturational constraints on language learning. *Cognitive Science, 14*, 11–28.

Norcia, A., & Tyler, C. (1985). Spatial frequency sweep VEP: Visual acuity during the first year of life. *Vision Research, 25*, 1399–1408.

Ohzawa, I., DeAngelis, G. C., & Freeman, R. D. (1990). Stereoscopic depth discrimination in the visual cortex: Neurons ideally suited as disparity detectors. *Science, 249*, 1037–1041.

Petrig, B., Julesz, B., Kropfl, W., Baumgartner, G., & Anliker, M. (1981). Development of stereopsis and cortical binocularity in human infants: Electrophysiological evidence. *Science, 213*, 1402–1405.

Piaget, J. (1952). *The origins of intelligence in children.* New York: International Universities Press.

Press, W. H., Teukolsky, S. A., Vetterling, W. T., & Flannery, B. P. (1992). *Numerical recipes in C: The art of scientific computing.* Cambridge: Cambridge University Press.

Qian, N. (1994). Computing stereo disparity and motion with known binocular cell properties. *Neural Computation, 6*, 390–404.

Quam, L. H. (1986). *Hierarchical warp stereo* (Technical Report 402). Menlo Park, CA: Artificial Intelligence Center, SRI International.

Rohde, D. L. T., & Plaut, D. C. (1999). Language acquisition in the absence of explicit negative evidence: How important is starting small? *Cognition, 72*, 67–109.

Shatz, C. J. (1996). Emergence of order in visual system development. *Proceedings of the National Academy of Sciences USA, 93*, 602–608.

Sietsma, J., & Dow, R. J. F. (1991). Creating artificial neural networks that generalize. *Neural Networks, 4*, 67–79.

Smallman, H. S. (1995). Fine-to-coarse scale disambiguation in stereopsis. *Vision Research, 34*, 2971–2982.

Turkewitz, G., & Kenney, P. A. (1982). Limitations on input as a basis for neural organization and perceptual development: A preliminary statement. *Developmental Psychobiology, 15*, 357–368.

Webb, A. R. (1994). Functional approximation by feedforward networks: A least-squares approach to generalization. *IEEE Transactions on Neural Networks, 5*, 363–371.

CHAPTER NINE

Learning and brain development:
A neural constructivist perspective

Steven R. Quartz
California Institute of Technology, Pasadena, CA, USA

THE PROBLEM OF DEVELOPMENTAL CHANGE

Relating brain and cognitive development

How human cognitive development relates to brain development remains poorly understood. For much of their history, developmental psychology and developmental neurobiology have been relatively independent of one another, owing in part to the widespread belief that cognitive development was explicable without reference to underlying substrates. This disciplinary isolation was predicated on a distinction between learning and maturation, whereby developmental psychologists studied processes of learning, which involved environmental interaction, while developmental neurobiologists studied processes of intrinsic maturation. The possibility that this cardinal distinction between learning and maturation might itself be misleading was rarely, if ever, considered. Hence, the possibility that cognitive processes of learning might play a role in regulating the growth of neural structures remains unexplored, both in terms of the degree of its empirical support and its implications for theories of cognitive development. Yet, this possibility holds a number of intriguing ramifications. If cognitive processes of learning do indeed play a role in regulating the growth of neural structures, then this would substantially alter the properties of what has come to be known as the "learning mechanism" in cognitive development (see Wexler & Culicover, 1980). In particular, it would demonstrate that the learning mechanism is nonstationary, meaning that its acquisition properties are time-dependent and change dynamically as a function of learning episodes. This would substantially alter how cognitive skills are acquired and would have to be taken into account in order to construct satisfactory theories of cognitive development. Because such a learning mechanism would introduce a number of time-dependent properties, which introduce many complications to the understanding of acquisition, there have been many attempts to exclude it on methodological grounds (Chomsky, 1980; Macnamara, 1982; Pinker, 1984). Primary among these attempts was Chomsky's (1980) argument that language acquisition could be idealised as an instantaneous process without affecting its learning properties.

These arguments, along with others, resulted in the relative neglect of the issue of nonstationarity in development. Primary among the other reasons for this neglect was the role of the traditional computational framework in cognitive science. This drew a strong distinction between software and hardware, again discounting the physical substrates of cognition as mere implementation. Since the equivalent computational function could be implemented in distinct physical systems, it was argued that the implementational level did not constrain theories sufficiently. Rather, the explanation of cognitive processes was considered autonomous from the substrates of cognition (Pylyshyn, 1984).

With the emergence of cognitive neuroscience, owing in part to advances in noninvasive probes of human brain function such as functional magnetic resonance imaging, theories of cognitive function are increasingly integrative across cognitive and neural levels. This integrative approach has been facilitated by an alternative computational approach to cognitive processes. In contrast to the traditional, functionalist computational framework, the resurgence of neural network research has blurred the strong distinction between hardware and software, making the interaction between cognitive processes and the physical substrates of cognition a central explanatory concern.

Cognitive and computational neuroscience provide the foundation for the recent emergence of a nascent developmental cognitive neuroscience (Elman et al., 1996; Johnson, 1997; Quartz & Sejnowski, 1997). The central goal of developmental cognitive neuroscience is to employ the research methodologies of cognitive and computational neuroscience to characterise how cognitive and neural levels interact during development. In this chapter, I take up the possibility of a nonstationary learning mechanism in cognitive development from the perspective of developmental cognitive neuroscience, and, specifically, from the perspective of a view I have referred to as neural constructivism (Quartz, 1999; Quartz & Sejnowski, 1997). From this perspective, I investigate the empirical evidence for such a learning mechanism and analyse some of its implications for theories of cognitive development. As I explore, a powerful feature of developmental cognitive neuroscience is that it integrates behavioural, computational, neurobiological, and evolutionary perspectives on development—which together first appear to present conflicting results. I refer to these as developmental paradoxes. Attempting to resolve these paradoxes can lead to new insights into the nature of development. Specifically, I will consider the issue of a nonstationary learning mechanism from the perspective of a developmental paradox that results from considering neurobiological and learning-theoretic perspectives on development. To provide a brief overview, learning-theoretic results indicate the strong need for constraints on a learning mechanism: A general learning mechanism appears too unconstrained to learn efficiently in all but the most restricted contexts. Results in developmental neurobiology, however, suggest that the cortex is relatively free of rigid domain-specific constraints. Somehow, these two apparently conflicting results must be reconciled. An exploration of this involves abandoning the traditional notion of constraints as static encoding of domain-specific information and instead requires characterising a more dynamic set of constraints that include those implicitly in place in the developmental trajectory itself. The dominant view of constraints on development regards them to be domain-specific limitations regarding the task domain. This view, however, neglects the process of developmental change, as these constraints are static ones. By seriously considering the centrality of nonstationarity in development, it is possible to derive a dynamic set of constraints that include the interaction between activity-dependent growth mechanisms and intrinsic developmental pathways; an initially small hypothesis space; the contribution of generic initial cortical circuitry; conduction velocities; subcortical organisation; learning rates; and hierarchical development.

In exploring the role of these constraints in development, I will present a theory of "constructive learning", which is at the core of neural constructivism and which begins to characterise the properties of nonstationarity in cognitive development. Rather than the more dominant view of learning as statistical inference, constructive learning addresses a prior, and more fundamental, issue: the origin of the representations that make learning as statistical inference possible at all. Constructive learning is seen to be a form of learning as representation construction whereby cognitive processes of learning play a role in regulating the construction of neural structures. Although the properties of such processes are only beginning to be explored, I will present reasons for why they hold important implications for theories of cognitive development.

Constructive learning focuses on the interplay between cognitive processes of learning and neural development, whereby patterns of environmentally derived neural activity help regulate neural growth. To understand the properties of constructive learning, however, it is necessary to characterise the operation of these processes at multiple levels of organisation, from the cellular to the systems level. Although there is a tendency to treat the brain as a homogeneous device, it is composed of multiple systems that employ multiple acquisition strategies. Thus, after characterising constructive learning at the cellular level, I will turn to consider constructive learning at the systems level, where it plays an important role in dynamically constraining development. As I explore this notion of constraint, I will suggest that the traditional view of the human cognitive architecture has obscured the fact that the brain is a hierarchical behavioural system, in which some elements direct the development of others, and thereby make the brain's acquisition properties highly time-dependent. In particular, I will explore the midbrain dopamine system's role both as a mediator of early behaviours and in directing the development of complex prefrontally mediated capacities. Together, evidence from many levels of organisation in the developing brain demonstrates that acquisition cannot be understood without characterising the dynamics of developmental change, from the cellular level of activity-dependent neural growth to the divergent acquisition strategies of multiple brain systems and their interaction.

Development as a formal problem

As suggested above, developmental cognitive neuroscience attempts to integrate multiple disciplinary perspectives, spanning from cellular and molecular approaches to neural development to evolutionary analyses of developmental programs. A fruitful approach to a complex phenomenon such as development is to explore each of these perspectives with an eye towards determining whether they present incompatibilities with one another and, if so, how these may be resolved. The first perspective I examine considers development as a formal, learning-theoretic problem. At its most general, cognitive development involves a process by which an organism constructs representations that both guide adaptive behaviour and facilitate alterations in representational structures through experience. The process of fitting representations to a particular ecological niche involves both phylogenetic and ontogenetic strategies, which at a high level of abstraction instantiate similar strategies of error correction, although on different time-scales (see Koza, 1992). A great deal of debate concerns the relative contribution of these two processes to cognitive development, as manifest in the innateness debate (Elman et al., 1996; Fodor, 1983).

A central issue of this debate concerns the need for domain-specific constraints on development: whether it is possible to learn in some domain without building in important assumptions about the nature of that domain *a priori*. An influential insight into this issue stemmed from learning theory based on Gold's (1967) treatment of language identification in the limit. Gold established upper bounds, or worst-case scenario results, by asking what a general learner could acquire when presented with example sentences of some language. Gold supposed that the learner's task was to conjecture a hypothesis regarding the grammar that might generate that language. The learner was said to identify the language in the limit if it eventually chose a grammar that was consistent with every string. Gold's model viewed learning as a process of selective induction, that is, learning as a search through a hypothesis space that the learner posits. The major implication of Gold's work was that unconstrained learning was prohibitive. Simple counting arguments show that the probability of a learner searching through a fixed hypothesis space to successfully learn a concept chosen at random is exponentially small (reviewed in Dietterich, 1990). For this reason, the hypothesis space must be an exponentially small subset of possible concepts (see Blumer, Ehrenfeucht, Haussler, & Warmuth, 1988).

The negative learning results stemming from Gold's work played an important role in shaping theories of cognitive development, particularly those influenced by Chomsky's arguments regarding language acquisition. These arguments, in turn, have played a prominent role in stressing the importance of phylogenetic constraints on development (for a consideration of these arguments in evolutionary psychology, see Tooby & Cosmides, 1992). Indeed, these considerations have figured centrally in popularising the view that infants must possess domain-specific knowledge to facilitate acquisition, typically taking the form of special organs, or modules.

A challenge to this position began to emerge in the late 1980s, as neural network research grew in popularity. In particular, the claim that such algorithms as back-propagation learned internal representations as a function of exposure to some domain attracted a great deal of attention. Since the networks in question typically began with a randomised set of weights, a popular interpretation was that such networks did not require domain-specific constraints to learn successfully (for an evaluation of this claim, see Quartz, 1993). Part of the promise surrounding the rise of neural network research concerned the potential of neural network learning algorithms to minimise the requirement for a richly structured initial state.

Many of these insights into the learning properties of neural network algorithms were based on experimental investigations. As more theoretical work was pursued, it became apparent that the early claims of neural network researchers were not accurate (see Geman, Bienenstock, & Doursat, 1992). Like other learning algorithms, neural network algorithms confronted a basic trade-off between the two contributors to error: bias and variance. Bias is a measure of how close the learner's best concept in its representational space approximates the target function (the thing to be learned). Variance refers to the actual distance between what the learner has learned so far and the target function. To make this a bit more concrete, a small neural network will be highly biased in that the class of functions allowed by weight adjustments is very small. If the target function is poorly approximated by this class of functions, then the bias will contribute to error. By making a network large, and hence flexible in terms of what it can represent (by decreasing bias), the contribution of variance to error typically increases. That is, the network has many more possible states, and so is likely to be far away from the function of interest. This means that very large training sets will be required to learn because many examples will be required to rule out all the possible functions. As Geman et al. (1992) state, this results in a dilemma—essentially the same impasse that led to nativist theories: Highly biased learners will work only if they have been carefully chosen for the particular problem at hand whereas flexible learners seem to place too high a demand on training time and resources. Geman et al. (1992) state, "learning complex tasks is essentially impossible without the a priori introduction of carefully designed biases into the machine's architecture."

Another important insight to emerge from this perspective involves the importance of separating learning into two distinct problems: (1) learning as statistical inference; and, (2) learning as the construction of an efficient set of representations that make statistical inference possible at all. In natural systems, this latter problem is the critical problem of development.

Conclusions from the formal perspective

The formal, learning-theoretic perspective on development suggests that a developmental system must be highly constrained. Although cognitive psychologists remained largely uncommitted to the specific form such constraints might take in neural terms, the plausibility of nativist proposals ultimately depends on whether they are consistent with known structures and mechanisms. The most straightforward and popular proposal regarding constrained learning is via modules, which encode domain-specific representations. Since knowledge in the brain is believed to be encoded by the pattern and weights of synaptic connections, the most straightforward and popular translation of such representational encodings in terms of the brain involves encoding information in the microstructure of neural circuits (see Pinker, 1994, for statements of this strategy). This is, of course, only one of any number of concrete proposals regarding how domain-specific information could be innately encoded in the brain (for discussion, see Elman et al., 1996), but its popularity merits attention. Indeed, if the claim is about what is innately given as domain-specific representations, then it is difficult to know how such representational knowledge could be encoded if not via patterns of connectivity.

From the perspective of developmental cognitive neuroscience, the relevant question to ask is: what form do learning constraints take, and is the dominant, domain-specific encoding strategy consistent with evidence from neurobiology?

Adding neurobiological constraints

One of the virtues of the representation-microstructure proposal is that it results in testable predictions: (1) that regions of cortex, to the extent that they instantiate different domain-specific modules, should differ in terms of their microstructure; and (2) that a representationally constrained module should be limited in terms of the sorts of domains it can represent. The latter is simply another way of saying that since modules are required in order to constrain possible representations, such a constrained device is not general or multipurpose. If a module is general purpose, then it undermines the reasons for positing it in the first place.

Do the properties of the cortex confirm the above two predictions? Consider the striking differences between the basic structure of the language domain and intuitive psychology. The former involves such concepts as phonemes, form classes, and noun versus verb, whereas the latter involves such concepts as self-propelledness and agency. Can the same device uncover the structure of these disparate problem spaces, or do these problem spaces require their own specialised representations, at least some of which must be innately encoded?

The question of whether such domains as language and intuitive psychology have enough in common for their acquisition to be dealt with by a unitary mechanism is difficult to resolve at present, since the neural basis of these capacities is poorly understood. However, recent neuroimaging studies in primary sensory areas bear on this issue. For example, Sadato et al. (1996) and Sadato et al. (1998) have investigated the neural basis of Braille discrimination tasks in congenitally blind patients. They determined that the visual cortex of these blind subjects mediates the sensory processing demanded by the Braille discrimination tasks. The question of whether visual cortex is functionally involved in the task itself was determined by transcranial magnetic stimulation of occipital cortex in blind subjects (Cohen et al., 1997). A magnetic pulse delivered to visual cortex during the discrimination task produced processing errors, demonstrating the functional involvement of visual cortex in the task. At the neural level, it appears that the tactile processing pathways usually linked to the secondary somatosensory area are rerouted in blind subjects to the ventral occipital cortical regions originally reserved for visual shape discrimination.

Although these results do not in themselves address the issue of representational biases in various cortical regions, the capacity of developing cortical regions to become functional within a novel sensory domain indicates that cortical regions have the capacity to develop representations for multiple problem spaces, as presumably tactile discrimination and visual shape discrimination require their own representations. Indeed, it is interesting that this representational flexibility is seen in primary sensory areas. One might suspect that if a high degree of domain-specific representational knowledge were built in anywhere in the brain, it would be in primary sensory areas. For one, these structures have a long evolutionary history, with homologous structures across a wide variety of species. Also, the structure of the visual and tactile world is relatively stable, suggesting that *a priori* representations would have little probability of mismatch with the world.

The emerging evidence from developmental neurobiology points toward broad regional differences across areas of cortex. These intrinsic factors regulate the differentiation of cells and act in concert with patterns of input activity to determine the functional properties of cortex (Huffman et al., 1999; Pallas, 2001; Wilson & Rubenstein, 2000). As I consider next, these principles of cortical organisation are in striking contrast to principles of subcortical organisation, where the representation-microstructure proposal receives more support. The difference between the principles of cortical and subcortical organisation demonstrates that there is little support for the proposal that substantial domain-specific information is encoded *a priori* in the microstructure of cortical circuits.

Resolving the developmental paradox

It is important to consider what inferences are justified by the lack of *a priori* representational encodings in cortex. Does this, for example, warrant a *tabula rasa* view of acquisition? It is important to note that a relatively unconstrained cortex in terms of its microstructure in no way implies that the brain is an unconstrained learning device. This fallacious implication relies on the common practice of discussing the brain as though it were a homogeneous device. However, the human brain is a structure composed of multiple neural systems, instantiating multiple acquisition strategies. Understanding cognitive development requires understanding how these multiple acquisition strategies interact in a time-dependent manner as they unfold during development, as I explore in detail below.

As the principles of cortical organisation are different from those of subcortical structures, the finding that there is little support for the proposal of a modular cortex has little bearing on the issue of modularity in subcortical structures. For example, in a series of striking experiments Balaban (1997) was able to transfer the chicken crow vocalisation to the quail by transplanting a region of the hypothalamus. As Balaban (1997, p. 2006) notes, "a simple model in which crowing differences are due to evolutionary changes in a single higher brain area is not tenable." Instead, major subcomponents of the behavioural difference were transferred independently with interspecies transplantation of separate subcortical regions. By contrast, no one has yet succeeded in transferring any species-specific behaviour between animals by transplanting part of the forebrain. Therefore, there is evidence for modularity in the brain, but it exists only in the hypothalamus and other subcortical structures. This is significant for cognitive theorists and developmental scientists. Although the cortex has received the most attention by cognitive neuroscientists, the subcortical generation of complex behaviour is an often overlooked constraint on cortical representation. For example, Dixson (1998) reviews at length the contribution of subcortical structures in the generation of complex primate sexual behaviour. From a developmental perspective, subcortical structures, which are developmentally precocial, may play both a critical role in providing early behavioural and cognitive competencies and a central but overlooked role in directing, or bootstrapping, the emergence of cortical representations; I consider this in the section 'Supervised, unsupervised, and self-supervised learning' (see p. 296).

The highly localised functions attributable to specific regions of the hypothalamus and many other subcortical structures are in marked contrast to the way that functions in the cortex are widely distributed. For example, vision is distributed over half the cortex and polysensory and association areas are the hallmarks of cortical organisation in mammals and especially primates. The contrast between cortical and subcortical organisation suggests that biology can produce modularity when nature wants to and that the anatomical correlate is highly conserved dedicated circuits. Interestingly, these species-specific differences are expressed by the same set of genes, which are common from frogs to humans (reviewed in Hirth & Reichert, 1999; Reichert & Simeone, 1999). What appears to vary is the subset of cells that these genes are expressed in and how they are modulated by other signals. For example, the species-specific affiliative behaviour of an asocial species of vole can be transformed to that of the highly social prairie vole by changing the pattern of expression of vasopressin receptors in a transgenic vole to that found in prairie voles (Young, Nilsen, Waymire, MacGregor, & Insel, 1999). If the cortex were organised in this highly modular manner, one would suspect that experimental results would have established such themes, as they have for subcortical structures. However, what has been seen so far is broad areal specification (Rubenstein et al., 1999), suggesting that the themes of cortical organisation are very different indeed.

The striking contrast between cortical and subcortical organisation shifts the development focus away from static encodings of information to a variety of dynamic constraints. These dynamic constraints operate at a number of levels of organisation and suggest that the developmental process itself can be a highly constrained process in terms of its systemic properties and in how its dynamics constrain the emergence of representations. In what follows, I first consider the nature of such constraints at the cellular level.

CONSTRUCTIVE LEARNING AND THE
TIME-DEPENDENT PROPERTIES OF
DEVELOPING CORTEX

Contrasting selective induction and constructive induction

The model of acquisition I have considered thus far implements learning as a process of selective induction, whose essential feature is that learning is a search through a fixed hypothesis space. An alternative framework treats learning as a process of constructive induction (for a review, see Quartz & Sejnowski, 1997). According to this framework, the learner begins with an initially restricted hypothesis space and constructs a more complex one as some function of exposure to a problem domain. Constructive induction provides a markedly different answer to the question of the source of the representations underlying acquisition. Rather than presupposing a set of representations in the initial state, constructive induction regards these representations to be the developmental consequence of environmental interaction.

From a theoretical perspective, White (1990) demonstrated that a network that adds units at an appropriate rate relative to its experience is a consistent nonparametric estimator. This asymptotic property means that it can learn essentially any arbitrary mapping. The intuition behind this result, which plays a central role in characterising constructive learning, follows a general nonparametric strategy: slowly increase representational capacity by reducing bias at a rate that also reduces variance. Since network bias depends on the number of units, as a network grows, its approximation capacities increase. The secret is regulating the rate of growth so that the contribution of variance to error does not increase. Encouraging bounds on the rate of convergence have been obtained (Barron, 1994).

White's demonstration of the power of neural networks depends on allowing the network to grow as it learns. In fact, many of the limitations encountered by neural networks are due to a fixed architecture. Judd (1988), for example, demonstrated that learning the weights in a neural network, what is known as the loading problem, is an NP-complete problem, and therefore computationally intractable, a result that extended to architectures of just three nodes (Blum & Rivest, 1988). These results suggest that severe problems may be lurking behind the early success of network learning. As Blum and Rivest (1988) note, however, these results stem from the fixed architecture property of the networks under consideration. By contrast, the loading problem becomes polynomial (feasible) if the network is allowed to add hidden units. This suggests fundamentally different learning properties for networks that can add structure during learning. This has been confirmed by studies such as that of Redding, Kowalczyk, and Downs (1993), who presented a constructivist neural network algorithm that can learn very general problems in polynomial time by building its architecture to suit the demands of the specific problem. Since the construction of the learner's hypothesis space is sensitive to the problem domain facing the learner, this is a way of tailoring the hypothesis space to suit the demands of the problem at hand. This allows the particular structure of the problem domain to determine the connectivity and complexity of the network. Since the network has the capacity to respond to the structure of the environment in this way, the original high bias is reduced through increases in network complexity, which allows the network to represent more complex functions. Hence, the need to find a good representation beforehand is replaced by the flexibility of a system that can respond to the structure of some task by building its representation class as it samples that structure to learn any polynomial learnable class of concepts. Research on constructive algorithms has become increasingly sophisticated (reviewed in Quinlan, 1998).

Constructive induction and the brain

Given that constructive induction has intriguing learning properties, it is important to consider whether there is evidence for such processes in brain development. Since its beginnings, developmental neurobiology has been embroiled in debate over whether neural structures are added progressively over the developmental time course, or whether developmental processes are analogous to those seen in population biology, where an initial overproduction of structures or individuals is acted on by selective mechanisms (see Purves, White, & Riddle, 1996, for a summary of this debate). In developmental neurobiology, the most programmatic statements of such a view are known as selectionist models, whereby the initial production of neural structures is regulated by intrinsic mechanisms whose main purpose is to create a diversity of representations for a later, activity-dependent process of selective elimination to act on, eliminating those structures that do not mirror the informational structure of the environment appropriately (Changeux & Danchin, 1976; Edelman, 1987). From a learning-theoretic perspective, these exuberant structures can be regarded as a hypothesis space that contains the target function as a proper subset.

To distinguish between the selectionist and constructivist models of development, two issues must be addressed:

(1) To what extent is neural development characterised by a progressive increase in some measure of representational complexity.
(2) Is this increase dependent on environmental interaction at a level of requisite specificity?

If there is confirming evidence for both (1) and (2), then the constructivist model—and processes of constructive induction—would apply to the developing brain.

With regard to (1), in previous work (reviewed in Quartz, 1999), I examined the developmental time course of synaptic numbers, axonal processes, and dendritic arbors and concluded that the bulk of the evidence favours progressive increases in these measures coinciding with the major periods of cognitive development (below, I consider in more detail the issue of which structural measure is most appropriate as a measure of representational complexity). Much of this research was based on traditional neurobiological methods, culled from research on a variety of species. More recently, paediatric neuroradiology has made promising advances in the application of structural magnetic resonance imaging to human brain development. Indeed, recent longitudinal studies of brain development using magnetic resonance imaging (MRI) have demonstrated preadolescent increases in cortical grey matter in all cortical lobes (Giedd et al., 1999; Thompson et al., 2000).

Given this evidence for progressive increases in representational structures during periods of cognitive development, it is important to consider issue (2): Is the progressive increase in representational structures mediated by activity-dependent mechanisms? If so, then this would indicate that the development of these representational structures is sensitive to the informational structure of the environment, and so could be considered a cognitive process of learning. Regarding this possibility, I reviewed neurobiological results spanning over 30 years that support the role for activity-dependent mechanisms in the progressive construction of neural circuits (Quartz, 1999).

These experimental results shed light on another central issue, that of the relation between structural measures and representational complexity. A central assumption of developmental neurobiology and much of cognitive and computational neuroscience is that the synapse is the basic computational unit of the brain. For this reason, developmental neurobiologists have been concerned with changes in synaptic numbers over the developmental time course (e.g. Rakic, Bourgeois, Eckenhoff, Zecevic, & Goldman-Rakic, 1986). Likewise, many computational models employ a fixed architecture and regard long-term changes in connection strengths as the main modifiable parameter, reflecting a central tenet of brain function that information is stored in the patterning of synaptic weight values. The central result of the cellular basis of learning—synaptic plasticity—has been the discovery of long-term potentiation (Bliss & Lomo, 1973), which has contributed to the view that information is stored in the pattern of synaptic weights. According to this view, learning is mediated by correlated patterns of firing that induce long-term increases in the strength of connections between neurons. The rise of connectionist network modelling has contributed to the view that learning involves the long-term modification of connection strengths between neurons, as computational studies demonstrated the power of computing by adjusting connection strengths in a fixed architecture. Theoretical analyses of these learning algorithms also demonstrated the powerful statistical methods they implemented. The combination of experimental, computational, and theoretical analyses has made the claim that connection strengths are the main modifiable parameters extremely widespread, viewing learning as involving a modification of this encoding of information.

As Poirazi and Mel (2001) note, much new evidence weakens the link between synaptic weights and information representation and processing in the brain. Perhaps the most important source of evidence, and one central to developmental issues, concerns the nonlinear summation properties of many dendrites. The dendrites of pyramidal cells contain numerous voltage-dependent channels that play an important role in determining the cell's information-processing function. Most importantly, a variety of channels, including NMDA, Na^+, and Ca^{2+}channels, are capable of amplifying synaptic inputs and generating fast and slow dendritic spikes. Numerous laboratories have localised active nonlinear responses to synaptic inputs within the dendritic arbor (Bernardo, Masukawa, & Prince, 1982; Golding & Spruston, 1998) and even within a single thin dendritic branch (Schiller, Major, Koester, & Schiller, 2000). These nonlinear properties complicate the notion of a connection strength, since the weight of a given synaptic contact will be dependent on the activity of neighbouring synapses.

These considerations suggest that the dendritic arbor itself is the basic unit of computation in cortex (for an extended discussion, see Quartz & Sejnowski, 1997).[1] Structural alterations in the axodendritic interface, particularly the growth and retraction of dendritic arbors, would be expected to have a significant impact on information processing. Indeed, rather than regard the learning of internal representations to be primarily a process of weight adjustment, structural alterations in the axodendritic interface could be a primary mechanism whereby the representational properties of cortex are constructed (see also Poirazi & Mel, 2001, for an extended discussion). From a developmental perspective, an important issue thus concerns the processes that regulate the growth of the axodendritic interface and their relation to cognitive processes of learning.

Recent cellular work provides the strongest evidence to date for the role of patterned activity in the development of neural structures. Specifically, recent advances in microscopy that allow the continuous monitoring of cellular components at high resolution (Engert & Bonhoeffer, 1999; Maletic-Savatic, Malinow, & Svoboda, 1999; reviewed in Wong & Wong, 2000), have revealed a highly dynamic view of development at the cellular level, and provide strong evidence for the instructive role of activity in neural development.

---

[1] More technically, the main unit would include the axodendritic interface, although the main information processing functions of interest would be dendritic integration.

Previously, it had been difficult to determine the level of specificity which such activity played in the construction of neural structures. Specifically, it was difficult to differentiate between a permissive role for activity, whereby the mere presence of activity was sufficient to induce growth, or whether activity played an instructive role by regulating growth according to learning rules at specific sites. These new results demonstrate that activity is not simply permissive in its regulation of development. Rather, as Maletic-Savatic et al. (1999) have demonstrated, temporally correlated activity between pre- and postsynaptic elements that induces long-term potentiation results in the highly spatially defined local sprouting of dendritic elements, in agreement with Hebb's original postulate, in its developmental context (Hebb, 1949).

Considered together, the reviewed work provides strong evidence that cortical development is not characterised by an early overproduction of neural elements followed by selective elimination, nor is it one exhausted by mechanisms of selective elimination operating on transient, exuberant structures. Rather, neural development during the acquisition of major cognitive skills is best characterised as a progressive construction of neural structures, in which environmentally derived activity plays a role in the construction of neural circuits. This revised view of the role of activity in the construction of neural circuits forms the basis for neural constructivism: which examines how representational structures are progressively elaborated during development through activity-dependent growth mechanisms, in interaction with intrinsic developmental programmes. From the perspective of cognitive development, the far-reaching interaction between neural growth and environmentally derived neural activity undermines the distinction between biological maturation and learning. In place of this dichotomy, "constructive learning" appears to be an important theme in development, and from a learning-theoretic perspective possesses more powerful acquisition properties than traditional accounts of cognitive development.

As I intimated above, constructive learning is aimed at a problem natural systems face that is in many ways more fundamental than the problem of learning as statistical inference. Development can be divided into two distinct phases: the first involves the development of representations while the second involves utilising those representations to learn efficiently, which continues into the mature state. A study in the owl (Knudsen, 1998) highlights the role of early experience as a constructor of the representations that facilitate learning later in life. The optic tectum of barn owls contains a multimodal map of space. In particular, auditory visual neurons in the optic tectum associate values of auditory spatial cues with locations in the visual field. This association is accomplished through matching the tuning of tectal neurons for interaural time differences with their visual receptive fields. During development, but not adulthood, there is considerable plasticity in this system, allowing for a wide range of associations to be learned. When

juvenile animals were fitted with goggles that shift the visual field, the resulting abnormal associations were learned. Knudsen (1998) demonstrated that
the range of associations adult owls could learn is greatly expanded in those
animals that had learned abnormal associations during development.

Towards resolving the developmental paradox

Constructive learning provides insight into how the apparent conflict
between learning-theoretic and neurobiological constraints may be resolved.
Learning-theoretic results pointed to the need for a highly constrained
learner, whereas neurobiological results indicated that cortex has a surprising
degree of plasticity and likely embeds few intrinsic domain-specific constraints. Given the central role of constructive learning in brain and cognitive
development, the static constraints of traditional innateness views appear
overly simplistic. Rather than conceiving of constraints in terms of restricting
a fixed hypothesis space, it appears that neurobiological and learning-
theoretic constraints must be resolved by considering time-dependent constraints on developing cortex. Such constraints include the interaction
between activity-dependent growth mechanisms, intrinsic developmental
pathways, an initially small hypothesis space, and the contribution of generic
initial cortical circuitry, conduction velocities, subcortical organisation,
learning rates, and hierarchical development.

To understand how the constraints I have enumerated above operate, it
will be necessary to characterise the dynamics of development and its time-
dependent properties. That is, it will be necessary to understand how these
constraints shape the developmental trajectory. For example, what are the
implications of a limited initial architecture for the acquisition properties of a
learning system? Whereas traditional accounts suggested that these limitations weakened the learning system, neural network modelling casts these
limitations in a new, advantageous, light (Elman, 1993). An initially restricted
network must pass through a phase of limited representational power during
early exposure to some problem and then build successively more powerful
representational structures. Thus, these early limitations may actually help
the system first learn the lower-order structure of some problem domain and
subsequently use what it has learned to bootstrap itself into more complex
knowledge of that domain (reviewed in Plunkett, Karmiloff-Smith, Bates, &
Elman, 1997).

Such considerations suggest that the developmental trajectory that is
determined by the dynamics of the constraints enumerated above play an
important but neglected role in constraining development. Thus, understanding the process of developmental change, rather than simply its initial state or
final outcome, is paramount in developmental science. It is here that the study
of self-organising systems provides a number of important insights. For

example, self-organising systems have helped to explicate the developmental role of spontaneous neural activity, which is known to play a role in constructing neural circuits (reviewed in Wong, 1999). As Linsker demonstrated (reviewed in Linsker, 1990), randomly generated activity—what appears as essentially noise—can create feature filters given the functional properties that neural circuits possess in combination with their geometrical properties (e.g. interaction functions such that nearby activity is excitatory and inhibitory with increasing distance). Ordered structure is thus an emergent property of the dynamics and geometrical organisation of such systems. Below, I consider in more detail how order may be generated from the dynamic interaction of brain systems.

DYNAMIC DEVELOPMENTAL CONSTRAINTS

Hierarchical development

Given the evidence for constructive processes at the cellular level, it is important to consider how these are related to larger levels of organisation in the brain. One of the most intriguing time-dependent developmental constraints is hierarchical development. Although many features of Piaget's developmental view have come under extensive criticism, the core idea that development involves the expansion of hierarchically organised sequential operations, beginning with perceptual and sensorimotor functions and becoming more combinatorially complex, remains popular. For example, Luciana and Nelson (1998) recently examined the developmental emergence of functions involved in prefrontally guided working memory systems in 4- to 8-year-old children. The development of such memory systems, which is thought to involve particularly the dorsolateral region of prefrontal cortex, appears to proceed dimensionally, beginning with the refinement of basic perceptual and sensorimotor functions and culminating with the emergence of distributed networks that integrate complex processing demands. This is a paradigmatic case of time-dependent development, in which increasingly complex representations are built as a function of exposure to problem domains. As recently as a few years ago, however, it was unclear whether cortical development proceeded in a manner that was consistent with hierarchical development. According to the influential results of Rakic et al. (1986) cortical development followed a pattern of concurrent synaptogenesis. This influential view was based on electron microscopic studies of synaptogenesis in the rhesus monkey. This view suggested that the entire cerebral cortex develops as a whole and that the establishment of cell-to-cell communication may be orchestrated by a single genetic or humoral signal. As Rackic et al. (1986) point out, this view ruled out a hierarchical view of cortical development, that is, a developmental ordering from the sensory periphery to higher associational areas. This theory of concurrent synaptogenesis was difficult to reconcile with other structural measures, including patterns of myelination and dendritic arborization, which showed a regional, or heterochronic, pattern of development.

More recent work has indicated that synaptogenesis in human development is not concurrent across different regions of cortex (Huttenlocher & Dabholkar, 1997), but rather follows a regional pattern. According to this finding, human cortical synaptogenesis occurs regionally and in accord with the hierarchical developmental schedule observed for axonal growth, dendritic growth, and myelination. Assimilating the developmental schedule for these various measures, it appears that primary sensory and motor cortical areas are both closer to their mature measures at birth and reach those measures earlier than do areas of association in temporal and parietal regions, and prefrontal cortex.

Recent, MRI studies have shed light on this issue. For example, Thompson et al. (2000) found that regions of cortex develop at different rates. These studies suggest that the brain develops hierarchically, with early sensory regions developing before more complex representations in association areas (Quartz, 1999). This regional pattern of cortical development, proceeding from the sensory periphery to higher association areas, is particularly intriguing given that cortical representations are arranged hierarchically in a way that matches this regional hierarchy. According to Fuster (1997, p. 451), "the cortical substrate of memory, and of knowledge in general, can be viewed as the upward expansion of a hierarchy of neural structures." Although the existence of extensive feedback connections suggests that the notion of a strict hierarchy must be qualified, cortical areas closer to the sensory periphery encode lower-order, or more elementary, representations than do areas that are further removed, which involve more distributed networks lacking the topographical organisation of lower areas. All three sensory modalities—vision, touch and audition—involve what Fuster (1997, p. 455) refers to as a "hierarchical stacking of perceptual memory categories in progressively higher and more widely distributed networks." All three modalities then converge on polysensory association cortex and the limbic structures of the temporal lobe, particularly the hippocampus. This hierarchical organisation of representations combined with its hierarchical developmental pattern lends support to the view of development as a cascade of increasingly complex representational structures, in which construction in some regions depends on the prior development of others.

FROM HIERARCHICAL DEVELOPMENT TO A BEHAVIOURAL SYSTEMS VIEW

Supervised, unsupervised, and self-supervised learning

As mentioned above, the brain is composed of multiple brain systems that instantiate multiple acquisition strategies. The hierarchical organisation of these systems suggests that some structures may constrain the development of others by directing their development. Just as a structure such as primary visual cortex can be constrained by the nature of the sensory modality innervating it (Katz & Shatz, 1996), so too some neural structures can be constrained by the pattern of input from other neural structures. In the case of primary visual cortex, it is generally believed that incoming sensory information, reflected in patterns of activity, is utilised in an unsupervised mode. Unsupervised learning, or self-organisation in its developmental context, involves developing an efficient internal model of the salient statistical structure of the environment. For example, Hebbian learning can be understood in the context of principal component analysis, which is a method of efficiently representing the correlational structure of the environment. Over the last few years, significant progress have been made in exploring unsupervised learning algorithms for neural network models (Hinton & Sejnowski, 1999). Unlike the earlier supervised learning algorithms, which required a detailed teacher to provide feedback on performance, the goal of unsupervised learning is to extract an efficient internal representation of the statistical structure implicit in the stream of inputs. Babies are barraged by sensory inputs in the womb and their environment after birth is filled with latent information about that environment. During development, unsupervised learning could shape circuits in the early stages of sensory processing to more efficiently represent the environment; in the adult brain, similar forms of implicit learning could provide cues to help guide behaviour.

While computational neurobiologists investigate unsupervised learning in analyses of the developing visual system, cognitive scientists typically investigate supervised algorithms in connectionist style architectures (Shultz, Mareschal, & Schmidt, 1994; for a review, see Plunkett et al., 1997). An additional class of learning algorithm—reinforcement, or self-supervised algorithms—may be utilised by one neural region to direct the development of another. As Piaget stressed, a central theme of development involves the developing system's active exploration of its environment whereby learning is mediated through the consequences of its actions on that environment. This places a premium on the presence of reward systems that both engage a developing system in its environment and drive learning through the patterns of reward (and punishment) that such engagement brings about. Elsewhere (Quartz, 2003), I have suggested that evolutionary considerations support a behavioural systems model of the brain that regards the brain as a hierarchical control structure, where reward plays a central computational role and where this hierarchical organisation is evident both developmentally and evolutionarily.

Neural reward structures

A key source of evidence regarding this view is that despite the apparent diversity of nervous systems, most share a deep structure, or common design principles. Even the simplest motile organisms require control structures to regulate goal-directed behaviour necessary for survival in a variable environment (for discussion, see Allman, 1999). For example, although the bacterium *Escherichia coli* does not possess a nervous system, it does possess control structures for sensory responses, memory, and motility that underlie its capacity to alter behaviour in response to environmental conditions. The capacity to approach nutritive stimuli and avoid aversive stimuli in the maintenance of life-history functions is the hallmark of behavioural systems across phyla. Whereas chemotaxis in bacteria involves a single step from sensory transduction to motor behaviour, some multicellular organisms embody control structures that involve intercellular communication via hormonal signalling, while others possess nervous systems with control structures that add layers of mediating control between sensory transduction and motor behaviour.

There are several alternative design possibilities for biological control structures. One is to make a closed system, in the sense of linking fixed behavioural patterns between internal goal states and their environmental targets. Although there are many examples of this strategy (Gallistel, 1990), there are more powerful and flexible control structures. For example, one such strategy involves leaving the path from internal goal state to target state open and discoverable via learning. Principal among this latter design strategy are reinforcement-based systems that are capable of learning an environment's reward structure.[2]

A variety of experimental techniques, ranging from psychopharmacology to neural imaging, have demonstrated the striking ubiquity and conservation of reward structures across species. At virtually all levels of the human nervous system, for example, reward systems can be found that play a central role in goal-directed behaviour (Schultz, 2000). Here, I focus on one such system, the midbrain dopamine system. The midbrain dopamine system projects principally from the ventral tegmental area to the nucleus accumbens

---

[2] Although this strategy emphasises learning, it is important to bear in mind that it requires a primitive set of target states that have intrinsic reward value to the organism (classically known as unconditional stimuli).

and the temporal and frontal cortex. Studies utilising self-stimulation para-digms have revealed that activation of this system is highly reinforcing, often with laboratory animals preferring to self-stimulate this system than eat, or copulate with a receptive partner (reviewed in Wise, 1996). Most addictive substances involve this system, giving rise to the hedonic theory of dopamine as the signal underlying pleasure (but see Garris et al., 1999).

Given what I have previously stated regarding the possibility that control structures are highly conserved, it is interesting to note, as Figure 9.1 illustrates, the striking homology between the dopamine system in humans and a reward system in the honeybee. The honeybee suboesophogeal ganglion contains an identified neuron, VUMmx1, which delivers information about reward during classical conditioning experiments via the neurotransmitter, octopamine, which is similar in molecular structure to dopamine (Hammer, 1993).

Both experimental and computational work on the role of VUMmx1 in honeybee foraging has provided important insights into the signal carried by octopamine, and into the functional significance of the system (Montague, Dayan, Person, & Sejnowski, 1995; Real, 1991). Rather than simply carrying information regarding reward, it appears that octopamine signals informa-tion regarding prediction errors. Whereas reward is traditionally a behavioural notion, prediction is a computational notion. The difference between certain rewarding outcomes and their predictions can be used to guide adaptive behaviour. A system that learns through prediction learning need not have the path from goal to reward specified, unlike fixed behavioural patterns, such as stimulus–response learning. Instead, the path from goals to rewards may be left open and discoverable via learning, resulting in flexible

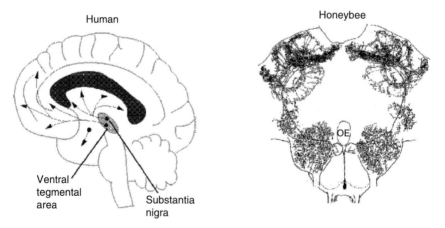

Figure 9.1.   Neuromodulatory (octopamine) neurons in the honeybee brain and dopamine pro-jections in the human brain play homologous roles. Neural activity in these neurons distributes information about expected reward. OE = cell body.

action. Evolution, then, may shape the pattern of basic rewards animals are motivated to obtain, but the behavioural path is left open to discovery, as are more complex relations among predictors. In this sense, brains are prediction machines that use information gathered from past experience to predict future events important for survival (reviewed in Montague & Quartz, 1999).

Experiments utilising neurophysiological recording in behaving monkeys by Schultz and colleagues demonstrate that the midbrain dopamine system plays an important role in prediction learning in the mammalian brain (Schultz, Apicella, & Ljungberg, 1993). When these monkeys were presented with various appetitive stimuli, dopaminergic neurons responded with short, phasic activations, which typically lasted for only a few repeated presentations. In an important finding, however, Schultz and colleagues found that when the rewarding stimuli were preceded by an auditory or visual cue, dopamine neurons changed their time of activation to just after the time of cue onset. In contrast, when the reward did not follow the conditioned stimulus, dopamine neurons were depressed below their basal firing rate exactly at the time the reward should have occurred. These results indicate that the dopamine signal encodes expectations regarding the delivery of reward. That is, the output of dopamine neurons code for an error between the actual reward received and predictions of the time and magnitude of reward. Like the octopamine signal in the honeybee, the dopamine signal codes a prediction error that can be used in learning and in action selection. This mode of action is equivalent to temporal difference learning, a thoroughly examined form of reinforcement learning (Sutton & Barto, 1998) that learns the predictive structure of an environment. Simulations demonstrate that despite the apparent simplicity of this model, it is a very powerful learner, capable of learning master-level backgammon, for example (Tesauro, 1995).

The developmental relation between the midbrain dopamine system and prefrontal cortex

It is deeply intriguing to note where the midbrain dopamine system projects to in the human brain. In particular, what is most intriguing is the fact that it projects to the dorsolateral prefrontal, premotor, and parietal cortices, which are structures believed to mediate goal representations, and to the orbitofrontal cortex, which is believed to mediate the representation of relative reward value and reward expectation (for a review, see Schultz, 2000). A great deal of attention has centred on the dorsolateral and orbitofrontal prefrontal cortices as structures implicated in crucial components of human cognition, particularly social cognition and theory of mind (Stone, Baron-Cohen, & Knight, 1998), symbolic learning (Deacon, 1997), representations of self (Craik et al., 1999), and executive function and behavioural inhibition (Norman & Shallice, 1986).

It is important to question the functional significance of the fact that a phylogenetically old part of the brain projects to a—relatively—phylogenetic newcomer. According to neural constructivism, these structures constitute a hierarchically organised control structure, where additional layers of control have been added to the evolutionarily conserved dopamine system and where this hierarchical organisation is evident developmentally as well. To see how, it is important to examine the developmental links between these components, as I explore in more detail below.

Diamond and colleagues (reviewed in Diamond, 1998) have demonstrated that a functional midbrain dopaminergic system is necessary for normal development of prefrontal functions. The most compelling evidence regarding this developmental dependence stems from studies of phenylketonuria (PKU). Patients suffering from PKU do not naturally produce a particular enzyme, phenylalanine hydroxylase, which converts the essential amino acid phenylalanine to another amino acid, tyrosine, the precursor of dopamine; when untreated, PKU leads to severe mental retardation. Diamond and colleagues found that lowered levels of tyrosine uniquely affect the cognitive functions dependent on prefrontal cortex because of the special sensitivity of prefrontally projecting dopamine neurons to small decreases in tyrosine. In a 4-year longitudinal study, they found that PKU children performed worse than matched controls, their own siblings, and children from the general population on tasks that required the working memory and inhibitory control abilities dependent on dorsolateral prefrontal cortex. However, these PKU children performed well on control tasks that were not mediated by the prefrontal cortex (Diamond, Prevor, Callender, & Druin, 1997).

The hierarchical organisation of the control structures that constitute the human cognitive architecture is apparent developmentally, with human cognition and behaviour becoming increasingly mediated by frontal structures. In contrast to the early functional involvement of midbrain dopamine systems, prefrontal structures develop relatively late and exhibit a protracted development that continues into adolescence. Thus, behaviour and cognition increasingly come under the mediation of frontal structures from subcortical structures across development, a process sometimes referred to as frontalisation of behaviour (Rubia et al., 2000). For example, executive function is a control mechanism that guides, coordinates, and updates behaviour in a flexible fashion, particularly in novel or complex tasks (Norman & Shallice, 1986). This requires that information related to behavioural goals be actively represented and maintained so that these representations may guide behaviour toward goal-directed activities. In humans, executive function follows a special developmental trajectory, reflecting an evolutionary reorganisation of prefrontal structures and their development. Between 7.5 and 12 months of age, infants show a developmental progression on A-not-B

(Diamond, 1985), delayed response (Diamond & Doar, 1989), and object retrieval tasks (Diamond, 1998). There is substantial evidence that these tasks are mediated by dorsolateral prefrontal cortex and rely on working memory, neural representations of goal-related information, and behavioural inhibition (Goldman-Rakic, 1990; Petrides, 1995). Further, various sources of evidence indicate that dopamine is necessary for successful performance on these tasks (Sawaguchi & Goldman-Rakic, 1994).

Although there is strong evidence that an intact dopamine system is necessary for the developmental emergence of prefrontal functions, a largely unresolved question concerns the specific nature of this developmental link. One particularly intriguing possibility is that the dopamine signal serves as a learning signal that guides the construction of prefrontal structures during development. Computational work on the midbrain dopamine system suggests such a learning role with strong analogies to temporal difference learning, a form of reinforcement learning (Sutton & Barto, 1998). A key notion underlying reinforcement learning is that of learning through interacting with one's environment. For example, a major source of knowledge stems from an infant's interactions with its environment, which produces a wealth of information about cause and effect, about the consequences of actions, and about what to do to achieve goals—all without the need for an explicit teacher. Of course, Piaget also emphasised the central importance of the developing child's agency and active exploration with its environment in his constructivist theory of cognitive development.

Learning through interacting with one's environment requires structures that direct the system to its environment. According to the view I have been outlining here, this is mediated in part by the midbrain dopamine system. One clue for this role derives from studies of the neurobiology of personality, which view personality as deriving from motivational systems. From this perspective, the midbrain dopamine system constitutes a behavioural facilitation system that underlies fundamental properties of personality, specifically extraversion and positive emotionality (Depue & Collins, 1999). From a developmental perspective, this behavioural facilitation system appears to be operative at an early age and notably underlies major dimensions of temperament, along with other diffuse ascending systems, such as noradrenergic and serotonergic systems. Thus, given this system's computational properties, and its role as a behavioural facilitation system early in postnatal development, this system is ideally situated to be involved in the reinforcement or self-supervised construction of prefrontal structures underlying complex behavioural control.

This computational role can be illustrated by comparing reinforcement models of learning to models of self-organisation, or unsupervised learning. The best-known account of unsupervised learning is Hebbian learning, which in its simplest form is:

$$\Delta w_{kj}(n) = \eta y_k(n) x_j(n) \tag{9.1}$$

where a synaptic weight w_{kj} of neuron k with presynaptic and postsynaptic signals denoted by x_j and y_k respectively are altered at time-step n and where η is a positive constant that determines the rate of learning. Algorithms such as equation 9.1, and a variety of modifications, essentially find efficient representations of salient environmental information by implementing such data-reduction strategies as principal component analysis. Such algorithms can be modified to become reinforcement learning algorithms by making weight updates dependent on the Hebbian correlation of a prediction error and the presynaptic activity at the previous timestep. This takes the following form:

$$w(i,t-1)_{\text{new}} = w(i,t-1)_{\text{prev}} + \eta x(i,t-1)\delta(t) \tag{9.2}$$

where $x(i, t-1)$ represents presynaptic activity at connection i and time $t-1$, η is a learning rate, and $w(i, t-1)_{\text{prev}}$ is the previous value of the weight representing time-step $t-1$. The term $\delta(t)$ is a prediction error term (Figure 9.2) and is the difference between a prediction of reward and the actual reward, represented as the output of the dopaminergic projection to cortex in the simulation framework. The addition of this term changes the Hebbian framework to a predictive Hebbian one (Montague & Sejnowski, 1994) and is the essential computed differential in the temporal differences method of reinforcement learning (Sutton & Barto, 1998; Figure 9.2). Such methods share close connections with dynamic programming (Bellman, 1957).

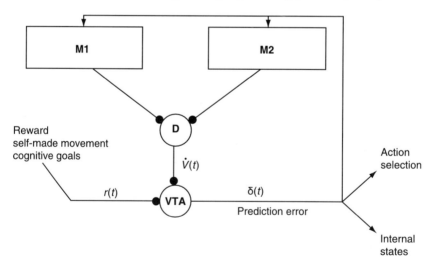

Figure 9.2. Architecture of prediction learning. M1 and M2 represent two different cortical modalities whose output is assumed to arrive at the ventral tegmental area (VTA) in the form of a temporal derivative $\dot{V}(t)$. Information about reward $r(t)$ also converges on the VTA. The VTA output is taken as a simple linear sum $\delta(t) = r(t) + \dot{V}(t)$. The output connections of the VTA make the prediction error $\delta(t)$ simultaneously available to structures constructing the predictions.

The developmental link between the midbrain dopamine system and pre-frontal structures suggests that complex developmental skills decompose into developmental precursors, which may often be mediated by structures that are distinct from those mediating the mature state. For example, face process-ing is believed to be mediated by subcortical structures during early postnatal development, but it subsequently shifts to cortical sites (reviewed in Johnson, 1997). The framework I have outlined above suggests a possible way of boot-strapping a system into such complex representations by biasing development through making the system selectively attentive to faces (for a review of the relation between reward structures and selective attention, see Dayan, Kakade, & Montague, 2000). An economical means of implementing such a strategy would be by making faces, or primitive template representations of them, rewarding to the system, thereby designing a system that preferentially attends to faces. It is clear that human infants possess such behavioural biases (Meltzoff & Moore, 1977), which may be implemented through projections to midbrain dopamine systems that constitute unconditioned stimuli.

Although still at an early stage, investigations into how one brain region may direct the development of another through such learning procedures as temporal differences learning offer a new framework for analysing the dynamics of developmental change. Current work in my laboratory involves exploring the relationship between these algorithms and neural outgrowth. It is intriguing to note that dendritic structures in prefrontal cortex display a protracted development (Figure 9.3) and that dopamine may modulate this development by acting trophically (Levitt, Harvey, Friedman, Simansky, & Murphy, 1997). These links merit further research.

Environmental structure and brain development

In examining the relationship between structured neural activity and neural development, neural constructivism stresses the importance of environmental structure and information in the developmental process. Although innateness views discounted such sources in various poverty of the stimulus arguments, there are good reasons to believe this discounting was premature (see Cowie, 1998). Indeed, as a number of investigators have recently stressed (Donald, 2000; Tomasello, 1999), it appears that human cognitive development depends on an extremely rich social and cultural interaction. Although pre-frontal function has traditionally been most closely associated with purely cognitive functions, its central involvement in social cognition has become increasingly apparent in recent years (Damasio, 1994). Indeed, one potential reason for protracted development lies in the difficulty of developing the social competence necessary for complex social life. There is now good evi-dence to indicate that one component of social competence—theory of mind—depends at least in part on the appropriate social exposure for its

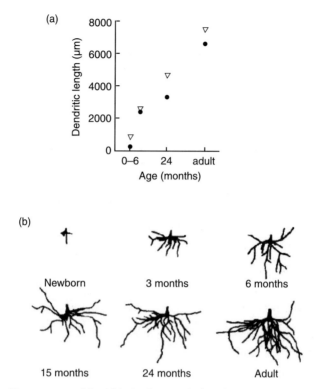

Figure 9.3. Human postnatal dendritic development in dorsolateral prefrontal cortex. The total dendritic length of basal dendrites (a) of layer III and V pyramidal cells develops over a protracted period. Camera lucida drawings (b) of layer V basal dendrites reveal the extent of this protracted postnatal development. (Modified from Schade, J. P. & van Groenigan, W. B. (1961) Structural organization of the human cerebral cortex: I. Maturation of the middle frontal gyrus *Acta Anatomica* 47: 72–111.) Reprinted with permission.

development, as many deaf children show delays on theory of mind tasks (Peterson & Siegal, 1995; Russell et al., 1998). This is believed to be due to the fact that parents of deaf children are typically naïve signers, and so household social interactions are limited by communicative ability. Constructive learning, then, may be one particularly powerful route to building complex cognitive and social skills through allowing the structure of the environment to play a central role in cognitive development.

ACKNOWLEDGEMENTS

This research was supported by National Science Foundation Career Grant 0093757.

REFERENCES

Allman, J. (1999). *Evolving brains*. San Franciso: Freeman.

Balaban, E. (1997). Changes in multiple brain regions underlie species differences in a complex, congenital behavior. *Proceedings of the National Academy of Sciences USA, 94,* 2001–2006.

Barron, A. R. (1994). Approximation and estimation bounds for artificial neural networks. *Machine Learning 14,* 115–33.

Bernardo, L. S., Masukawa, L. M., & Prince, D. A. (1982). Electrophysiology of isolated hippocampal pyramidal dendrites. *Journal of Neuroscience, 2,* 14–22.

Bliss, T. V. P., & Lomo, T. (1973). Long-lasting potentiation of synaptic transmission in the dentate area of the anesthetized rabbit following stimulation of the perforant path. *Journal of Physiology (London), 232,* 331–356.

Blum, A., & Rivest, R. L. (1988). Training a 3-node neural network is NP-complete. In D. S. Touretzky (Ed.), Advances in neural information processing systems (pp. 494–505). San Francisco: Morgan Kaufmann.

Blumer, A., Ehrenfeucht, A., Haussler, D., & Warmuth, M. (1988). *Learnability and the Vapnik–Chervonenkis dimension*. Technical Report UCSC-CRL-87-20.

Changeux, J. P., & Danchin, A. (1976). Selective stabilisation of developing synapses as a mechanism for the specification of neuronal networks. *Nature, 264,* 705–12.

Chomsky, N. (1980). Rules and representations. *Behavioral and Brain Sciences, 3,* 1–61.

Cohen, L. G., Celnik, P., Pascual-Leone, A., Corwell, B., Falz, L., Dambrosia, J. et al. (1997). Functional relevance of cross-modal plasticity in blind humans. *Nature, 389,* 180–183.

Cowie, F. (1998). *What's within? Nativism reconsidered*. Oxford: Oxford University Press.

Craik, F. I. M., Moroz, T. M., Moscovitch, M., Stuss, D. T., Winocur, G., Tulving, E., & Kapur, S. (1999). In search of the self: A positron emission tomography study. *Psychological Science, 10,* 26–34.

Damasio, A. R. (1994). Descartes' error: Emotion, reason, and the human brain. New York: G. P. Putnam.

Dayan, P., Kakade, S., & Montague, P. R. (2000). Learning and selective attention. *Nature Neuroscience, 3,* 1218–1223.

Deacon, T. W. (1997). *The symbolic species: The co-evolution of language and the brain*. New York: W. W. Norton.

Depue, R. A., & Collins, P. F. (1999). Neurobiology of the structure of personality: Dopamine, facilitation of incentive motivation, and extraversion. *Behavioral and Brain Sciences, 22,* 491–569.

Diamond, A. (1985). Development of the ability to use recall to guide action, as indicated by infants' performance on AB. *Child Development, 56,* 868–883.

Diamond, A. (1998). Evidence for the importance of dopamine for prefrontal cortex functions early in life. In A. C. Roberts, T. W. Robbins, & L. Weiskrantz (Eds.), *The prefrontal cortex: Executive and cognitive functions* (pp. 144–164). New York: Oxford University Press.

Diamond, A., & Doar, B. (1989). The performance of human infants on a measure of frontal cortex function, the delayed response task. *Developmental Psychobiology, 22,* 271–294.

Diamond, A., Prevor, M. B., Callender, G., & Druin, D. P. (1997). Prefrontal cortex cognitive deficits in children treated early and continuously for PKU. *Monographs of the Society for Research in Child Development, 62,* 1–205.

Dietterich, T. G. (1990). Machine learning. *Annual Review of Computer Science, 4,* 255–306.

Dixson, A. F. (1998). *Primate sexuality: Comparative studies of the prosimians, monkeys, apes, and human beings*. Oxford: Oxford University Press.

Donald, M. (2000). A mind so rare: The evolution of human consciousness. New York: W. W. Norton.

Edelman, G. (1987). *Neural Darwinism: The theory of neuronal group selection.* New York: Basic Books.

Elman, J. L. (1993). Learning and development in neural networks: The importance of starting small. *Cognition, 48*, 71–99.

Elman, J. L., Bates, E. A., Johnson, M. H., Karmiloff-Smith, A., Parisi, D., & Plunkett, K. (1996). *Rethinking innateness: A connectionist perspective on development.* Cambridge, MA: MIT Press.

Engert, F., & Bonhoeffer, T. (1999). Dendritic spine changes associated with hippocampal long-term synaptic plasticity. *Nature, 399*, 66–70.

Fodor, J. A. (1983). *Modularity of mind: An essay on faculty psychology.* Cambridge, MA: MIT Press.

Fuster, J. M. (1997). Network memory. *Trends in Neurosciences, 20*, 451–459.

Gallistel, C. R. (1990). *The organization of learning.* Cambridge, MA: MIT Press.

Garris, P. A., Kilpatrick, M., Bunin, M. A., Michael, D., Walker, Q. D., & Wightman, R. M. (1999). Dissociation of dopamine release in the nucleus accumbens from intracranial self-stimulation. *Nature, 398*, 67–69.

Geman, S., Bienenstock, E., & Doursat, R. (1992). Neural networks and the bias/variance dilemma. *Neural Computation, 4*, 1–58.

Giedd, J. N., Blumenthal, J., Jeffries, N. O., Castellanos, F. X., Liu, H., Zijdenbos, A. et al. (1999). Brain development during childhood and adolescence: A longitudinal MRI study. *Nature Neuroscience, 2*, 861–863.

Gold, E. M. (1967). Language identification in the limit. *Information and Control, 10*, 447–74.

Golding, N. L., & Spruston, N. (1998). Dendritic sodium spikes are variable triggers of axonal action potentials in hippocampal CA1 pyramidal neurons. *Neuron, 21*, 1189–1200.

Goldman-Rakic, P. S. (1990). Cortical localization of working memory. In J. L. McGaugh, N. M. Weinberger, & G. Lynch (Eds.), *Brain organization and memory: Cells, systems, and circuits* (pp. 285–298). New York: Oxford University Press.

Hammer, M. (1993). An identified neuron mediates the unconditioned stimulus in associative olfactory learning in honeybees. *Nature, 366*, 59–63.

Hebb, D. O. (1949). *The organization of behavior; a neuropsychological theory.* New York: Wiley.

Hinton, G. E., & Sejnowski, T. J. (1999). *Unsupervised learning: Foundations of neural computation.* Cambridge, MA: MIT Press.

Hirth, F., & Reichert, H. (1999). Conserved genetic programs in insect and mammalian brain development. *Bioessays, 21*, 684.

Huffman, K. J., Molnár, Z., Van Dellen, A., Kahn, D. M., Blakemore, C., & Krubitzer, L. (1999). Formation of cortical fields on a reduced cortical sheet. *Journal of Neuroscience, 19*, 9939–9952.

Huttenlocher, P. R., & Dabholkar, A. S. (1997). Regional differences in synaptogenesis in human cerebral cortex. *Journal of Comparative Neurology, 387*, 167–178.

Johnson, M. H. (1997). *Developmental cognitive neuroscience: An Introduction.* Oxford: Blackwell Science.

Judd, S. (1988). On the complexity of loading shallow neural networks. *Journal of Complexity, 4*, 177–92.

Katz, L. C., & Shatz, C. J. (1996). Synaptic activity and the construction of cortical circuits. *Science, 274*, 1133–1138.

Knudsen, E. I. (1998). Capacity for plasticity in the adult owl auditory system expanded by juvenile experience *Science, 279*, 1531–1533.

Koza, J. (1992). *Genetic programming: On the programming of computers by means of natural selection.* Cambridge, MA: Bradford Books.

Levitt, P., Harvey, J. A., Friedman, E., Simansky, K., & Murphy, E. H. (1997). New evidence for neurotransmitter influences on brain development. *Trends in Neurosciences, 20*, 269–274.

Linsker, R. (1990). Perceptual neural organization: Some approaches based on network models and information theory. *Annual Review of Neuroscience, 13*, 257–281.

Luciana, M., & Nelson, C. A. (1998). The functional emergence of prefrontally guided working memory systems in four- to eight-year-old children *Neuropsychologia, 36*, 273–293.

Macnamara, J. (1982). *Names for things: A study of child language.* Cambridge, MA: MIT Press.

Maletic-Savatic, M., Malinow, R., & Svoboda, K. (1999). Rapid dendritic morphogenesis in CA1 hippocampal dendrites induced by synaptic activity. *Science, 283*, 1923–1927.

Meltzoff, A. N., & Moore, M. K. (1977). Imitation of facial and manual gestures by human neonates. *Science, 298*, 75–78.

Montague, P. R., Dayan, P., Person, C., & Sejnowski, T.J. (1995). Bee foraging in uncertain environments using predictive Hebbian learning. *Nature, 377*, 725–728.

Montague, P. R., & Quartz, S. R. (1999). Computational approaches to neural reward and development. *Mental Retardation & Developmental Disabilities Research Reviews, 5*, 86–99.

Montague, P. R., & Sejnowski, T. J. (1994). The predictive brain: Temporal coincidence and temporal order in synaptic learning mechanisms. *Learning and Memory, 1*, 1–33.

Norman, D. A., & Shallice, T. (1986). Attention to action: Willed and automatic control of behavior. In R. J. Davidson, G.E. Schwartz, & D. Shapiro (Eds.), *Consciousness and self-regulation* (pp. 1–18). New York: Plenum Press.

Pallas, S. L. (2001). Intrinsic and extrinsic factors shaping cortical identity. *Trends in Neurosciences, 24*, 417–423.

Peterson, C. C., & Siegal, M. (1995). Deafness, conversation and theory of mind. *Journal of Child Psychology and Psychiatry, 36*, 459–474.

Petrides, M. (1995). Functional organization of the human frontal cortex for mnemonic processing: Evidence from neuroimaging studies. In *Structure and functions of the human prefrontal cortex* (pp. 85–96). New York: New York Academy of Sciences.

Pinker, S. (1984). *Language learnability and language development.* Cambridge, MA: Harvard University Press.

Pinker, S. (1994). *The language instinct.* New York: William Morrow.

Plunkett, K., Karmiloff-Smith, A., Bates, E., & Elman, J. L. (1997). Connectionism and developmental psychology *Journal of Child Psychology, Psychiatry, and Allied Disciplines, 38*, 53–80.

Poirazi, P., & Mel, B. W. (2001). Impact of active dendrites and structural plasticity on the memory capacity of neural tissue. *Neuron, 29*, 779–796.

Purves, D., White, L. E., & Riddle, D. R. (1996). Is neural development Darwinian? *Trends in Neurosciences, 19*, 460–64.

Pylyshyn, Z. (1984). *Computation and cognition: Toward a foundation for cognitive science.* Cambridge, MA: Bradford Books.

Quartz, S. R. (1993). Nativism, neural networks, and the plausibility of constructivism. *Cognition, 48*, 123–44.

Quartz, S. R. (1999). The constructivist brain. *Trends in Cognitive Sciences, 3*, 48–57.

Quartz, S. R. (2003). Toward a developmental evolutionary psychology: Genes, development, and the evolution of the human cognitive architecture. In S. Scher & M. Rauscher (Eds.), *Evolutionary psychology: Alternative approaches*, (pp. 185–210). Dordrecht: Kluwer.

Quartz, S. R., & Sejnowski, T. J. (1997). The neural basis of cognitive development: A constructivist manifesto. *Behavioral and Brain Sciences, 20*, 537–596.

Quinlan, P. T. (1998). Structural change and development in real and artificial neural networks. *Neural Networks, 11*, 577–599.

Rakic, P., Bourgeois, J. P., Eckenhoff, M. F., Zecevic, N., & Goldman-Rakic, P. S. (1986). Concurrent overproduction of synapses in diverse regions of the primate cerebral cortex. *Science, 232*, 232–35.

Real, L. A. (1991). Animal choice behavior and the evolution of cognitive architecture. *Science, 253*, 980–986.

Redding, N. J., Kowalczyk, A., & Downs, T. (1993). Constructive higher-order network algorithm that is polynomial time. *Neural Networks, 6*, 997–1010.

Reichert, H., & Simeone, A. (1999). Conserved usage of gap and homeotic genes in patterning the CNS. *Current Opinion in Neurobiology, 9*, 589–595.

Rubenstein, J. L., Anderson, S., Shi, L., Miyashita-Lin, E., Bulfone, A., & Hevner, R. (1999). Genetic control of cortical regionalization and connectivity. *Cerebral Cortex, 9*, 524–532.

Rubia, K., Overmeyer, S., Taylor, E., Brammer, M., Williams, S. C. R., Simmons, A. et al. (2000). Functional frontalisation with age: Mapping neurodevelopmental trajectories with fMRI. *Neuroscience & Biobehavioral Reviews, 24*, 13–19.

Russell, P. A., Hosie, J. A., Gray, C. D., Scott, C., Hunter, N., Banks, J. S., & Macaulay, M. C. (1998). The development of theory of mind in deaf children. *Journal of Child Psychology and Psychiatry, 39*, 903–910.

Sadato, N., Pascual-Leone, A., Grafman, J., Deiber, M. P., Ibañez, V., & Hallett, M. (1998). Neural networks for Braille reading by the blind. *Brain, 121*, 1213–1229.

Sadato, N., Pascual-Leone, A., Grafman, J., Ibañez, V., Deiber, M. P., Dold, G., & Hallett, M. (1996). Activation of the primary visual cortex by Braille reading in blind subjects. *Nature, 380*, 526–528.

Sawaguchi, T., & Goldman-Rakic, P. S. (1994). The role of D1-dopamine receptor in working memory: Local injections of dopamine antagonists into the prefrontal cortex of rhesus monkeys performing an oculomotor delayed-response task. *Journal of Neurophysiology, 71*, 515–528.

Schade, J. P., & van Groenigan, W. B. (1961). Structural organization of the human cerebral cortex: I. Maturation of the middle frontal gyrus. *Acta Anatomica, 47*, 72–111.

Schiller, J., Major, G., Koester, H. J., & Schiller, Y. (2000). NMDA spikes in basal dendrites of cortical pyramidal neurons. *Nature, 404*, 285–289.

Schultz, W. (2000). Multiple reward signals in the brain. *Nature Review Neuroscience, 1*, 199–207.

Schultz, W., Apicella, P., & Ljungberg, T. (1993). Responses of monkey dopamine neurons to reward and conditioned stimuli during successive steps of learning a delayed response task. *Journal of Neuroscience, 13*, 900–913.

Shultz, T. R., Mareschal, D., & Schmidt, W. C. (1994). Modeling cognitive development on balance scale phenomena. *Machine Learning, 16*, 57–86.

Stone, V. E., Baron-Cohen, S., & Knight, R. T. (1998). Frontal lobe contributions to theory of mind. *Journal of Cognitive Neuroscience, 10*, 640–656.

Sutton, R. S., & Barto, A. G. (1998). *Reinforcement learning: An introduction.* Cambridge, MA: MIT Press.

Tesauro, G. (1995). Temporal difference learning and TD-Gammon. *Communications of the ACM, 38*, 58–68.

Thompson, P. M., Giedd, J. N., Woods, R. P., MacDonald, D., Evans, A. C., & Toga, A. W. (2000). Growth patterns in the developing brain detected by using continuum mechanical tensor maps. *Nature, 404*, 190–193.

Tomasello, M. (1999). *The cultural origins of human cognition.* Cambridge, MA: Harvard University Press.

Tooby, J., & Cosmides, L. (1992). The psychological foundations of culture. In J. H. Barkow, L. Cosmides, & J. Tooby (Eds.), *The adapted mind: Evolutionary psychology and the generation of culture* (pp. 19–136). New York: Oxford University Press.

Wexler, K., & Culicover, P. (1980). *Formal principles of language acquisition.* Cambridge, MA: MIT Press.

White, H. (1990). Connectionist nonparametric regression: Multilayer feedforward networks can learn arbitrary mappings. *Neural Networks, 3*, 535–49.

Wilson, S. W., & Rubenstein, J. (2000). Induction and dorsoventral patterning of the telencephalon. *Neuron, 28*, 641.

Wise, R. A. (1996). Addictive drugs and brain stimulation reward. *Annual Review of Neuroscience, 19*, 319–340.

Wong, R. O. (1999). Retinal waves and visual system development. *Annual Review of Neuroscience, 22*, 29–47.

Wong, W. T. & Wong, R. O. (2000). Rapid dendritic movements during synapse formation and rearrangement. *Current Opinion in Neurobiology, 10*, 118–124.

Young, L. J., Nilsen, R., Waymire, K. G., MacGregor, G. R., & Insel, T. R. (1999). Increased affiliative response to vasopressin in mice expressing the V1a receptor from a monogamous vole. *Nature, 400*, 766–768.

CHAPTER TEN

Cross-modal neural development

Mark T. Wallace
Wake Forest University School of Medicine, North Carolina, USA

CROSS-MODAL PERCEPTUAL AND BEHAVIOURAL PROCESSES

We live in a multisensory world. In this world, our sensory organs are continually bombarded with stimuli that originate from a variety of sources. To form a unified view of our sensory world, our nervous system must synthesise this information into a coherent behavioural and perceptual gestalt.

Although the cross-modal synthesis that gives rise to this unified whole is a process of which we are typically unaware, a number of perceptual examples highlight the ongoing interactions between the senses. Perhaps the most familiar of these is the ventriloquism effect, in which the visual cues generated by the moving lips of the dummy bias our localisation of the auditory stimulus (i.e. the words of the ventriloquist; Howard & Templeton, 1966). Although we know that the ventriloquist is actually doing the talking, we are struck nonetheless by the compelling nature of this illusion. A related example is our ability to attribute voices to specific characters on the movie screen or television, despite the fact that these voices all originate from the same location, and one that can be quite distant from the appropriate visual cues. In another family of cross-modal illusions, collectively referred to as the McGurk effect, a unique product is generated by the synthesis of discordant visual and auditory cues (McGurk & MacDonald, 1976). Thus, pairing the sight of a speaker's lips reciting the syllables "ga-ga" with the auditory syllables "ba-ba" results in a unique percept—"da-da." Although it is commonly held that vision is the dominant or driving modality in many of these illusions, it has recently been shown that audition can have a profound influence on our visual perceptions as well (Shams, Kamitani, & Shimojo, 2000). In this illusion, a unitary visual event (i.e. a single flash) is perceived as multiple flashes when paired with two or more auditory stimuli (i.e. beeps).

Such cross-modal interactions are not unique to vision and audition. In fact, a number of examples serve to illustrate that each of the senses has the ability to influence information processing in the other senses. For example, rotation of a subject in a darkened room, which serves to stimulate the vestibular sense, strongly influences both our visual and auditory perceptions. In the simplest illustration of this effect, the orientation of a line appears to change during the rotation of the subject in the dark, even though the physical stimulus remains the same (Day & Wade, 1966). In the "parchment skin illusion", changing the frequency of sounds heard by a subject strongly modulates their tactile perceptions (Jousmaki & Hari, 1998). Here, the same tactile stimulus can be perceived as rough or smooth, depending on the characteristics of a coincidentally presented auditory stimulus. The list of such perceptual cross-modal interactions is quite long, and beyond the scope of this review. Nonetheless, their presence serves to highlight the profound interactions that are ongoing between the senses in normal human perception.

In fact, a number of individuals experience cross-modal interactions that lie outside of the realm of those normally experienced. Such interactions, collectively referred to as synaesthesia, take an overwhelming variety of forms (Cytowic, 1989). In these individuals, stimulation in one sense results in a perception in an unstimulated sense. One of the more common forms of synaesthesia is an association between colours and spoken letters or words. In such instances, subjects report a strong linkage between specific auditory stimuli and specific colours. For example, the sound of the letter B or the word "bat" may give rise to a visual perception of blue, whereas the sound of the letter S or the word "safe" may give rise to the visual perception of yellow. As more data is gathered, it appears that the prevalence of synaesthesia is significantly higher than previously thought, with some estimates suggesting that it may be found in as many as one in every two thousand persons (Grossenbacher & Lovelace, 2001). Although the underlying neural basis of this interesting syndrome remains a mystery, many believe that it has a developmental aetiology.

Cross-modal interactions, although perhaps most illustrative and dramatic in the perceptual realm, are also apparent in simpler behaviours. Thus, it has been shown that simple reaction times to either a visual or an auditory stimulus can be significantly speeded by the concurrent presentation of stimuli in both modalities (Andreassi & Greco, 1975; Bernstein, Clark, & Edelstein, 1969; Gielen, Schmidt, & Van den Heuvel, 1983; Hershenson, 1962; Hughes, Reuter-Lorenz, Nozawa, & Fendrich, 1994; Morrell, 1968). Similarly, the latencies of saccadic eye movements are shortened by such multisensory stimulus combinations (Corneil, Van Wanrooij, Munoz, & Van Opstal, 2002; Frens, Van Opstal, & Van der Willigen, 1995; Goldring, Dorris, Corneil, Ballantyne, & Munoz, 1996; Harrington & Peck, 1998; Hughes et al., 1994; Nozawa, Reuter-Lorenz, & Hughes, 1994; Perrott, Saberi, Brown, & Strybel, 1990). In fact, these speeded responses have been shown to be faster than predictions based on probability summation of the two modality-specific responses, arguing for an interaction between these inputs at some point in the nervous system (Hughes et al., 1994; Nozawa et al., 1994).

Despite the ubiquity of these cross-modal phenomena, the neural bases for such interactions have, until recently, been the subject of limited study. However, in the last 15 years, concerted attempts have been made to begin to parse out how the nervous system synthesises information from multiple sensory modalities. Not surprisingly, this work has focused on areas of the brain in which there is a significant convergence of information from two or more sensory modalities. Although the list of such areas is quite long (and continues to grow; see Stein & Meredith, 1993, for a review), the greatest insights that have been gleaned about multisensory neural processes have been obtained from a midbrain structure, the superior colliculus.

THE ADULT SUPERIOR COLLICULUS AS A MODEL FOR STUDYING MULTISENSORY PROCESSING

For many years, the superior colliculus (SC) has been known to play an important role in both sensory and motor processes. Visual, auditory, and somatosensory inputs converge on this structure, and they do so in a very systematic manner. As a result of this convergence, multiple topographic representations or "maps" of sensory space are formed, each of which is aligned or registered with the other (see Stein & Meredith, 1993). As a consequence of this organisation, a sensory stimulus in front of the animal, regardless of sensory modality, will result in a locus of activity in the front (i.e. rostral) portion of the SC. Conversely, a stimulus in temporal or peripheral space (or on the caudal body surface) will preferentially activate neurons in the caudal SC. The second dimension of sensory space, elevation, is represented systematically along the medial–lateral axis of the SC. In this dimension, the medial portion of the SC represents upper or superior sensory space, and the lateral portion represents lower or inferior space.

As described above, the SC has been implicated in both sensory and motor function, and may well play an important role in the transformation of sensory information into the motor signals or commands that direct the eyes, ears and head towards a stimulus of interest (Stein, Magalhaes-Castro, & Kruger, 1976). Highlighting this presumptive role for the SC in such sensorimotor transformations, the sensory maps described above have been found to be in register with a motor map(s) in the same layers. A motor map for eye movements has been defined by electrical stimulation studies of the SC. Here, activation of a specific SC location results in an eye movement of a defined direction and amplitude (McHaffie & Stein, 1982; Robinson, 1972; Schiller & Stryker, 1972; Stein, Goldberg, & Clamann, 1976). The vectors of these stimulation-induced eye movements are systematically ordered in the SC, such that stimulation of the rostral SC gives rise to small amplitude saccades, whereas stimulation of the caudal SC gives rise to large amplitude saccades. In a similar manner, stimulation of the medial SC results in upward-directed eye movements, and stimulation of the lateral SC results in downward-directed eye movements. In addition to this eye movement map, in animals with mobile ears, such as the cat, a map of ear movements has been detailed as well (Stein & Clamann, 1981). Such an organisation allows for an efficient link between the spatial locus of sensory information and the appropriate motor commands to move toward that location. As an example, a sensory stimulus in far peripheral space (regardless of modality) will activate neurons in the caudal SC, a location that codes for large amplitude movements of the eyes and head. Such movements would serve to bring the stimulus onto the foveal representation.

Sensory inputs from multiple modalities not only converge on the SC as a structure, in many instances they converge on individual neurons, creating a substantial population of neurons that are responsive to stimuli from multiple modalities—"multisensory" neurons. As a simple consequence of receiving input from more than one sensory modality, multisensory neurons have multiple receptive fields, one for each of the effective modalities. Reflecting (and possibly giving rise to) the topographic register between the modalities described above, each of the receptive fields in a multisensory neuron is in register (Figure 10.1). Thus, a visual–auditory neuron with a visual receptive field in frontal space will have an auditory receptive field in frontal space as well. Similarly, a visual–somatosensory neuron with a somatosensory receptive field on the rump will have its visual receptive field in peripheral space. As we'll see below, this receptive field register appears to be an important determinant in how these neurons will respond when they are presented with stimuli from two or more modalities.

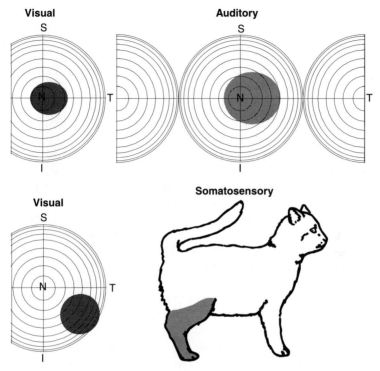

Figure 10.1.   The individual receptive fields of multisensory superior colliculus (SC) neurons exhibit good spatial overlap. Shading shows the receptive fields of a representative visual–auditory (top) and visual–somatosensory (bottom) neuron. The convention for representing auditory space is that the central sphere depicts frontal auditory space, and the two lateral hemispheres (that have been split and folded forward) depict caudal space. I, inferior; N, nasal; S, superior; T, temporal.

MULTISENSORY INTEGRATION AT THE NEURONAL LEVEL

In many respects, the response properties of multisensory SC neurons look very similar to their modality-specific neighbours. Thus, visually responsive neurons, regardless of whether they are exclusively visual or multisensory, are similar in regard to the vigour of their responses, how much they habituate to repeated stimulus presentations, their directional and velocity preferences, and so on. This holds true for auditory and somatosensory responses as well. However, such similarities end when one examines the manner in which these neurons respond when stimuli are presented from more than a single modality. The responses of multisensory SC neurons can be, and often are, dramatically different when they are subjected to stimuli from multiple sensory modalities (Meredith, Nemitz, & Stein, 1987; Meredith & Stein, 1986a, 1986b). For

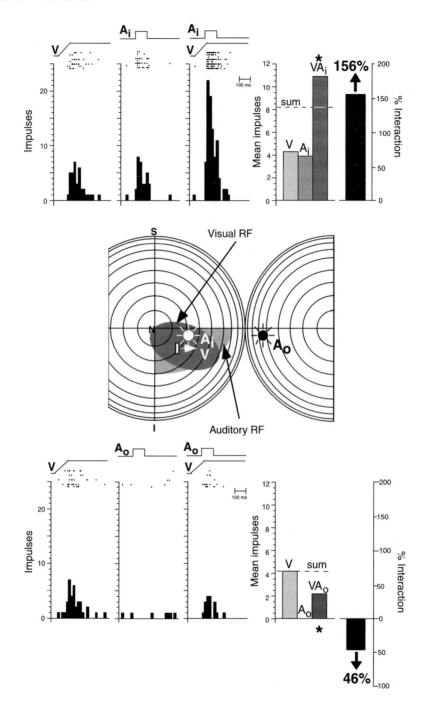

example, in a visual–auditory neuron, the pairing of visual and auditory stimuli can result in a response that is significantly greater than the responses to either of the stimuli presented alone. This response enhancement can even exceed the response predicted by summing the two modality-specific (i.e. visual alone, auditory alone) responses (Figure 10.2). Conversely, responses can be dramatically reduced by multisensory stimulus pairings (Figure 10.2). This response depression can be so strong as to completely eliminate sensory responses.

Response enhancements and depressions in multisensory neurons appear to follow a predictable set of principles, dictated in large measure by the spatial, temporal, and physical characteristics of the stimuli that are combined. Thus, stimuli that are presented together within their respective receptive fields (and thus, given the overlap described above, likely to have originated from the same event) typically result in response enhancements (Meredith & Stein, 1986a). Conversely, if one of the stimuli is presented outside of its receptive field, either response depression or no interaction is seen. The presence or absence of this response depression appears to be dependent on the presence of an inhibitory surround outside of the classical excitatory receptive field (Kadunce, Vaughan, Wallace, Benedek & Stein, 1997). In addition to space, time plays a key role in the generation of multi-sensory interactions. Thus, multisensory stimuli that are presented together within a certain temporal window will tend to give rise to response enhance-ments, whereas outside of this window interactions are no longer seen (Meredith et al., 1987). Somewhat surprisingly, these windows can be quite long by neural standards, spanning many hundreds of milliseconds. Finally, stimulus effectiveness has also been shown to play an important role in multi-sensory integration. Specifically, it has been found that stimuli that are highly effective on their own in generating a neuronal response typically give rise to little or no enhancement when paired with a stimulus from a second modality (Meredith & Stein, 1986b). However, as stimuli become increasingly less effective in activating the neuron when presented alone, the proportionate

Figure 10.2. Response enhancement and response depression in a visual–auditory SC neuron. In the centre are shown the receptive fields (RF) (shading) and the stimulus locations (icons) for tests of multisensory integration. Rasters and peristimulus time histograms on the top show that the movement of a visual stimulus (moving bar of light) within the receptive field (V; depicted by ramp) elicited a modest response in this neuron (each dot represents an action potential; each line of dots a single stimulus sweep; histograms the summed activity sorted in 20 ms bins). Similarly, presentation of an auditory stimulus (broadband noise burst) within the receptive field (A_i) elicited a modest response. However, when these same stimuli were paired, a large enhancement of response was seen. Summary bar graphs on the right show that this enhance-ment was 156 per cent of the best modality-specific response, and exceeded the sum of the two modality-specific responses. In contrast, presentation of the auditory stimulus outside of the receptive field (A_o) resulted in a significant depression of the response to the same visual stimulus (bottom). $*p < .05$.

gain from pairing them increases. Such a finding makes intuitive sense, in that stimuli that are very strong on their own need little added benefit from a second stimulus in a different modality. However, as individual stimulus effectiveness declines, signal ambiguity rises, increasing the potential information that can be gained with a second channel of sensory information.

That this integration is more than the product of simply having two stimuli presented together within a neuron's receptive field(s), but is unique to the fact that information is present in two *different* modalities, has been demonstrated by presenting two stimuli from the same modality within the receptive field of a multisensory neuron (Stein & Meredith, 1993). Thus, pairing two visual stimuli fails to give rise to the response enhancements that characterise multisensory interactions. In fact, such pairings most often give rise to responses that fail to reach that predicted by summing the individual responses, suggesting a within-modality occlusive effect.

MULTISENSORY INTEGRATION AT THE BEHAVIOURAL LEVEL

Somewhat remarkably, these changes at the neuronal level are mirrored by changes in the behaviour of animals when they are presented with stimuli from more than a single sensory modality (Stein, Huneycutt, & Meredith, 1988; Stein, Meredith, Huneycutt, & McDade, 1989). To examine this, cats were first trained to approach a visual stimulus (i.e. an illuminated light-emitting diode—LED) to receive a food reward. Once the animals got very good at this task (i.e. they went to the correct location more than 95 per cent of the time), the intensity of the LED was lowered until the animals were working at or near their behavioural threshold (i.e. 50 per cent correct responses). Now, the impact of an auditory stimulus (which was either neutral or that the animal had been trained to ignore) on these responses was evaluated. When the auditory stimulus was paired with the visual stimulus at the same location in space, behavioural responses were enhanced (i.e. correct responses increased). On the other hand, if this pairing was done with the visual and auditory stimuli at different locations, behavioural responses were depressed. As is seen in the responses of single neurons, under many circumstances the behavioural changes could be substantially different from either of the component responses. For example, whereas the presentation of a visual stimulus at one location might result in a 50 per cent response rate, and the presentation of an auditory stimulus at that same location might give only a 10 per cent response rate, the pairing of these stimuli could give rise to response rates exceeding 90 per cent.

THE ROLE OF CORTEX IN MULTISENSORY INTEGRATION

How does a multisensory SC neuron transform its modality-specific inputs into a product that can be dramatically different from these inputs? Although on first blush this might be seen as a simple consequence of receiving convergent sensory inputs from different modalities, and one can envisage an intrinsic property of SC neurons that might mediate such integration, several lines of evidence suggest this not to be the case. First, not all multisensory SC neurons generate the response enhancements and depressions described above. For example, in cats—the most extensively studied model species for examining these interactions—upwards of 20 per cent of all multisensory neurons appear to lack this integrative capacity (Jiang, Wallace, Jiang, Vaughan, & Stein, 2001: recent data suggest a similar proportion of non-integrative multisensory neurons in the monkey SC; Wallace & Stein, 1997; Wallace, Wilkinson, & Stein, 1996). Second, early in postnatal development, all multisensory neurons lack the ability to integrate multisensory stimuli like the adult (see below). Consequently, it appears that multisensory integration is not a *de facto* property of receiving convergent sensory inputs from multiple modalities.

To better characterise the origins of multisensory integration in SC neurons, it was necessary to first focus on the convergent inputs that give rise to the multisensory character of these neurons. This analysis started by examining inputs from the cerebral cortex, given that prior anatomical studies had shown extensive projections from several cortical areas to the multisensory layers of the SC (Clemo & Stein, 1984; Harting, Updyke, & Van Lieshout, 1992; Huerta & Harting, 1984; McHaffie, Kruger, Clemo, & Stein, 1988; Meredith & Clemo, 1989; Norita et al., 1986; Segal & Beckstead, 1984; Stein, Spencer, & Edwards, 1983). Additionally, cortical inputs seemed a good candidate, based on the speculation that they might provide a higher-order means of modulating multisensory processes in the brainstem. To examine the potential role of cortex in mediating such processing, physiological studies in the cat first focused on the cortex of the anterior ectosylvian sulcus (AES). In this work, the effects of reversible deactivation (i.e. cryogenic blockade) of AES on the responses of SC neurons were examined (Wallace & Stein, 1994). Quite dramatically, it was found that deactivation of AES had a very specific effect on many multisensory SC neurons. Whereas the modality-specific responses of these neurons were relatively unaffected (e.g. a visual–auditory neuron continued to respond to the visual or auditory stimulus as it had prior to deactivation), multisensory integration was severely compromised during deactivation of AES. In a number of instances, deactivation of AES abolished the integration of cross-modal cues—the multisensory SC neuron responded to the stimulus combination as it did to one or the other of the component stimuli (Figure 10.3). As soon as the deactivation was reversed (by rewarming the cortex), multisensory integration returned. Extending this finding, it has recently been shown that a second cortical area, the cortex of the rostral lateral suprasylvian sulcus (rLS), plays an additional role in modulating these integrated multisensory responses (Jiang et al., 2001).

This work has suggested two classes of input onto multisensory SC neurons (Figure 10.4). The first, in large measure derived from subcortical and more primary cortical sources, results in the creation of a multisensory neuron by the sheer nature of the convergence of modality-specific inputs. However, such inputs are unable to support the large changes in neuronal responsiveness that characterise multisensory integration. This property is dependent on a second set of inputs, which are derived from association cortical areas such as AES and rLS. In support of this model, recent anatom-ical work has shown that whereas subcortical inputs onto SC neurons terminate on distal dendrites, cortical inputs terminate more proximally (Harting, Feig, & Van Lieshout, 1997). Such an architecture is ideally suited for allowing cortical inputs to gate the access of subcortical inputs to the soma, and thus the large changes in response seen in response to multisensory stimulus combinations.

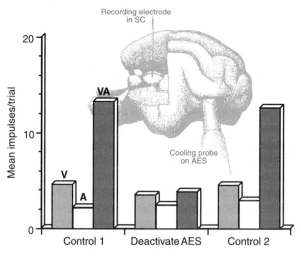

Figure 10.3. Reversible deactivation of association cortex (AES) eliminates multisensory inte-gration in superior colliculus (SC) neurons. Summary bar graphs show the responses of a visual–auditory neuron to modality-specific (i.e. V alone, A alone) and multisensory (VA) stimuli before (control 1), during (deactivate AES) and after (control 2) deactivation of AES by means of a cooling probe (paradigm is shown in background). Note the enhanced multisensory response in the two control conditions and the loss of this enhancement during deactivation.

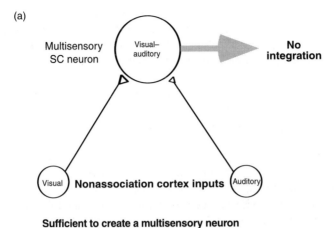

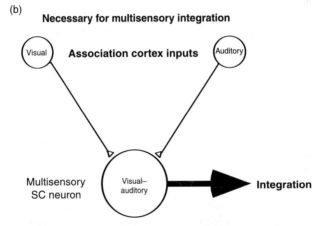

Figure 10.4. A model of the proposed circuit for the creation of multisensory superior colliculus (SC) neurons. See text for details. (Adapted from Wallace & Stein, 1994.) Copyright © 1994 The American Physiological Society. Reproduced with permission.

Again, paralleling these neuronal findings, behavioural studies have supported the importance of these cortical areas for multisensory processes. Thus, when AES is deactivated in a behaving animal (which is done by means of injections of the anaesthetic agent lidocaine through a cannula implanted in AES), multisensory orientation behaviours are severely impacted (Wilkinson, Meredith, & Stein, 1996). Specifically, the behavioural enhancements and depressions seen to spatially coincident and spatially disparate stimuli are abolished. As in the physiological experiments described above, responses to the component modality stimuli (i.e. visual or auditory) remain relatively unaffected during deactivation. Similar results have recently been shown with deactivation of rLS cortex (Jiang, Jiang & Stein, 2002). The strong ties between these behavioural results and the physiological data strongly support the importance of the SC for multisensory orientation behaviours, as well as the importance of cortex in gating these events.

THE UNIVERSALITY OF MULTISENSORY INTEGRATION

Although the most substantial data set concerning the neural substrates for multisensory processes has been collected from the midbrain of the cat, growing evidence suggests that the manner in which these multisensory neurons respond is not unique to either the cat or the SC. For example, in the monkey SC, a favourite model for studies examining the neural bases of saccadic (i.e. ballistic) eye and head movements, many of the same multisensory characteristics have been found (Bell, Corneil, Meredith & Munoz, 2001; Frens & Van Opstal, 1998; Wallace et al., 1996). Like in the cat, multisensory neurons are plentiful in the monkey SC, have overlapping receptive fields, and integrate multisensory cues in a manner that is dependent on the spatial, temporal, and physical characteristics of the stimuli presented. In fact, recent advances in imaging methodologies have provided a view into multisensory processes in the human SC. Using fMRI, Calvert and colleagues (Calvert, Campbell, & Brammer, 2000) have shown increases in the blood oxygenation signal (an indirect measure of neural activity) in the midbrain during the presentation of spatially coincident stimuli, and concomitant decreases in this signal during the presentation of spatially disparate stimuli.

As highlighted earlier, the convergence of sensory information from different modalities is not unique to the SC, and characterises many areas of the brain. In several of these areas, examination of the response characteristics of multisensory neurons has revealed striking similarities with those in the SC. Thus, in the rat, cat, and monkey, multisensory neurons have been identified in several cortical areas. In each, individual multisensory neurons show a good correspondence in the receptive fields for each of their effective modalities (Bruce, Desimone, & Gross, 1981; Duhamel, Colby, & Goldberg, 1998; Fogassi, Gallese, Fadiga, Luppino, Matelli, & Rizzolatti, 1996; Graziano, Hu, & Gross, 1997; Graziano, Reiss, & Gross, 1999; Ramachandran, Wallace, Clemo, & Stein, 1993; Rizzolatti, Scandolara, Matelli, & Gentilucci, 1981; Wallace, Meredith, & Stein, 1992). In the AES cortex of the cat, multisensory neurons have been shown to exhibit significant response enhancements and depressions, changes that have been found to be dependent on the spatial and temporal relationships of the stimuli, as well as their effectiveness in eliciting a response (Wallace et al., 1992). In humans, population studies using event-related potentials, magnetoencephalography (MEG), positron emission tomography (PET), and fMRI have identified cortical regions that show substantial changes during multisensory stimulation (Bense, Stephan, Yousry, Brandt & Dieterich, 2001; Bushara, Grafman & Hallett, 2001; Calvert et al., 2000; Foxe, Morocz, Murray, Higgins, Javitt, & Schroeder, 2000; Giard & Peronnet, 1999). Each of these studies has suggested that the basis for these changes might lie in modulations of activity within a substantial population of multisensory neurons within these structures.

THE DEVELOPMENT OF HUMAN MULTISENSORY PROCESSES

Although a good deal of work has gone into detailing the neural and behavioural characteristics of multisensory neurons and multisensory integration in the adult brain, surprisingly little research has been focused on understanding the development of these intriguing cross-modal processes. This is despite the presence of a substantial and long-contested debate in the human developmental psychology literature as to the sensory character of the newborn and infant brain. Framing the debate by its extremes is, on the one hand the belief that the early human brain is extraordinarily multisensory, with early perceptual processes being driven by relatively undifferentiated sensory events. Support for this view comes from evidence of cross-modal matching in newborns (Meltzoff & Borton, 1979; Meltzoff & Moore, 1977), their ability to make eye movements towards auditory stimuli (Butterworth & Castillo, 1976), as well as their capacity to equate auditory and visual inputs on the basis of intensity (Lewkowicz & Turkewitz, 1980). Other evidence, although confounded by the fact that it can't be shown immediately after birth, but only in the months after birth, has been taken as further support of early human multisensory capabilities. This includes the ability to perceive temporal synchrony in the visual and auditory components of a multisensory stimulus (Bahrick, 1994; Lewkowicz, 1986, 1992a, 1992b), as well as the common duration of the visual and auditory components of a multisensory stimulus (Lewkowicz, 1986). Indeed, it has been argued that the human infant is an obligate synaesthete, initially "confusing" or "blending" the senses together (Maurer & Maurer, 1988).

In contrast to this viewpoint is the belief that the senses are largely segregated at birth, and that it is only with the passage of time and its consequent sensory experiences that associations between the senses are made. Championed by Piaget and others (Birch & Lefford, 1963, 1967; Piaget, 1952), experimental evidence for this has come largely in the form of studies which have shown a failure to integrate multisensory cues in early human infants (Bahrick, 1992, 1994; Humphrey & Tees, 1980; Lewkowicz, 1985, 1994; Spelke, 1994). Analogous to the genetic versus epigenetic debates that framed much discussion as to the biological bases of human behaviour in the twentieth century, the answer to the question is likely to lie somewhere in the middle. In the context of the current question, we can envision a developmental chronology in which simple cross-modal distinctions (rate, duration, etc.) can be made in relatively young infants (i.e. 4–6 months), whereas distinctions based on more complex stimulus attributes (synchrony, etc.) appear later as a consequence of greater cross-modal experience (Lewkowicz, 2000).

Despite the importance of these issues in furthering our understanding of human development, animal model studies have focused in large measure on the maturation of individual sensory systems. Through these studies we have learned a great deal as to the normal developmental timetable in these sensory systems, and we have even been able in some instances to relate these findings to the development of human perceptual and behavioural processes. However, if we are to ultimately understand the maturation of perception and behaviour, it is also necessary to study the development of intersensory function at the neuronal level.

THE SUPERIOR COLLICULUS: A MODEL FOR SENSORY DEVELOPMENT

Given the strong base of knowledge about multisensory function that has been derived from the adult SC, it seems the logical place to start an examination of multisensory development. Predictions based on the idea of early multisensory interactions (what some have referred to as "primitive unity") would find the neonatal SC replete with multisensory neurons. In fact, this has been found to not be the case.

Much like in other mammalian species (see Gottlieb, 1971), the cat shows a developmental chronology of sensory function (Stein, Labos, & Kruger, 1973; Wallace & Stein, 1997). At birth, the only sensory responses in the SC are in response to somatosensory (tactile) cues. Late in the first postnatal week, the first auditory responses appear. It is not until the third postnatal week that visual response are seen in what will become the multisensory layers of the SC (visual responses are seen much earlier in the superficial SC, but these layers lack any multisensory function). This chronology closely parallels the behavioural repertoire of the animal (Fox, 1970; Levine, Hull, & Buchwald, 1980; Villablanca & Olmstead, 1979). The earliest exploratory behaviours of the newborn kitten are mediated by somatosensory cues and involve finding the mother's nipple in search of milk. Responses to auditory stimuli are seen next, as the kitten becomes more aware of cues in extrapersonal space. Finally, as the animal begins to explore the space away from the mother, it becomes increasingly responsive to stimuli in the visual world.

THE DEVELOPMENT OF MULTISENSORY NEURONS

As would be predicted on the basis of the sensory chronology described above, the first multisensory neurons in the cat SC respond to somatosensory and auditory cues (Wallace & Stein, 1997). Although they appear during the second postnatal week, the incidence of such neurons is initially quite low. Soon after the development of visual responses in the deep SC, visually responsive multisensory neurons are found. Again, the incidence of such neurons starts out very low. As postnatal development proceeds, the population of multisensory neurons rises gradually, to where they become nearly two thirds of the sensory-responsive neurons in the deep SC by 4 months after birth (Figure 10.5).

The characteristics of these early multisensory SC neurons are very different from their adult counterparts. These neurons have very large receptive fields; consequently, they respond to stimuli over large regions of sensory space. In the 2–3 months after birth, there is a gradual decline in the size of these receptive fields (Figure 10.6). The rate of this decline in receptive field size appears to be similar for each of the represented modalities. One striking effect of this reduction is an increasingly apparent registry between the receptive fields of the different modalities in these multisensory neurons. This

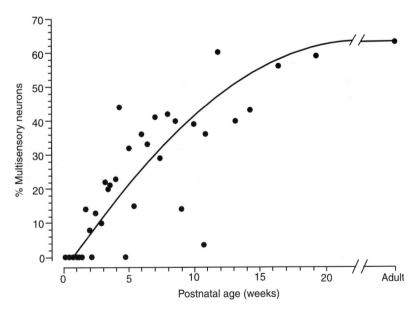

Figure 10.5.   The population of multisensory superior colliculus (SC) neurons grows over a protracted period of postnatal development. Plotted is the incidence of multisensory neurons in the deep layers of the cat SC as a function of postnatal age. (Adapted from Wallace & Stein, 1997.) Copyright © 1997 by the Society for Neuroscience. Reproduced with permission.

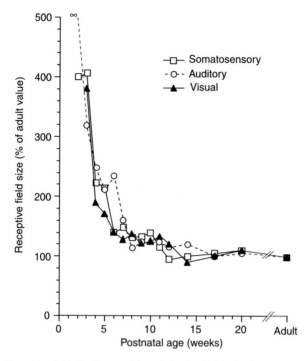

Figure 10.6. Receptive fields decline precipitously in size during the first 4–8 weeks of postnatal development. The mean size of receptive fields in cat SC for each of the represented modalities (vision, audition, somatosensation) is plotted as a function of postnatal age. (Adapted from Wallace & Stein, 1997.) Copyright © 1997 by the Society for Neuroscience. Reproduced with permission.

increasing spatial fidelity appears to have important implications for the manner in which these neurons synthesise multisensory cues (see below).

Perhaps the most interesting feature of the earliest multisensory neurons is not their receptive fields but rather the manner in which they respond to stimuli from multiple modalities. Very different from their adult counterparts, neonatal multisensory neurons respond to a multisensory combination much like they respond to the individual modality-specific stimuli (Figure 10.7). Consequently, such neurons are said to lack the capacity for multisensory integration. However, once again this situation changes with the passage of time. As development progresses, neurons with the ability to exhibit multisensory integration appear in increasing numbers, reflecting a transition from the nonintegrative state to their adult integrative state. For any given neuron, this transition appears to happen very abruptly, and once it takes place the integrative characteristics of the neuron are quite mature. Despite the rapid nature of this switch in any given neuron, for the entire multisensory population this transition is rather gradual, occupying the first 2–3 months of postnatal life.

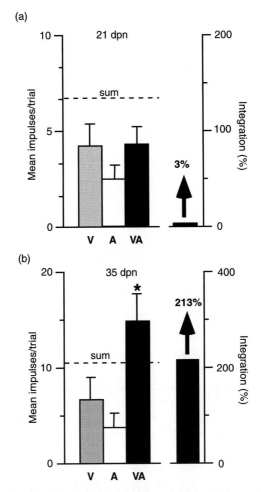

Figure 10.7.   Multisensory integration is absent in the earliest multisensory superior colliculus (SC) neurons, and appears in the first neurons several weeks later. Summary bar graphs show the modality-specific and multisensory responses, as well as the percentage enhancement, for representative visual-auditory neurons at 21 (top) and 35 (bottom) days postnatal (dpn). Note that whereas the neuron in the 21 dpn animal showed a comparable response to the multisensory (VA) and to the visual (V) stimulus, the neuron in the 35 dpn animal showed a significantly enhanced response to the multisensory stimulus. A, auditory, * $p < .05$.

As a consequence of this transition, the earliest integrating multisensory neurons typically exhibit response enhancements to stimuli placed within their respective receptive fields (Figure 10.7), and will often exhibit response depressions when one of the stimuli is moved outside of its receptive field. Furthermore, like their adult counterparts, the enhancements and depressions seen in these early multisensory neurons are of a magnitude equivalent to what is seen in the adult, and are dependent on the effectiveness of the stimuli in eliciting a response. However, these early multisensory neurons differ from the adult in one important respect. This is in the temporal window within which they will generate multisensory interactions. Whereas in adults, such windows typically span several hundred milliseconds (and can often be much longer: Meredith et al., 1987), in the neonate this window is substantially smaller (Wallace & Stein, 1997). In fact, in a number of the earliest neurons to exhibit integration, multisensory interactions could only be generated at one temporal combination (Figure 10.8).

Although the reason for this temporal difference between the neonate and the adult remains unknown, one possibility is that the limited sensory capacity (and consequent behavioural repertoire) of the young kitten constrains the size of their sensory world. Specifically, since temporal asynchronies are potential means by which information about stimulus distance can be conveyed (think of the differences in the speed of travel of light and sound), a narrower temporal window may signal (or even give rise to) a smaller behavioural window. Consistent with this is the finding that the most prevalent temporal asynchrony that results in multisensory enhancement in early visual–auditory neurons is 50 ms (with the visual stimulus leading by this amount). Such a temporal window could be envisioned to represent close peripersonal space, where the visual and auditory signals arrive at the retina and cochlea at about the same time. Because visual information takes approximately an additional 50 ms to arrive at the SC (largely a result of the complex processing in the retina), this asynchrony results in the simultaneous activation of the visual and auditory channels onto a given SC neuron. As development progresses, this temporal window gradually expands, possibly signalling the increasing importance of stimuli occurring at a distance from the animal.

THE DEVELOPMENT OF INFLUENCES FROM CORTEX

The rapid transition of maturing multisensory SC neurons from the non-integrating to the integrating state suggests the presence of a developmental "switch" that could mediate this dramatic change in response profile. Given the evidence from the adult concerning the importance of cortical influences for the integrative characteristics of SC neurons, one possibility was that this transition reflected the functional maturation of these important corticotectal pathways. Although projections from the AES to the SC are apparent at birth, such projections undergo substantial remodelling during early postnatal development (McHaffie et al., 1988). To test the role of these corticotectal inputs in mediating multisensory processes in the early SC, experiments closely resembling those conducted in the adult and described above were performed. In these studies, in multisensory SC neurons prior to the

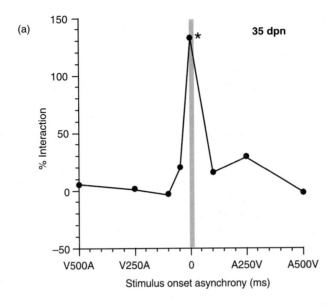

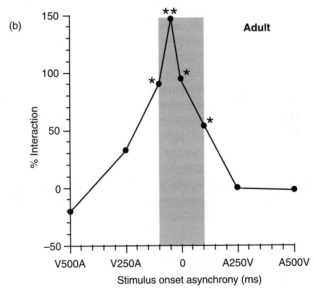

Figure 10.8. The temporal window for multisensory integration is narrower in neonatal animals. Plotted for two representative visual–auditory neurons, one in the neonate (top; 35 days postnatal; dpn) and one in the adult (bottom), is the percentage change in the multisensory response as function of stimulus onset asynchrony (SOA). In this convention, V250A represents a visual stimulus onset that precedes the auditory stimulus onset by 250 ms, and so on. Note that whereas in the neonate a significant interaction is seen only at simultaneity (shading), the interactive window is substantially broader in the adult. * $p < .05$.

appearance of their integrative capacity, reversible deactivation of AES cortex had little effect on sensory responses (Wallace & Stein, 2000a). However, as soon as a neonatal SC neuron exhibited the capacity to integrate cross-modal cues, that integration could be abolished by deactivation of AES (Figure 10.9). As in the adult, such deactivation has little effect on the modality-specific responses of these integrating multisensory neurons. These results strongly suggest that the appearance of multisensory integration in developing SC neurons is a result of the functional maturation of inputs from cortex. Consequently, the protracted time frame for the complete maturation of multisensory integration in the SC is likely to reflect the gradual maturation of the relevant areas of cortex; a process that is likely to be sculpted dramatically by early postnatal experiences (see below).

MULTISENSORY DEVELOPMENT IN NONHUMAN PRIMATES

Although the cat has been the most extensively studied species for examining the developmental chronology of multisensory neurons and their integrative capabilities, recent work has examined these issues in a nonhuman primate model, the rhesus monkey (Wallace et al., 1997; Wallace & Stein, 2001). Because of the more precocial nature of this species, one possibility was that multisensory development would be far advanced at birth relative to the cat. In some regards this turned out to be true. Thus, all sensory modalities represented in the adult SC (i.e. visual, auditory, somatosensory) are present at birth in the SC of the newborn monkey (Wallace, McHaffie, & Stein, 1997). Although enlarged relative to the adult, receptive fields in the newborn monkey SC are proportionately much smaller than those found in the newborn cat. Not surprisingly, given the presence of inputs from three modalities, multisensory neurons are present in the newborn monkey SC. However, the incidence of these neurons was reduced compared to the adult, and, like the earliest multisensory neurons in the cat SC, they lacked the ability to synthesise multisensory cues. When examined from a comparative perspective, the SC of the newborn monkey in many ways resembles the SC of the 2- to 4-week-old cat: it has a complement of multisensory neurons that have enlarged receptive fields, and that lack the multisensory integrative features that characterise adult SC neurons. Longitudinal studies are now necessary to detail the appearance of multisensory integration in this population.

THE ROLE OF EXPERIENCE IN MULTISENSORY DEVELOPMENT

As should be clear from the previous discussion, regardless of the precocial or altricial nature of the species examined, a substantial amount of multisensory development takes place after birth. Such a finding suggests that sensory

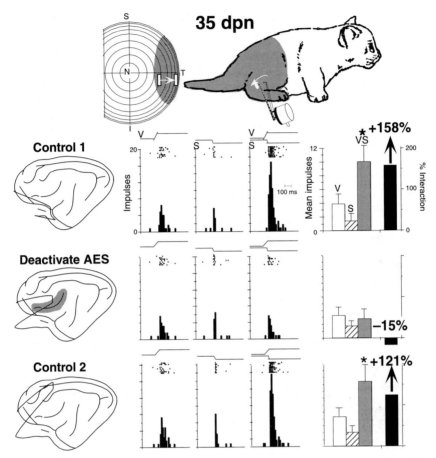

Figure 10.9. In neonates, as soon as multisensory integration is evident in superior colliculus (SC) neurons, it can be affected by deactivation of association cortex. Conventions are the same as in previous figures. On the top are shown the receptive fields (shading) for this visual–somatosensory neuron in a 35 days postnatal (dpn) animal. The three sets of rasters, peristimulus time histograms, and summary bar graphs show this neuron's modality-specific and multisensory responses before (control 1), during (deactivate AES), and after (control 2) cortical deactivation. Note the abolition of multisensory enhancement during AES deactivation, and the relative lack of effect of such deactivation on the modality-specific responses of this neuron. * $p < .05$.

experience may be a critical contributor in the maturation of multisensory processes, particularly given the importance of cortex in gating the developmental appearance of multisensory integration. After birth, sensory experiences change rapidly and continually as the animal's behavioural repertoire becomes increasingly complex. However, for obvious reasons, in normal development it is difficult to parse out the relative contributions of postnatal experience from those events that are simply following a predetermined maturational timetable. To examine this issue, it is necessary to alter experience in some manner and look at the consequent effects on sensory and multisensory development.

To shed light on this question, we have recently manipulated sensory experience by raising cats in complete darkness from birth to adulthood (Wallace, Hairston, & Stein, 2001; Wallace & Stein, 2000b). Such manipulations have been shown to have profound effects on the development of the visual system, delaying or eliminating many of the experience- and activity-based cues that drive the functional organisation of this sensory system (for a review of these effects see Daw, Reid, Wang, & Flavin, 1995). However, in addition to its effects on the visual system, such deprivation should also preclude the normal visual–nonvisual interactions that take place during development. The effects of altering visual experience on the auditory representation in the SC have been described previously in the barn owl (Knudsen & Brainard, 1991), ferret (King, Hutchings, Moore, & Blakemore, 1988), and guinea pig (Withington-Wray, Binns, & Keating, 1990). These studies, although showing the importance of visual signals in "instructing" the formation of the auditory space map, did not look at the impact of such manipulations on multisensory processes. We have recently embarked on studies to examine these effects.

In dark-reared cats, visual deprivation from birth reduces but does not eliminate visual responses in the deep SC (Wallace et al., 2001; Wallace & Stein, 2000b). Thus, whereas the incidence of visually responsive neurons in the adult cat SC is normally around 75 per cent (Wallace & Stein, 1996), the value in dark-reared animals is closer to 50 per cent (Figure 10.10). Visual receptive fields in these animals are significantly enlarged, and the normal visual topography is disrupted. Despite these changes, multisensory neurons are still quite common (Figure 10.10). When compared with normal animals, the receptive fields of these multisensory neurons are very large and lack the characteristic receptive field register.

When presented with combinations of visual and nonvisual stimuli, SC neurons in dark-reared animals show none of the response enhancements or depressions seen under normal circumstances (Figure 10.11). These neurons respond to the combination of stimuli much like they respond to either of the modality-specific stimuli. This is true regardless of the spatial, temporal or physical characteristics of the paired stimuli.

These experiments have provided the first evidence for the importance of sensory experience in the development of multisensory integration. On the basis of this finding it is tempting to speculate that experience plays a major role in shaping the maturation of cortical circuitry, and that changes in cortical organisation brought about by experiential manipulation or deprivation will be reflected in the integrative characteristics of elements in the SC. To examine this it will next be necessary to examine the functional state of the

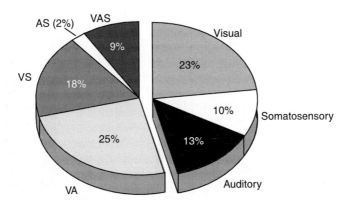

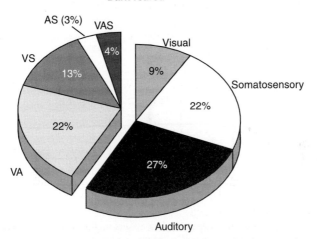

Figure 10.10. Dark-rearing affects the modality distribution of neurons in the deep superior colliculus (SC). The top pie chart plots the deep SC modality distribution for a group of normally reared animals. The left side of the pie represents the multisensory component of the population. The bottom pie chart plots the modality distribution for a group of animals raised from birth until adulthood in complete darkness. In these animals, note the decline in the visual population, the increase in the other modality-specific neurons (i.e. somatosensory, auditory), and the retention of a substantial multisensory population. VA, visual-auditory; VS, visual-somatosensory; AS, auditory-somatosensory; VAS, visual-auditory-somatosensory.

corticotectal circuits critical in gating multisensory integration. A simple prediction is that such connections will be nonfunctional in these experientially deprived animals, mirroring the state of the early neonatal brain. Thus, only with the acquisition of appropriate (and meaningful) cross-modal

Normal visual–nonvisual experience

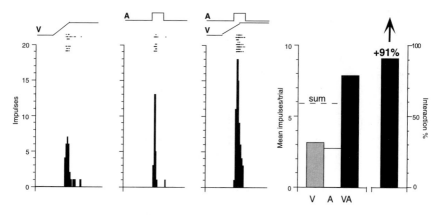

No visual–nonvisual experience

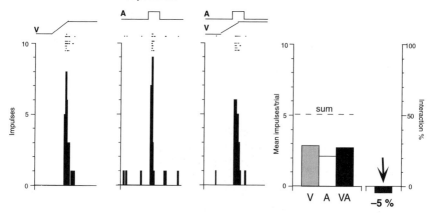

Figure 10.11. Dark-rearing compromises visual–nonvisual multisensory integration. Conventions are the same as in previous figures. On the top is shown an example of multisensory enhancement in a visual–auditory (VA) neuron from a normally-reared animal. On the bottom is shown the lack of such integration in a dark-reared animal. Note the robust modality-specific responses in this neuron, but the complete absence of any response enhancement. A, auditory; V, visual.

experiences will the functional maturation of these important projection pathways occur.

An additional question that can be examined in this experimental series is the plastic capacity of the adult brain to compensate for the changes brought about by this lack of early postnatal experience. Stated simply, if animals raised in the dark are reintroduced to a normal environment as adults, will multisensory integration appear in the SC? This question is at the core of one of the most exciting areas of contemporary neurobiological inquiry—what is the plastic capacity of the adult brain?

For many years, dogma held that the capacity of the adult brain for change was exceedingly limited. Much of this argument was structured around the notion that the adult brain produces very few new neurons, and that the capacity of mature neurons to make new connections was fairly limited. This idea was supported by the limited recovery of function seen following damage to the central nervous system. However, more recent work has begun to challenge this concept of the static adult brain, and has raised intriguing questions about the ability of the senses to substitute for one another.

CROSS-MODAL PLASTICITY

Although normal development results in the types of cross-modal organisation described above, alterations in sensory experience can result in the creation of cross-modal interactions outside of the realm of those normally seen. This phenomenon has a number of manifestations. Perhaps the most extensively studied example of induced cross-modal plasticity has been demonstrated in the ferret. In this altricial species, visual projections can be induced to grow into auditory structures by means of surgical manipulations done soon after birth (Roe, Pallas, Hahm, & Sur, 1990; Sur, Garraghty, & Roe, 1988). When examined as adults, these projections can be shown to be functional and to relay sensory information from the modality that has been induced to grow into the "inappropriate" target. Hence, in these "rewired" animals, primary auditory cortex is responsive to visual cues. Rather than being organised haphazardly, these novel pathways show a remarkable degree of organisation reminiscent of their normal target cortex (Roe, Pallas, Kwon, & Sur, 1992; Sharma, Angelucci, & Sur, 2000). Thus, like in primary visual cortex, visually responsive neurons in primary auditory cortex (AI) of the rewired ferrets show orientation and direction selectivity, and form a map of visual space. Perhaps most exciting, however, is the recent evidence showing that such redirected projections have the capacity to support visual behaviours (von Melchner, Pallas, & Sur, 2000). These experiments suggest that primary cortical areas are not prespecified, but rather look to their inputs for organisational cues.

Similarly, work in humans has suggested a potential for cortical reorganisation outside of the bounds of traditional expectations. Thus, in early deaf individuals, studies have suggested that auditory cortex can be, at least in part, captured by inputs from other sensory modalities (Neville, Schmidt, & Kutas, 1983). Electrophysiological and neuroimaging studies in early blind individuals have suggested a similar reorganisation of visual cortex. Thus, event-related potential (ERP) recordings have revealed foci of activation over visual cortex during auditory and somatosensory stimulation (Kujala, Alho, Huotilainen, Ilmoniemi, Lehtokoski, & Leinonen et al., 1997; Roder, Rosler, Hennighausen, & Nacker, 1996). Similar results have now been shown using PET and fMRI neuroimaging methods (Arno, De Volder, Vanlierde, Wanet-Defalque, Streel, & Robert et al., 2001; Sadato, Pascual-Leone, Grafman, Ibanez, Deiber, & Dold et al., 1996; Weeks, Horwitz, Aziz-Sultan, Tian, Wessinger, & Cohen et al., 2000). Although controversial, these reorganised projections have been suggested to underlie the heightened skills in the remaining modalities of individuals with early loss of one modality (Lessard, Pare, Lepore, & Lassonde, 1998; Roder, Teder-Salejarvi, Sterr, Rosler, Hill-yard, & Neville, 1999). To examine the functionality of these reorganised projections, Cohen and colleagues used transcranial magnetic stimulation (TMS) to reversibly deactivate occipital cortex during a Braille-reading task in blind individuals (Cohen, Celnik, Pascual-Leone, Corwell, Falz, & Dambrosia et al., 1997). Such stimulation disrupted the ability of these individuals to read Braille letters, while having no effect on tactile discrimination in a control population.

Such compensatory plasticity is also seen in the cat, although the locus of the change appears to lie more in the realm of association as opposed to primary cortical areas. Thus, Rauschecker and colleagues (Rauschecker & Korte, 1993) have found that the modality distribution of AES cortex changes dramatically in response to early visual deprivation, with a loss of visually responsive neurons and a corresponding gain in the auditory-responsive population. In addition, the spatial tuning of auditory neurons is enhanced, a finding which may explain the improved auditory localisation in these animals (Korte & Rauschecker, 1993; Rauschecker & Kneipert, 1994).

TOWARDS A CONNECTIONIST MODEL OF CROSS-MODAL DEVELOPMENT

The plastic changes that take place across the different sensory modalities in both development and adulthood point to the flexibility in the neural processes that underlie sensory-directed behaviours and the creation of perceptual gestalts. From the developmental perspective, the critical importance of postnatal sensory experience for the generation of "normal" multisensory processes illustrates the hierarchical nature of cross-modal development. Thus, from the earlier discussion, we can readily envisage a two-stage process resulting in the formation of a mature multisensory circuit. In the first step, which is generated in large measure prenatally, and which I will label intrinsic, the convergence of inputs from different sensory sources creates the necessary multisensory framework (i.e. a population of neurons with input from two or more modalities). In the second step, which occurs during postnatal development, and which I will call extrinsic, higher-order inputs provide the gating mechanism for nonlinear interactions in these neurons—the robust and dramatic changes in activity that have become the hallmark of multisensory integration. As with the development of most systems, this extrinsic step matures over an extended time frame, during which corresponding complexity and competence appear in the animal's behavioural repertoire. As opposed to the intrinsic circuitry, the extrinsic elements of this system are highly malleable and are sculpted dramatically by sensory experience. Thus, in the absence of certain cross-modal experiences, such as what happens under conditions of dark-rearing, normal multisensory integration fails to develop. This is presumed to be the result of the imposed immaturity of association cortex that results from the absence of visual experience, and the consequent lack of functional maturation of the gating inputs to subcortex.

Recently, a new interest has emerged in modelling multisensory processes with an eye toward the circuit relationships that characterise this system. Several classes of model, structured around the biological constraints of the SC circuitry, have been applied to this question. One of the most intriguing of these is based on Bayes's rule, and proposes that the SC neuron uses its sensory inputs to compute the probability of the presence (or absence) of a target (Anastasio, Patton, & Belkacem-Boussaid, 2000). Although this work has focused to date on trying to model these interactions in the mature nervous system, the insights that will be gleaned will no doubt have applicability for the developing system as well.

From a connectionist perspective, we can thus relate the functional appearance of multisensory behaviours to the interactive development of these circuits. Only upon their maturation is the synergism that characterises multisensory processes fully realised. It is with the coordinated action of these subcortical and cortical circuits that the true benefits of multisensory integration are apparent. These include the speeding of reactions to cross-modal stimuli, their greater detectability and salience, and the perceptual binding of stimuli from different modalities to form a continuous and seamless sensory gestalt.

CONCLUDING REMARKS

The development of cross-modal processes, like the development of each of the different sensory systems, is critically dependent on the experiences gathered during early postnatal life. Such experiences shape the manner in which stimuli from the different modalities are combined within the nervous system, as well as dictating the salience of these cross-modal combinations. Altering the normal associations between stimuli from the different senses compromises the ability of the nervous system to effectively utilise multiple sensory channels for behavioural and perceptual gain. Nonetheless, such changes appear to set in motion a cascade of events that may enhance the processing capabilities of the remaining modality(ies), compensating, at least in part, for the lost modality-specific and multisensory information. Although these data attest to the remarkably plastic nature of the developing brain, recent work in a variety of systems suggests that the adult brain may also have a significant capacity for such reorganisation. Characterising this adult plasticity in sensory and multisensory processes represents an exciting new realm in neuroscience research, and one that has profound implications for the treatment of nervous system disorders and damage.

REFERENCES

Anastasio, T. J., Patton, P. E., & Belkacem-Boussaid, K. (2000). Using Bayes' rule to model multisensory enhancement in the superior colliculus. *Neural Computation, 12,* 1165–1187.

Andreassi, J. L., & Greco, J. R. (1975). Effects of bisensory stimulation on reaction time and the evoked cortical potential. *Physiological Psychology, 3,* 189–194.

Arno, P., De Volder, A. G., Vanlierde, A., Wanet-Defalque, M. C., Streel, E., Robert, A. et al. (2001). Occipital activation by pattern recognition in the early blind using auditory substitution for vision. *Neuroimage, 13,* 632–645.

Bahrick, L. E. (1992). Infants' perceptual differentiation of amodal and modality-specific audio-visual relations. *Journal of Experimental Child Psychology, 53,* 180–199.

Bahrick, L. E. (1994). The development of infants' sensitivity to arbitrary intermodal relations. *Ecological Psychology, 2,* 111–123.

Bell, A. H., Corneil, B. D., Meredith, M. A. & Munoz, D. P. (2001). The influence of stimulus properties on multisensory processing in the awake primate superior colliculus. *Canadian Journal of Experimental Psychology, 55,* 123–132.

Bense, S., Stephan, T., Yousry, T. A., Brandt, T., & Dieterich, M. (2001). Multisensory cortical signal increases and decreases during vestibular galvanic stimulation (fMRI). *Journal of Neurophysiology, 85,* 886–899.

Bernstein, I. H., Clark, M. H., & Edelstein, B. A. (1969). Effects of an auditory signal on visual reaction time. *Journal of Experimental Psychology, 80,* 567–569.

Birch, H., & Lefford, A. (1963). Intersensory development in children. *Monographs of the Society for Research in Child Development, 28* (5, Serial No. 89), 1–47.

Birch, H., & Lefford, A. (1967). Visual differentiation, intersensory integration, and voluntary motor control. *Monographs of the Society for Research in Child Development, 32* (1, Serial No. 110), 1–42.

Bruce, C., Desimone, R., & Gross, C. G. (1981). Visual properties of neurons in a polysensory area in superior temporal sulcus of the macaque. *Journal of Neurophysiology, 46,* 369–384.

Bushara, K. O., Grafman, J., & Hallett, M. (2001). Neural correlates of auditory–visual stimulus onset asynchrony detection. *Journal of Neuroscience, 21,* 300–304.

Butterworth, G., & Castillo, M. (1976). Coordination of auditory and visual space in newborn human infants. *Perception, 5,* 155–160.

Calvert, G. A., Campbell, R., & Brammer, M. J. (2000). Evidence from functional magnetic resonance imaging of crossmodal binding in the human heteromodal cortex. *Current Biology, 10,* 649–657.

Clemo, H. R., & Stein, B. E. (1984). Topographic organization of somatosensory corticotectal influences in cat. *Journal of Neurophysiology, 51,* 843–858.

Cohen, L. G., Celnik, P., Pascual-Leone, A., Corwell, B., Falz, L., Dambrosia, J. et al. (1997). Functional relevance of cross-modal plasticity in blind humans. *Nature, 389,* 180–183.

Corneil, B. D., Van Wanrooij, M., Munoz, D. P. & Van Opstal, A. J. (2002). Auditory-visual interactions subserving goal-direct saccades in a complex scene. *Journal of Neurophysiology*, *88*, 438–454.

Cytowic, R. E. (1989). *Synesthesia: A union of the senses*. New York: Springer-Verlag.

Daw, N. W., Reid, S. N., Wang, X. F., & Flavin, H. J. (1995). Factors that are critical for plasticity in the visual cortex. *Ciba Foundation Symposium*, *193*, 258–276.

Day, R. H., & Wade, N. J. (1966). Visual spatial aftereffect from prolonged head-tilt. *Science*, *154*, 1201–1202.

Duhamel, J. R., Colby, C. L., & Goldberg, M. E. (1998). Ventral intraparietal area of the macaque: Congruent visual and somatic response properties. *Journal of Neurophysioloy*, *79*, 126–136.

Fogassi, L., Gallese, V., Fadiga, L., Luppino, G., Matelli, M., & Rizzolatti, G. (1996). Coding of peripersonal space in inferior premotor cortex (area F4). *Journal of Neurophysioloy*, *76*, 141–157.

Fox, M. W. (1970). Reflex development and behavioural organization. In W. A. Himwich (Ed.), *Developmental neurobiology* (pp. 553–580). Springfield, IL: Thomas.

Foxe, J. J., Morocz, I. A., Murray, M. M., Higgins, B. A., Javitt, D. C., & Schroeder, C. E. (2000). Multisensory auditory–somatosensory interactions in early cortical processing revealed by high-density electrical mapping. *Cognitive Brain Research*, *10*, 77–83.

Frens, M. A., & Van Opstal, A. J. (1998). Visual–auditory interactions modulate saccade-related activity in monkey superior colliculus. *Brain Research Bulletin*, *46*, 211–224.

Frens, M. A., Van Opstal, A. J., & Van der Willigen, R. F. (1995). Spatial and temporal factors determine auditory–visual interactions in human saccadic eye movements. *Perception & Psychophysics*, *57*, 802–816.

Giard, M. H., & Peronnet, F. (1999). Auditory–visual integration during multimodal object recognition in humans: A behavioral and electrophysiological study. *Journal of Cognitive Neuroscience*, *11*, 473–490.

Gielen, S. C., Schmidt, R. A., & Van den Heuvel, P. J. (1983). On the nature of intersensory facilitation of reaction time. *Perception & Psychophysics*, *34*, 161–168.

Goldring, J. E., Dorris, M. C., Corneil, B. D., Ballantyne, P. A., & Munoz, D. P. (1996). Combined eye-head gaze shifts to visual and auditory targets in humans. *Experimental Brain Research*, *111*, 68–78.

Gottlieb, G. (1971). Ontogenesis of sensory function in birds and mammals. In E. Tobach, L. R. Aronson, & E. Shaw (Eds.), *The biopsychology of development* (pp. 67–128). New York: Academic Press.

Graziano, M. S., Hu, X. T., & Gross, C. G. (1997). Visuospatial properties of ventral premotor cortex. *Journal of Neurophysiology*, *77*, 2268–2292.

Graziano, M. S., Reiss, L. A., & Gross, C. G. (1999). A neuronal representation of the location of nearby sounds. *Nature*, *397*, 428–430.

Grossenbacher, P. G., & Lovelace, C. T. (2001). Mechanisms of synesthesia: Cognitive and physiological constraints. *Trends in Cognitive Science*, *5*, 36–41.

Harrington, L. K., & Peck, C. K. (1998). Spatial disparity affects visual–auditory interactions in human sensorimotor processing. *Experimental Brain Research*, *122*, 247–252.

Harting, J. K., Feig, S., & Van Lieshout, D. P. (1997). Cortical somatosensory and trigeminal inputs to the cat superior colliculus: Light and electron microscopic analyses. *Journal of Comparative Neurology*, *388*, 313–326.

Harting, J. K., Updyke, B. V., & Van Lieshout, D. P. (1992). Corticotectal projections in the cat: Anterograde transport studies of twenty-five cortical areas. *Journal of Comparative Neurology*, *324*, 379–414.

Hershenson, M. (1962). Reaction time as a measure of intersensory facilitation. *Journal of Experimental Psychology*, *63*, 289–293.

Howard, I. P., & Templeton, W. B. (1966). *Human spatial orientation*. London: Wiley.

Huerta, M., & Harting, J. (1984). The mammalian superior colliculus: Studies of its morphology and connections. In H. Vanegas (Ed.), *Comparative neurology of the optic tectum* (pp. 687–773). New York: Plenum.

Hughes, H. C., Reuter-Lorenz, P. A., Nozawa, G., & Fendrich, R. (1994). Visual–auditory interactions in sensorimotor processing: Saccades versus manual responses. *Journal of Experimental Psychology: Human Perception and Performance, 20*, 131–153.

Humphrey, K., & Tees, R. (1980). Auditory–visual coordination in infancy: Some limitations of the preference methodology. *Bulletin of the Psychonomic Society, 16*, 213–216.

Jiang, W., Jiang, H. & Stein, B. E. (2002). Two corticotectal areas facilitate multisensory orientation behaviour. *Journal of Cognitive Neuroscience, 14*, 1240–1255.

Jiang, W., Wallace, M. T., Jiang, H., Vaughan, J. W., & Stein, B. E. (2001). Two cortical areas mediate multisensory integration in superior colliculus neurons. *Journal of Neurophysiology, 85*, 506–522.

Jousmaki, V., & Hari, R. (1998). Parchment-skin illusion: Sound biased touch. *Current Biology, 8*, R190.

Kadunce, D. C., Vaughan, J. W., Wallace, M. T., Benedek, G., & Stein, B. E. (1997). Mechanisms of within- and cross-modality suppression in the superior colliculus. *Journal of Neurophysiology, 78*, 2834–2847.

King, A. J., Hutchings, M. E., Moore, D. R., & Blakemore, C. (1988). Developmental plasticity in the visual and auditory representations in the mammalian superior colliculus. *Nature, 332*, 73–76.

Knudsen, E. I., & Brainard, M. S. (1991). Visual instruction of the neural map of auditory space in the developing optic tectum. *Science, 253*, 85–87.

Korte, M., & Rauschecker, J. P. (1993). Auditory spatial tuning of cortical neurons is sharpened in cats with early blindness. *Journal of Neurophysiology, 70*, 1717–1721.

Kujala, T., Alho, K., Huotilainen, M., Ilmoniemi, R. J., Lehtokoski, A., Leinonen, A. et al. (1997). Electrophysiological evidence for cross-modal plasticity in humans with early- and late-onset blindness. *Psychophysiology, 34*, 213–216.

Lessard, N., Pare, M., Lepore, F., & Lassonde, M. (1998). Early-blind human subjects localize sound sources better than sighted subjects. *Nature, 395*, 278–280.

Levine, M. S., Hull, C. D., & Buchwald, N. A. (1980). Development of motor activity in kittens. *Developmental Psychobiology, 13*, 357–371.

Lewkowicz, D. J. (1985). Bisensory response to temporal frequency in 4-month-old infants. *Developmental Psychology, 21*, 306–317.

Lewkowicz, D. J. (1986). Developmental changes in infants' bisensory response to synchronous durations. *Infant Behavior and Development, 9*, 335–353.

Lewkowicz, D. J. (1992a). Infants' responsiveness to the auditory and visual attributes of a sounding/moving stimulus. *Perception & Psychophysics, 52*, 519–528.

Lewkowicz, D. J. (1992b). Infants' response to temporally based intersensory equivalence: The effect of synchronous sounds on visual preferences for moving stimuli. *Behavior and Development, 15*, 297–324.

Lewkowicz, D. J. (1994). Limitations on infants' response to rate-based auditory–visual relations. *Developmental Psychology, 30*, 880–892.

Lewkowicz, D. J. (2000). The development of intersensory temporal perception: An epigenetic systems/limitations view. *Psychology Bulletin, 126*, 281–308.

Lewkowicz, D. J., & Turkewitz, G. (1980). Cross-modal equivalence in early infancy: Auditory–visual intensity matching. *Developmental Psychology, 16*, 597–607.

Maurer, D., & Maurer, C. (1988). *The world of the newborn*. New York: Basic Books.

McGurk, H., & MacDonald, J. (1976). Hearing lips and seeing voices. *Nature, 264*, 746–748.

McHaffie, J. G., Kruger, L., Clemo, H. R., & Stein, B. E. (1988). Corticothalamic and corticotectal somatosensory projections from the anterior ectosylvian sulcus (SIV cortex) in neonatal cats: An anatomical demonstration with HRP and 3H-leucine. *Journal of Comparative Neurology, 274,* 115–126.

McHaffie, J. G., & Stein, B. E. (1982). Eye movements evoked by electrical stimulation in the superior colliculus of rats and hamsters. *Brain Research, 247,* 243–253.

Meltzoff, A. N., & Borton, R. W. (1979). Intermodal matching by human neonates. *Nature, 282,* 403–404.

Meltzoff, A. N., & Moore, M. K. (1977). Imitation of facial and manual gestures by human neonates. *Science, 198,* 74–78.

Meredith, M. A., & Clemo, H. R. (1989). Auditory cortical projection from the anterior ectosylvian sulcus (Field AES) to the superior colliculus in the cat: An anatomical and electrophysiological study. *Journal of Comparative Neurology, 289,* 687–707.

Meredith, M. A., Nemitz, J. W., & Stein, B. E. (1987). Determinants of multisensory integration in superior colliculus neurons. 1: Temporal factors. *Journal of Neuroscience, 7,* 3215–3229.

Meredith, M. A., & Stein, B. E. (1986a). Spatial factors determine the activity of multisensory neurons in cat superior colliculus. *Brain Research, 365,* 350–354.

Meredith, M. A., & Stein, B. E. (1986b). Visual, auditory, and somatosensory convergence on cells in superior colliculus results in multisensory integration. *Journal of Neurophysiology, 56,* 640–662.

Morrell, L. K. (1968). Cross-modality effects upon choice reaction time. *Psychonom Science, 11,* 129–130.

Neville, H. J., Schmidt, A., & Kutas, M. (1983). Altered visual-evoked potentials in congenitally deaf adults. *Brain Research, 266,* 127–132.

Norita, M., Mucke, L., Benedek, G., Albowitz, B., Katoh, Y., & Creutzfeldt, O. D. (1986). Connections of the anterior ectosylvian visual area (AEV). *Experimental Brain Research, 62,* 225–240.

Nozawa, G., Reuter-Lorenz, P. A., & Hughes, H. C. (1994). Parallel and serial processes in the human oculomotor system: Bimodal integration and express saccades. *Biological Cybernetics, 72,* 19–34.

Perrott, D. R., Saberi, K., Brown, K., & Strybel, T. Z. (1990). Auditory psychomotor coordination and visual search performance. *Perception & Psychophysics, 48,* 214–226.

Piaget, J. (1952). *The origins of intelligence in children.* New York: International Universities Press.

Ramachandran, R., Wallace, M. T., Clemo, H. R., & Stein, B. E. (1993). Multisensory convergence and integration in rat cortex. *Society of Neuroscience Abstracts, 19,* 1447.

Rauschecker, J. P., & Kniepert, U. (1994). Auditory localization behavior in visually deprived cats. *European Journal of Neuroscience, 6,* 149–160.

Rauschecker, J. P., & Korte, M. (1993). Auditory compensation for early blindness in cat cerebral cortex. *Journal of Neuroscience, 13,* 4538–4548.

Rizzolatti, G., Scandolara, C., Matelli, M., & Gentilucci, M. (1981). Afferent properties of periarcuate neurons in macaque monkeys. II. Visual responses. *Behavioral Brain Research, 2,* 147–163.

Robinson, D. A. (1972). Eye movements evoked by collicular stimulation in the alert monkey. *Vision Research, 12,* 1795–1808.

Roder, B., Rosler, F., Hennighausen, E., & Nacker, F. (1996). Event-related potentials during auditory and somatosensory discrimination in sighted and blind human subjects. *Cognitive Brain Research, 4,* 77–93.

Roder, B., Teder-Salejarvi, W., Sterr, A., Rosler, F., Hillyard, S. A., & Neville, H. J. (1999). Improved auditory spatial tuning in blind humans. *Nature, 400,* 162–166.

Roe, A. W., Pallas, S. L., Hahm, J. O., & Sur, M. (1990). A map of visual space induced in primary auditory cortex. *Science, 250,* 818–820.

Roe, A. W., Pallas, S. L., Kwon, Y. H., & Sur, M. (1992). Visual projections routed to the auditory pathway in ferrets: Receptive fields of visual neurons in primary auditory cortex. *Journal of Neuroscience, 12*, 3651–3664.

Sadato, N., Pascual-Leone, A., Grafman, J., Ibañez, V., Deiber, M. P., Dold, G., & Hallett, M. (1996). Activation of the primary visual cortex by Braille reading in blind subjects. *Nature, 380*, 526–528.

Schiller, P. H., & Stryker, M. (1972). Single-unit recording and stimulation in superior colliculus of the alert rhesus monkey. *Journal of Neurophysiology, 35*, 915–924.

Segal, R. L., & Beckstead, R. M. (1984). The lateral suprasylvian corticotectal projection in cats. *Journal of Comparative Neurology, 225*, 259–275.

Shams, L., Kamitani, Y., & Shimojo, S. (2000). Illusions. What you see is what you hear. *Nature, 408*, 788.

Sharma, J., Angelucci, A., & Sur, M. (2000). Induction of visual orientation modules in auditory cortex. *Nature, 404*, 841–847.

Spelke, E. S. (1994). Preferential looking and intermodal perception in infancy. *Infant Behavior and Development, 17*, 284–286.

Stein, B. E., & Clamann, H. P. (1981). Control of pinna movements and sensorimotor register in cat superior colliculus. *Brain Behavior and Evolution, 19*, 180–192.

Stein, B. E., Goldberg, S. J., & Clamann, H. P. (1976). The control of eye movements by the superior colliculus in the alert cat. *Brain Research, 118*, 469–474.

Stein, B. E., Huneycutt, W. S., & Meredith, M. A. (1988). Neurons and behavior: The same rules of multisensory integration apply. *Brain Research, 448*, 355–358.

Stein, B. E., Labos, E., & Kruger, L. (1973). Sequence of changes in properties of neurons of superior colliculus of the kitten during maturation. *Journal of Neurophysiology, 36*, 667–679.

Stein, B. E., Magalhaes-Castro, B., & Kruger, L. (1976). Relationship between visual and tactile representations in cat superior colliculus. *Journal of Neurophysiology, 39*, 401–419.

Stein, B. E., & Meredith, M. A. (1993). *The merging of the senses.* Cambridge, MA: MIT Press.

Stein, B., Meredith, M., Huneycutt, W., & McDade, L. (1989). Behavioral indices of multisensory integration: Orientation to visual cues is affected by auditory stimuli. *Journal of Cognitive Neuroscience, 1*, 12–24.

Stein, B. E., Spencer, R. F., & Edwards, S. B. (1983). Corticotectal and corticothalamic efferent projections of SIV somatosensory cortex in cat. *Journal of Neurophysiology, 50*, 896–909.

Sur, M., Garraghty, P. E., & Roe, A. W. (1988). Experimentally induced visual projections into auditory thalamus and cortex. *Science, 242*, 1437–1441.

Villablanca, J. R., & Olmstead, C. E. (1979). Neurological development of kittens. *Developmental Psychobiology, 12*, 101–127.

von Melchner, L., Pallas, S. L., & Sur, M. (2000). Visual behaviour mediated by retinal projections directed to the auditory pathway. *Nature, 404*, 871–876.

Wallace, M. T. Hairston, W.D., & Stein, B. E. (2001). Long-term effects of dark-rearing on multisensory processing. *Society of Neuroscience Abstracts, 27*, 1340.

Wallace, M. T., McHaffie, J. G., & Stein, B. E. (1997). Visual response properties and visuotopic representation in the newborn monkey superior colliculus. *Journal of Neurophysiology, 78*, 2732–2741.

Wallace, M. T., Meredith, M. A., & Stein, B. E. (1992). Integration of multiple sensory modalities in cat cortex. *Experimental Brain Research, 91*, 484–488.

Wallace, M. T., & Stein, B. E. (1994). Cross-modal synthesis in the midbrain depends on input from cortex. *Journal of Neurophysiology, 71*, 429–432.

Wallace, M. T., & Stein, B. E. (1996). Sensory organization of the superior colliculus in cat and monkey. *Progress in Brain Research, 112*, 301–311.

Wallace, M. T., & Stein, B. E. (1997). Development of multisensory neurons and multisensory integration in cat superior colliculus. *Journal of Neuroscience, 17*, 2429–2444.

Wallace, M. T., & Stein, B. E. (2000a). Onset of cross-modal synthesis in the neonatal superior colliculus is gated by the development of cortical influences. *Journal of Neurophysiology, 83,* 3578–3582.

Wallace, M. T., & Stein, B. E. (2000b). The role of experience in the development of multisensory integration. *Society of Neuroscience Abstracts, 26,* 1220.

Wallace, M.T., & Stein, B. E. (2001). Sensory and multisensory responses in the newborn monkey superior colliculus. *Journal of Neuroscience, 21,* 8886–8894.

Wallace, M. T., Wilkinson, L. K., & Stein, B. E. (1996). Representation and integration of multiple sensory inputs in primate superior colliculus. *Journal of Neurophysiology, 76,* 1246–1266.

Weeks, R., Horwitz, B., Aziz-Sultan, A., Tian, B., Wessinger, C. M., Cohen, L. G., Hallett, M., & Rauschecker, J. P. (2000). A positron emission tomographic study of auditory localization in the congenitally blind. *Journal of Neuroscience, 20,* 2664–2672.

Wilkinson, L. K., Meredith, M. A., & Stein, B. E. (1996). The role of anterior ectosylvian cortex in cross-modality orientation and approach behavior. *Experimental Brain Research, 112,* 1–10.

Withington-Wray, D. J., Binns, K. E., & Keating, M. J. (1990). The maturation of the superior collicular map of auditory space in the guinea pig is disrupted by developmental visual deprivation. *European Journal of Neuroscience, 2,* 682–692.

CHAPTER ELEVEN

Evolutionary connectionism

Peter McLeod and Bodo Maass
Department of Experimental Psychology, University of Oxford, UK.

Connectionist models usually start with a predetermined architecture—a set number of units with a fixed pattern of connectivity between them. The network develops in response to its environment by adapting the strengths of the connections with a learning algorithm. The final state of the network is determined by the initial architecture, the environment and the learning algorithm.

Evolutionary connectionism is a different approach to the way a network develops. Information about the network is stored in a "genome". What is stored varies from simulation to simulation but might include any, or all of, the structure of the network (i.e. what's connected to what), the weights of the connections, and the learning rule for each connection. The network develops by a process that mimics evolution by natural selection. Networks derived from variants of an initial genome perform a task and those that are more successful are selected to produce the next generation. New genomes are created either by mutation of the genomes of the selected networks or by splitting and rejoining the genomes as in sexual reproduction. The networks derived from the new genomes then perform the task. Those that are successful provide the genomes that will be the basis of the next generation of networks and so on.

There is no guarantee that this process will produce a network that can perform the task. But, if a successful network does emerge, it is not one whose structure was decided in advance by the experimenter. Nor is there a learning algorithm that knows the goal towards which the network should move and changes the weights to direct the network towards that goal. The structure and weights of the successful network are the result of blind evolutionary forces, capitalising on anything that led to improved performance in previous generations.

Evolutionary connectionism is a powerful technique. A conventional connectionist model searches the weight space associated with its architecture to try to find a set of weights that can solve the problem it faces. An evolutionary network also searches the space of possible architectures given the resource limitations of numbers of units, possible learning rules, and so on, that the simulation was provided with. Naturally, this technique can discover networks that solve difficult problems. Perhaps more surprisingly, by allowing the evolutionary process to discard unnecessary units, it can discover simple solutions to difficult problems. Our intuitions about the difficulty of the information processing problems facing the developing child can bear little relationship to what the associationist mechanisms of connectionist networks discover about the environments they are placed in.

We will follow three simulations. They share the same overall approach but the information stored in the genome, and hence the way the network evolves, is different in each case. In the first simulation only the weights of a fixed structure evolve; in the second the weights, the structure, and the learning rule for each connection evolve; in the third the weights and the structure evolve.

The first simulation demonstrates how a network that initially produces random behaviour can find a set of weights that produce goal-oriented behaviour without the guidance of a learning algorithm. Evolution of weights provides an alternative to a gradient-descent learning algorithm such as back-propagation for solving a problem with a multilayer network.

The second simulation models the relationship between innate and acquired knowledge in an infant learning to recognise speech. The structure of the network evolves and this evolving structure is handed on to the next generation, simulating the processes that, across evolution, have given rise to the information-processing mechanism the infant has at birth. This structure is modified by the environment it enters, simulating the effects of acoustic experience on the infant. In this example, unlike the other two, the networks are allowed to adapt to the environment in which they are placed. The speech they hear changes the weights of connections in the network. Those networks that are better at distinguishing between different phonemes after brief exposure to speech are selected to produce the next generation. (They pass on only their initial structure, not what they learn.) The result is the evolution of networks that have no wired-in representation of the acoustic features that underlie speech recognition but which start to develop such representations after a few minutes of exposure to language. The speed with which they can do this shows that categorical perception of speech within a few hours of birth, often presented as a demonstration that speech recognition mechanisms have an innate representation of the features that underlie speech, could be the result of an innate mechanism capable of ultra-rapid learning in the presence of speech.

The third simulation is of a child learning to catch—a classic example of an implicit learning task. Evolutionary connectionist models offer a natural approach to understanding the acquisition of behaviour that develops without an explicit teacher. Like a child, the networks are not told *how* to catch a ball, but those that get nearest to the ball when it lands are selected to produce the next generation. The simulation demonstrates how a network can discover a solution to a complex perceptual–motor coordination problem without having a teacher that knows a solution to the problem in advance and changes the weights of connections until the network embodies that solution. The simple solution that it discovers for an apparently complex problem suggests how this problem might be solved by people.

This chapter will discuss the general principles of evolutionary connectionism rather than the technical details of genome design and selection. For a discussion of specific evolutionary algorithms see Goldberg (1989).

WEIGHT EVOLUTION AND THE EMERGENCE OF GOAL-DIRECTED BEHAVIOUR

The way that evolutionary networks develop can be seen in a simple simulation that shows how goal-directed behaviour can evolve from random behaviour in the absence of a learning rule. Nolfi, Elman, and Parisi (1994) modelled an organism that wandered through a two-dimensional world where food was distributed at random. It consumed any food it bumped into. The organism's behaviour was controlled by a feedforward network with input, hidden, and output units. The input units received information about the direction of the nearest food and about the organism's last action. The activity of the output units determined the direction of the organism's next step, forwards, left, or right.

An initial network was created with random connection weights. Variants of this were produced by mutation of the weight matrix and allowed to wander through the world. The organisms that consumed the most food in a given number of steps were selected and, after random mutation of their weight matrices, became the next generation. The rate of consumption of food increased steadily across generations. Figure 11.1 shows typical pathways through the environment for first- and fiftieth-generation organisms. The first-generation organism moves through the environment bumping into food (F) by chance. The fiftieth-generation organism appears to have a clear-cut goal of moving towards the nearest food. Individual organisms were not taught to move towards food. That is, there was no weight change during the life of an organism. Selection and weight mutation across generations achieved the

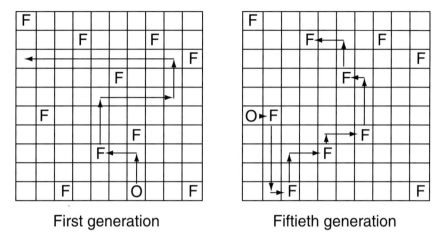

First generation   Fiftieth generation

Figure 11.1.   Paths taken from randomly selected start points (O) with the same food pattern for organisms in the first and fiftieth generations. (Based on Nolfi, Elman, & Parisi, 1994.)

same result that would have been achieved in a single organism by a learning algorithm that changed the weights of connections so that movement towards food would become more likely

The weights of the connections in an individual organism place it somewhere in a weight versus fitness space (where fitness is a measure of success in eating food). This is shown schematically in Figure 11.2 with a weight space of two dimensions. The surface shows the fitness associated with every possible combination of weights. (Of course, the networks are in a higher dimensional space as they have many more than two weights, but the principle is the same.) High values of fitness correspond to weight patterns that produce activation of the output units that drives the organism towards food; low values correspond to weight patterns which are not effective at driving the network towards food. The position of a parent organism is indicated by +. Random mutation of the weight matrix creates a set of organisms that occupy positions in weight space around it indicated by the oval. The mutated organisms that get weights corresponding to higher fitness (i.e. lower points on the surface) are more effective at finding food. These will be selected and their genomes will be the basis of the next set of mutated variants.

The overall result across generations is the development of a weight pattern that causes the organism to move towards low points on the weight versus fitness surface. That is, to move towards food. This is similar in effect to the process of error reduction by weight change that a gradient-descent learning algorithm achieves across trials within a single network. However, random mutation and selection can be a more effective way of discovering the global minimum of the weight versus fitness space than gradient descent. A

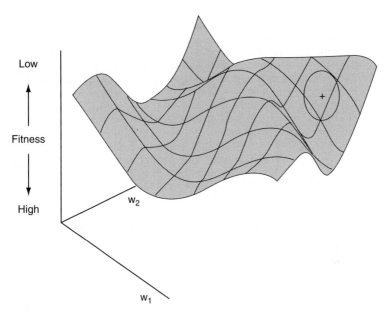

Figure 11.2.   A surface showing the fitness of all possible combinations of two weights. + marks the position in weight space and corresponding fitness of a parent network. The oval shows the area of the surface that may be explored by its mutated offspring.

gradient-descent algorithm works on a single network, moving it in the direction of steepest descent from its current position. This can lead the network to a local minimum in the weight space where it stays. The creation and testing of a set of networks by random mutation of the original weight matrix allows the fitness associated with a range of positions in weight space to be assessed. Consequently, the danger of the simulation getting stuck in a local minimum is reduced. Back-propagation is often considered to be an undesirable learning algorithm in simulations where one of the aims is biological plausibility. This form of evolution demonstrates how training of multilayer networks by gradient descent can be achieved without back-propagation.

The evolutionary advantage of the ability to learn

In an intriguing twist to this simulation Nolfi et al. (1994) added a second pair of output units. The activation level of these was interpreted as the network's prediction of what the angle and distance of the nearest food would be after it had made its next move. On each trial, the output of these units was compared with the actual angle and distance to the nearest food after it had moved and the discrepancy used to change the weights by back-propagation. Note that these weight changes were not related to the organism's success in eating, only to its success in prediction. The selection procedure worked as before—those organisms that were most successful at bumping into food were chosen to produce the next generation. The next generation was produced by mutating the *original* weight matrix of successful networks—not the matrix that had developed as a result of learning the prediction task. There was no Lamarckian inheritance of acquired characteristics in this simulation.

The networks developed the ability to move towards food more quickly than those in the first simulation, which were not trained to predict. It might seem obvious that organisms that can predict the position of food would be better at moving towards it. But, in fact, the prediction units did not influence the direction in which the organism moved. They were just another pair of output units—they could not help the network to move towards food. So the possession of a capacity (predicting the direction of food after a movement) that did not influence the behaviour that was the basis of selection (moving towards food) led to a selective advantage for the organism!

This apparently paradoxical result can be understood by considering the position of competing networks in the weight versus fitness space. Figure 11.3 shows two networks that have different weight matrices (so they are at different

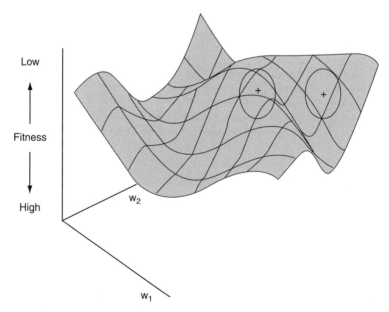

Figure 11.3.   The position of two networks on a weight versus fitness surface. The ovals show the regions of this surface explored as they learn the prediction task.

positions on the surface, shown by the +s) but which are equally effective at finding food. That is, they have the same value of fitness. The learning algorithm for the prediction task changes the network weights, causing each network to move from its starting position into the nearby region of weight space during its life time. The movement is to a position that produces better prediction. If, by chance, this also leads to better food consumption, that network is more likely to be selected to breed the next generation. Thus the weight changes that produce better prediction also, incidentally, identify networks that are close to a region of weight space that will produce more effective eating behaviour (i.e. to low points on the surface). The weight changes acquired during learning that led to more effective eating are not passed on. But the chance mutation may take the next generation network into this region, leading to more effective eating behaviour. Thus the capacity to learn—that is, allowing an organism to explore its own weight space—can lead to the selection of networks for reproduction that have the potential for more effective behaviour in future generations, even though what is learnt by an individual is not passed on.

EVOLUTION OF LEARNING RULES AND THE RECOGNITION OF SPEECH

The first simulation placed new networks into the same environment as their parents. Each one was tested to see how well it performed the task but it did not learn as a result of its experiences. In the next simulation, each network adapts to the environment it experiences by changing its weights. Fitness is measured by how quickly a network adapts. The structure the successful networks started with is passed on to the next generation, not the weights acquired during learning. The question is whether a general network structure that is good at adapting quickly to the sort of problem presented by an environment can evolve across generations, even when the environmental experiences of parent and child differ.

The form of this simulation was driven by the observation that infants show categorical perception of speech sounds within a few hours of birth. That is, they treat sounds such as /p/ and /b/, which lie on either side of a speech category boundary, as different, and those within a category, such as variants of /p/, as the same even when the acoustic differences between the /p/ and /b/ are less than those between the variants of /p/. What is more, they show categorical perception of sounds in categories that do not occur in the language environment into which they are born. The natural conclusion is that infants are born with an acoustic analysis system into which the structures necessary to detect the contrasts which distinguish the elements of human speech are prewired. That is, they have an innate representation of the acoustic features that divide speech sounds in categories. However, there is an alternative to this view. Jusczyk and Bertoncini (1988) suggested that the hard-wiring that allows categorical perception shortly after birth might be of structures that are acutely sensitive to the acoustic contrasts that distinguish elements in natural languages, but that the particular form they take will depend on the language environment into which the infant is born. On this view, the innate wiring is seen as setting up structures that guide the direction development will take after exposure to speech rather than as determining the development itself (a distinction explored in detail by Elman, Bates, Johnson, Karmiloff-Smith, Parisi, & Plunkett, 1996).

Given that infants show categorical perception a few hours after birth, the structures would have to start representing speech contrasts after very little experience of language. Nakisa and Plunkett (1998) devised an evolutionary connectionist simulation to see whether structures could evolve that would show ultra-rapid acquisition of feature-detection ability after exposure to language. They exposed networks to speech and their connection weights changed in response to their experience. After a few minutes exposure to speech and adaptation by weight change, their response to novel speech was tested. Those networks that had developed sensitivity to the features that underlie the categories into which speech sounds are classed were selected. These networks provided the genomes to create the networks for the next generation after random splitting and reconnection. Successful networks handed on the genes that determined their structure to the next generation but not the connection weights that they had acquired through their exposure to speech. New networks all started with random connections.

The simulation

The general architecture is illustrated in Figure 11.4. Each network had 64 input units and 8 output units. The input was the amplitude of the speech spectrum of English sentences sampled in 64 frequency bands between 0 and 8 kHz. Eight output units were chosen as this is claimed to be the number of features necessary for distinguishing human speech sounds. The 64 input units were divided into 16 groups of 4 with mutually inhibitory connections between the units within each group. Given this basic architecture, a family of 50 variants was produced for each generation by randomising the following parameters:

(1) Each input group was connected to each of the 8 output units with a connection probability of 0.2. Output units could have recurrent connections to themselves but could not be connected to input units. Thus the network was feedforward (with the exception of possible recurrent activity of output units) with no hidden units.
(2) Associated with each connection was a learning rule. The basic

Featural output

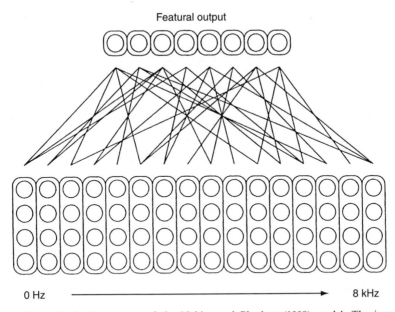

0 Hz ——————————————→ 8 kHz

Figure 11.4. The basic structure of the Nakisa and Plunkett (1998) model. The input is speech, broken into 64 bands between 0 and 8 kHz. The output is interpreted as speech features. (Reproduced with permission from Nakisa & Plunkett, 1998.)

learning rules contained Hebbian, anti-Hebbian, and weight decay elements. That is, the rule increased or decreased the strength of a connection depending on the activity of the units on either side of the connection and the current strength of the connection. The use of a learning rule that only uses information local to the connection being modified is an important constraint in making this a plausible simulation of processes that might occur in infants, as such learning is known to take place in the brain (Rolls & Treves, 1998). A pool of possible rules was created by varying the weighting of the Hebbian, anti-Hebbian, and weight decay components, and the learning rate constant. A rule was selected at random from this pool for each connection.

(3) Each input group or output unit had a time decay parameter determining how quickly its activation decayed.

The connectivity of each input group or output unit, the learning rule and learning rate constant for each connection, and the time decay associated with each unit was stored in the genome.

Training and evaluation

The input to the network came from a digitised set of short English sentences divided into 10 ms samples. The energy in each of the 64 frequency bands in the first 10 ms sample was presented to the input units and the resulting activity spread through the network. The weight of each connection was then adjusted depending on the activity of the units on either side of the connection and the current connection weight, according to the learning rule for that connection. Activity decayed in each unit according to its time decay parameter, the next 10-ms sample was presented to the input units, activity propagated and weights were adjusted according to activity levels, until the end of the sentence. This procedure was followed for 30 sentences, corresponding to about 2 minutes of speech. The sentences were taken at random from a large corpus so each network experienced a different sample of speech during training.

At this point training stopped and the network was tested on new sentences with the connection weights established during exposure to the training sentences. The test took a phonemic transcription of the new sentences and recorded the pattern of activity on the output units at the midpoint of each phoneme. The fitness of each network was computed with a function that favoured those that produced a similar pattern of activation at the output units for occurrences of the same phoneme and different patterns for different phonemes. Thus successful networks were those that had found a way of identifying the features that underlie the categorisation of speech sounds. The genomes of successful networks were split and rejoined to produce the next generation of networks.

Performance

After a few thousand generations, networks evolved that, after 2 minutes exposure to language, produced similar output patterns for the same phonemes and different output patterns for different phonemes. The simulation shows that the evolution of a structure that can build feature detectors for speech in response to very brief exposure to speech, despite starting with random connections weights, is possible. This is the "innately guided" principle proposed by Jusczyk and Bertoncini (1988) and by Elman et al. (1996).

Nakisa and Plunkett demonstrated three ways in which successful networks behaved like infants. First, they showed categorical perception. That is, small differences at input caused large changes in the output of the network if they occurred across a phonemic boundary. Prior to training, the networks did not show this shift. Second, they performed equally well in any language, not just the one they were trained on. Networks were trained on a variety of languages such as Cantonese or Urdu and then tested on English. Like infants, their ability to respond appropriately to the English test sentences was more or less equivalent after training in any language. Third, successful networks grouped phonemes into clusters in a way that is reminiscent of the behaviour of adult English speakers. That is, the network divided the input patterns into categories, producing similar output for different phonemes within a category and dissimilar output for phonemes falling in different categories. The categories were stops, fricatives, voiced consonants, and vowels, similar to the categories used by English-speaking adults.

Nakisa and Plunkett's demonstration that a structure with the ability to learn very rapidly in response to speech input exists does not, of course, prove that infants are born with such a structure. However, the similarity of the behaviour of the networks to that of infants is striking. There is also some similarity between what happens in the simulation and normal human development. We, as a species, have evolved to recognise speech. The structural evolution in the simulation might mimic the processes which have taken place during human evolution. What the network learns during its lifetime mimics what the individual child learns with the structure it has acquired through evolution. This is an effective way to learn as evolution starts the child with a structure that is already quite close to a global minimum so it is unlikely to get stuck in a local minimum as it learns.

STRUCTURAL EVOLUTION AND THE DISCOVERY OF A VISUAL–MOTOR COORDINATION ALGORITHM

The first simulation showed how a network can acquire a simple skill—moving towards visually specified points in the environment—by evolution of weights rather than by weight change following a learning rule. In this example we will follow a simulation in which the skill to be acquired is more complex—watching a ball hit in the air and moving to the right place to catch it before it hits the ground. Here, there is no equivalent of the simple algorithm in the first example to solve the problem. If the network always moves towards the ball it will fail to catch those that are going to go over its head (if it has the same limitations on maximum running speed as a human fielder). The network must learn to move towards the place where the ball will land, not towards the ball. If the ball is going to land in front of it, it must move towards the ball; if it is going to land behind, it must move away from the ball. Similarly, it must learn to move at an appropriate speed. If the ball is going to land near, it can move slowly. But if the ball is going to land far away it must move fast, as soon as possible, to maximise its chances of catching the ball.

The ease with which many children learn to catch may make this task sound easier than it is! A typical problem for a fielder in a game like cricket or baseball is illustrated in Figure 11.5. This shows the trajectories of three balls

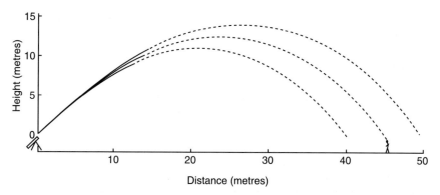

Figure 11.5.   The trajectories of three balls projected at 45° and velocities of approximately 22, 24 and 26 m/s towards a fielder 45 m away. The solid lines show the first 840 ms of each flight; the dashed lines the remainder.

projected with the same initial launch angle and slightly different velocities towards a fielder 45 m away. They will land 5 m in front of, at, or 5 m behind the fielder. The solid line shows the trajectory of each ball for the first 840 m; the dashed line shows the rest of the flight. Within 840 m of the ball being launched, a competent fielder would have started to run forward for the ball on the lower trajectory and back for the one on the higher. Yet the only difference between the trajectories at this time is the difference between the longest and shortest solid lines. The fielder must learn how to use this information to predict whether the ball will land behind or in front, and start moving in the appropriate direction.

McLeod and Dienes (1996) studied skilled fielders catching balls on trajectories such as those shown in Figure 11.5 and showed that they ran at a speed that kept the acceleration of the tangent of the angle of elevation of gaze to the ball at zero. (The angle of elevation of gaze is the angle above the horizontal through which the fielder has to raise his or her gaze to keep his or her eye on the ball.)[1] Although the fielder's behaviour is consistent with use of this algorithm, it sounds somewhat implausible as a human interception strategy. The tangent of an angle is an unlikely quantity for the nervous system to compute and people are not good at detecting acceleration.

Maass (1997) gave this problem to an evolutionary network—trying to catch balls thrown on similar trajectories and from a similar distance to those used by McLeod and Dienes—to see whether the network could learn to catch the ball and, if so, whether it would run in the same way as human

---

[1] Successful interception requires that the angle of gaze to the ball increases during its flight (for reasons explained in McLeod & Dienes, 1996) but it must not reach 90° or the ball will go over the fielder's head. Nulling the acceleration of the tangent of the angle of gaze achieves both these goals.

fielders. As we shall see, not only does the network produce catching behaviour that is similar to that of skilled human fielders but it also runs at a speed that keeps the acceleration of the tangent of the angle of gaze at zero, just like the fielders. The way that the network implements this apparently obscure algorithm may reflect the mechanism used by people. In fact, the simulation shows that it is much simpler to implement than it might appear and requires neither the computation of a tangent nor the detection of acceleration.

Learning to catch is an example of unsupervised learning—no one tells a child how to catch a ball. The child is told what the goal is—to try to intercept the ball before it hits the ground—and to keep its eye on the ball. It is then left to discover how to convert the sensory information that comes from watching the ball into appropriate actions for moving to the right place to catch it. To simulate what is learnt when an untutored skill is acquired we must not presuppose a solution and use an error correction algorithm to teach that solution to the network. We must see what the network can discover for itself in an environment with the same stimuli and feedback that are available to a child. A child watches balls thrown towards it, so the network is given the information the child would get from watching the ball. The child attempts to move towards the place where the ball will land and gets feedback about how close it was to the ball when it landed, so this is the feedback that is used as the basis of selection among network variants. Those that get near to the ball are used as the basis for the next generation.

The simulation

Figure 11.6 shows the general structure of the simulation. Realistic ball trajectories (i.e. ones that allow for the effects of wind resistance on the flight of the ball) were generated. The angle of elevation of gaze (α) from the network to the ball was calculated and successive values of α at time intervals of 0.15 s used as input to the network. The network's output was interpreted as the acceleration of the viewing point.

The structure of the network was encoded in a genome consisting of a set of genes, one for each unit in the network. The information in the gene defined the computational properties of that unit. It indicated which other units it was connected to, the strength of the connections, the bias of the unit and the slope of its sigmoidal activation function. The gene also held a parameter to indicate whether or not it was active. If this parameter was switched off in the random mutation phase the unit simply passed its input on without any modification. That is, it was lost as a computational unit to the network. The network parameters chosen *a priori* were: (1) the maximum number of input units (i.e. the number of previous angles of gaze that the network could use in its computation)—set at 3; (2) the maximum number of hidden units;

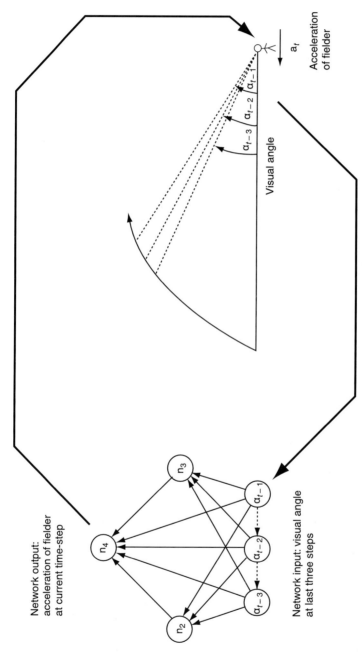

Network output:
acceleration of fielder
at current time-step

Network input: visual angle
at last three steps

Visual angle

Acceleration
of fielder

Figure 11.6. The network as a fielder. The network watches balls thrown towards it, generating an angle of elevation of gaze at α, time t. The three most recent angles of gaze are the input to the network (indicated by the lower solid arrow). They feed through to produce an output that is interpreted as an acceleration of the viewing point (indicated by the upper solid arrow). The movement of the viewing point influences the new value of α. The network discovers a movement strategy that controls the rate of change of α in a way that ensures that the ball will be intercepted.

and (3) the constraint of feedforward architecture. The parameters that were allowed to change during evolution were the number of input and hidden units, which units were connected to which, and the weights of the connections.

Training

Each network was presented with the angle of gaze it would get from watching the trajectories of 20 balls launched with an initial angle randomly chosen from the range 40° to 50° and the initial velocity from the range 21 m/s to 27 m/s. The networks started 45 m away from the projection point, waited for 0.5 s before starting to move and were allowed a maximum acceleration of 3 m/s², a maximum speed of 6 m/s when running forwards and 4 m/s when running back. (The pause time and values for maximum velocity and acceleration were based on the performance of the human fielders reported by McLeod & Dienes, 1996.) From the new position of the ball and the network the next angle of elevation of gaze was calculated and became the input to the first input unit at the next time-step. This was repeated until the ball hit the ground or went over the network.

Evaluation

The fitness of individual networks was evaluated by seeing how close they came on average to the place where the ball landed in the 20 trajectories they faced. After a population of 100 networks had been evaluated the next generation of 100 networks was created. Fitness-proportionate selection was used such that if the fitness of network A was twice that of network B then A's genome would be twice as likely to be selected for the reproduction pool as B's. For each new network two parents were selected at random. The parent genomes were divided at a random crossover point that could be at the boundary between any two genes. The child genome received the genetic information of the first parent up to the crossover point and from the second parent afterwards. A few elements of the new genome were then changed to new random values. This mutation ensured that new genes entered the population so the process of evolution was more than just a reorganisation of an unchanging gene pool.

Performance

Many networks that could intercept 100 per cent of the balls thrown at them (defined as a mean terminal error of less than 10 cm) evolved. Figure 11.7 shows a comparison between the running patterns produced by a skilled human fielder studied by McLeod and Dienes (left-hand side) and those

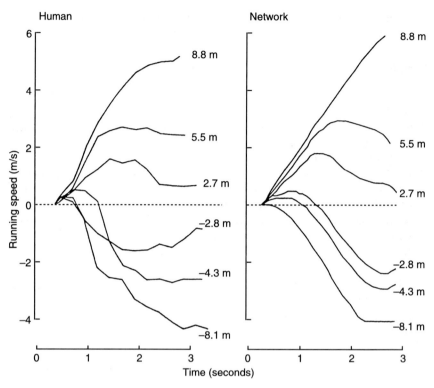

Figure 11.7. Left: the running speed, as a function of time, of a human fielder running to catch balls falling 8.8 m, 5.5 m, or 2.7 m in front, or 2.8 m, 4.3 m, or 8.1 m behind. Right: the running speed of the network when faced with balls on the same trajectories as the human. The network got to within less than 10 cm of each ball.

produced by a successful network (right-hand side) when balls were hit on the same trajectory to the network as they had been to the human. The curves show the fielder's/network's velocity throughout the catch, ending at the time when the ball was caught. The number after the curve indicates how many metres the fielder/network had to run to catch the ball.

The network produces behaviour that, at a qualitative level, is strikingly similar to that of the fielder: (1) They are both moving at the moment when they intercept the ball, that is, they do not predict where the ball will land, go there, and wait for it; rather the interception algorithm takes them to the point where the ball will fall at the precise time that the ball arrives; (2) there is no consistent running pattern. They do not, for example, run to the catching point at constant velocity. If they have to run 8 m they accelerate continuously. For balls landing 4–6 m away they accelerate and then run at a roughly constant velocity. For balls landing nearer they accelerate, then decelerate, and are almost stationary when they intercept the ball; (3) when the ball is going overhead they sometimes takes an initial step in the wrong direction.

What controls the speed at which the network runs?

Figure 11.8 shows a successful network. Surprisingly, this network has dropped one input node during evolution. Although this was not common among successful networks, we will study this one because it is easy to demonstrate graphically how a network with two input nodes achieves interception.

Watching the ball generates values of α, which change with time. The left of Figure 11.9 shows a set of α versus time values for a ball trajectory. Successive values of α, α_t and α_{t-1}, become the input to the network. The right of Figure 11.9 shows the sign of the network's output, which determines the acceleration of the viewing point, as a function of the two most recent inputs. The network has divided the input space into two regions. For one the output is positive and the network accelerates backwards; for the other it is negative and it accelerates forwards.

The regions are separated by a boundary representing those values of (α_t, α_{t-1}) for which the network produces a zero output (i.e. for which it continues to move at its current velocity). A line at 45° through the origin, representing $\alpha_t = \alpha_{t-1}$, has been superimposed on the output space. A comparison of the

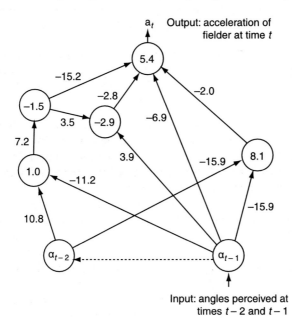

Figure 11.8. A successful network which uses only two consecutive angles as input. The numbers by the connections indicate the weights and the numbers in the units the biases.

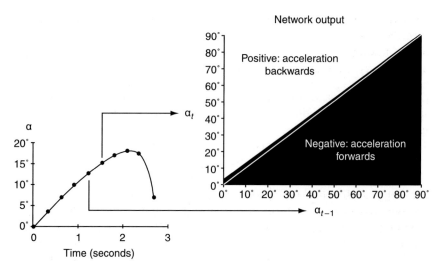

Figure 11.9.   The sign of the network's output as a function of the last two inputs.

null output boundary with this line is the key to understanding what the network is doing. The boundary lies above the $\alpha_t = \alpha_{t-1}$ line, so null output requires that α_t exceeds α_{t-1}. Thus the network will continue to move at its current speed (i.e. it won't accelerate either backwards or forwards) provided α increases in one time-step by an amount that corresponds to the height of the null output boundary at the current value of α_{t-1} above the corresponding point on the $\alpha_t = \alpha_{t-1}$ line. The null output line becomes closer to the $\alpha_t = \alpha_{t-1}$ line as α increases, so the amount by which α must grow in one time-step to produce a null output declines as α increases. As α becomes large the null output boundary approaches the $\alpha_t = \alpha_{t-1}$ line so the network will try to run at a speed that prevents any further change in α. If α_t grows more quickly than the critical amount, (α_t, α_{t-1}) will lie above the null output line and the network will accelerate away from the ball. This will slow the growth of α. If α_t grows more slowly than the critical amount (or starts to decline), (α_t, α_{t-1}) will lie below the null output line and the network will accelerate towards the ball. This will increase α. Thus, the network operates as a negative feedback servo, adjusting its velocity so that α increases throughout the flight but at a decreasing rate as α increases.

Inferring human strategies from those of networks

The simulation shows that given angle of gaze as an input and no feedback other than whether they were near to the ball when it landed, networks evolve that can discover a strategy that ensures interception of balls thrown towards them. The key to the strategy is that they move at a speed that allows the angle of gaze to the ball to increase (i.e. it runs at a speed such that α_t always exceeds α_{t-1}). This is an efficient strategy because it ensures that the network moves towards the place where the ball will land, even when that means moving away from the ball (see McLeod & Dienes, 1996). This strategy must be controlled to prevent the angle of gaze from exceeding 90°, because at this point the ball passes overhead. The network does this by reducing the target rate of increase of α as α increases. Provided it can run fast enough, α will never reach 90°.

If the acceleration of the tangent of α is plotted for the network it turns out that, just like human fielders, the network adjusts its speed to keep the acceleration of tan α close to zero. However, as is clear from Figure 11.9, the network is computing neither the tangent of α nor its acceleration. The output boundary produces behaviour that makes the network look as if it is keeping the acceleration of the tangent at zero. The network appears to find the same solution to catching the ball that people do, and shows a simple way in which the method could be implemented.

This example demonstrates a strength of the evolutionary connectionist approach. Modellers using conventional connectionist techniques try to teach networks to solve tasks in a particular way using a predetermined architecture which may be unnecessarily complex. Left to themselves, an evolutionary simulation may find a simpler solution to the problem.

Human learning and evolution

The simulation found an algorithm which solves the problem of interception—allow the angle of gaze to increase but at a decreasing rate. This is the same algorithm that skilled fielders use. Does the selection method mimic human learning? Presumably not at the biological level. But at the cognitive level the simulation is similar to trial and error learning—trying out a variety of strategies and discarding those that are less successful. Learning by testing out the efficiency of a large selection of rival information processing structures is the basis of the classic "exhaustion of methods" model of improvement with practice proposed by Crossman (1959). Such a method reproduces the ubiquitous finding that the improvement in skill is a power function of the amount of practice.

However, it is possible that children have less learning to do than these networks. It seems unlikely that we are predisposed by our evolutionary heritage to learn to catch, but it is possible that we are predisposed to learn how to *avoid* objects thrown towards us. Those of our ancestors who were good at this may have been more likely to survive than those who were not. Children may be born with innate structures that are particularly sensitive to the information provided by watching trajectories of objects on a collision course. What they have to learn when they learn to catch is to stand the output of such a mechanism on its head and move towards the collision point rather than away from it. But the basic computational mechanism needed for this operation may already be in place.

CONCLUSION

Evolutionary connectionism is a powerful technique for finding solutions to difficult problems. Researchers using the technique often comment on their surprise at the solutions their simulations discover. In a simulation that showed that, under certain conditions, the structures necessary for the basic cortical computational primitives of pattern association, competitive learning, and autoassociation can emerge from collections of interconnected neurons, Rolls and Stringer (2000) commented "we were surprised by the power of the genetic search [to find] unanticipated solutions to problems by combining genes originally provided in the genome . . . for quite different anticipated uses." And who would have thought, before the demonstration by Nakisa and Plunkett, that a network starting with random weights could begin to identify speech features after 2 minutes exposure to speech? And who would have thought that a network could mimic the behaviour of people who appeared to be computing the acceleration of the tangent of their angle of gaze without computing either an acceleration or a tangent?

These demonstrations do not prove that the computational structures discovered by the evolutionary connectionist process exist in the brain. But the behaviour of the networks that have been produced by selection, random resplicing of genomes, and genome mutation is similar to that of humans. It is not clear what it is about such procedures that mimics human learning, but the structures it produces do seem to capture some fundamental aspects of human behaviour.

REFERENCES

Crossman, E. (1959). A theory of the acquisition of speed-skill. *Ergonomics, 2*, 153–166.

Elman, J., Bates, E., Johnson, M., Karmiloff-Smith, A., Parisi, D., & Plunkett, K. (1996). *Rethinking innateness: A connectionist perspective on development.* Cambridge, MA: MIT Press.

Goldberg, D. (1989). *Genetic algorithms in search, optimization and machine learning.* Reading, UK: Addison Wesley.

Jusczyk, P., & Bertoncini, J. (1988). Viewing the development of speech perception as an innately guided process. *Learning and Speech, 31*, 217–238.

Maass, B. (1997). *The role of image velocity in ball catching strategies: A genetic connectionist account.* Unpublished undergraduate dissertation. Department of Experimental Psychology, Oxford University, UK.

McLeod, P., & Dienes, Z. (1996). Do fielders know where to go to catch the ball or only how to get there? *Journal of Experimental Psychology: Human Perception and Performance, 22*, 531–543.

Nakisa, R., & Plunkett, K. (1998). Evolution of a rapidly learned representation for speech. *Language and Cognitive Processes, 13*, 105–128.

Nolfi, S., Elman, J., & Parisi, D. (1994). Learning and evolution in neural networks. *Adaptive Behavior, 3*, 5–28.

Rolls, E. T., & Stringer, S. M. (2000). On the design of neural networks in the brain by genetic evolution. *Progress in Neurobiology, 61*, 557–579.

Rolls, E. T., & Treves, A. (1998). *Neural networks and brain function.* Oxford: Oxford University Press.

Author index

Page numbers in italic indicate actual references as opposed to text citations.

Kohler, K. J. *184*
Kohonen, T. 123, 125, 127, *147, 148,* 225, *230*
Korman, M. 152, *186*
Korte, M. 336, *340, 341*
Kosslyn, S. M. 180, *186*
Kovacs, I. *230*
Kowalczyk, A. 288, *308*
Koza, J. 282, *306*
Krogh, A. 125, *147*
Kropfl, W. 262, *277*
Krubitzer, L. 286, *306*
Kruger, L. 314, 319, 328, *340, 342*
Kucera, H. 129, *146*
Kuczaj, S. 115, *147*
Kuhl, P. K. 153, *186*
Kuhn, D. *147*
Kujala, T. 336, *340*
Kutas, M. 335, *341*
Kwon, Y. H. 335, *342*

La Mendola, N. P. 152, 157, 158, 160, 173, *184*
Labos, E. 324, *342*
Lacerda, F. *113,* 153, *186*
Lachter, J. 117, 123, *147*
Lalonde, C. E. 52, *81*
Lashley, K. S. 31, *40*
Lassonde, M. 336, *340*
Lavie, N. 95, *111*
Lebiere, C. 14, 19, *40,* 109, *112,* 136, *146,* 181, *185*
Lefford, A. 323, *338*
Lehiste, I. 151, *186*
Lehtokoski, A. 336, *340*
Leinbach, J. 115, 122, 130, *147*
Leinonen, A. 336, *340*
Lenneberg, E. H. 189, *230*
Lepore, F. 336, *340*
Lessard, N. 336, *340*
Lev, M. 190, 205, 212, 215, 216, 217, 226, *230*
Levine, M. S. 35, *40,* 324, *340*
Levitt, P. 303, *306*
Levy, J. 159, 160, 171, 177, 179, *184*
Lewkowicz, D. J. 323, 324, *340*
Lhermitte, F. 85, *112*

Li, P. 7, 8, 115, 116, 120, 121, 122, 123, 124, 125, 128, 129, 130, 132, 136, 137, 139, 141, 144, *146, 147*
Liben, L. S. 77, *80*
Lieberman, I. 190, 205, 212, 215, 216, 217, 226, *230*
Lifter, K. 116, *146*
Lin, T. 204, 224, *230*
Lindbolm, B. 153, *186*
Ling, C. 115, *147*
Linsker, R. 294, *307*
Liu, H. 290, *306*
Ljungberg, T. 299, *308*
Lomo, T. 290, *305*
Long, M. 189, 224, 227, *230*
Loose, J. J. 77, *80*
Lovelace, C. T. 312, *339*
Luce, D. R. 196, *230*
Luce, P. A. 155, 164, *184, 186*
Luciana, M. *79, 113,* 294, *307*
Lund, K. 116, 124, 130, *146, 147*
Luppino, G. 322, *339*
Lynch, G. *306*

Maass, B. 10, 345, 356, *364*
Macaulay, M. C. 304, *308*
MacDonald, D. 290, 295, *308*
MacDonald, J. 311, *340*
MacDonald, M. 144, *148*
MacGregor, G. R. 287, *309*
MacKay, I. R. A. 227, *229*
Macnamara, J. 280, *307*
Macomber, J. 85, *114*
MacWhinney, B. 115, 116, 121, 122, 123, 124, 125, 127, 128, 130, 132, 136, *145, 146, 147, 186, 231*
Magalhaes-Castro, B. 314, *342*
Major, G. 291, *308*
Maletic-Savatic, M. 291, 292, *307*
Malinow, R. 291, 292, *307*
Mallot, H. A. 263, *277*
Mansfield, R. J. W. *81*
Marchand, H. 118, *148*
Marchman, V. 54, *80,* 115, *148,* 225, 228, *230*
Marcovitch, S. 109, *113*
Marcus, G. F. 1, 9, *11,* 115, *148,* 181,

Munakata, Y. 4, 7, 39, 58, 77, *80*, 83, 84, 86, 88, 89, 90, 92, 94, 97, 101, 102, 103, 104, 107, 108, 110, 111, *112, 113, 114*
Munoz, D. P. 313, *339*
Munro, M. J. 227, *229*
Munro, P. 46, *79*
Murphy, E. H. 303, *306*
Murray, M. M. 323, *339*
Murre, J. M. *147*

Naatanen, R. 336, *340*
Nacker, F. 336, *341*
Nagaraja, S. S. 225, *231*
Nakisa, R. 352, 353, 354, 355, 364, *365*
Nanez, J. E. 66, *79*
Negishi, M. 234, *255*
Nelson, C. A. *79, 113*, 294, *307*
Nemitz, J. W. 315, 317, 328, *341*
Nersessian, N. J. 16, *41*
Neville, H. J. 335, 336, *341*
Newport, E. L. 9, *12*, 144, *148*, 156, 158, 159, 167, *185, 186*, 189, 190, 191, 202, 205, 206, 207, 208, 209, 211, 212, 218, 223, 225, 226, 227, 228, *230*, 233, 239, 245, 253, *255*, 258, *277*
Newsome, M. 156, *185*
Nikanne, U. *255*
Nilsen, R. 287, *309*
Nodine, C. F. *40*
Noetzel, W. 161, 181, *186*
Nolfi, S. 347, 349, *365*
Noll, D. C. 87, *111*
Norcia, A. 259, 262, *277*
Norita, M. 319, *341*
Norman, D. A. 299, 300, *307*
Norris, D. 152, 157, 165, 166, 167, 172, *184, 186*
Novak, M. 85, *111*
Nowlan, S. J. 264, *276*
Nozawa, G. 313, *340, 341*
Nystrom, L. E. 87, *111*

Ohzawa, I. 265, *277*
Olmstead, C. E. 324, *342*
Olver, R. R. 29, *39*

O'Reilly, R. C. 8, *12*, 85, 88, 101, 107, *112, 113*, 153, *186*, 225, *230*
Oshima-Takane, Y. 23, *41*
Overmeyer, S. 300, *308*
Oviatt, S. L. 163, *186*

Page, M. 2, *12*, 167, *186*
Pallas, S. L. 286, *307*, 335, 341, *342*
Palmer, R. 125, *147*
Papert, S. 43, *80*
Papousek, M. 152, *185*
Parault, S. J. 190, 205, 218, 219, 226, *229*
Pare, M. 336, *340*
Parisi, D. 39, *40*, 44, 77, *79, 81*, 111, 112, 144, 146, 153, *185*, 202, *229*, 280, 282, 284, *306*, 347, 349, 352, 354, 364, *365*
Parsons, T. 119, *148*
Pascual-Leone, A. 285, *305, 308,* 336, *338, 342*
Pascual-Leone, J. 31, 37, *41*
Passingham, R. E. 58, *80*
Patton, P. E. 337, *338*
Paus, T. 290, *306*
Peck, C. K. 313, *339*
Pegg, J. E. 52, *81*
Pennington, B. F. 85, *114*
Pentland, A. P. 167, *186*
Perlstein, W. M. 87, *111*
Peronnet, F. 323, *339*
Perrott, D. R. 313, *341*
Person, C. 298, *307*
Perthick, S. J. 162, 170, *185*
Peterson, C. C. 304, *307*
Petrides, M. 87, *114*, 301, *307*
Petrig, B. 262, *277*
Petsche, T. *41*
Piaget, J. 5, 13, 14, 15, 16, 17, 18, 22, 23, 24, 25, 28, 29, 30, 31, 37, 38, 39, 40, *41*, 58, *80*, 83, 84, 85, 88, 105, 111, 112, *114*, 257, 277, 294, 296, 301, 323, *341*
Piattelli-Palmarini, M. *40, 41*
Pine, J. M. 225, *230*
Pinker, S. 115, 136, *148*, 163, 167, *186*, 234, *255*, 280, 284, *307*

Subject index

abstraction 14–18, 22, 30, 36, 37, 282

accommodation 14–17, 22, 30, 36, 36–38

active memory 86–88, 90, 93, 94, 96, 100–109

active-latent account 86–88, 97, 100, 107, 109, 110

activity-dependent 2, 281, 282, 289, 290, 292, 293

activity-independent 2

acuity 258, 262, 275, 277

AES 319–322, 328, 336, 341

age-of-acquisition 189

A-Not-B 4, 5, 84, 85, 87, 88–91, 94, 96, 99, 101, 102, 109, 112, 114, 300

anti-Hebbian 240, 251, 353

artificial language 54, 159, 168, 173, 230, 253

assimilation 14–17, 22, 30, 36–38

associative learning 53, 57, 76–78, 135, 138

atelic verbs 116

attractor 239–241, 247

autoencoder 46, 52, 53, 57, 76

Backpropagation 1, 5, 8, 11, 18, 47, 54, 61, 79, 117, 123, 125, 136, 153, 166, 168, 196, 200, 277, 346, 349, 350

balance-beam 5

basic-level 45

bias unit 21

binding problem 167, 242

binocular disparity 10, 259, 262–264, 266–269, 275, 276

brain development 1–6, 10, 257, 277, 279, 289, 290, 306

candidate unit 19

card sorting 85, 88, 97–114

cascade-correlation (CC) 6, 7, 14, 18–24, 27–37, 40, 41, 136, 146

catastrophic interference 225

categorisation 7, 43–52, 76–80, 108, 354

CCC 109, 110, 130

CHILDES 124, 129, 131, 144, 147

cognitive architecture 17, 38, 282, 300, 307

cognitive change 13–17, 37, 38

cognitive development 4, 7, 12–16, 24,

381